MAURITIUS, REUNION & SEYCHELLES

Discovery
CHANNEL

APA PUBLICATIONS

Part of the Langenscheidt Publishing Group

INSIGHT GUIDE
MAURITIUS RÉUNION & SEYCHELLES

Editorial
Project Editor
Emily Hatchwell
Managing Editor
Cathy Muscat
Editorial Director
Brian Bell

Distribution

UK & Ireland
GeoCenter International Ltd
The Viables Centre, Harrow Way
Basingstoke, Hants RG22 4BJ
Fax: (44) 1256 817988

United States
Langenscheidt Publishers, Inc.
46–35 54th Road, Maspeth, NY 11378
Fax: 1 (718) 784 0640

Canada
Thomas Allen & Son Ltd
390 Steelcase Road East
Markham, Ontario L3R 1G2
Fax: (1) 905 475 6747

Australia
Universal Press
1 Waterloo Road
Macquarie Park, NSW 2113
Fax: (61) 2 9888 9074

New Zealand
Hema Maps New Zealand Ltd (HNZ)
Unit D, 24 Ra ORA Drive
East Tamaki, Auckland
Fax: (64) 9 273 6479

Worldwide
**Apa Publications GmbH & Co.
Verlag KG (Singapore branch)**
38 Joo Koon Road, Singapore 628990
Tel: (65) 6865 1600. Fax: (65) 6861 6438

Printing

Insight Print Services (Pte) Ltd
38 Joo Koon Road, Singapore 628990
Tel: (65) 6865 1600. Fax: (65) 6861 6438

©2003 Apa Publications GmbH & Co.
Verlag KG (Singapore branch)
All Rights Reserved

First Edition 2000
Updated 2003

CONTACTING THE EDITORS
We would appreciate it if readers
would alert us to errors or out-
dated information by writing to:
**Insight Guides, P.O. Box 7910,
London SE1 1WE, England.
Fax: (44) 20 7403 0290.
insight@apaguide.co.uk**
NO part of this book may be reproduced,
stored in a retrieval system or transmitted
in any form or means electronic, mech-
anical, photocopying, recording or otherwise, without prior written permission of
Apa Publications. Brief text quotations
with use of photographs are exempted
for book review purposes only. Information has been obtained from sources
believed to be reliable, but its accuracy
and completeness, and the opinions
based thereon, are not guaranteed.

www.insightguides.com

ABOUT THIS BOOK

This guidebook combines the interests and enthusiasms of two of the world's best-known information providers: Insight Guides, whose titles have set the standard for visual travel guides since 1970, and Discovery Channel, the world's premier source of nonfiction television programming.

The editors of Insight Guides provide both practical advice and general understanding about a destination's history, culture and people. Discovery Channel and its popular website, www.discovery.com, help millions of viewers explore their world from the comfort of their own home and also encourage them to explore it first-hand.

This book is carefully structured to convey an understanding of the islands and their culture as well as to guide readers through the principal sights and activities:

◆ The **Features** section, indicated by a yellow bar at the top of each page, covers the history and culture of the islands in a series of informative essays.

◆ The main **Places** section, indicated by a blue bar, is a complete guide to the sights and areas worth visiting. Places of special interest are coordinated by number with the maps.

◆ The **Travel Tips** listings section, with an orange bar, provides a handy point of reference for information on travel.

EXPLORE YOUR WORLD
Discovery
CHANNEL

The contributors

Insight Guide: Mauritius, Réunion and Seychelles was edited by **Emily Hatchwell**, a London-based editor who also assembled a widespread team of writers and expert contributors, and by **Cathy Muscat**, a managing editor at Insight Guides.

MAURITIUS, RODRIGUES AND RÉUNION

Mauritian-born **Katerina Roberts** and her husband, **Eric Roberts** are travel writers and photographers specialising in the Indian Ocean. After years of visiting and writing about the Mascarene Islands, they were perfectly placed to complete the Places and Features sections, and compile the corresponding information for the Travel Tips. They also supplied many of the outstanding photographs.

The chapters *People of the Indian Ocean, The Impact of Tourism* and *Sailors and Explorers – Discoverers of the Mascarenes* were written by historian **Dr Marina Carter**, who has spent much of the past 10 years living in Mauritius, writing about the island's history and its people. Many of the archive photographs are from her own personal collection.

Carl Jones, passionate ornithologist and conservationist, and a key figure in saving the pink pigeon and Mauritius kestrel from extinction, wrote the chapters on flora and fauna: *Bats, Birds and Banyan Trees* and *Volcanic Habitats*.

Jane Anderson, travel editor for *You & Your Wedding* magazine, wrote *Romancing the Isles*, and supplied the corresponding Travel Tips information. Mauritian journalist, **Jacques Lee,** contributed *The Mauritians, Sega* and *Lingua Franca* features.

SEYCHELLES

Judith and **Adrian Skerrett** are keen naturalists and active conservationists who spend much of their time in Seychelles. Authors of several guides on Seychelles, including the *Insight Pocket Guide to Seychelles*, they wrote the majority of chapters and travel tips for the Seychelles section, and supplied a number of the photographs.

David Rowat, marine biologist and managing director of Seychelles Underwater Centre, contributed the chapters on *Marine Life* and the Seychelles' *Underwater World*.

Special thanks to **Nigel Tisdall** for his contribution to the Seychelles section, to **Caroline Radula-Scott** for her help editing a number of features and the Travel Tips, to **Lynn Bresler** for proofreading and to **Elizabeth Cook** for compiling the index.

Map Legend

▬ ▪▪	International Boundary
▬ ▬ ▬	Administrative Boundary
▬▪▬	National Park/Reserve
▬ ▬ ▬	Ferry Route
✈ ✈	Airport: International/ Regional
🚌	Bus Station
⊙	Tourist Information
✉	Post Office
🕇 ✝ ⳨	Church/Ruins
✝	Monastery
☪	Mosque
✡	Synagogue
🏰 🏯	Castle/Ruins
∴	Archaeological Site
∩	Cave
🗿	Statue/Monument
★	Place of Interest

The main places of interest in the Places section are coordinated by number with a full-colour map (e.g. ❶), and a symbol at the top of every right-hand page tells you where to find the map.

INSIGHT GUIDE
MAURITIUS RÉUNION & SEYCHELLES

CONTENTS

INDIAN OCEAN ISLANDS

The main attraction may be the white beaches and crystal waters, but beyond the palm trees there are cultures to explore

Visitors who have already been to both Mauritius and Seychelles always have a firm favourite. "The beaches are better on the Seychelles", "But the people are so wonderful in Mauritius… and I've never seen such hotels…", "But what about the diving?"

And what about Réunion? Few mention this corner of France in the Indian Ocean, with its breathtaking volcanic landscapes. Réunion, with Mauritius, forms part of the Mascarenes, along with Rodrigues, an isolated outpost of Mauritius with unspoilt beaches and a particular serenity.

All these Western Indian Ocean islands share the same history to a certain point – all were colonised and cultivated with tea, sugar or vanilla plantations, and their populations are the descendants of explorers and colonists, slaves and indentured labourers. So, Creole of one form or another is spoken in all of them, and some of their songs and dances share similar roots, as do their cuisines. But there is also great diversity, both culturally and in the experience that they give to tourists.

The cultural diversity of these islands, whose roots spread across three continents, is more visible in the Mascarenes than in Seychelles. The culture of Mauritius, from politics to cooking, is heavily influenced by Asian customs and beliefs, while Rodrigues aligns itself more to the people and character of Africa. In Réunion, where culture is rooted firmly in Gallic tradition, boulangeries sell baguettes and croissants alongside creole snacks.

Seychelles, made up of many islands, has cultural diversity as well as chart-topping beaches and birdlife to make birdwatchers weep; the government's commitment to conservation has resulted in almost half the total landmass being given over to nature reserves and national parks.

This guide sets out to both bring out the truth behind clichés that are so often attached to these tropical islands, and also to introduce the lesser-known islands and features of the region. ❑

PRECEDING PAGES: fishermen sorting the catch, Seychelles; chefs at La Pirogue displaying fresh produce, Mauritius; Touessrok's bar manager tests the *rhum arrangé*, Mauritius; kids with kites, Seychelles.
LEFT: a welcoming Rodriguan smile.

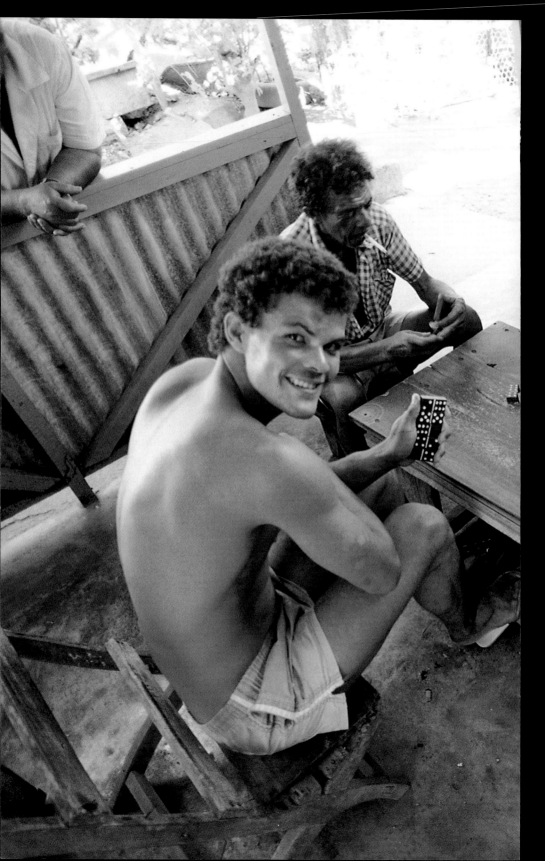

PEOPLE OF THE INDIAN OCEAN

All Indian Ocean islanders are descended from immigrants – whether pioneers or pirates, settlers or slaves – and at least three continents are represented among them

The only thing that distinguishes a Mauritian or Seychellois away from home is the lovely French lilt of their English. Otherwise you could be forgiven for believing that you are meeting a person of European, Asian or East African origin. And, leaping across a few generations, you would be right. The diversity, intermingling and surviving distinctions of the ethnic groups, who have arrived over the past 400 years, create the intriguing hotch potch of cultures and physiognomies which characterise the Western Indian Ocean peoples today.

Polyglot ports

Travellers to the islands of the southwest Indian Ocean often remarked on the ethnic diversity of the inhabitants. Charles Darwin, visiting Mauritius in 1836 on the *Beagle* noted that "the various races of men walking in the streets afford the most interesting spectacle". He would have seen Arab and Persian traders dressed in long, flowing robes, Malagasy with elaborate hair-styles, turban and langouti clad Indians and Chinese shopkeepers with long plaits.

It was the piecemeal settlement of the islands which helps to explain the diversity of the inhabitants. In the 17th and 18th centuries, small groups of French prisoners and pioneers, along with a few Malagasy, Indians and Malays, set up bases, initially in the Mascarenes, and later in Seychelles and Rodrigues. With the importation of women from these same regions, the foundations of "white" and "coloured" communities were laid. Free immigrants were offered grants of land and encouraged to produce cash crops such as cotton, coffee or spices for export to Europe, or to cultivate foodstuffs and raise livestock which could be used to provision the ships calling at the islands on their way to or from the Indies.

PRECEDING PAGES: domino players, Seychelles.
LEFT: Indian Ocean life through the eyes of Seychelles artist, Michael Adams.
RIGHT: Malagasy women *circa* 1860.

Merchants, adventurers, pirates and refugees from many nations were soon attracted to these new centres of trade and maritime construction, and the demand for skilled labour spiralled. Asians were cheaper to employ than Europeans, and agreements signed with Indian artisans led to the establishment of a wealthy free

ARTISTS' IMPRESSIONS

In the days before photography, artists travelled from place to place, capturing and publishing famous moments – such as the conquest of an island (for example, R. Temple's drawings of the British conquest of Mauritius in 1810), or sketching and labelling "types" of exotic peoples for a curious European audience who knew very little about life in the tropics. L.A. Roussin and A. D'Hastrel published *Albums of Réunion* in 1863 and 1847 respectively, while Alfred Richard illustrated individuals as diverse as the "Persian Groom", the "Indian Labourer" and the "Muslim Barber" for his *Types de l'Île Maurice* published in 1850.

"Malabar" class in the islands by the late 18th century. The crews of sailing ships were also frequently sourced from Asia, and were known as "Lascars". Many were Muslims. To this day the terms "Malabar" and "Lascar" are local slang for Hindus and Muslims respectively, but visitors should avoid using them, as they can also be considered terms of insult.

Slaves and convicts from countries as diverse as Guinea, the Canary Islands, Bengal, Java and Timor were also off-loaded from passing ships to the labour-hungry colonists. From the mid-18th century, however, organised slaving voyages brought large numbers of Mozambicans

and Malagasy to the islands, so that they became the dominant ethnic groups, swallowing up the diverse pre-19th century minorities into a Creole population that increasingly reflected this East African cultural heritage.

Asian immigrants

The conversion of Mauritius and Réunion into plantation societies in the late 18th and early 19th centuries led to the large-scale introduction of estate workers, chiefly from India. Mauritius recruited indentured labour from several states: Biharis and Tamils were the most numerous; Marathis and Telegus arrived in

smaller numbers. Réunion recruited mostly Tamils. Principally Hindus, some Muslim and Christian Indians were also indentured. Smaller numbers of African and Chinese labourers arrived over the same period. In the 1860s and 1870s several thousand "Liberated Africans" were brought to Seychelles and Mauritius. They are thought to have mostly come from Malawi.

Merchants and other service migrants followed these population flows: Gujarati merchants and Chinese traders (chiefly Hakka and Cantonese speaking) established themselves in wholesale and retail first on Mauritius and then across the region. Chinese women did not immigrate in large numbers until the turn of the 20th century, and the earlier relationships established by Chinese men produced a substantial Creole-Chinese population on the islands.

Seychelles and Rodrigues, less well suited by size and terrain to sugar cane cultivation, received fewer Asian immigrants and have remained principally Creole societies.

Old inequalities, new attitudes

The Mascarene and Seychelles island groups are all ex-slave societies in which the three tiers of the population – whites, coloureds and slaves – were clearly demarcated and discouraged from intermarrying. Distinctions, grounded in

Tamils have taken Christian first names, has been relaxed recently leading to a rediscovery of separate Hindu and Creole identities.

The ethnic compartmentalisation of present-day Mauritian society is more apparent. Here, a white settler class has survived and maintains its ethnic exclusiveness by marrying within its ranks and with acceptable outsiders – typically white Europeans and, increasingly, white South Africans, who have a shared experience of enclave status in a multi-cultural environment. The old three-tier society has been replaced by one of five or more subgroups which each claim specific caste, religious, and regional distinc-

membership of these "colour coded" groups remain, in varying degrees, on all the islands.

Vestiges of this old hierarchical society seem to have little relevance in modern Réunion and Seychelles, where intermarriage is now the norm, with equality of opportunity an official policy. A light-skinned élite nevertheless remains influential in Seychelles politics and society, while in Réunion, a new class of z'oreilles (white metropolitan French) is complained of as having favoured status. Integrationist French policy in Réunion which ensured that generations of

LEFT: tea pickers in Seychelles.
RIGHT: Rodriguan boys and Mauritian girls.

CREOLE OR KREOL

The term "Creole" might seem to be a catch-all to the uninitiated and needs to be explained. In its historical sense, the word meant someone born on an island and was applied to white as well as coloured inhabitants. Thus Napoleon's consort, Josephine de Beauharnais, was a French Creole of Martinique. Nowadays, the term "Creole" has become associated with a specific community usually considered to derive from the fusion of African with other ethnic groups. In these societies a colonial language often became the basis of a new lingua franca or "creole". To avoid confusion, the language is often spelt Kreol, as it is throughout this book.

tions, maintained through intermarriage. Most Mauritian communities view marriage with a foreigner as a preferable option to an alliance with a Mauritian of another ethnic group. Intermarriage is not unusual, but it is not yet the norm. Politically, ethnic divisions are reinforced by a constitution which provides electoral safeguards for minorities and by a tradition which has grown up since Independence of selecting candidates and even ministers according to their community. To date, every prime minister of Mauritius has come from the Vaish subcaste of the North Indian Hindu community, numerically the most powerful ethnic group in Mauritius.

> **BLUE BLOOD**
>
> Some French Mauritian families are genuine descendants of aristocrats who fled the French Revolution, while more outlandish claims of noble descent from Arab princesses and heroic corsairs can be heard in rum shops across the islands.

Distinctive traditions

Despite a shared history, and collective musical, linguistic and other traditions, each of the Indian Ocean islands has evolved a unique brand of Kreol and a distinctive set of social customs and religious practices. The African cultural heritage is strongest in Seychelles and Rodrigues where the proportion of Afro-Creoles is highest. Réunion is greatly influenced by France and the Francophone world – the zouk rhythms of Martinique are as popular as Paris fashions. In Mauritius, the preponderance of people of Indian origin means that cinemas here are as likely to show Hindi as French films, the sari and the *shalwar kamiz* (trousers and tunic) are common forms of dress, and bhojpuri bands compete with sega and European music for the hearts and minds of the island's youth. The ubiquitous red flags or *jhandi* which can be seen in front of houses throughout the island signify that the occupants are Sanatanist or orthodox Hindus – an eloquent symbol of the cultural dominance of this community in modern Mauritius.

While there are latent tensions between ethnic groups, the Indian Ocean islands are characterised more by syncretism, and participation in each other's celebrations, than by communal conflict. Many non-Tamils make vows to participate in the Cavadee fire-walking ceremonies *(see pages 80–81)* and people of all religions light candles at the Catholic shrines.

Superstition and sorcery cut across ethnic divides: individuals perceived to possess the requisite skills – from traditional practitioners of alternative medicine to specialists in the art of black magic – attract followers from every community, and may be called in to administer remedies, settle quarrels and banish evil spirits.

The food of the islands is the best expression of this shared ethnic heritage: creole cuisine incorporates European, Asian and African influences and offers dishes to suit every palate, from creamy gratins, to Indian-style curries and Chinese-style fried noodles. ❑

> **BRAIN TEASERS**
>
> Kreol *sirandanes* or riddles are a legacy of the African storytelling traditions that are now disappearing in the Indian Ocean islands. When someone had a few riddles to tell they would shout "*Sirandane!*", their audience would reply "*Sampek!*" and the brain teasing session would begin. Here are some typical examples:
> *Dileau dibout? Canne.*   Standing water? A sugar cane.
> *Dileau pendant? Coco.*   Hanging water? A coconut.
> *Menace dimoun, napas koze? Ledoigt.*
>   I threaten but I do not speak? A finger.
> *Ki lalangue ki zames ti menti? Lalangue zanimaux.*
>   Whose tongue never lies? An animal's.

LEFT: Hindu marriage ceremony.

Lingua Franca

As a legacy of their shared history of settlement during periods of French rule, the mother-tongue of the inhabitants of the Seychelles and Mascarene islands is Kreol. The various forms of Kreol spoken have evolved from adaptations of French to which a sprinkling of words and speech patterns from the other languages of immigrants has been added.

The formative period of Indian Ocean Kreol in the late 17th and 18th centuries has left its mark on the language. The Breton origins of many early French settlers means that traces of their regional language survive into modern Kreol while the influence of Malagasy immigrants is reflected in local words such as *frangourin* or cane sugar juice and which derives from the Malagasy term *fangorinana*. South Indians who arrived on the islands in the 18th century as slaves and artisans have left their mark not only in the delicious curries of the region but also in culinary terms. The herb known as *kaloupile* in Réunion, *karipoule* in Mauritius and *karipile* in Seychelles is derived from the Tamil word *kariveppilai* or curry leaf. The creole dish known as *rougaille* is also derived from the Tamil word *urkukay* meaning pickled vegetable.

Over time, different islands have developed particular speech patterns. Seychelles Kreol is said to be more sing-song in style, while Réunion Kreol has been exposed to greater influence from the Francophone world, particularly the French Caribbean. Mauritian Kreol uses many words deriving from its large population of North Indian origin. Expressions such as "nisa" (feeling high), "jalsa" (amusement) and "paise" (money) derive from the bhojpuri dialect spoken widely in rural Indian villages on the island. English league football is a popular spectator sport in Mauritius and Seychelles where terms such as "offside" and "goal kick" are commonly used by Kreol speakers.

The emphasis given to Kreol in the various islands is strongly linked to political factors. Because Réunion is a *département* of France, the French language is given priority, and is used in all official communications and in the written media. In Mauritius and Seychelles, where French rule was succeeded by British government, English is the official language. In Seychelles, however, Kreol also has this status and is given equality of treatment in

the media and government institutions. A Kreol Institute has even been established on Mahé to nurture the language. In Mauritius, as in Réunion, Kreol is spoken but rarely written.

For all the islands, these varying political solutions to the language question pose further problems. Middle-class Seychellois complain that the prominence given to Kreol restricts the opportunities for their children to become proficient in French. Réunion suffers from being a Francophone island in an Indian Ocean which is largely Anglophone. Mauritius, with its multiplicity of competing Asian ancestral languages and chiefly French media, is continually struggling with internal dis-

sent and controversy. The island is becoming increasingly Francophone while the education system is slanted towards the use of both English and Oriental languages.

As a rule, English is widely understood in Seychelles and Mauritius, but not in Réunion. French is the preferred language of communication in Mauritius and Réunion, but will not be appreciated by all Seychellois. Switching from English to French and back will not daunt a Mauritian who can usually reply in kind! A few words of basic Kreol acquired in any of the islands, should provide a channel of easy communication in all of them. ❏

● *A quick pronunciation guide and glossary of basic terms and phrases appear on page 376.*

RIGHT: exchanging news and views.

THE IMPACT OF TOURISM

Seychelles and Mauritius continue to lure the rich and famous, Réunion remains a well-kept secret from all but the French, and Rodrigues is yet to be "discovered"

The development of tourism is relatively recent in the Western Indian Ocean and its growth and quality have been carefully monitored. Planners, all too aware that the islands' natural assets are what attract visitors, have kept conservation very much at the forefront of their development schemes. There are no sprawling miles of concrete coastal resorts here, and the isolated location of the islands, together with high standards of service and beautiful natural beaches, mean that the tropical island paradise experience as presented in the brochures and glossy magazines actually lives up to expectations.

Battling for pole position

Trendiness has been a key factor in determining the way tourism has evolved both in Mauritius and Seychelles which are at different stages of development. Seychelles was the first island group to be popular with European visitors and, by 1979, tourism was the chief earner. Sporadic political conflict, however, as in Madagascar and the Comores, slowed economic growth in Seychelles while Mauritius remained stable. Despite the coup d'état and succeeding radical governments, Seychelles still attracts a steady stream of holidaymakers. The beaches are as stunning as ever and are often rated among the world's best in travellers' surveys *(see page 33)*. Nevertheless, this has not been enough to stop Seychelles from being overtaken by Mauritius which has been riding the crest of a popularity wave for some years now.

The Mauritian tourist industry has concentrated all its energies on developing the luxury end of the market, building splendid hotels and gaining a reputation for excellent service. Since 1993, the island has outstripped Seychelles in tourist numbers and currently welcomes around half a million tourists a year (Seychelles visi-

PRECEDING PAGES: waterskiing at La Pirogue on the west coast of Mauritius.
LEFT: Berjaya Hotel on Le Morne peninsula, Mauritius.
RIGHT: verandah of the Casino des Îles, Seychelles.

tors numbered 132,000 in 2002). Indications are that this figure will double in the next 20 years, to equal and maybe exceed its own population.

State vs the private sector

Politics has also affected the development of tourism in the region. The state has a deeper

level of involvement in tourism on "socialist" Seychelles than on "capitalist" Mauritius. While it was the government that initiated tourist development in Seychelles, the role of the private sector in the building of exclusive resorts in Mauritius was significant. Seychelles' population of 82,000 is low compared to Mauritius which has one million inhabitants, so labour and production costs are less advantageous. In addition to this, the wages of workers in the Seychelles hotel sector are regulated, as are the number of privately owned guest houses and the prices they can charge.

All of these factors contribute to a higher cost of living than on Mauritius. Seychelles recognises the fact that to maintain its appeal and the high quality people have come to expect, it needs to begin reinvesting. Currently, Seychelles has more middle than top of the range hotels, but prices are still high. However, the recent opening of the Lemuria Resort on Praslin, complete with 18-hole golf course, reflect moves to compete in the luxury hotel market. Lemuria has been followed by two more five-star resorts, Banyan Tree opened on Mahé in 2001 and Beachcomber on St Anne in 2002. Also in 2002, Lemuria added eight new luxury villas plus, for the super-rich, a four-bedroom Presidential Suite.

Celebrity spotting

Whatever the economic and political ups and downs, both Mauritius and Seychelles are still hot favourites among the rich and famous. Celebrities in search of an exclusive destination the paparazzi can't get to, opt for Seychelles where whole islands can be hired out – Frégate, Félicité and d'Arros, all privately owned, are perfect hideaways for those who can afford to pay for the privilege of having a tropical island to themselves. Among the more recent celebrity tourists were Pierce Brosnan who stayed on Frégate (an island with the perfect James Bond profile), Michael Douglas who cruised the

COASTAL FORTS AND QUARANTINE SITES

The Indian Ocean islanders feared two things above all else – enemy attack, which their small populations could not easily fend off, and the introduction of contagious disease, which frequently decimated their numbers. The dangers came from visiting ships, and elaborate measures were taken to protect their coastlines. Defence and quarantine buildings were erected on shores and islets – precisely those areas that are most in vogue today as tourist sites. Flat Island off the north coast of Mauritius was a quarantine station, while Seychelles' Île Curieuse was once a leper colony. Some hotels have incorporated these ruins into their grounds. Le Canonnier hotel in

Mauritius is built on the site of an important fortress and a quarantine station. The old defence walls are now an integral part of the hotel and the mounted cannon still point out to sea. Maritim Hotel, further along the coast, offers guests and non-residents the opportunity to walk around its 18th-century ruins of a French arsenal. Mauritius also has some of the best preserved Martello towers in the world (see page 145).

On your travels, you may come across the ruins of old lime kilns. The French spent a great deal of time and manpower in the manufacture of lime, which they used for the building of roads and in construction work.

islands on his own luxury yacht, Tony Blair who has chosen La Digue as a family holiday retreat on more than one occasion, and Paul McCartney who honeymooned here in 2002. The Sultan of Bahrain has a home in Seychelles, and the Miss World Competition has been staged here on more than one occasion; its co-ordinators exploited the paradise cliché to the full, billing the event as a unique opportunity to see "the most beautiful girls on earth in the most beautiful place on earth".

STAR RATING

It used to be said that Mauritius is a 3-star destination with 5-star hotels while Seychelles is a 5-star destination with 3-star hotels, but Seychelles facilities are rapidly catching up.

and world class chefs. Supermodels, footballers, pop stars and film stars regularly appear in glossy magazines, captured languishing in their designer swimwear by the poolside cafés and seaside bars of Mauritius' most fashionable hotels. Old favourites, the Touessrok (where England goalkeeper David Seaman had his honeymoon) and St Géran (holiday haunt of ex-Spice Girl Gerri Halliwell), compete with newer glitzy resorts such as the Prince Maurice and the Residence. Playwright Harold Pinter is a

With its larger tourist industry, Mauritius has more five-star hotels than Seychelles. Seychelles had no five-star facilities until the late 1990s, but this has since changed dramatically and new hotels have capitalised on the twin advantages of more private islands and better beaches than Mauritius. Both countries have several hotels in the "leading hotels in the world" category. They cater to every whim of their celebrity guests, providing security, a high standard of service

LEFT: Prince Edward tries his hand at waterskiing at La Pirogue, during a royal visit to Mauritius.
RIGHT: beach-side breakfast at the Paradise Sun Hotel, Anse Volbert, Praslin.

regular at the Royal Palm hotel, also a favourite with visiting heads of state. Lesser mortals can usually persuade the security guards at the entrance gates to let them in for lunch or afternoon tea, if the hotel isn't full.

A "once-in-a-lifetime" holiday

In principle, these islands are luxury destinations. A two week holiday at a good hotel on Seychelles or Mauritius can cost several thousand pounds per person. That said, you don't have to be a celebrity or tycoon to enjoy the best that the region has to offer. There are so many small islands in the Seychelles group that anyone can find their own "private" cove complete with swaying palms, fine white sand and turquoise lagoon. Cruising the granitics sounds like an expensive luxury but there are a range of options available for those with a more limited budget. Honeymooners and others looking to splash out on an exceptional holiday, can spend their fortnight on islands such as La Digue, where cars are rarely seen, or enjoy the utter isolation of Denis or Frégate where your very own island wedding can be arranged. Cousine is also an exclusive hideaway with four to eight rooms which can be reached by helicopter.

The tourist industry on Mauritius targets the well-heeled lover of luxury and exclusivity – no

charter flights are allowed to land here. This is the destination of choice for those who want to exploit the service and amenities of a five-star hotel and the tropical beach on its doorstep to the full. Such luxury comes at a price, but the hotels are exquisite and they've got the service down to a fine art. The key to a successful holiday on Mauritius lies in choosing the right hotel to suit you, both in terms of style and location. It's even worth staying in more than one just to compare experiences.

Natural assets

While both places have been effectively marketed as idyllic beach holiday destinations, the islands' other natural assets have been widely exploited to draw in people looking for more than just a "sun, sea and sand" experience. The Seychelles government is anxious to attract the "discerning and environmentally aware" tourist. Top of its list of highlights are two UNESCO World Heritage Sites – the Vallée de Mai on Praslin and the far flung Aldabra Atoll. Other designated bird sanctuaries and tropical forests attract twitchers and trekkers, while live-aboard cruises around the Outer Islands are becoming increasingly popular.

In Mauritius, watersports are big business. The island is renowned for its good game fishing and its annual World Marlin Fishing competition is a big event on the fishing calendar. It has also developed into a top diving destination and most of the big hotels operate their own dive centres.

The flora and fauna of Seychelles and Mascarenes is in many respects unique and, like all small island ecologies, endangered. Coral reefs are notoriously fragile and prone to destruction

THE WORLD'S BEST HOTELS

The hotels of Seychelles and Mauritius are the Indian Ocean's best assets. In 2003, a Special Edition of Swiss magazine *Bilanz*, noted that while Sardinia, Hawaii, Kenya and Florida have all had their time as the world's hot spots, the centre of gravity for the best hotel resorts in the world has now shifted to Seychelles and Mauritius. This conclusion was based on a survey of travel consultants, business leaders and leading travel agents, and confirmed by reference to the top magazines *Condé Nast Traveller*, *Institutional Investor*, *Travel & Leisure* and *Tatler*. Number one in the world in the Swiss survey was Lemuria Resort of Praslin, Seychelles, singled out for its luxurious facilities and spectacular grounds and beaches. Le Prince Maurice of Mauritius came a close second. The roll of honour also included the Seychelles hotels of Frégate Island Private (fifth) and Banyan Tree Resort (twenty-first) together with Mauritius hotels Le Saint Géran (ninth) and The Oberoi (twenty-fourth). Indeed, other top hotels of Seychelles and Mauritius must also vie for a position on any list of the best hotels in the world. Mauritius still has more five-star hotels, including Tousserok (a honeymooners favourite upgraded and re-launched in 2002) and Royal Palm. Seychelles can boast Sainte Anne Resort and Alphonse Resort, both worthy of special mention.

by over-zealous exploitation. Seychelles has a long tradition of eco-tourism, with several islands declared nature reserves and access to them limited to the daytime. Mauritius is belatedly recognising the advantages of exploiting the few remaining areas on which unique species have survived. Thankfully, it's now following the example set by the Seychelles government in requiring permits for visits to some of its islets and in opening them up to responsible, supervised nature tours. Île aux Aigrettes, off the southeast coast, is home to the only remaining example of coastal savannah which the dodo and other local birds found a natural habitat, and tours have recently been set up by the Mauritius Wildlife Foundation *(see page 129).*

Holidaying on a budget

Back-packers are not encouraged, but there are ways of staying more cheaply on the islands. The resorts of Grand Baie/Pereybère and Flic-en-Flac in Mauritius offer numerous flats and guest houses where a studio can be rented for just a few pounds a day. Once you have paid for your flight, this is the one island in the region where you can live more cheaply than at home, and some seasonal workers from European coastal resorts choose to spend the winter here, staying for the three to six months which is allowed them on a tourist visa. Prices of imported goods are higher than in Europe, but essential foodstuffs are subsidised, and if you bring your own luxury items, you can live very cheaply.

Seychelles also has a number of small guest houses; though not particularly cheap compared to other countries, they are less expensive than hotels, the service is much more personal and standards are generally high. Self-catering establishments are also good quality, and shopping for yourself brings down costs: shop prices for drinks are half those charged by hotels, while local produce including fish is inexpensive.

Adventure playground

Réunion is the most expensive of the Indian Ocean islands because its economy is artificially boosted with regular injections of French capital. Prices are up to 30 percent higher here than in

France. It has long been popular with French visitors – as an overseas *département* there are no customs or immigration checks for arrivals from the metropolis (mainland France) – but its lack of coral-fringed beaches and monolingualism have lessened the island's appeal to non-French tourists. The Réunionnais themselves often take their annual holidays on Mauritius where, beyond the big hotels, the cost of living is much lower.

As its coastline doesn't fit the tropical island profile, Réunion has escaped invasion from international tourists. Most of us still need persuading that hiking – even to an active volcano

LEFT: appetising display of fresh fish and seafood.
RIGHT: the sega performances staged at hotels are formalised versions of the traditional slave dance.

– is more fun than lounging by a palm-fringed lagoon, and the island's breathtaking landscape remains a well-kept secret from all but the French and the ardent adventure traveller.

The tourist authorities were quick to recognise and exploit its potential as a paradise for back-packers and thrill seekers, and over the years they have built up an efficient infrastructure. The trail network is well-mapped and maintained, as are the purpose-built mountain lodges or *gîtes*. The adventure sport potential

BOLLYWOOD'S BEACHES

Fans of Hindi cinema have a good chance of glimpsing their screen idols in Mauritius where Bollywood films are almost constantly in production.

has been developed to the full. Other than trekking, organisations and facilities for mountain-biking, climbing, horse-riding, canyoning, canoeing, even bungee-jumping can be found all over the island

Réunion has also countered its shortcomings with the marketing of its colonial heritage which it seems to have preserved far better than its neighbours. Plantations and colonial houses have been faithfully restored and opened to the public. However, despite the opportunites for cultural heritage tourism that the rich history and diverse population of Mauritius offer, museum development and tours of cultural and historic sites remains unsophisticated.

The forgotten island

Rodrigues, granted regional autonomy in 2002, is the minuscule and often forgotten partner in the twin-island Republic of Mauritius. Until not so long ago, the island could be reached only by a cargo vessel which docked at Port Mathurin just once a month and only the most determined travellers reached its rugged shores. Nowadays, the modern *Mauritius Pride*, makes the crossing two or three times a month, bringing in islanders and tourists on short breaks.

Tour operators are beginning to turn their attentions to Rodrigues, but tourism is still very much in its infancy here and further development seems to be hampered by the difficulties of air access, water shortages and concern about its infrastructure. Light aircraft make regular flights to and from Mauritius and visitors from Réunion can either fly direct or opt to overnight in Mauritius before continuing to Rodrigues.

The Association of Rodrigues Tourism Operators is a body of guesthouse and hotel managers, tour operators, car hire companies and shopkeepers who, in conjunction with the Mauritius Tourism Promotion Authority, are promoting cultural and niche tourism, with some success. Their organised activities include staying in islanders' homes, going to folklore shows, walking, fishing and diving. The gigantic lagoon for which Rodrigues is famous, is an unspoilt haven for divers, and is currently the subject of detailed research by scientists studying the Indian Ocean's unique coral islands.

Rodrigues remains uncrowded and unspoiled. There are no high rise hotels or malls, and chickens still roam the capital's streets. Interestingly, the island is visited mostly by Mauritians looking for a relaxing weekend break and small numbers of European and South African tourists travelling from Mauritius who are keen to discover another facet of life in the Mascarenes.

An extended airport runway built in 2002 with European funding allows direct flights from Réunion, and the popularity of Rodrigues is on the rise. Developers will one day home in on its beaches, but hopefully with the sensitivity to the natural environment that is essential to the survival of such a small island. ❑

LEFT: cleaning the pool before the tourists arrive.

Seychelles' Top Ten

In 1987, the film *Castaway* was released. It was based on the true story of two Londoners who dreamed of living for a year on an exotic tropical island, but unfortunately the beaches on the real island, which lies between Papua New Guinea and Australia, weren't photogenic enough. The director, Nicolas Roeg, looked around the world for the perfect tropical paradise. Where were the ultimate beaches on earth? His eyes settled on the perfect arc of white sand at Anse Kerlan on Praslin, lapped by crystal clear blue waters and surrounded by lush tropical vegetation. The film starred Oliver Reed and Amanda Donahue, but according to one review: "...they weren't the real stars of *Castaway*. The real star was the beach".

The beaches of Seychelles are a legend. The German travel magazine, *Reise & Preise* conducted a recent survey to rate the world's most fabulous beaches. Thousands of its readers responded to the "Beach Test", rating sand, surf, sunbathing, accessibility, water quality and so on. Many beaches and many countries were listed, but Seychelles emerged the clear winner, with six of the top twelve beaches in the world. In a supplementary list of insider tips for those beaches rarely mentioned in the guidebooks (this one excepted), Seychelles again dominated with two of the world's top five. No other country had more than one slot in the same category. "There is no doubt," concluded the magazine "that the best beaches in the world can be found in Seychelles."

Top of the league table is **Anse Lazio**, followed at number two by its close neighbour **Anse Georgette**, both on Praslin. La Digue also had two entries, **Anse Source d'Argent** at number five and **Grande Anse** at twelve. Frégate Island's **Anse Victorin** was rated at number seven and Mahé's **Anse Intendance** at nine. In the supplementary rankings, **Anse Soleil** on Mahé and **Anse Cocos** on La Digue completed the roll of honour.

Seychelles is never absent from similar polls. Anse Source d'Argent was recently voted the best beach in the world by the UK's *Independent* newspaper, Condé Nast's *Traveler* magazine and the American cable TV station, the Travel Channel.

The stark white sands, swaying palms and emerald seas of these and other idyllic coastal stretches

RIGHT: Anse Lazio on Praslin, voted "best beach in the world".

are the answer to many a film-maker's, not to mention advertiser's dream. Roman Polanski chose to shoot scenes for his swashbuckling adventure film, *Pirates*, on Frégate, while Sylvia Kristel stuck with Anse Source d'Argent for the erotic romance, *Emmanuelle in Paradise*. Take a closer look at the classic paradise backdrop to any fashion shoot, TV or glossy magazine ad, and there's a good chance you'll recognise a Seychelles hotspot.

The truth is, when beaches are this good it is difficult to choose. There are beaches for every mood. Romantic beaches to wander along, surf-lashed beaches to frolic in, fish-rich waters to snorkel in, child-friendly beaches on the edge of sleepy

lagoons, lively beaches with watersports and restaurants, and beaches where you'll not see a soul all day except perhaps for a fisherman launching his pirogue. Mahé's **Beau Vallon**, though the most developed beach in Seychelles, retains a majestic beauty. It remains uncrowded and unspoilt relative to most destinations. At the other extreme of sophistication are the remote **Outer Islands**. The little-visited islands of St François, Desroches, Alphonse, Farquhar and Assomption all have stunning beaches awaiting discovery. Small resorts and liveaboard cruising are slowly opening up this corner of Eden so that next time a poll is conducted, there will be even more Seychelles contenders to add to the list. ❑

ROMANCING THE ISLES

Weddings and honeymoons in the Indian Ocean are increasingly popular, often with family and friends in tow. Forward planning is the key to their success

The lure of Mauritius and Seychelles comes in many guises for brides and grooms to be. (As Réunion operates under French rule, European visitors are forbidden by its residency laws to marry here.) More often than not, it's the desire to escape all the hassle and cost of a formal white wedding at home that tempts couples overseas. Apart from an idyllic setting and perfect climate, these islands offer the freedom to kick off your shoes and tie the knot barefoot in the sand if the mood takes you.

Mauritius and Seychelles have so far managed to avoid the tackiness to which other destinations have succumbed. Unlike many Caribbean resorts where lace-clad newlyweds often bump into each other, most hotels here prefer to limit ceremonies to one per day.

Tying the knot

Weddings are generally civil, the ceremony held either under a gazebo beside the beach or in a hotel garden. Church weddings are possible, but they involve a little more organisation and often an extra cost for hiring the church. However, provided the hotel or tour operator is willing to make the arrangements, there's nothing to stop more adventurous couples getting married anywhere they choose. In Mauritius, couples can helicopter into the highlands for a ceremony at the Varangue Sur Morne near the Black River Gorges with awesome views of the dramatic landscape and turquoise ocean. Or they can board a catamaran decked out in bougainvillaea for a wedding on the water. The Coco Beach resort even offers the possibility of getting married under water. In Seychelles, at resorts such as Denis or Frégate, you can have your own private island wedding, providing your budget stretches that far.

The key to a successful Indian Ocean wedding is finding the right tour operator *(see Travel Tips for a list of reputable organisations)*. Travel agents and the respective tourist boards should be aware of who features what. In most cases, there is little or nothing to organise except the provision of the necessary documents, and the arrangement of a few details like hair appointments, flowers, wedding cake and choosing between say a sunset cruise or a romantic dinner.

Mauritius has a sophisticated wedding scene with its four- and five-star international resorts well equipped to organise ceremonies, many with dedicated wedding co-ordinators who guide couples through all their arrangements. Seychelles may not be as slick as Mauritius when it comes to organising weddings, but in many ways this adds to its charm. With its pristine beaches, dramatic peaks and rain forest, not to mention the notorious coco de mer "love nut", Seychelles is just as seductive.

Trends show that weddings abroad are on the increase and more and more couples are accompanied by friends and family. The beauty of the Indian Ocean is that once the wedding

LEFT: white wedding on Mahé.
RIGHT: fertility statue: for the benefit of newlyweds staying at the Touessrok hotel.

is over, guests can stay on for a holiday while newlyweds can honeymoon on another island, take an island-hopping cruise, go on safari in Africa (not a long plane-ride away) or go for a spell on Réunion – a great contrast to Mauritius or Seychelles with its dramatic volcanic scenery and intensely French culture.

The average two-week wedding and honeymoon in the Indian Ocean costs in the region of £4,000 (US$6,000) per couple. If the wedding party is big enough, some of the larger hotels may waive the cost of the wedding package (usually £350–£600 / $500–$850) – but you'll need to book well in advance.

Top Mauritian venues

Foreigners marrying in Mauritius can incorporate elements of traditional weddings into their ceremonies if they wish, but must advise the hotel as to what they want.

The two hotel groups which dominate the island are Beachcomber and Sun International. Both are well geared up for weddings and take care to make couples feel special. Most of the other upmarket hotels on the island such as La Residence, Les Pavillons and Le Prince Maurice resorts also cater for weddings. Another possible location is the Domaine Les Pailles, a re-creation of an 18th-century sugar estate that

WEDDING DOS AND DON'TS

Do...

● book well in advance and plan your wedding date at least three days after your arrival so you can acclimatise and get all the details and legal paperwork completed.

● choose wedding clothes that are lightweight; natural fibres are best for the tropics.

● hang your wedding dress or suit in a steamy bathroom on arrival to remove creases. Alternatively, ask the airline permission to hang your wedding attire in the cabin.

● check exactly what's included in your wedding package and whether you want any extras such as live music.

● take out wedding and travel insurance.

Don't...

● get sunburnt before the wedding.

● wear new or tight shoes as your feet will expand in the heat.

● get worked up. Formalities often work at a slower pace in a hot climate.

● expect the earth. As weddings abroad are usually very quick, it's worth organising something special after the ceremony such as a sunset cruise, especially if it's just the two of you.

● plan your wedding in the hottest months or the rainy season and check the weather before you go.

lies in the shadow of Le Pouce mountain. Couples can be brought here by horse and cart and have five restaurants to choose from for their reception, or they can head for the mountains.

Sunset weddings

In Seychelles there are registrars on the main islands of Mahé, Praslin and La Digue. However, resorts on the other islands can also assist with wedding arrangements, including photography if required.

BEAT THE RUSH

Couples wanting to marry in Mauritius and Seychelles send their requests as much as 18 months in advance. November and December are particularly popular months, so book early to avoid disappointment.

Most hotels in Seychelles welcome weddings. As they tend to be smaller than in other destinations, they lend themselves to intimate gatherings. Coco de Mer on Praslin decorates its wooden pier with local flowers and banana leaves to create a wedding venue over the water. A wedding just before sunset allows the photographer to capture some stunning sunset shots. Some of the best-known hotels for weddings on Mahé are the Plantation Club, the Berjaya hotels, Coral Strand and Le Northolme. Over on Praslin

Foreign couples can marry anywhere they want although strictly speaking they are not supposed to marry on the distinctive white sand beaches. However, hotels such as the Plantation Club have pavilions or gazebos beside the beach. A favourite beach wedding setting is Anse Source d'Argent on La Digue. Anse Lazio on Praslin, proclaimed best beach in the world by style guru Giorgio Armani, is equally idyllic. Foreigners can also marry in church, but for an extra charge.

LEFT: honeymooners at the Coco de Mer Hotel on Praslin.
RIGHT: sunset photo shoot.

favourites include Coco de Mer Hotel and the Black Parrot Suites, La Reserve, L'Archipel, Indian Ocean Lodge and the new Lemuria Resort. On La Digue couples can arrive by ox cart to their wedding at Patatran Village, or Hotel L'Ocean for example. As there are so many islands to choose from, it's worth considering marrying on one island such as Mahé or Praslin and honeymooning on another, or even island hopping by air or sea.

Those who really want to get away from it all can make arrangements on several of the small outer islands: Denis has its own tiny wedding chapel; Desroches, Alphonse and Frégate Island Private all fit the tropical paradise bill. ❑

MARINE LIFE

Not far beneath the surface of the Indian Ocean lies a fascinating world, teeming with life and colour and easy to explore – all you need is a mask, snorkel and fins

For many people the "Underwater World" is a strange and inaccessible place, full of mystery and danger. While it is true that most of the submarine environment will remain an area that few have the opportunity to experience, the temperature and generally favourable conditions make the shallow waters easy to explore. The most popular holiday destinations in the Indian Ocean are on the coast and have easy access to the sea. Mauritius is encircled by an almost continuous reef barrier, interrupted only to the south between Le Souffleur and Souillac; many of the Seychelles islands support fringing coral reefs, while some experts maintain that Rodrigues' corals are even better than the Seychelles'.

Tidal zone

The first type of terrain you are likely to come across is the tidal zone. Here at sea level, rock pools host a number of small fish species adapted to the inter-tidal way of life. Prominent among these are the rock skippers, small brown blennies and gobies which have modified fins that act as suckers, allowing them to cling to the rocks as the surf sweeps back and forth.

Many species of crustaceans are found only in these refuges. Most striking of the rock pool treasures are the crabs which scurry nimbly from rock to rock, such as the aptly named Sally Lightfoot. Barnacles spend their life attached to rocks. From their cone-shaped structure, they extend hairy paddle-like legs that beat to create a current bringing nutrient-rich water to their mouths.

Sandy areas

As you wade into the sea and peer through the water, the sand beneath the surface looks like a submarine desert when compared to the busy reefs beyond. But look a little closer and you'll

---

PRECEDING PAGES: sea anemones sheltering clownfish, which never stray far from home.
LEFT: Aldabra's underwater world.
RIGHT: sea cucumber.

spot some interesting sea creatures. Often the most obvious are the slow-moving crawlers such as crabs, sea urchins and sea cucumbers, the long sausage-like objects littered around many sandy bottom areas. These creatures are the caretakers of the seabed and feed on detritus and algae in the sand's surface layer. The

small submarine "volcanoes" characteristic of some areas are built by marine worms, generally hidden from view.

Flat-fish species, such as the peacock flounder, are difficult to see. Generally well camouflaged, they only give themselves away when they glide off in search of another resting spot. Various types of ray also inhabit sandy bottom areas, especially in the shallow lagoons. They can be quite large, measuring up to 2 metres (6½ ft) across their wide wing-like disc. You have to look quite hard to spot a resting ray as they often cover themselves with a coating of sand, but their whiplike tails, which tend to stick out of the sand like flagpoles, often give them away. While the sting ray is indeed well equipped with a sting mechanism in his barbed tail, it is used purely for defence and divers and snorkellers should have no fear of attack unless they provoke the animal or tread on it. A few minutes spent watching a sting ray hunting through the sand for molluscs and crabs can be very rewarding. Manta rays are among the biggest Indian Ocean fish and feed on plankton and small fish. They are quite harmless and a joy to watch as they sail gracefully through the water.

SECURITY BLANKET

Many parrotfish sleep in a mucus "bubble", which they blow around themselves as an early warning system of approaching danger.

A number of the unique animals inhabiting the sandy seabed are often mistaken for plants; sea pens, for example, have a feather or plume-like structure on a fleshy stalk which protrudes from the sand. The "plume" is in fact an intricate structure of arms that is rotated to face into any water currents and strain out plankton and other particles of food.

Look out for areas of algae or sea-grass which provide food and shelter for a number of animals. Wrasse are often found feeding here and you may even come across a charismatic little seahorse clinging to the grass with his tail.

Sea-grass beds are also visited by larger algal browsers, notably the green turtle, the larger of the two turtle species found in this region. Watching the turtles feeding is one of the rare opportunities you will have of observing them at close quarters. The other prime time for a good sighting is when the female turtles come up the beach to lay their eggs.

Rock reefs

Rock reefs are another easily accessible and productive zone in the Indian Ocean and provide the habitat for a profusion of marine life. The rocks themselves are often covered in a variety of marine plants and creatures ranging from subtly coloured encrusting hard corals, barnacles and limpets to brightly coloured sponges and soft corals, so much so that little of the actual rock surface may be visible. Each of these encrusting structures is itself host to a number of other creatures and provides a micro-ecosystem on the reef. In soft coral formations look out for small fish such as gobies and blennies that often mimic the colour of the coral for protection. They actually nest on the corals and feed on zooplankton. The hard coral formations are home to a number of brightly coloured fish species including hawk-fish, damselfish and small scorpion or rock-fishes, all benefiting from the protection that the branching structures provide. Various crabs also use the branching corals for shelter, such as the red-spotted crab and hermit crab which hides in its borrowed shell for protection.

Many fish species hide in the gaps and crevasses between the rocks of the reef for protection from predators and can be found feeding above the reef during the day. Along the reef you are sure to see brightly coloured surgeon-fish that graze algae off the rocks, often just below the wave zone. Their name derives from the sharp spines found at the base of their tail which is why fishermen are extra careful when handling them.

Coral reefs

Coral reefs are the submarine equivalent of the rain forest and have the greatest diversity of marine life. They are formed by tiny animals, coral polyps, which secrete a hard external casing of calcium. Successive generations build on top of each other to form the limestone of the reef with just the outer surface covered with the living corals.

There are a vast number of hard coral formations. The real reef builders are known as "massive" corals. They form enormous rounded coral heads which coalesce to form reefs. Other hard corals are highly branched, with delicately ornate structures, giving rise to such evocative names as staghorn, elk-horn and table horn.

While the stony corals secrete a calcium casing, many of the soft coral species grow on even more complex structures. Some – the colourful tree corals, for example – support their bodies called fire coral. If you brush against one, the potent sting it inflicts on your skin feels like the burn from a stinging nettle.

DANGEROUS BEAUTY

Cone shells with their beautiful intricate designs are among the most attractive shells in the world. But beware! Never pick one up by the thin end, for its poison is deadly.

Sea anemones

Related to the corals are the sea anemones – a bit like giant coral polyps without the external shell. These creatures are generally hidden within cracks and ledges of the reef but a few species are conspicuously stuck to the surface of the rocks. They are mostly host anemones and are almost always associated with

with a latticework of tiny calcium needles. Others produce a horny resilient material called gorgonin and develop into long spiral whip corals or intricate fans. These grow at right angles to the current and act as living sieves, filtering out food particles as the water flows through.

All corals are really predatory animals and their polyps have tentacles that are armed with stinging cells that stun microscopic prey. Most of these stings are harmless to humans, but the one coral to learn to recognise and avoid is the so-

the anemone fish, also known as the clown fish. Theirs is a classic symbiotic relationship: the anemone fish gains shelter and protection from the anemone, and in return the anemone gets scraps of food from the resident fish. Although the anemone fish is able to develop a protection to the anemone's stings they are still a powerful deterrent to a would-be predator. The exact mechanism of the anemone-fish's immunity is not clearly understood but it is thought that the mucus coating covering the scales of the fish which it wears like a coat absorbs small amounts of the anemone's sting; the anemone begins to accept this coated fish as being itself and thus no longer tries to sting it.

LEFT: a green turtle: clumsy on land, graceful in the water.
RIGHT: giant potato cod, motionless on the seabed.

Kaleidoscope of colours

For many snorkellers, and even divers, it is the brightly coloured and most visible fish which gather in the shallower waters around and above the reef that leave the strongest impression. Many of these fish are in fact deep water species which come into the shallows to feed. Colourful schools of fusiliers, known locally as mackerel, have the characteristic "fishy" shape of a torpedo-like body with small fins, and feed on phyto-plankton above the reefs. Most of the common species have bright blue body colourings with a mixture of stripes and flashes ranging from yellow through to pink,

which shimmer in a vivid colour display as the school moves.

On the reef itself the two most colourful species are the angelfish and butterfly fish both of which have bodies which are flattened from side to side when viewed from ahead and are almost circular when viewed in profile. Butterfly fish are generally small, around 8–15 cm (3–6 in) across the disc and are predominantly algal and coral grazers; most have body colours which are yellow, black or white. Angelfish species are larger in size, up to 25 cm (10 in), and display a wide range of markings. They also have different patterns in juvenile forms compared to the final adult phases and so add enormously to the colour of the living reef.

A larger visitor to the coral reef is the hawksbill turtle; this is probably the most commonly found marine turtle species in this region and takes its name from its hooked hawk-like beak which it uses to carve chunks off sponges and soft coral formations. In some areas of Seychelles these turtles may be be found nesting on the beaches in daylight – a very unusual sight.

Just like a rock reef, the coral reef offers shelter and protection to a vast number of species as well as being a food source for some of its residents. Some fish are especially adapted to feeding on coral polyps, such as certain butterfly fish and filefish; others feed on small shrimp and other invertebrates that shelter between the branches, such as the razor or shrimpfish.

Molluscs are frequent residents; the most obvious of these are the brightly coloured nudibranchs, or sea slugs. Despite their small size they are the most apparent because of their bright coloration that warns would-be predators that they do not taste good and might be poisonous. A number of shelled molluscs can be found during the day as well but many have highly camouflaged shells to conceal them so they can be difficult to find.

Other animals actually live within the limestone of the coral colony; these include the tube or "feather-duster" worms that are evident from their coloured fans which extend above the surface of the coral colony to trap particles. Some are spectacularly formed into twin spiral cones, as in the Christmas-tree worm, and these pretty structures are often brightly coloured. All fan worms are sensitive to changes in light and as such will disappear into their tubes on the sudden appearance of a snorkeller or diver.

In the deep

The open ocean is a very different and much more inaccessible environment. The deep waters and their currents support creatures from microscopic plankton to some of the largest animals on the planet but often the concentration of individuals is very low. Due to the constraints of deep water activities, most people will only get the chance to see these creatures when they come to the surface. Luckily, some places seem to have special properties that encourage deep water species to aggregate at the surface; in

CHEMICAL WEAPONS

Many molluscs secrete chemical substances which, without being poisonous, are distasteful enough to put off a would-be predator.

of the air performing aerial twists and acrobatics. In some instances these places are special feeding or breeding areas and although the animals may appear to be easily approachable in organised encounter programmes, there are strict codes of conduct to ensure the safety of visitors and the protection of the animals concerned.

Some deep water species are generally only seen when landed by fishing boats; these big game species such as sailfish, marlin, wahoo and dorado are relatively abundant but are sel-

these areas it is possible to find whales and dolphins at specific times of the year.

Dolphins are one group that visitors are likely to come across on boat journeys around the islands, although in-water encounters are unfortunately a rare occurrence. There are a number of species in this area and the larger bottlenose and common dolphins are most often seen. In more remote areas there are local populations of the smaller species, notably spinner dolphins, which are readily recognisable by the habit of the youngsters to leap out

dom seen in their natural environment. Other deep water animals are sometimes washed ashore by the ocean currents. These include several varieties of medusa or jelly-fish; characteristically these have a clear gelatinous bell-shaped body and like their coral cousins they have a ring of stinging tentacles. While some jellyfish are harmless others can deliver a powerful and possibly lethal sting and so contact should be avoided.

The Indian Ocean offers a huge diversity of life. Whether you choose to scuba dive, snorkel or take a glass-bottom boat trip, a glimpse into this magical underwater world will most certainly be a highlight of your trip. ❑

LEFT: one of many colourful species of butterfly fish.
RIGHT: potato lips grouper.

TROPICAL ISLAND BLOOMS

From delicate orchids and hibiscus to vibrant bougainvillaea and flaming red flamboyants, the richness and variety of plant life are astounding

When the first explorers set eyes on the Indian Ocean islands, it was the luxuriant forests and sweet-smelling colourful plants that led them to believe they had found Eden. In Mauritius, three centuries of human habitation have brought plantations, roads and logging, and destroyed many of the island's plants. In Seychelles, the shorter human history, absence of plantations and mountainous islands have helped preserve the environment. Réunion, too, was more fortunate: its rocky and mountainous landscape is more inaccessible, so large areas of its natural forests have remained untouched.

Although many species are still endangered, the islands' flora remains rich: Mauritius has 685 native species of which 311 are endemic; Réunion has 700 indigenous species of which 161 are endemic; Seychelles, too has a remarkable flora. Of more than 1,100 species, over 400 are native, with 75 endemic to the granitic islands and a further 43 found only in the Aldabra group.

BOTANICAL GARDENS

All the islands have botanical gardens where visitors can admire and learn about the abundant plant life. Mauritius has the famous Pamplemousses gardens near Port-Louis, the Curepipe Botanical Gardens and Le Pétrin Native Garden in the Black River Gorges area; Réunion has the Conservatoire Botanique National in St-Leu and the Jardin de l'Etat near St-Denis; and in Seychelles you can visit the Botanical Gardens and the Jardin du Roi spice gardens, both on Mahé.

△ **PASSIFLORA**
Luxuriant passion fruit vines grow all over Seychelles. The fruit is used for juices.

▷ **QUEEN OF THE TROPICS**
The delicate hibiscus flower comes in myriad colours, but the bloom only lasts for one day.

◁ BLOOMING BUSINESS

The growing of anthuriums is big business in Mauritius. The waxy blooms come in a variety of colours and sizes, and last for several weeks.

△ LOTUS BLOSSOM

One of around 500 plant species you can see in Mauritius' famous Pamplemousses Gardens, not far from the capital, Port-Louis.

◁ A BLAZE OF COLOUR

With its dense canopy of bright red flowers, the flamboyant tree in bloom is an impressive sight. It flowers between November and January.

▽ BIRD-OF-PARADISE

The stem of this most distinctive of tropical plants calls to mind the long neck of a bird, while its vibrant blossoms are like the tuft of feathers on the bird's crown – hence the name.

△ MAY FLOWER

The essential oil from geraniums cultivated in Réunion is considered by the perfume industry to be the best in the world.

▷ SWEET AROMA

The exquisite-smelling vanilla orchid opens only for a few hours in the morning.

LA VANILLE BOURBON

Vanilla was introduced to Réunion from Central America in 1819, but attempts at natural pollination failed. Then, in 1841, a 12-year-old slave called Edmund Albius discovered that flowers could be pollinated by grafting. By the end of the 19th century Réunion was churning out 100 tons a year. Annual production has dropped significantly since then, but the island remains one of the world's leading producers. Cultivation is concentrated on the lush eastern side of the island where the warm, wet conditions are ideal. The pods are harvested between June and September, about eight months after pollination. Still green, they are scalded in boiling water then laid out in the sun to dry. Now brown, the pods are then left in airtight containers for eight months during which time they develop their strong aroma.

don Josao 24

ñ furtado

ão

.co depai ua

Simaoda neijna

don .co f coutinho

moronga cõ

EA POS ESTEVE O DOM PEDRO
CASTELOBRA MCOOMESMOA

niculao gu   zarte

dõp de castlo   Rco

@dsecasco

g de rrusa

Ant.º de sousa

f.co fiz leme

baltezar gil cz

lionel d lin

f.co fiz

am.to lobo

rjda de sousa

f.co fiz

THE MASCARENES

The Mascarene islands each offer very different landscapes
and completely different experiences

Named after the Portuguese admiral, Pedro Mascarenhas, whose fleet anchored by the uninhabited islands nearly 500 years ago, the Mascarenes had lain undisturbed since they rose from the sea in a series of volcanic eruptions millions of years before. Even so, their discovery hardly led to a mad rush to colonise. And as far as tourism is concerned, they were never more than a dot on the map until a trickle of visitors started in the 1970s.

For most people, Mauritius is, of course, the best known island, but the French have been holidaying in Réunion for years. If you're in Mauritius, the 35-minute hop to St-Denis is easy and you can see some of the best of the island in just two or three days if time is limited. For Mauritius regulars, the short hop to Rodrigues is becoming an increasingly attractive proposition.

Mauritius is, in many ways, the archetypal romantic idyll with gorgeous fine-sanded beaches, hotels whose standards would put most of their counterparts around the world to shame, and everything else laid on to ensure you forget all your worries. With such a reputation for pampering its visitors, it is perhaps not surprising that the island's exclusive beachside hotels attract so many of the world's rich and famous.

Rodrigues, an integral part of Mauritius, lies 640 km (400 miles) east and is markedly different from the motherland in character and culture. This is the place to come for a taste of authentic island life. Being so isolated and still relatively inaccessible, it remains unspoilt – so far at least. There are no high-rise buildings, shopping malls or Bondi-style beaches here: just rugged beauty, a warm and welcoming people and plenty of peace and quiet.

Just 160 km (100 miles) southwest of Mauritius is Réunion, where the first thing to strike you as your plane makes its descent into St-Denis is the awesome nature of the landscape, whose volcano and cirques force most islanders to live along the coast. No one should come here and not explore inland and upwards, but wherever you go you will be entertained by the bizarre spectacle of trying to work out where classic Frenchness ends and local creole culture begins.

Few people discover all the islands of the Mascarenes in one trip, but whichever you choose, adopt a little creole insouciance along the way. Take it easy. ❑

PRECEDING PAGES: aerial view of the luxury Coco Beach Hotel at Belle Mare, Mauritius; Portuguese fleet en route to the East Indies, 1533.
LEFT: along for the ride; fishermen ferry passengers between the Touessrok hotel and Île aux Cerfs.

Decisive Dates

EARLY DISCOVERERS

10th–12th centuries Arabs sight the Mascarenes and produce the first rough maps and descriptions of them.

15th century The Arab names of Dina Arobi, Dina Margabim and Dina Moraze for Mauritius, Réunion and Rodrigues, appear on early world maps. The Arab traders did not settle.

1498 Vasco da Gama rounds the Cape of Good Hope en route to the Indies. More Portuguese expeditions follow.

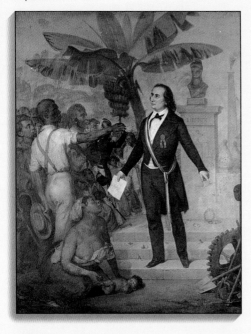

1505 Mascarenes appear on Portuguese maps; probably renamed by Diego Diaz.

1507 Portuguese navigator, Diego Fernandez Perera, names Mauritius "Ilha do Cirne".

1513 The islands are named after the officer commanding Portuguese fleets of discovery in the region, Pedro Mascarenhas.

1528 A Portuguese seaman, Diogo Rodriguez, visits Rodrigues and gives the island his name.

THE DUTCH YEARS

1598 First Dutch landing at Port South East in Ilha do Cirne. Annexed to Holland and renamed Mauritius after Prince Maurice of Nassau, son of William of Orange.

1600–20 Founding of first East India trading companies.

1601 First Dutch landing in Rodrigues.

1619 Dutch East India Company established in Batavia (Java).

1638–1710 Dutch settle at Port South East, Mauritius but abandon it after several attempts to colonise. First slaves imported from Madagascar. Sugar cane, deer, pigs from Java introduced.

1642 The French (under Governor Pronis) take possession of Rodrigues and Réunion which they name Mascareigne and later Bourbon.

1652 Dutch East India Company establish another settlement at Cape of Good Hope.

1663 First official occupation by French settlers in Bourbon.

1688 Last recorded sighting of dodo on Mauritius.

1691–93 François Leguat and nine adventurers become Rodrigues' first settlers. They stay on the island for two years.

THE FRENCH PERIOD

1710 The Dutch leave Mauritius.

1715 French annex Mauritius and call it Île de France. Control of the island is held by the French East India Company (Compagnie des Indes Orientales).

1721–1810 French occupy Île de France. Slaves from Madagascar, Africa and Asia imported to work sugar cane plantations.

1735 Mahé de Labourdonnais takes over as governor of the Mascarene Islands, basing himself on Île de France. He expands port and builds first sugar mill, hospital and road network.

1740–48 War of the Austrian Succession.

1742 Lazare Picault leads an expedition to chart the islands northeast of Madagascar, reporting to Mahé de Labourdonnais. Previously charted by the Portuguese as the Seven Sisters, they were renamed Seychelles after Vicomte Jean Moreau de Séchelles, the French Controller General.

1756–63 The Seven Years' War so seriously affects French interests in the Indian Ocean that by 1764 the French East India Company is forced to officially hand Île de France to the French crown.

1770 First settlement in Seychelles, on the island of Ste Anne.

1790 News of the French Revolution reaches the Mascarenes.

1794 Abolition of slavery declared in France.

1793–1805 Privateering reaches its peak in the Indian Ocean with huge losses to British East India Company. French Revolution leads to

creation of colonial assemblies in all the islands. Fear of losing their slaves provokes local resistance to French political emissaries. Île de France renamed Île Bonaparte and Bourbon renamed Réunion.
1799 Napoleon controls France. General Decaen is sent to repossess Île de France. Slavery is allowed to continue.

THE BRITISH PERIOD

1810 Weakened by Napoleonic wars, Île de France and Réunion capitulate to British naval forces. Île de France reverts to its former name, Mauritius.
1814 The Treaty of Paris places Mauritius, Rodrigues and Seychelles under British ownership while Réunion is handed back to the French.
1835 The British abolish slavery in Mauritius and compensate slave owners to the tune of £2 million. Indian indentured labourers, or "coolies", introduced to work the sugar cane plantations.
1848 Slavery abolished in Réunion.
1862 First railway in Mauritius.
1872 Royal Commission appointed to look into the problems of Indian immigrants.
1885 Mauritians William Newton and Virgile Naz found the Reform Movement, leading to the introduction of the country's own constitution.

THE MODERN AGE

1903 Seychelles is given the status of British Crown Colony.
1909 Indian immigration ceases and another Royal Commission appointed to make recommendations for political and social reform.
1936 Labour Party formed in Mauritius
1946 Réunion becomes an overseas French *département.*
1947 Mackenzie-Kennedy Constitution gives the right to vote to all Mauritians who can read and write.
1964 Formation of political parties in the Seychelles.
1968 Mauritius achieves independence from Great Britain and is admitted as a member of the Commonwealth. Rodrigues becomes a dependency of Mauritius. Sir Seewoosagur Ramgoolam is elected first prime minister.
1976 Republic of Seychelles declared under a

coalition government of Seychelles Democratic Party (SDP) and People's United Party (PUP). James Mancham becomes first president.
1977 A bloodless coup ousts Mancham. He is replaced by Albert René.
1981 Bungled coup in Seychelles by Colonel "Mad Mike" Hoare and a group of mercenaries posing as a South African rugby team.
1982 Sir Seewoosagur Ramgoolam defeated in general election in which all 60 seats are won by political alliance of Mouvement Militant Mauricien (MMM) and the Parti Socialiste Mauricien (PSM). Aneerood Jugnauth, leader of the MMM, becomes prime minister.

1992 Republic of Mauritius is declared. Rodrigues becomes an integral part of Mauritius. Jugnauth remains prime minister of the new republic.
1993 Multi-party elections held in Seychelles. Albert René remains prime minister
1995 Labour Party wins election. Navin Ramgoolam (son of the late Sir Seewoosagur) becomes prime minister of the Republic of Mauritius.
2000 Jugnauth elected Prime Minister. The removal of Chagos islanders from Chagos Archipelago by Britain between 1965–1971 declared unlawful by High Court in London.
2001 President Cassam Uteem resigns and is replaced by Karl Offman.
2002 Rodrigues granted regional autonomy. ❑

LEFT: declaration of the abolition of slavery in Réunion, 1848.
RIGHT: coverage of the 1995 elections, won by the Labour Party.

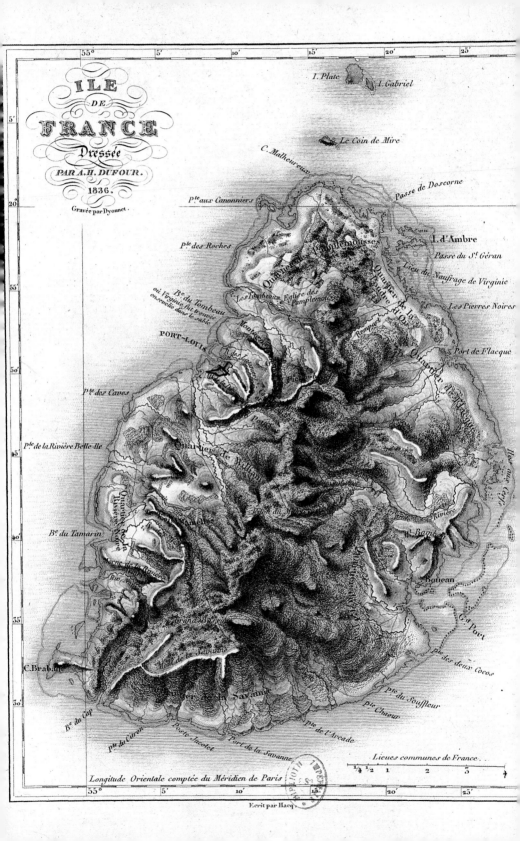

ILE DE FRANCE

Dressée

PAR A.H. DUFOUR.

1836.

Gravée par Dyonnet.

I. Plate   I. Gabriel

Le Coin de Mire

C. Malheureux

Passe de Doscorne

Pte aux Canonniers

I. d'Ambre

Pte des Roches   Passe du St Géran

Quartier des Pamplemousses   Lieu du Naufrage de Virginie

Les Pierres Noires

Bie du Tombeau
où Virginie fut trouvée
ensevelie dans le sable   Les Tombeaux Eglise des Pamplemousses   Quartier de la Grande Rivière

PORT-LOUIS   Rempart   Port de Flacque

Montagne   Quartier d'Flacque

Pte des Caves

Pte de la Rivière Belle-Ile   Quartier de Moka

Rivière

Bie du Tamarin   Be Bane

Quartier de la Rivière Noire   Boucan

Grand Bassin   Gd Port

Pte des deux Cocos

Haut de la Savanne   Pte du Souffleur

C. Brabant   Quartier de la Savanne   Pte Chaux

Bie du Cap   Pte de l'Arcade

Pte du Citron Poste Jacotet Port de la Savanne

Lieues communes de France

¼ ½ 1   2   3   4

Longitude Orientale comptée du Méridien de Paris.

Ecrit par Haeq.

SAILORS AND EXPLORERS: DISCOVERERS OF THE MASCARENES

From the Arabs and Portuguese, to the Dutch, French and English, the history of the Mascarenes has been determined by traders, explorers, colonisers and corsairs

The Mascarenes were all uninhabited until the arrival of European colonisers from the 16th century. Ever since, these islands have been subjected to the whims of European taste and ambitions which have determined their population, their pursuits and, to a large extent, their politics.

The Mascarenes are oceanic islands – they did not break away from continental land masses but developed independently as a result of volcanic action. Mauritius is the oldest at about 8 million years, Réunion and Rodrigues are around 3 and 2 million years old respectively. The islands are affected by volatile weather conditions; and the vagaries of trade winds and cyclones which blew countless sailing ships off course or onto reefs, meant that it was as likely accident and misfortune as intrepid exploration which provoked the first sightings of these small land masses in the southwestern Indian Ocean.

The earliest recorded proof of the identification and location of the islands is from Arab documents and maps. Writings dating back to the 12th century include descriptions of islands which may be the Mascarenes. In 1498, Vasco da Gama saw maps by Ibn Majid in which three islands southeast of Madagascar are named Dina Moraze, Dina Margabim and Dina Arobi, which roughly translate as "eastern", "western" and "deserted" islands.

It was not until the early 16th century that Portuguese explorers became the first recorded European visitors to the Mascarenes. They named Mauritius "Cirne", probably after one of their ships, Réunion "Santa Apolina" after the date of its discovery and Rodrigues, after the navigator Diego Rodriguez, the only one of the islands to retain its Portuguese name. The

Portuguese only occasionally used the Mascarenes route on their way to the Indies but it was a welcome place of respite for damaged ships and weary crews which found themselves blown towards these archetypal desert islands.

Dodos, tortoises and ebony

Still uninhabited in the early 17th century, the fertility and unspoilt nature of the Mascarene islands were extolled by Dutch, French and English visitors. Samuel Castleton, who first set eyes on Réunion in 1613, described thick forest, cascading waterfalls, fat eels in the rivers and plentiful turtles and birds. In homage to its natural beauty, he named the island "England's Forest". The Dutchman, Mandelslo, wrote that Mauritius teemed with figs, pomegranates, partridges and pigeons. There were no cats, pigs, goats, dogs or even rats – at least not until some escaped from ships wrecked near Mascarene shores.

LEFT: early map of Île de France.
RIGHT: engraving of a scene from the 18th-century novel *Paul et Virginie*, a romantic tale inspired by a shipwreck off Île d'Ambre.

These early visitors brought back drawings of a strange flightless bird, indigenous to Mauritius and Réunion. It was described as fat, clumsy and bigger than a turkey. In 1628, Emmanuel Altham sent a live specimen of this "strange fowle" home to his brother in Essex. This was the dodo *(see page 67)* whose relative, the solitaire, was found on Réunion and Rodrigues.

The ebony forests on Mauritius, and its two natural harbours, made it a colonial prize for European traders and explor-

WHAT'S IN A NAME?

The Mascarene Island group is named after the Portuguese navigator Pedro Mascarenhas. Like Columbus, he has probably been given more credit than his due, as he did not discover any of them.

groups combined with soldiers and sailors who deserted from the garrison and visiting ships' crews to form a counter-settlement in the forested interior. They launched frequent raids and arson attacks on the fort and farmers. The difficult conditions of the earlier settlers were made worse by seasonal cyclones, which ripped through their fragile wooden homesteads, and by the depradations of rats who ate the crops and stores. The ruins of the Dutch fort at Grand Port can be seen to this day, having only

ers. Annexed for the Netherlands in 1598, the Dutch felled much of the valuable black wood on the island, until a glut in the European market slowed the destruction.

Colonisation begins

The Dutch occupied Mauritius twice, between 1638 and 1658, and again from 1664 to 1710. Their first settlement was around the southeast harbour (where present-day Mahébourg is now situated). The garrison and commander, along with a small group of free farmers, brought convicts and slaves from Southeast Asia and Madagascar to help them with wood-cutting and crop cultivation. Runaways from these

been excavated in 1997 by archaeologists.

While the Dutch were establishing their settlement on Mauritius, the French had annexed the other Mascarene islands. Both nations supplemented piecemeal colonisation by sending unruly settlers from their bases at the Cape, Batavia and Madagascar into exile on the Mascarenes.

Bourbon, later renamed Réunion, was given its royal name by the French governor at Madagascar after hearing from a group of returned exiles of its beauty, abundance and healthiness. In 1654, the French attempted a permanent settlement of the island with a mixed group of French and Malagasy. They left four years later and Bourbon remained unoccupied until 1663.

The next group of settlers included three women, but disputes over them led to the creation of rival camps of French and Malagasy men. Attempts to send volunteers from France met with mixed results – many died en route.

Two events then proved a turning point for Bourbon: firstly the French were massacred on Madagascar, forcing the abandonment of that base, and secondly war with Holland closed off the Cape to French ships. Bourbon now became an important post for them on the Indies route. A governor was appointed from France, and, in a series of efforts to boost the size of the population, Indian convicts were imported, Indo-Portuguese women were induced to settle, and pirates, tired of a life of plunder, were invited to marry into the growing Bourbon community.

CRUSOE'S ISLAND

The Mascarenes were legendary refuges. Mandelslo's description of a man marooned on Mauritius in 1601 is said to have provided Daniel Defoe with inspiration for his tale Robinson Crusoe.

Paradise lost

The glowing description of Bourbon made by its first forced inhabitants had also inspired a group of Protestants, persecuted in France, to set up their Eden on the last remaining desert island of the Mascarenes. François Leguat was one of eight males who settled on Rodrigues until the effects of solitude and the lack of women led them to escape in a small boat to Mauritius. Utopia, it seemed, could not be achieved without sex.

The reality of life on a tropical desert island was far removed from the visions of recuperating sailors and persecuted Protestants. The small settlements, peopled with prisoners and pirates, neglected by the trading companies, presided over by frustrated commanders and weakly defended, found survival a struggle. Geographical constraints – isolation and unreliable weather – had been revealed to be major determinants of Mascarenes history.

The impact of these visitors from across the seas was immense. The fragile island ecologies were irreparably damaged by human settlement and the animals they imported that upset the natural balance. The coastal palms and the ebony forests were depleted. Eventually 30 species of birds, including the dodo and solitaire, and the large tortoises and turtles with whom they cohabited, would become extinct – casualties of the fragility of unique small island populations.

The Mascarene Islands have become the archetypal example of the destruction of ecological systems by outsiders. Once this process began, it took only a few decades for these small island "Edens" to vanish forever.

The French century

Between 1710, when the Dutch left, and 1810 when the British took control, the French had a century of uninterrupted supremacy in the Mascarenes. Over this period the islands served several purposes: as a rest and refuelling point for European ships on the Indies route, where goods could be traded and ships repaired; as cultivating grounds for spices and coffee; and as good vantage points for the study of astronomic phenomena.

Already established on Bourbon, in 1721 the French sent a party of colonists from there to settle on Mauritius, renamed Île de France. A governor and several hundred soldiers and

LEFT: the Dutch settlement at Vieux Grand Port.
RIGHT: Mauritius was named after Maurice of Nassau, son of William of Orange.

colonists were also sent from France, arriving the following year with 30 Malagasy slaves they had acquired en route. They settled in the southeast of the island, building on top of the Dutch ruins. Administered from Bourbon, both islands struggled to master their environment. One visitor to Île de France at this time sarcastically renamed it "Kingdom of the Rats", describing the discomfort of nights spent trying to ignore them crawling over his body.

SLAVE LABOUR

The French author of *Paul et Virginie*, Bernardin de Saint Pierre, observed: "I do not know whether coffee and sugar are necessary to the happiness of Europe, but they have certainly made much of the world miserable".

A decisive change occurred in the administration of the French Mascarenes in 1735, with the arrival of Mahé de Labourdonnais, and the decision to transfer the seat of government to Île de France. For the rest of the 18th century, Bourbon was relegated to what its colonists believed to be the inferior position of "granary", supplying food for its sister island, and watching as the latter developed into a substantial trading and naval repair post.

Labourdonnais aimed to transform Île de France into a flourishing colony, but his ambitious plans could not be achieved without labour, and from this period, the trickle of West Africans and Asians arriving with visiting ships was regularly supplemented by the organisa-

tion of slave trading voyages to East Africa and Madagascar, and the importation of skilled workers from India and France. With serious food shortages threatening the increased population, Labourdonnais introduced manioc to the Mascarenes, which became a staple food of slaves, and began the systematic plunder of tortoises from Rodrigues. This marked the beginning of the irreversible decline of its endemic land and marine fauna, a process accelerated by the periodic presence of naval squadrons.

By 1767 the French East India Company, suffering severe financial losses occasioned by years of warfare, gave up control of the Mascarenes to the French king. Port Louis was able to expand its trading activities which had been limited by the Company's monopolistic practices, and developed an air of prosperity and style which led to its designation as the "Paris of the Indian Ocean".

But this facade of culture, elegance and profit concealed an economy based on speculation and a society in which the presence of celebrated intellectuals and naturalists could not prevent the continuing destruction of nature and the differentiation of men by colour and chains.

The French had hoped to use the Mascarenes to further their interest in the spice trade and to cultivate tropical produce. Colonists were encouraged to grow coffee, cotton, indigo, cane, cinnamon, tea and pepper. Cloves and nutmegs were introduced. Many crops failed – eaten by birds, rats and monkeys or destroyed by adverse weather conditions. Coffee and spices grown on Bourbon nevertheless became the principal exports of the Mascarenes, while sugar cane was found to resist the onslaught of the elements best at Île de France. Its cultivation, expanding towards the end of the 18th century, was to become the defining feature of the Mascarenes in the 19th century.

Revolution and rebellion

French rule in the Mascarenes had instituted a kind of social apartheid which subjected slaves to the provisions of the Code Noir – a famous French law applied to their colonies which prevented the free coloured population from marrying white colonists. After 1789, the revolutionary fervour emanating from France swept away such laws and unleashed a chain of events in the French colonies which culminated in the breakaway of Haiti and provoked a rebellion in the Mascarenes.

News of the French Revolution did not reach the Indian Ocean islands until the following year, but once ships bearing the tricolour arrived, Colonial Assemblies were set up on the islands and the royal name of Bourbon was changed to Réunion. The revolution was not very bloody in the Mascarenes although one notable victim was MacNamara, a royalist naval officer who was hacked to death by a

– they were thrown out within three days. For a while the islands ruled themselves but not without serious disagreements which almost led to Réunion separating from its sister island.

The arrival of Napoleon on the political scene led to the re-establishment of slavery and in 1803 he sent General Decaen to rule, granting him absolute power over the Mascarenes. Réunion was promptly renamed Bonaparte Island but, once again, did not flourish in the shadow of Île de France. The rigid social and fiscal legislation introduced by Decaen was designed for, and discriminated in favour of, the latter.

mob in Port Louis. Restrictions on marriages between white and coloured colonists were lifted and the gulf between social groups was briefly narrowed.

In 1796, however, the Revolutionary government in France took matters too far for the liking of the colonists. Having proclaimed the abolition of slavery, France sent two representatives to the Mascarenes to put this into effect

LEFT: the horrors of slavery. Roughly translated, the French inscription beneath reads "all that serves your pleasure, is soaked with our tears".
RIGHT: engraving of Governor Mahé de Labourdonnais being welcomed by islanders.

MAHÉ DE LABOURDONNAIS

Mahé de Labourdonnais is fêted in Mauritius and his statue stands in the centre of Port Louis, its capital, because in a few short years he transformed this natural harbour into the beginnings of a flourishing port.

Some of the works he undertook are still in evidence today. The renovated mill and granary on the waterfront of Port Louis are vestiges of this formative period. Labourdonnais also built a hospital, established a road network and imported the first primitive sugar processing equipment to be used in Mauritius, which can still be seen in the grounds of Pamplemousses Botanical Gardens, formerly the site of his estates.

Pirates, traitors and spies

For Portuguese and particularly British ships plying the route to the Indies, the French Mascarenes were by now chiefly known for being a "nest of pirates". Between 1793 and 1802 more than a hundred captured ships were brought into Port Louis where the booty on offer attracted neutral peoples like the Danes and Americans. The port was also popular with sailors: the increasing cultivation of sugar cane meant that one of its by-products, rum, was widely available, and it was one of the few places on the Indies route, outside the Cape, where men did not heavily outnumber women,

and where the latter were reputed to be generous in distributing their favours.

These privateering activities led by the king of the corsairs, Robert Surcouf, were the chief reason why the British decided to target the Mascarenes. In 1806 they blockaded Île de France, where the celebrated British explorer and naturalist Matthew Flinders was then imprisoned. Flinders and other British prisoners and reconnaissance agents who had been sent ashore, were offered information and hospitality from colonists who were either royalist sympathisers or pragmatists.

This did not prevent the British from overestimating the strength of French forces. They sent an armada from Bombay and the Cape, which regrouped at Rodrigues and took Bourbon (later Réunion) in July 1810 without much struggle.

Île de France was not so easy a conquest. In August, the British were defeated after a three-day naval battle in Mahébourg bay, known as the battle of Grand Port. In November 1810 they returned to the attack with 70 ships and 10,000 troops, landing on the north coast and marching to the capital. Both sides recognised that the numerical superiority of the British was such as to make unnecessary bloodshed pointless. So Decaen negotiated an honourable capitulation.

After the conquest, Île de France and Bourbon were renamed Mauritius and Réunion. The British retained control of Réunion until 1814 when the Treaty of Paris returned the island to French rule. Louis XVIII is supposed to have commented to the British Minister who negotiated the deal: "You are leaving us the volcano and you are keeping the port".

Abolitionist movement

The British conquest of Mauritius and Rodrigues, undertaken for strategic motives, did not lead to a large influx of British settlers, and the Francophone character of the Mascarenes has consequently never been lost.

Early British colonial officials not only had to deal with a largely French settler class, but had to implement unpopular slave amelioration laws. The abolitionist movement, which had a massive following in Britain at this time, turned its attention to Mauritius at the worst possible moment for that colony. The island was in the process of converting itself into a plantation society and needed extra labour to clear land and plant canes. When John Jeremie, a known abolitionist, was sent to the island in 1832 to take up an important legal post, the colonists gave him a "welcome" akin to that received by the delegates from France during the Revolution. A general strike was organised which paralysed the capital and the fearful British governor ordered Jeremie to re-embark almost immediately. In response, the British built Fort Adelaide on a

MOUNTAIN REFUGE

In 1811 a slave revolt on Réunion led to the execution of 30 ringleaders. A later uprising in Mauritius was also snuffed out. But for as long as slavery was in force, the Mascarene mountains remained a refuge for runaways.

free labour could produce sugar as cheaply as slaves, by allowing the colony the first opportunity to import Indian workers under the indenture system – which tied labour immigrants to fixed wage contracts with penal clauses, so that if a labourer could or would not work he could be imprisoned. Almost half a million indentured workers were introduced in the 19th century, making Mauritius the largest recipient of Indian labour in the Empire and helping the island to achieve the position of

hill overlooking the capital – a striking symbol of colonial power designed to quell its unruly inhabitants. The colonists were appeased by a £2 million compensation package for their slaves (including those that had been illegally introduced) and the day of emancipation passed without incident in 1835.

Immigrant labour

In 1842 the British decided to make Mauritius the site of a "great experiment' to see whether

LEFT: "King of the Corsairs", Robert Surcouf, captures the British vessel, *Kent*, in the Bay of Bengal in 1800.
RIGHT: Indian labourers.

Britain's premier sugar colony within a decade.

Both Réunion and Mauritius had turned increasingly to sugar production as falling supplies from the British and French West Indies encouraged the newer colonies to fill the gap. Réunion was given the go ahead to import British Indian labour from 1860, and both islands continued to recruit smaller numbers of Chinese, Malagasy, Comorian and Mozambican workers. Africans rescued from slave ships by British naval cruisers were also offloaded at Mauritius and the Seychelles from the mid-19th century and "liberated" into lengthy apprenticeships with local employers.

Réunion adapted to socio-economic change

at a more gentle rate than Mauritius. It was slower to abolish slavery (abolition was declared in 1848, 13 years after Mauritius), and slower to develop into a mono-culture economy. Both islands, nevertheless, underwent a revo-lution of sorts, as mechanisation and centralisation of estates transformed them into plantation societies where plantocracies confronted increasing ranks of immigrant labour. Only Rod-rigues remained primarily an agricultural colony and did not experience the vast influx of Indian

labour which had transformed the demographic characteristics of its neighbours. Administered from Mauritius, Rodrigues was only rarely visited by British governors.

Indentured labourers were contracted to work at a fixed wage for a varying number of years. Breaches of contract were punishable by imprisonment, and the physical chastise-ment and limited mobility of Indian workers made their treatment akin to that of slaves. In 1872 and 1877 Commissions of Enquiry were sent to Mauritius and Réunion respectively to compile reports on the conditions of these workers, and they found much evidence of malpractice.

> **DEMON DRINK**
>
> Mark Twain, who visited Mauritius in 1896, noted a local saying about new settlers: "The first year they gather shells; the second year they gather shells and drink; the third year they do not gather shells".

Disease and disaster

When sugar prices began to fall in the last quarter of the 19th century, the distress of the enormously enlarged popula-tions of the islands increased their vulnerability to outbreaks of such deadly diseases as smallpox, cholera and malaria. In 1892, a fierce cyclone hit Mauritius, killing 1,260 people, and making 50,000 homeless, while Réunion experienced periodic eruptions of its active volcano. But the sequence of disasters did not end there – rats once again wreaked devastation on the Mascarenes as bubonic plague struck, and in 1902 a fly-borne parasite necessitated the slaughter of thousands of horses, mules and cattle in Mauritius. The islands were at their lowest ebb and were a far cry from the idyllic Edens encountered barely 200 years before.

With the sugar economy still in a state of depression, the flow of labour immigration had all but ended, but traders, principally Chinese and Gujarati, continued to settle in the Mas-carenes, and gradually took over the retail and wholesale sectors. On the other hand, emigra-tion began to take place from Réunion to Mada-gascar and from Mauritius to South Africa as colonists sought opportunities elsewhere.

Politically, progress was swift in Réunion which moved from a system of absolute gov-ernment to one of universal suffrage, and was given the right to be represented in the French Parliament from 1870. Mauritius, by contrast, did not have an elected legislative council until 1885. In both islands, however, a few wealthy planter families continued to wield dispropor-tionate influence.

Post-war Mascarenes

World War I brought an increase in sugar prices and a degree of prosperity was restored to the Mascarenes, but by the 1930s, the dis-affection among labourers had transformed into widely orchestrated strikes on both Mau-ritius and Réunion.

World War II affected the islands much more directly. The British hurriedly set up naval and air bases on Mauritius, while the Vichy régime, installed on Réunion, isolated the island and brought it to the verge of famine. Following the war, both islands were supplied with a regular air service, becoming increasingly accessible to visitors.

Réunion was given the status of a *département* or district of France in 1946 (along with Martinique, Guadeloupe and French Guyana). The flow of capital from France produced a socio-economic power shift from the planter class towards the growing public and commercial sectors of the economy.

Departmentalisation entailed a process of assimilation, which Réunion, little touched by

> **SUEZ CANAL**
>
> The cutting of the Suez Canal robbed the Mascarenes of strategic significance. Ironically, De Lesseps' wife was Mauritian and many of her compatriots worked on the construction of the Canal.

The 1980s was a period of political radicalism in Mauritius also with the rise of the left-wing Mouvement Militant Mauricien, the MMM, which gained a huge following under the banner of "one nation, one people". Both of these movements have ultimately been limited in their effects and the struggle to create a sense of national identity – Réunion against the linguistic and cultural hegemony of France, and Mauritius against the competing claims of ethnic identity – goes on.

the "negritude" movement of the French Caribbean to assert "black power", seemed initially disinclined to resist. However, since 1959 when the Communist Party was set up, there has always been a movement on the island fighting for the recognition of a distinctively Réunionese identity. This was partly achieved in 1981 when the acknowledgement of a "right to difference" produced a kind of cultural revolution to accompany the political departmentalisation revolution.

LEFT: Chinese immigrant women, *circa* 1910.
RIGHT: Independence Day celebrations in the Mauritian capital, Port Louis.

Independence

Independence was something of a brokered affair, with Britain willingly divesting itself of the island in 1968 in return for the British Indian Ocean Territory created from a group of smaller, dependent islands. The Americans were promptly leased one of these – Diego Garcia – for use as a military base, which has become of increasing importance to them in Indian Ocean geopolitics.

The growing recognition in Mauritius that independence would lead to rule by the Indian majority led to fears of Hinduisation policies, and the 1968 celebrations were marred by ethnic violence and the emigration of disaffected minorities. Between 1968 and 1982 the ruling Labour Party did indeed become increasingly identified with its Hindu power base, but it was the combination of corruption scandals, over-population and high unemployment, which swept the opposition MMM into office in the early 1980s. The shift to radicalism was short-lived. Since then, Mauritius has been governed by a series of coalitions of four principal parties – Labour, the MMM, the PMSD and the PSM – all of which have a pro-capitalist stance. In 1992, Mauritius became a Republic, and the Queen was replaced as head of state by a locally nominated president.

Rodrigues, formerly a dependency of Mauritius, became fully integrated as an electoral district in 1968, despite being further away than its French neighbour, Réunion, and sends MPs to the Mauritius Legislative Assembly.

Economically, the islands remain fragile, although Mauritius has gone furthest down the road towards economic diversification. Between 1951 and 1974 the economy was bolstered by the Commonwealth Sugar Agreement, which provided Mauritius with a quota of sugar that could be sold on the British market for an annually negotiated price. From 1985, Mauritius began earning more money exporting manufactured goods than from sugar exports.

The Franco-Mauritians have consolidated their economic role, expanding into the newer tourist and textile industries. Tourism increases in size every year, with currently around half a million annual visitors, and the financial services sector – the latest addition to the economy – has a promising future.

Some Rodriguans have sought a share in the development of their country's infrastructure by migrating to work on Mauritius, as their own island lags behind in resource-allocation – its economy remains largely agricultural and youth unemployment is high. The economic prosperity which has kept ethnic frustrations at bay in this two-island Republic has been indifferently redistributed, with the Afro-Creole populations on both islands feeling increasingly aggrieved. In 1999 widespread rioting on Mauritius constituted a clear signal that socio-economic disparities are reaching dangerous levels. It remains to be seen whether the Mauritian political élite will respond effectively.

Réunion inhabits a position midway between the developed and developing nations. Its health and education infrastructure are akin to those of "first world" states, while its economy lags far behind. Unlike Mauritius, Réunion has not been able to develop a significant Export Processing Zone because wages are too high. The island has its own appeal for tourists, but lacks the plentiful beaches which have made the Seychelles and Mauritius internationally known as holiday destinations. The Chaudron riots of February 1991 underscored the problems of social inequalities and high unemployment which persist in Réunion. Ironically, these disturbances occurred at a time when the French government had at last begun to address the demands of the overseas *départements* for social and economic parity. Réunion has also been active in forging a regional identity: taking part in projects of regional co-operation with its Indian Ocean neighbours.

The Mascarenes constitute one of the few regions where Francophony continues to make advances against the worldwide dominance of the English language. The French have clearly returned to their 18th-century bastion in the Indian Ocean, ready to stand their ground in the 21st century, less in military, than in political and cultural terms. ❑

LEFT: ex-President Cassam Uteem of Mauritius.

Death of the Dodo

The dodo is Mauritius' most famous export. This giant, flightless bird, which developed from the pigeon family and was killed off in the 17th century, has become a byword for stupidity and a symbol of man's destructiveness, throughout the world.

The dodo was first seen in Asia and Europe in the 17th century when Dutch sailors brought live specimens from Mauritius to the world's attention. Their name for the bird is thought to derive from Dutch words meaning "round arse". The Dutch described the bird as fearless of man, ungainly, so fat that it could not run, and so foolish that it did not recognise danger. In pre-Darwinian days, the dodo was seen as an example of a mistake made by God, and later as an evolutionary failure. In Grant's *History of Mauritius* published in England in 1801 it is described as a "feathered tortoise" which was an easy target for hunters.

For many years, contemporary paintings and written descriptions of the birds were practically all that were known of them – only a disputed claw and other remnants having survived from the birds brought to Europe. Naturalists began to argue that the dodo was a figment of sailors' rum-fuelled imagination. In the mid-19th century, however, dodo bones were dug up at Mare aux Songes (ironically, where the airport now stands) and models of the bird were constructed and placed in museums throughout the world. Lewis Carroll saw one such model at the University Museum in Oxford which evidently sparked his imagination – the flightless bird was immortalised in *Alice in Wonderland*.

With the reality of the dodo's existence, and its fame now firmly established, naturalists began to turn their attention to the bird itself. Travellers' accounts and cultural artefacts were re-examined along with the skeletal evidence this century. Bones unearthed in Rodrigues were found to belong to a similar bird with longer legs, named the solitaire. These findings vindicated the account of French Huguenot, Leguat, two centuries before.

The overweight, ungainly dodo was rehabilitated when it was discovered that the bird ate seasonally and was both fast and trim at other times of the year. The new slimline model of the dodo is now on display in several museums. Nat-

RIGHT: artist's impression of the dodo, extinct by 1861.

uralists also absolved the Dutch from the ignominy of killing the last dodo. While men were the catalyst of its destruction, it was the pigs, rats and monkeys they introduced to Mauritius which ate the eggs and chicks.

Some facts about the dodo remain to be elucidated. Travellers' accounts speak of a grey dodo in Mauritius and a white dodo in Réunion. Others assert that the dodo in Réunion was more like a solitaire. It is clear that a similar large bird to the dodo and solitaire was found on Réunion but no bone discoveries have been made to confirm the various theories. Scientists in the UK are now attempting to use new genetic techniques to re-

create the dodo, so we may one day see the bird back in what remains of its natural habitat. Until then, the dodo remains the world's most famous example of extinction, food for thought when we visit today's examples of rare species in Mauritius.

Île aux Aigrettes, just off the southeast coast of Mauritius, is thought to be the site of the dodo's extinction. Since 1987, the MWF (Mauritius Wildlife Foundation) have been working on restoring the island's original ecosystem. Obviously it's too late for the dodo, but the pink pigeon has been saved from the same fate and can be seen flying free here. Most hotels organise day-trips to the island and a percentage of the cost goes towards wildlife conservation. ❑

MAURITIUS

Mauritius, as its people will tell you, is a real tropical paradise,

but there's more to the island than its beaches and hotels

Bounded by a coastline littered with glittering beaches, protected by a virtually unbroken coral reef, Mauritius fulfils many people's fantasy of a tropical island paradise. Furthermore, with its excellent hotels that offer everything most visitors could possibly want in terms of watersports, food, entertainment, shops and, of course, weddings, it can be hard to drag yourself away to explore inland.

Mauritius does not have many single traditional tourist attractions – though there are notable exceptions, including the Botanical Gardens and some wonderful old plantation houses – but it is great fun to drive around among the coastal fishing communities or explore the verdant plateau at the heart of the island that was once the floor of a gigantic volcano which blew its top and left behind the jagged peaks and rock formations that are today so characterisitic of the island's scenery. Rainfall on the plateau feeds many rivers and streams, providing an abundant supply of water and irrigation for the sugar cane fields that cover most of the island's arable land.

One thing you will discover is that the quality of the service you receive in your hotel is not due just to good training, but to the genuine good nature of the mainly Hindu people of Mauritius. Brightly coloured Hindu temples and shrines pepper the landscape, often seen glistening in the sun, and those of Indian descent can still be seen wearing the traditional clothes of their forbears.

But Mauritius is all about a diversity of races and cultures living side by side. At the airport, new arrivals are surrounded by a flurry of officials who address their guests in English, accentuated with a French twang. As you change your foreign currency into rupees, Chinese, Indian and European bank clerks complete the transaction with such conversational ease that you may wonder if you haven't been accidentally misrouted to some other continent. Because of the multicultural nature of its society, hardly a week goes by without some celebration or religious ritual taking place from Tamil firewalking and Hindu body-piercing ceremonies, to Catholic pilgrimages and Chinese dragon dances.

But, in reality, whatever the attractions of the land and its people, you will always be drawn back to the sea. Whether you end up lazing by a lagoon, snorkelling or diving over the coral reef, playing with little fish or wrestling with big ones from the fighting chair, it is probably the delectable coast that will remain imprinted on your mind long after returning home. ❏

PRECEDING PAGES: fishing boat and sugar cane plantation.
LEFT: the beauty of Mauritius is not confined to the coast; inland the landscape is characterised by swaying green cane fields and low mountains.

THE MAURITIANS

The complexity of ethnic groups in Mauritius is bewildering, but Mauritians are always welcoming, and happy to explain the intricacies of their nation

I t is said that Mauritians only consider themselves such when abroad – at home they are first and foremost members of a community. Descended from immigrants from Europe, Asia and Africa, the ethnic mix of the island population is both fascinating and incredibly complex. Racism does not exist in Mauritius – or so its political leaders claim – but colour, creed and language continue to divide its people.

Origins, religions and cultures

The French colonial period which lasted just under a century, until 1810, has left an enduring legacy in Mauritius. The Franco-Mauritians are a distinctive community who trace their ancestry to the early white settlers and, while numerically very small, remain important in economic terms. Slaves and free labourers from Africa and Asia who also arrived in the 18th century are now mostly subsumed into the Creole population. Within this group, characterised not by ethnic homogeneity, but by a shared religion – Catholicism – an old hierarchy which favoured those of mixed origin and lighter skin still persists.

In the 19th century, during British rule, large-scale Indian immigration transformed the island's demography. Two-thirds of the population is now of Indian origin. These Indo-Mauritians are also not a homogeneous group, but are divided on regional, caste and religious lines. About 15 percent of the population are Muslims, mostly from Bihar – known, confusingly, as Calcuttyas, to distinguish them from the smaller, endogamous groups of mainly Gujarati Muslims. The Hindus, who number around 50 percent, also differentiate themselves along regional lines with a larger Bihari Hindu component and smaller Tamil, Telegu and Marathi minorities. The Bihari Hindus hold the trump card in terms of numbers, and play a key role in politics – every prime minister since Independence has been a member of this community.

LEFT: devotee at the annual Cavadee festival carrying a *sambo* of milk.
RIGHT: vegetable vendor.

Other small minorities include the 3,000 or so Chinese, who mostly came from the mid-19th century to engage in commerce, and still run many of the shops, whilst now also important in the professions and other sectors of the economy. The Chinese have embraced Catholicism, but many continue to practise Buddhist

traditions in the home. Even today, most Mauritians marry within their community, and although mixed weddings are becoming more common, shared religious belief remains a strong element in the choice of a life partner. Newer, charismatic churches, such as the Jehovah's Witnesses, are actively recruiting members from the various established communities.

Despite being a British colony between 1810 and 1968, the English did not settle in large numbers, and those who have remained, have generally intermarried into the Franco or Creole communities. The most visible legacy of British rule is on the roads where the British system of driving and signage is used.

A multi-lingual society

The mother tongue of most Mauritians is Kreol. The language of education and government is English, and that of the media overwhelmingly French. To add to this linguistic complexity, some Indo-Mauritians can only converse in Bhojpuri, a regional dialect based on Hindi, whilst the older generation of Chinese are more proficient in Cantonese or Hakka than their adoptive tongues. The so-called "ancestral languages" of Mauritians of Asian origin are actively promoted by members of these communities, and state controlled television and radio are obliged to broadcast in all the community languages. The island's cinemas show either Hollywood films dubbed in French, or Bollywood productions in Hindi.

In general, visitors to Mauritius will find that most islanders are reasonably proficient in English, though they are more at ease with French. Official forms that you may have to fill in at customs/immigration or at a police station are in English. Indo-Mauritians generally have at least a basic knowledge of Hindi, and if you attempt a few words in the island's lingua franca, Kreol, you will be sure to raise a smile (*for a short list of Kreol words and phrases, see page 376*).

FORMS OF ADDRESS

Human interaction in Mauritius is a compelling mix of the formal and the endearing. Old habits of deference linger in the custom of politely addressing even the children of those in positions of influence as *Mamzelle* and *Misié (Monsieur)*. A person of middle age might be hailed as *tonton/tantine* (uncle/auntie). Once on friendly terms, you might be jokingly referred to as a *cousin* or *cousine*. Indo-Mauritians have a whole range of specific terms for relatives on the paternal or maternal side, and some of these are in common use. For example, the first prime minister of Mauritius, Sir Seewoosagur Ramgoolam, is affectionately termed *chacha*, or uncle.

Public worship, private festivities

Religion is a way of life in Mauritius, and mosques, churches and temples have full and thriving congregations. The islanders put as much effort into the preparations for Hindu, Muslim or Catholic festivals as other societies do for their annual Carnivals. The biggest crowd-puller in Mauritius is still a pilgrimage and all the major religions organise such events. The island's public holidays take account of the different communities, so that at least one festival of every ethnic group is celebrated. Non-participating Mauritians may organise a family picnic at the beach on such occasions.

Weddings are another common weekend activity on the island. Hindu nuptials take place over several days, and innumerable sittings are organised in marquees for guests who are served vegetarian curries on a banana leaf. The bride will wear a traditional red or cream sari, and her groom – probably for the only time in his life – will don an ornate turban, and slippers. Muslim weddings are characterised in Mauritius by the serving of a biryani meal, accompanied by a soft drink, generally Pepsi. The ceremony, or *nikah*, is shorter than that of Hindus, and at some gatherings male and female guests are accommodated in separate

of quirky customs and taboos, ranging from cutting your toenails only at certain times of day to leaving out food to pacify malevolent spirits. Chinese Mauritians are partial to the number 9, as their car number-plates testify.

Local sorcerers, known as *longanistes* or *traiteurs*, have followers from diverse backgrounds, and are called in to settle quarrels, exact revenge, reverse bad luck and administer love potions. When one's spouse or lover loses interest, a rival may well be suspected of having used the services of a sorcerer. Cemeteries are powerful sites for such practitioners of magic, and they can often be seen at mid-

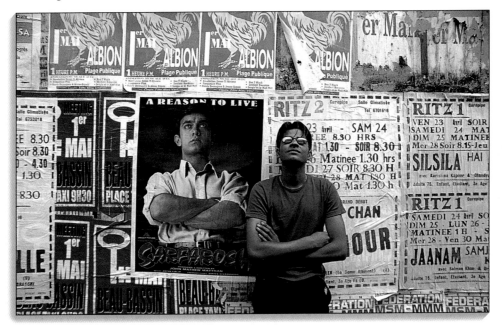

areas. Weddings of Catholics, be they Chinese, Creole or Franco-Mauritian, generally involve a ceremony at the local church, followed by a reception. Sooner or later, at most functions, the sega will be played when guests of all ages will indulge their love of dancing *(see page 79)*.

Folklore and superstition

Diverse beliefs and practices, some originating in the popular customs which African and Asian immigrants brought to the island, have persisted into modern-day Mauritius. There are all kinds

LEFT AND RIGHT: watching the world go by in Port Louis and Curepipe.

day, sacrificing a small chicken, breaking coconuts, and lighting candles or camphor sticks on the graves, surrounded by a small knot of followers.

The phenomenon of the loup garou, or werewolf, is a good example of how a popular belief can become a serious issue in Mauritius given propitious circumstances. In 1994 a serious cyclone, Hollanda, brought down most of the island's electricity pylons, leaving many areas without power for several weeks. During this time, the notion that a loup garou was on the loose took hold of the popular imagination. Women claimed to have been raped by the creature, and there were daily sightings. The loup garou became front page news for several weeks, and hysteria mounted daily, with women and children barricading themselves indoors. The police issued a communiqué, assuring people that it was tackling the problem, and only when the issue took on a communal dimension, with Muslims asserting that the werewolf was hiding in a Catholic shrine, and inter-religious tensions increasing, did the president intervene, disputing the existence of such a creature.

Community, class and generation

It is one of the peculiarities of Mauritian society, that any seemingly insignificant object can

KAYA

Joseph Reginald Topize was born in Roche Bois in 1960 and began his singing career in the early 1980s. He called himself "Kaya" after one of Bob Marley's albums and his dreadlocks and pot-smoking image struck a chord with young islanders who readily identified with "seggae", a fusion of reggae and sega. In 1999, Kaya's death in police custody, one of several in less than two years, sparked off communal riots on a scale not seen since Independence in 1967–8. He has become a symbol of discrimination against Afro-Creoles. The president, sensing that things could turn ugly, pleaded with the nation to form a human chain around the island to symbolise solidarity among Mauritian ethnic groups.

become an ethnic signifier. Here, the company you work for, the kind of car you drive, even the type of soft drink you buy, is often a decision governed by communal factors. The reason may simply be that the importer of a certain make of vehicle or product, is a member of your community, influencing your decision. There is a popular saying in Mauritian Kreol, "*sak zako bizin protez so montan*" (each monkey must protect his mountain) which refers to the tendency to put members of one's own ethnic group before others.

That tensions sparked by the prevalence of favouritism and nepotism do not erupt into more serious violence, can be attributed to the pragmatism of most Mauritians and to the elaborate balancing act performed by all governments. In fact, ministerial posts are assigned in cabinet so that members of competing caste and ethnic groups each have at least one representative. Alongside relatively recent strategies of ethnic lobbying, the old demon of racial discrimination still exists, however. Widespread rioting in 1999, following the suspicious deaths of a number of Afro-Creoles in police custody, highlighted the frustrations of this group, who are most affected by the persistence of racial stereotyping.

The generational differences in Mauritius are also marked, but may ultimately be an antidote to the long-standing divisions based on community and colour. School is a bastion of cultural mixing in a society with a large youth population, and increasing exposure of teenagers to Western media is impacting on old preconceptions. While most Mauritian girls still do not have the freedom of their Western counterparts, or even of their male peers, afternoon discotheques are providing a means of socialising which were not available to their mothers.

Mauritius today is a fascinating blend of the spiritual and the material, a place where the accountant working in the booming offshore sector will take a day off to participate in a religious pilgrimage, and who might buy a herbal infusion from a stallholder at the Port Louis bazaar who claims to know the remedies for all the world's ailments, which he will sip as he logs on to the internet, effortlessly combining "olde worlde" beliefs with an enthusiasm for all that modern technology has to offer. ❏

LEFT: natural cures for all ills.

Sega

Sega goes back at least to the early 18th century when it evolved as the soul dance of the African slaves as a form of escapism from the harsh reality of their daily lives. After a long week toiling in the cane fields, they would gather around a fire drinking alambic. Once fuelled by the rum, they became less inhibited and started to sing and dance what became known as the sega.

Sega has been described as "an erotic dance that leaves little to the imagination", as "provocative in the extreme" or even as "a simulated sexual act". The movements are sensuous and the flirtation real, but however tempestuous it becomes, the sensuality is controlled and it is never obscene.

The original sega instruments were made from anything the slaves could lay their hands on. The ravan (a goatskin tambour), maravan (a hollowed out tube filled with dried seeds) and triang (a triangular-shaped piece of old iron) were played, along with anything else that could produce a sound – pots and pans, empty bottles ond spoons. The ravan, maravan and triang are still played, but modern *ségatiers* also use guitars and keyboards.

The accompanying songs, often scattered with double entendres and sexual overtones, are an added amusement. In the past, these songs were also a way for the slaves to express their pent up feelings and vent their anger on their masters, whom they ridiculed in the lyrics.

Although its roots are in Africa, sega in its present form is found only in Mauritius, Rodrigues and Seychelles, and each place has its own particular version (see page 261). In classical Mauritian sega, or *sega typic*, the women begin the dancing. They hold out their bright, long skirts in both hands and sway to the rhythmic music, swinging their hips to reveal a glimpse of leg, enticing the men to join them. As more and more dancers join in, shuffling their feet and swaying to the powerful beat of the drums, the dance develops into a sort of courtship drama. Both men and women try to attract a partner of their choice. The women are teasing and provocative, changing partners, until they single out their man. The men stretch out their arms as if to catch a dancer they admire or to prevent their chosen partner from escaping. When at last a pair form, the woman leans backwards while the man

extends his body over hers, at which point the singers may encourage the dancers by shouting "enba! enba!", literally "get down!" Then they swap positions and the woman dances above the man while he lies on the floor inviting her to come lower and lower. The drumbeats become more frenzied as the dancers move closer to each other – they never touch. Onlookers may be forgiven for thinking that anything could happen next. But the crescendo of the drum reaches a dramatic climax and, on a last exciting beat, ceases.

Nowadays, classical sega in Mauritius is mostly associated with the Rivière Noire area on the west coast. Public holidays are the best time to try and

catch authentic performances; you may be lucky enough to see a group of locals gathered around a fire on the beach, drinking rum or wine, and spontaneously breaking into dance.

However, if the only sega performance you get to see is at your hotel, you may well wonder what the fuss is all about. "Sega hotel", as the locals call it, is a refined, formalised version of the dance. The men wear tight breeches or trousers rolled up about the knee with unbuttoned *corsair* shirts knotted at the waist. The women wear full, brightly coloured ankle-length skirts and short bodices with a bare midriff. It makes a pretty sight but is often nothing to get excited about – though you may be asked to join in. ❑

RIGHT: an outdoor sega performance at the Domaine les Pailles.

CEREMONIES AND CELEBRATIONS

With such a multicultural society, the festival calendar is full all year, but it's the colourful Hindu and Tamil celebrations that draw the big crowds

So many festivals are celebrated in Mauritius that visitors are bound to see one or more in any month of the year. The majority emanate from the Indian communities and they are great and colourful occasions of religious celebration.

Cavadee (Thai Poosam) is a Tamil festival which can be celebrated any time in January or February. It is an amazing if blood-curdling sight. Tamil devotees pierce their bodies with needles; some also partake in fire-walking ceremonies. The Cavadee – a wooden arch decorated with flowers with a brass pot of milk attached to each end – is carried in a procession to the temple where it is placed before the Tamil deity, Muruga.

Holi is a raucous two-day festival held in February or March. It begins with a bonfire on which an effigy of the evil demon Holika is burnt. Men, women and children then all join in squirting coloured water and smearing red and purple powders on each other's faces and hair.

Divali is the Hindu's happiest festival. Celebrated in October or November, at the darkest period of the autumn months, it marks the victory of Rama (an incarnation of Vishnu) over the demon Ravana and also commemorates Krishna's destruction of the demon Narakasuran. Candles and simple earthen lamps are lit around houses, gardens and even at business premises to brighten the moonless night.

△ **HINDU SHRINES**
Many shrines have been built on the banks of Grand Bassin. This one is to Lord Krishna and Rahna Radi.

◁ **DANCING FOR DIVALI**
Divali celebrates the victory of good over evil symbolised by the thousands of little lights that flicker in the night.

▷ **SWORD-WALKING**
Blessing of swords before a sword-walking ceremony, another form of penance, usually enacted between April and June.

◁ COLOURFUL CAVADEE
On the day of Thai Poosam several processions are held in the major towns. They usually start from a river and end at the temple.

△ BODY-PIERCING
As an act of penance, Tamil devotees pierce their faces and bodies with skewers and needles; some cover the whole torso and back.

△ FIRE-WALKING
Teemeedee, or fire-walking, is a Tamil and Hindu festival where worshippers walk over red-hot embers to the accompaniment of chants, apparently suffering no harm.

PILGRIMAGE TO GRAND BASSIN

In 1972 sacred water from the Ganges was poured into Grand Bassin lake, which is some 550 metres (1,800 ft) above sea level, after which it became known to the Hindus as Ganga Talao – the Lake of the Ganges. One of the most important festivals for the Mauritian Hindu community is Maha Shivaratri (February/March) which is celebrated in honour of Lord Shiva, also known as the upholder of the sacred Ganges. Following an all-night vigil, Hindu pilgrims, dressed in white, make their way to the lake carrying bamboo structures decorated with flowers and multi-coloured bells. At the lake, devotees offer prayers to Lord Shiva and other deities. Some bathe and many take the sacred water home. The whole colourful scene is reminiscent of the great rituals on the banks of India's holy Ganges.

◁ FACE-PAINTING
The festival of Holi is characterised by red, the colour of joy for Hindus. Be careful not to get caught in the line of fire during the water and powder battles – unless, of course, you want to join in the fun.

▽ JUICE BAR
Stands and stalls serving snacks and drinks are set up around the temple for non-fasting celebrants.

SUGAR AND SPICE

The local cuisine is an inspiring combination of Indian, Creole, French and Chinese influences, adapted to the local produce with great flair

The people of the Mascarene Islands, whose ancestors came from Europe, Africa, India and China, are dab hands at throwing together a bit of this and a bit of that and turning out a cuisine as richly diverse as its people. Ever since Mauritius was discovered in the 16th century, colonial powers popped in and out, each leaving their own gastronomic legacy. The Portuguese brought pigs and monkeys, the Dutch introduced deer, the French brought fruit trees and spices. The African slaves, meanwhile, kept fit on wild fruit and greens, pumping up their protein with fish, wild boar and bats, while the staple of the Indians and Chinese was rice, brought over from India. Out of this cultural melting pot came a unique cuisine.

Key ingredients

Rice is at the heart of both Mauritian and Réunionnais cuisine. Whether you dine in upmarket restaurants or gather round *en famille* you'll find mountains of it – plain boiled, fried or steeped in saffron. Noodles are a popular alternative and come in all shapes and sizes from the vermicelli-like *meefoon*, ideal for a light bite, to the gut-busting fried version, *mine frit*. As versatile as a plain pizza base, you can ring the changes with chicken, meat or seafood (the "*mine frit* special" comes with a bit of each).

Seafood here is as good as you would expect on a tropical island. It is prepared in a mouthwatering range of ways – fat shrimps and octopus, firm and flaky *cordonnier* (surgeon fish), *cateaux* (parrot fish) and the close-textured *licorne* come stewed, curried and fricaseed. *Carangue* (trevally fish), *bourgeois* (red snapper) and *vieille rouge* (grouper) are marinated in lemon juice, oil and spices and simply grilled. *Capitaine* (white snapper) is good in a bouillabaisse or oven-baked.

LEFT: fresh fish stall, Port Louis market.
RIGHT: preparing the pancake mixture for the lunchtime crowd.

Meat appears in similar guises. Beef, chicken and even the humble sausage are thrown into casseroles and curries. Venison, usually curried or served in a thick sauce, and *cochon marron* (wild boar), traditionally served with sweet potato are seasonal foods, reserved for special occasions.

Eating out

There are scores of restaurants, bars, cafés and fast food outlets to choose from. Restaurants usually close by 11 pm and booking is rarely necessary. Generally, the atmosphere is relaxed, the service good and, compared to hotel dining, prices are very reasonable.

Nearly every restaurant menu lists Indian, creole, Chinese and European dishes. Standard fare includes the spicy Indian *vindaye* curry and *briani*, a typical Muslim dish made with beef, venison or meaty fish; *bol renversée*, literally "upturned bowl", a quirky creole rice dish with slivers of pork, spicy sausage and chunks of chicken; *fooyang*, a Mauritianised Chinese omelette, filled with lobster, crab or prawn; *rougaille,* a Mediterranean type of stew made with any meat or fish cooked in a mixture of fried tomatoes, onions, garlic, herbs and ginger; *daube,* a smoother version of *rougaille.* Among the many exotic vegetables you'll come across are heart of palm (*coeur de palmiste*) or "millionaire's" salad, *gros pois* (fat butter beans), *bredes* (fresh greens), *lalo* (lady's fingers) and a variety of pumpkin and marrow.

Mauritians often pick up their lunch from street vendors who serve spicy snacks such as *gateaux piments* (fried lentils and chillis), curry-filled *samousas, dal puris* (lentil-based

pancakes filled with vegetables and sauces), along with a variety of soups and noodle dishes all eaten piping hot. A word of caution for newcomers. It's a good idea to give yourself a couple of days to acclimatise before sampling any roadside snacks, which can cause tummy upset.

Home cooking

If you are lucky enough to be invited to someone's home, go with an open mind and an empty stomach. You could be offered anything from smoked marlin or a spice-packed meat *massala,* to Indian-style pancakes (known as *puri, roti, chapati* and *farata,* depending on how they're cooked). Few islanders serve Creole food without rice. The Japanese "rice cooker" is as common in the Mauritian kitchen as the microwave is in Western homes. Another key utensil is the wok into which just about anything edible is thrown and stir-fried to perfection. Less common in an age of supermarkets and ready made spices is the curry stone, the Indian equivalent of a pestle and mortar, which is used to make *massala,* a curry paste made of ground turmeric, coriander, black pepper, nutmeg, ginger, garlic and as many chillis as the cook or guests can stand. Chillis turn up everywhere, either in a dish or as an accompaniment. Strengths vary, so be warned – they can set the unsuspecting mouth on fire.

Bread, cakes and fruit

Mauritians buy their bread fresh every day. In addition to crusty French-style loaves, most bakeries offer a choice of choux buns and sweet or savoury puff pastries, but other than the rich milk-based Indian sweetmeats, you won't find a great variety of cakes and puddings which are reserved for special occasions. Fruit is the most common dessert and home cooks are experts at throwing together fruity creations from their own back gardens: pawpaws, mangos and lychees parade alongside sweet pineapples, tiny gingli bananas, water melons and guavas.

Drinks

Some very palatable white and rosé wines are made in Mauritius from imported grape concentrate and labels to look for are Chateau Bel Ombre, Eureka and Saint Nicholas. The purist can buy imported South African and Australian wines at reasonable prices. French wine does not always travel well and is more expensive. The

MONKEY BUSINESS

The monkeys that inhabit the forests of Mauritius are not protected. They are still hunted for their meat, though the practice is becoming rare; unless you know an expert shot you're unlikely to taste the meat, which isn't for sale anywhere. However, some enterprising hunters are well paid for their troubles by licensed exporters who ship the live animals to overseas labs. Other local delicacies you won't find on the average tourist menu include curry made with *tenrec,* a type of hedgehog, curried *chauve-souris* or fruit bat, and *mouches jaunes…* crispy fried wasp larvae! However unappealing this may sound, people risk life and limb to shake them from their nests.

best beer brands to go for are the locally brewed Phoenix and Stella, and the slightly stronger Blue Marlin. Mauritian men drink whisky, usually Black Label, and neat rum. Rum cocktails and punches are popular with the women. The best local rum brand is Green Island.

Of the usual range of fizzy drinks on offer, Pepsi reigns supreme. Fresh fruit juices are popular and Indian *lassi* is a refreshing yoghurt and water drink.

Tea comes in a variety of vanilla flavoured strengths. If you prefer vanilla-free tea, a choice of local brands are available. Most hotels and restaurants offer filter coffee, cappuccino and

lagoon is Nature's larder from which lobster and crab are simply steamed; prawns are served plain or smothered in chilli-rich tomato sauce. *Cono-cono*, similar to the whelk, makes a light lunch when mixed with salad, while freshly caught fish, cooked Chinese style in ginger and garlic, wakens tired taste buds. But for a typical Rodriguan meal, try *carri de poulet aux grains*, chicken curry with red beans and mashed maize served on fluffy white rice.

There is no such thing as genetically modified vegetables in Rodrigues and the meat, poultry and fish are additive-free. Onions, limes, lemons and chillis form the basis of the

espresso. The locally produced Chamarel coffee is palatable, but pricey because it is produced in small quantities. The smaller restaurants and snack bars tend to serve instant coffee.

Rodriguan specialities

Octopus fishing is one of Rodrigues' greatest industries so it's hardly surprising that this cephalopod turns up as a tasty fried, grilled, casseroled or curried tit-bit on most of Port Mathurin's restaurant menus. The massive

---

LEFT: sweet and sticky cakes are often on the menu.
RIGHT: street vendors serving up hot snacks – the spicier the better.

famous mind-blowing *chatinis* (chutney) and *achards* (sun dried pickles). Some of the hottest chillis on earth are grown in the back gardens of Rodrigues; crammed into bottles and preserved for posterity, the tiny green ones are so ragingly hot that Mauritians and Réunionnais make special trips to bring them home.

The little luxuries of life may be absent in Rodrigues, decent coffee being one of them, but there's no lack of sticky puddings. Many of these are creolised versions of old-fashioned stodgy British puddings, such as *pain frit* (fried bread sprinkled with sugar), *gâteau patate* (sweet potato cake), *gâteau manioc* (manioc pudding) and *pudding maïs* (maize pudding). ❑

BATS, BIRDS AND BANYAN TREES

With the help of conservationists, the native wildlife is starting to flourish
in the protected parks and reserves of Mauritius and Rodrigues

For the naturalist, tropical oceanic islands are akin to a Pandora's box of the unique and strange. Once upon a time, Mauritius and Rodrigues were home to flightless birds, giant tortoises and dwarf lizards, but today there are other species, equally remarkable in their own way, that still live on these islands and surrounding islets isolated in the Indian Ocean.

Originally, wildlife had to get here by flying, swimming or hitching a ride and many species are now endemic. But since the nearest land mass is Madagascar, 855 km (550 miles) away, the only mammals that made it over on their own were bats and sea mammals. Due to the lack of land predators, reptiles evolved from the latter and birds had no problem establishing themselves here bringing seeds from other lands which grew up into hardwood forests. In the 17th century, humans arrived, triggering the demise of many species of flora and fauna.

All is not lost...

During the past 50 years, conservationists have been hard at work, and their endeavours can be now be witnessed in small protected areas, such as the Black River Gorges, supporting the remaining original forests that are home to the island's wildlife.

Giant fruit bats are still going strong and the Mauritian fruit bat is a truly stunning animal with a wingspan of about a metre (nearly 4 ft) and a furred body which varies from dark brown to a gorgeous golden orange. Around 20,000 of these bats range over the island at night and feed on fruits in gardens and forests. By day they sleep in gorges or on mountain sides hanging on trees in huge colonies of up to a thousand. A roost can be seen beneath the Black River viewpoint.

Most of the mammals on Mauritius have been introduced. The Javan deer and the black feral pigs are common in the forest and are hunted for food. The deer are also farmed, as the meat is very popular. One of the most interesting of the introduced mammals is the tenrec, a nocturnal insectivore, similar to a hedgehog, from Madagascar and commonly seen crossing or squashed on roads. Monkeys, long-tailed

WILDLIFE WATCH

In the Black River Gorges National Park several forests shelter a large proportion of Mauritian endemic wildlife. Well mapped out trails allow visitors to see these endangered animals and plants, now part of a major conservation programme. Go to the Visitor Centre, near Black River, or the Pétrin Information Centre (near Grand Bassin) for details of walks and sites to explore.

The Île aux Aigrettes nature reserve off Mahébourg is gradually being restored to its pristine state. The island is covered with coastal forest and is home to a population of pink pigeons that are easy to see. Visits can be arranged through your hotel.

LEFT: the fruit bat, with its big eyes and furry head, is popularly known as a "flying fox".
RIGHT: an ornate day gecko basking in the Macchabee Forest.

macaques from Java, abound in the forests and woods. About 60,000 in all, they are a terrible pest, damaging native plants and destroying bird nests. Nevertheless they are very interesting and intelligent animals and a good place to see them up close is next to the sacred lake of Grand Bassin where they are fed by visitors.

> **BLONDE BATS**
>
> The Rodrigues fruit bat, known as the blonde bat due to a pale tuft of fur on its head, was saved from extinction in the 1970s by the late naturalist Gerald Durrell.

Pesky vermin

The black rat, feral cat and mongoose have contributed the most to the demise of the endemic wildlife. The rats climb the trees and raid birds'

Giant tortoises and tiny lizards

Since pristine Mauritius had no land mammals many of the reptiles evolved to fill their niche. Two species of giant tortoise have gone but have been replaced by the Aldabra giant tortoise *(see page 266)* which roam in the parks. Queen Victoria had them brought to Mauritius after Charles Darwin advised that the last population on Aldabra should be protected in captive herds. Some may even be original immigrants.

Out of the island's many native and endemic

nests and damage the fruit on native trees. Similar to the African wildcat, the spotted tabby cat with russet orange ears has an appetite for birds.

The lesser Indian mongoose, most common in the dry lowlands, was introduced in 1900 to control the rats. The founding population of 16 males and three females quickly multiplied and soon wiped out several populations of game birds. Their diet is eclectic, including insects, lizards, rats and birds but a favoured food is the toad which most animals find poisonous. The discovery of a young endangered Mauritius kestrel in the stomach of a mongoose also revealed that they played a large part in the falcon's struggle for survival.

geckos and skinks (a smooth, shiny lizard), the nocturnal house gecko is the most common and the Phelsuma day gecko the most spectacular. A group of bright green and red lizards, the latter lives on coconut palms and banana plants, avoiding the greedy eye of mynah birds.

The house gecko can also be seen in gardens along with the common Agama lizard, known erroneously as a chameleon. There are some real chameleons in Mauritius, but not many.

Contrary to popular belief, snakes do live on the main island of Mauritius, although none of them is poisonous. There are two species of blind, worm-like, burrowing snakes and a larger wolf snake, which bites if handled but as it rarely reaches half a metre (2 ft) in length it does little harm.

Free from rats, Round Island is home to a whole community of native reptiles, including three species of skinks and two Phelsuma geckos, one of which is a Durrell's night gecko, named after the late naturalist Gerald Durrell, who made Round Island famous in his book *Golden Bats and Pink Pigeons*. Two rare types of endemic boa live here as well, but one of these, the burrowing boa, has not been seen since 1975. This island is so important that visits can only be made with special permission. However, there are plans to establish additional

The remaining survivors are the Mascarene cave swiftlet, Mascarene swallow, Mauritius cuckoo shrike, Mauritius black bulbul, Mauritius fody, paradise flycatcher and two types of white-eyes. The swiftlet breeds in lava tunnels but has been in decline for many years as its nest is considered a delicacy for bird's nest soup. There are, however, still 2,000–4,000 birds on Mauritius which can be seen flying in flocks over any part of the island. The heavily built swallow keeps to the dry southwest and is most active in the late afternoon when it feeds on flying insects. The only other endemic bird that you are likely to see around and about is the grey white-eye, a tiny

populations of some of the reptiles on other islands such as Île aux Aigrettes.

Surviving birds

There are 11 surviving species of land birds endemic to the islands of the southwest Indian Ocean, and seven of them are endemic to Mauritius. The most well known are the Mauritius kestrel, pink pigeon and echo parakeet, for these have been the subjects of a conservation programme for more than 25 years *(see page 91)*.

(see page 91).

LEFT: a herd of Javan deer.
RIGHT: the yellow weaver bird, one of many colourful birds you can spot flitting around hotels and houses.

MAURITIUS WILDLIFE FOUNDATION

Formed in 1984 by Gerald Durrell and other naturalists, the Mauritius Wildlife Foundation is a charity dedicated to the conservation of the native wildlife of Mauritius, Rodrigues and their islands. It is most well known for its work on the Mauritius kestrel, pink pigeon and echo parakeet, but is also working on protecting endemic passerines and the endangered reptiles of Round Island, and Rodrigues' golden fruit bat. Several small islands have been restored by the foundation. Île aux Aigrettes, for example, has been cleared of rats and many weeds and the MWF is now in the process of replacing the missing fauna and flora.

grey bird with a white rump that travels in small flocks and is known as a *pic-pic*. You would be lucky to see any of the other birds, which are all perching songbirds (passerines), unless you specifically go to look for them in the forests of the Black River Gorges and Bassin Blanc.

The woods along Cascade Pigeons River and at Solitude on Rodrigues are home to two of the world's rarest birds: the endemic warbler which only has about 25 pairs left and the striking yellow and orange fody with about 200 pairs.

> **ISLAND FLOWER**
>
> The beautiful boucle d'oreille *(Trochetia boutoniana)*, meaning earring, is the national flower of Mauritius. However, it can only be seen in cultivated sites.

The colourful birds commonly seen around the hotels and houses have mostly been introduced to Mauritius. Many of these may seem very familiar since they are common cage birds that long ago escaped from captivity and established themselves in the wild. The most prolific are the mynah bird, the elegant, crested red-whiskered bulbul, the bright red Madagascar fody and the yellow village weaver.

Coastal creatures

Nesting on the small islands around Mauritius are boobies, sooty terns and noddies, as well as several species of petrel. A wonderful sight to see is the elegant, rare red-tailed tropic bird which nests in cliffs on Gunner's Quoin, Flat Island and Round Island. But its more common smaller cousin, the white-tailed tropic bird *(paille-en-queue)* can be watched from the Black River viewpoint.

Fourteen species of whales and dolphins have been recorded around the Mascarene coasts. Spinner and bottle-nose dolphins can often be seen from the shore and in Tamarin Bay, beyond the reef. The chances of seeing dolphins on a boat trip are high and you may also see sperm whales off the west coast. A school of humpbacked whales return to the waters between the mainland and Round Island, during July and August most years, probably to breed.

At one time dugongs, or sea cows, lived in the lagoons around Mauritius and Rodrigues feeding on sea- grass. These sea beauties are believed to have been the creatures sea-weary sailors mistook for mermaids, but it didn't stop them from being hunted. Luckily, some still survive off Madagascar in the Mozambique Channel.

Fascinating flora

The native hardwood forests of Mauritius are now largely limited to the mountain tops and deep in gorges, where they could not be exploited for their timber. Only five percent of the island is forested, and only small areas of that are in good condition. Nevertheless, Mauritius has 685 species of native plants of which 311 are endemic and most are endangered.

It is a sobering thought that Mauritius has some of the rarest plants in the world. The palm *Hyophorbe amauricaulis* is down to its last plant, surviving in the Curepipe Botanical Garden. Rodrigues is hanging on to its last specimen of café marron *(Ramosmania heterophylla)* but we are too late for the *Pyramid pandanus*, which succumbed to Cyclone Hollanda in 1993.

Many of those that haven't survived have been supplanted by alien plants, such as the Chinese guava and *Lantana camara* that have run riot, suffocating seedlings. The familiar casuarina tree seen lining the beaches was brought from Malaysia as a windbreak and the mighty banyan tree with dangling roots, so typical of tropical forests, comes from India. ❑

LEFT: lesser noddies in a two-storey nest, Île aux Cocos.

To the Rescue

Mauritius is most famous for its birds and in particular for its extinct birds – the dodo being the best known, but there are many other birds that have vanished, including a large black flightless parrot, the largest parrot ever known, a blue pigeon, some ducks, owls, more parrots and others. Indeed scientists still argue about the numbers of species that have disappeared.

However, since the mid-1970s three birds – the Mauritius kestrel, the pink pigeon and the echo parakeet – have been rescued from the edge of extinction by a group of conservationists, led by the ornithologist Carl Jones along with Gerald Durrell's Jersey Wildlife Preservation Trust (JWPT).

The Mauritius kestrel *(Falco punctatus)* is a small falcon which lives in the forested gorges and mountains, feeds on bright green day geckos and nests in cliff holes. In 1974 there were only four wild birds, and only one pair were breeding. The rescue operation was started by breeding birds in captivity. Over several years, eggs were harvested from the last pair – every time a clutch of eggs was taken from the wild kestrels, they would lay again, increasing their productivity. Many of the young reared from harvested eggs were released back into the wild together with birds that were also bred in captivity. These were fed and provided with nest boxes and protected from predators such as the mongoose and feral cats. The released kestrels began to breed well and between 1984 and 1994, 331 birds were put back into the Black River Gorges and tracts of forest that had not had kestrels for decades. Today it is believed there are between 500 and 800 birds.

Almost as rare as the kestrel, the pink pigeon *(Nesoenas mayeri)* was believed by some to be extinct. But in the 1970s a population was found in an isolated pocket of woodland near Bassin Blanc. These birds were slowly declining because rats and monkeys were stealing their eggs or they were being caught by feral cats. By 1990 there were only 10 birds left in the wild but a small population had been established in captivity and since then the captive-bred birds have been released into the wild, boosting the numbers. A programme controlling the introduced predators has also been put in

force. The pigeons have responded dramatically to these initiatives and the population has increased to more than 370 birds, but the pink pigeon still has a long way to go before it is safe.

The work with the kestrel and pigeon may have been tough but the problems were minor compared to those encountered rescuing the echo parakeet *(Psittacula echo)*. This emerald green parrot – distinguishable from the introduced ring-necked parakeet by its shorter tail, more rounded wing and darker green – had the distinction of being the world's rarest parrot, until recently. In 1987 there were thought to be only eight left, with only two females. The problem was their low breeding rate.

Working under the auspices of the MWF *(see page 89)*, conservationists tried rearing the young and eggs taken from wild nests that seemed doomed to failure. Many died until they learned how to nurture them with a good diet (plenty of fresh fruit and vegetables), filtered water and scrupulous hygiene. The wild parakeets were provided with extra food and their nest sites in hollow trees improved. The nesting birds were guarded against predators and their nesting cavities regularly cleaned out and treated with insecticide, to kill the nest flies that sucked out the babies' blood. The population increased slowly and now the future looks good, with around 120 echo parakeets flying free along the Macchabee Ridge in the Black River Gorges National Park. ❏

RIGHT: once the world's rarest bird, there are now more than 500 Mauritius kestrels flying around the island – some even nesting in people's gardens.

INTO THE BLUE

The sea is central to leisure time in the Mascarenes. The Réunionnais surf on it,
the Rodriguans fish in it and the Mauritians love to sit, eat and chat by it

Mauritians may not always swim in the sea but they certainly love to be beside it, on it and sometimes under it. At week-ends huge parties head for the beach armed with picnic hampers, curry pots and all the necessary accoutrements for a day or two's relaxation in the lagoon.

Tourism has brought new and exciting activities to these translucent Indian Ocean waters. Most hotels offer free windsurfing, waterskiing and boating, but scuba diving, big game fishing and parasailing come at a price. If you don't want to go as far as learning to dive, the tranquil lagoons are perfect for snorkelling. Otherwise there are plenty of kayaks, canoes and pedalos to keep you amused and rides in glass-bottom boats for bird's eye views of life in the lagoon without getting your feet wet.

Beyond the reef is the game fisherman's sporting ground where wahoo, shark, marlin, tuna and other big fish prowl the depths of their deep blue domain. They have few enemies, but even the great speed and strength of a blue marlin requires some cunning to outwit that most determined of ocean predators – The Deep Sea Fisherman. The business of sport fishing is bigger, bolder and more macho in Mauritius than in Réunion or Seychelles *(see page 97)*.

The best dive sites

The waters around Mauritius offer some exciting diving experiences. There are dozens of sites to choose from where shoals of small reef fish, such as blackspotted sweetlip, humpbacked snapper and squirrel fish play hide and seek; or you could venture further out for sightings of hammerhead shark, ray and barracuda.

The best dive sites, no more than an hour's boat ride away, are found off the west coast near Flic en Flac *(see page 143)* and include some wonderful wrecks. Well worth exploring are *Kei Sei 113* and *Tug 11*, sunk in the late

1980s to form artificial reefs and now inhabited by giant moray eels and a vast community of colourful reef fish.

On the east coast, organised diving is rather more limited due to prevailing winds and exposed seas and nearly all diving takes place in or around passes through the reef. However,

the region has excellent facilities at dive centres attached to the St Géran, Belle Mare, Hotel Ambre and Le Touessrok hotels. When weather conditions become too unpleasant for diving in this area, clients are transported to Grand Baie in the north, where nearly a dozen sites – including the wreck, *The Silver Star*, sunk in 1992 to form an artificial reef – can be easily reached by boat.

Diving conditions in the south of the island are best in the sheltered lagoon at Blue Bay where you can dive all year round in complete safety for sightings of weirdly shaped corals and dancing reef fish. Experienced divers can choose from several sites beyond the reef where

LEFT: snorkelling and sailing in the shallow waters of a limpid lagoon.
RIGHT: bird's-eye view of Île aux Cerfs.

caves and tunnels attract shoals of kingfish, crayfish and black-tip sharks.

Snorkelling

While authorities argue that safeguards and restrictions are in place to protect the lagoons, such as a ban on dynamite fishing, collecting shells and corals from the seabed and spear fishing, many islanders complain of increased pollution and impaired visibility. However, there is still an amazing marine world to be discovered just below the surface. Snorkelling is just as popular as diving. Hours of pleasure can be had gliding silently over shallow reefs to observe the many creatures which live there. Hotel boathouses provide free snorkelling equipment for their guests, though these are not always in tip-top condition. If you've been bitten by the snorkelling bug, you might want to invest in your own equipment. Good quality masks, fins and goggles are on sale everywhere.

A walk on the wet side

One way of discovering the seabed in complete safety for R750 is to take an undersea walk or "helmet dive". Undersea walking began in the Bahamas in 1948, but the idea was patented and brought to Mauritius in 1990. Following

TAKE THE PLUNGE

Mauritius' warm waters and rich marine life make it the perfect place to learn to dive. Dive centres attached to hotels are affiliated to CMAS (World Underwater Federation), PADI (Professional Association of Diving Instructors), NAUI (National Association of Underwater Instructors) and BSAC (British Sub-Aqua Club) and operate under strict safety rules, providing all the equipment you need and multilingual instructors.

Most dive centres offer a brief resort course designed to test your affinity with the sport. For more in-depth training, you can enrol on an intensive 5-day course leading to an Open Water One certificate, followed by a number of qualifying dives. Children are specially catered for, with themed dives introducing them to the wonders of the ocean.

Experienced divers can expect to pay up to R900 for a day dive and R1,200 for a night dive, although packages of 5 and 10 dives are better value at around R4,000 and R8,000 respectively. *(See Travel Tips for a list of recommended dive centres.)*

Diving accidents are rare but if you get into trouble, arrangements are quickly made to convey you to the island's recompression chamber at the paramilitary Special Mobile Force (SMF) Headquarters at Vacoas (tel: 686 1011), about an hour's drive from the coast.

the success of the first company, Captain Nemo's Undersea Walk (tel: 263 7819) in Grand Baie, others followed including Aquaventure (tel: 422 7983) at Île aux Cerfs.

Undersea walking attracts people of every age and ability, including non-swimmers and young children. A boat ferries you to a floating dive platform inside the reef where a glass fronted steel helmet is placed over your head and rests loosely on your shoulders. Initially it feels heavy but once you are under water it

LANDING A MARLIN

The best time for catching marlin is from October to April, although big game fisherwoman, Birgit Rudolph, says "You never know when a big one is coming".

Submarine safari

To observe the colourful corals teeming with fish, and stay dry, join an hour-long submarine safari from Grand Baie (Blue Safari; tel: 263 3333). You can also hire the submarine for a private party or night dive; it can even be used as a venue for an underwater wedding.

Unmissable for families with young children is a trip in *Nessie*. This semi-submersible boat can be booked through hotels and tour operators and guarantees viewings of marine life gliding

becomes relatively weightless. Compressed air is then pumped into the helmet and filtered out through valves ensuring a fresh air supply and preventing the water from seeping up to your face. You can even chat to your fellow undersea walkers, and contact-lens or glasses wearers need not worry. Experienced guides stroll with you through a garden of spectacular coral inhabited by giant clam and flowering anenomes, and let you hand-feed the shoals of zebra fish.

LEFT: diving off *The Charming Lady*.
RIGHT: facilities for waterskiing, and other watersports, are available all over the Mauritius coast.

LETHAL WEAPON

The stone fish *(Synancea verucosa)*, known locally as the laff, lurks like a barnacle of basalt in mud and rock, clamping its upturned mouth on whatever takes its fancy. Hollow dorsal spines emit a highly toxic poison causing excruciating pain and swelling, and days of incapacity to anyone unfortunate enough to step on one. In some cases the injury can even prove fatal. In case of injury, clean the wound and seek medical help immediately.

Wearing plastic water shoes when wading through mud and rocks is essential, not only to protect your feet from the laff's noxious spines, but also to avoid cutting yourself on sharp rocks and corals.

through a riot of ornamental vegetation, in the comfort and safety of an air-conditioned compartment attached to the hull.

Cruising

Most hotels offer free use of hobie cats, windsurfing boards and kayaks for pottering about inside the lagoon. But to experience the real McCoy, you could spend a day sailing along the coast with an experienced crew in a luxury catamaran or yacht. You can join in pulling a few ropes or just relax on deck and watch the shapes and shadows of miniature mountains unfold. Full-day tours cost around R1,600 per

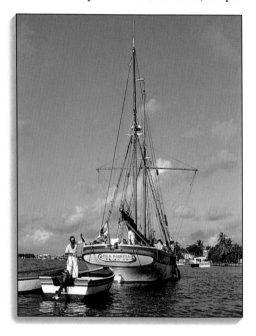

person and include lunch and soft drinks and can be booked through your hotel. *(See Travel Tips for list of operators.)*

Unspoilt Rodrigues

When it comes to corals, many experienced divers maintain that Rodrigues wins over on Seychelles. In *Islands in a Forgotten Sea*, author T.V. Bulpin refers to the scenery outside the lagoon as "dreamlike jungles of coral reefs" while Jacques Degremont, instructor at Cotton Bay, believes the island's waters are far superior to anything he has seen in Mauritius, especially since 1998 when many Indian Ocean corals died because of the rise in water temperature caused by El Niño. Because of its southerly location, Rodrigues escaped the worst of the El Niño effect. Today pristine sites in crystal-clear waters can be enjoyed for most months of the year outside the cyclone season.

One of the best sites for both divers and snorkellers is The Aquarium, inside the lagoon near Cotton Bay, where you need only slip over the side of the boat to see beautiful coral outcrops infested with brightly coloured reef fish. Just beyond the reef, at Aquarium Passe, lie canyons inhabited by shoals of king and unicorn fish. You may even spot some turtles.

Two hotel dive centres at Cotton Bay (tel: 831 6000) and Mourouk (tel: 831 3350) provide equipment and instruction with qualified PADI instructors. Both are affiliated to international dive associations. Rates here are slightly higher than in Mauritius, but groups tend to be smaller and more intimate. As the island does not have a recompression chamber, dives deeper than 30 metres (100 ft) are never undertaken and precautionary decompression stops are compulsory for those deeper than 12 metres (40 ft).

The range of other watersports on offer in Rodrigues is similar to Mauritius, though there is no parasailing or waterskiing because the lagoon is too shallow. Big game fishing was only introduced to Rodrigues in 1997, and is still in its infancy, but the unpolluted waters attract yellow fin tuna, dog tooth tuna, skipjack, dolphin fish, blue, black and striped marlins and sizable sailfish. With just five big game fishing boats to choose from and an entire ocean to play in, your chances of hooking "The Big One" are high. ❑

THE SHOALS OF CAPRICORN

Initiated by the Royal Geographical Society, the Shoals of Capricorn is a major marine science research programme into shallow water environments. British oceanographers are currently investigating the massive Seychelles Mauritius plateau and the adjacent Rodrigues trench. Larger than the Great Barrier Reef, longer than the Red Sea and covering an area of around 115,000 sq km (44,000 sq miles), it is one of earth's few submerged features clearly visible from space. If you're in Rodrigues you can see the work they are doing by dropping in at the Shoals education centre next to the Fisheries Office at Pointe Monier, to the west of the capital, Port Mathurin.

LEFT: the restored 19th-century vessel, *Isla Mauritia*, carries tourists on day trips around the coast.

The Big Ones

Big game fishing is big business in Mauritius all year round. It's no secret that the numbers of fish in Mauritian waters have dropped in recent years, and that sea temperatures have certainly been lower than usual, which most scientists are putting down to the effects of La Niña. Nevertheless, the seas are still rich in game and some of the top big fishing grounds in the world are around here.

The best season for black and blue marlin is usually from October to the end of March or April. Mauritius holds the world record for blue marlin at 648 kg (1,430 lb). Yellow fin tuna traditionally migrate in massive shoals to Mauritian waters between March and April. They can weigh anything between 63 and 90 kg (140–200 lb). Then in September the ocean sees prolific runs of wahoo which are reputed to be the fastest moving fish in the sea, sailfish averaging at around 45 kg (100 lb) which literally fly through the air when hooked and furiously fight for their freedom, not to mention bonito, better known to the supermarket shopper as skipjack tuna. Then, of course, there are the different species of shark from blue, hammer-head, mako and tiger, to black fin and white fin.

Most of the big hotels have their own boats and there are a number of boat clubs that operate fishing excursions for tourists. The largest fleets are based at the Corsaire Club at Trou aux Biches and the Hotel Club Centre de Peche at Black River, but if you're staying at Le Paradis Hotel at Le Morne in the southwest, you can get to the fishing grounds from the fishing centre at the hotel jetty, just a 20-minute ride away. The luxury craft are all equipped with ship to shore radio, trolling equipment for live and artificial lures, life-saving rafts and jackets and everything you would expect from an experienced skipper and deck hand.

If you're up to flexing your muscles with a marlin, just sit back in a fighting chair, strap on your harness and wait for the big moment. There really is nothing quite like the thrill of the chase to get the adrenalin levels pumping when a marlin strikes. These majestic, hugely powerful fish don't give themselves up easily and if they are hooked and landed, the winners pose for pictures alongside their catch.

RIGHT: a proud moment – landing a 23 kg (50 lb) yellow fin tuna.

You may prefer just to sit back and scan the ocean for signs of marlin or shark fins while the professionals prepare themselves for a fight. If you're just going along for the ride, the sun deck of any big game fishing boat is designed for a long sultry day at sea. You need do nothing more strenuous than cover yourself with high factor sun cream and equip yourself with a cool drink.

As for the catch, it can be returned to the sea, but expect to pay a hefty charge since many big game fishing operators rely on the income generated from selling it to the local market. Smoke houses in the Black River area process and package marlin, which is similar in taste and texture to smoked salmon

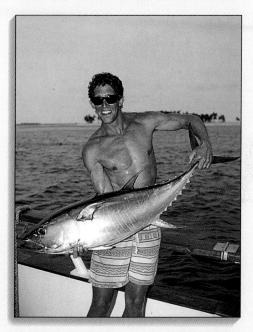

and is perfect served with a twist of lemon and black pepper. But if you really want to taste your own catch then smaller fish, such as bonito, can be cooked to order by the chef at your hotel.

If you're keen to take your prize marlin home as a trophy then a professional taxidermist can do the job for you. It might look a little out of place in your living room and you could wait up to six months for the process to be completed, but if you just want to see what one looks like, there's a fine specimen hanging from the rafters of the Blue Marlin Restaurant at Le Paradis Hotel.

Most boats take up to 9 passengers and the average daily rate is around R10,000 per person. ❏
● *For a list of reputable organisations see Travel Tips.*

PLACES

A detailed guide to Mauritius, with principal sites
clearly cross-referenced by number to the maps

The most important decision you will have to make when planning a visit to Mauritius is where to base yourself. The most established "resorts" lie on the northwest coast – in particular Grand Baie, the island's only conventional resort, with a choice of hotels and nightclubs, bars, shopping centres and a lively beach area. The appeal of nearby Trou-aux-Biches focuses on the main hotel, but between here and Port Louis, small side roads lead to a series of more isolated hotels. These are about as close to Port Louis as you can get, so are useful if you're in Mauritius on business.

The west coast resorts, renowned for year-round fine weather and magical sunsets, offer some of the best diving and watersports, and are well located if you are keen to explore. The main centres are Flic en Flac and nearby Wolmar, and the Morne peninsula, which has some of the island's finest beaches. Within easy reach are the wild and dramatic Black River Gorges, a perfect place for walking. Organised treks are led by local guides and may even offer the chance to glimpse one of Mauritius' endangered birds. The western hotels are also well placed for forays to the rugged south coast, which provides a temporary escape from the tourist trails of the north. Wild and windswept, it's best to hire a car to get around and explore the isolated fishing communities, lonely beaches, rolling sugar fields and old colonial residences.

For some, the east coast may feel too isolated. People come here to enjoy the top-class hotels, including the world famous Touessrok and St Géran hotels, the superb beaches around Belle Mare and Trou d'Eau Douce and the lovely offshore islands.

There is a small concentration of hotels near Mahébourg in the southeast corner of the island – a handy spot for the airport, trips along the unspoilt south and east coasts, and the Naval Museum.

While for tourists the coast is the source of Mauritius' appeal, local people aspire to live in the plateau towns sprawled across the centre of the island. Though not obviously attractive, these communities show the real Mauritius, where ordinary folk go about their daily business.

It is possible to go to Mauritius and not even visit the capital, Port Louis, as the airport is on the other side of the island. Mauritians are proud of the rejuvenation of the waterfront, which has brought new restaurants and shops and boosted the nightlife. For newcomers, however, the big appeal of the city is the central market and the chance to take in a dose of contemporary island life.

Rodrigues requires an effort to visit, and generally attracts only wanderers, walkers and escapists. What it lacks in sophistication is compensated for by the warmth of the islanders; if you want a simple, no-frills insight into remote island life, go now before things change. ❏

PRECEDING PAGES: majestic peak of Montagne du Rempart, as seen from Tamarin.
LEFT: carved wooden door of the Jummah Mosque, the island's main mosque.

PORT LOUIS

The capital of Mauritius may lack obvious appeal, but the busy streets, the jumble of new and scruffy old buildings, and the old-fashioned market are worth exploring

Map on page 104

N ot so long ago, when office workers chorused "pens down at 4pm" and left the stifling heat of the capital for the cooler uplands, Port Louis simply shut up shop and went to bed. The city was as dead as a dodo and, save for late-night gambling with Sino-Mauritians and newly arrived sailors in the now defunct casino, there was nothing else to do. Since then, Port Louis has undergone something of a transformation – or, as the locals would say, a "lifting", a hand-me-down expression acquired from the British, meaning a face lift. This is thanks largely to the development of the new Caudan Waterfront, which, with its trendy designer shops, al fresco cafés, cinemas, club and 24-hour casino, has become the focal point of the city – and is generally considered the main attraction for tourists.

But anyone not interested in shopping is likely to find more of interest in the rest of the city, with its jumble of new and decrepit old buildings, mosques, churches and temples, Chinese and Muslim quarters and race course, and above all the lively, old-fashioned market. There is enough to keep you busy for half a day at least. Remember though, that between November and April the city can be uncomfortably hot.

LEFT: the shiny new Caudan Waterfront, hub of the capital.
BELOW: old Port Louis still attracts shoppers.

History of an island port

Port Louis started out in 1722, when the infant French East India Company transferred its headquarters from the old Dutch settlement at Warwyck Bay (now Mahébourg) to what was then North West Harbour. It was renamed Port Louis after Louis XV of France. From its early days, fortune seekers descended on the city prompting an 18th-century traveller to note that it contained "a sort of scum of bankrupts, ruined adventurers, swindlers and rascals of all kinds". Those characters have long gone but, for all the modernity of air-conditioned shopping malls and fast food outlets, the past has not been completely erased.

Under the British, Port Louis developed into a major port for sailing ships, but by the late 1800s, with the introduction of the steamer and the opening of the Suez Canal, the city had lost much of its appeal, while outbreaks of disease, cyclones and fire caused many of its folk to flee to the healthier climate of the uplands.

A look across the Caudan Basin today, with its cargo and freighter ships, reminds you that Port Louis is still very much a working port and commercial centre. Many thousands pour into the city each day to work, congesting the roads with traffic and adding to the resident population of 150,000 – all packed into 10 sq km (4 sq miles). It is no surprise that Port Louis, like most modern capitals, is crowded, dirty and noisy. But the Moka mountains behind, and the sea in front, provide a resplendent setting.

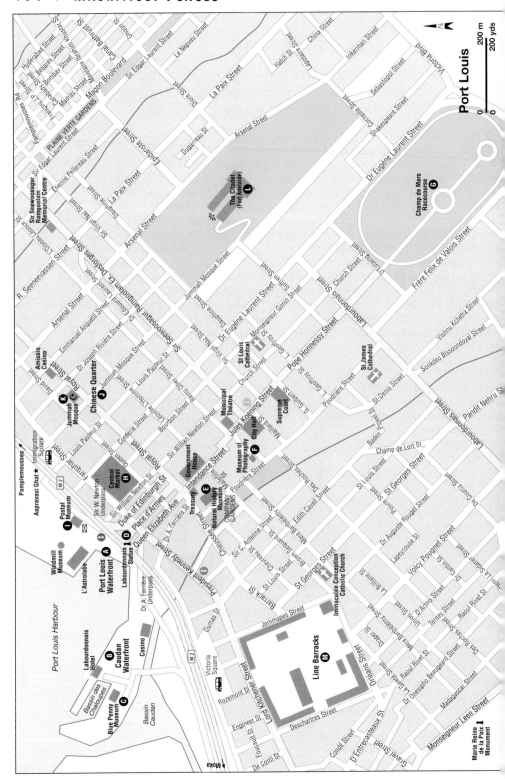

Port Louis

On the waterfront

The new waterfront development is officially divided into two sections – the large, privately run Caudan Waterfront and the smaller, government-run Port Louis Waterfront. A good place to start a walking tour of the city is from the **Port Louis Waterfront Ⓐ**, where you'll find the **Tourist Office** (open Mon–Fri 9am–5pm, Sat 9am–3pm; tel: 208 6397), which has maps and brochures, and a small shopping mall.

A waterfront tour on the fun train costs just a few rupees.

The most curious sight in this area is the **Windmill Museum** (open Mon–Fri 10–noon and 1–3pm; free). A windmill was first built on this spot by the French in the 18th century, and it was France which donated the mechanism inside the modern reconstruction and which also supplies the grain used in occasional demonstrations. The collection of old photographs and the video focus on the transformation of the waterfront.

Over on the **Caudan Waterfront Ⓑ**, beyond the complex of shops and restaurants, rises the vast **Labourdonnais Hotel**. Patronised mainly by international businessmen, the hotel is not a bad pitstop in the evening – particularly if you're flush with rupees from the nearby casino.

One of the best views of the city is from the sea, and you can take a **harbour cruise** from just outside the Labourdonnais. The pleasure boat chugs past a panoramic view of a delectable landfall of peaks and knolls. Looking inland, from right to left, the bulk of Signal Mountain dominates the city. Next, Le Pouce (The Thumb) rises from the south wing of the Moka Range in a "thumbs up" sign. The most distinctive peak of all, whose pinnacle looks like the cloak-shrouded shoulders of a man, comes in the form of **Pieter Both**, named after the Dutch Admiral who drowned off the coast. Closer to the city to the north is a knoll known as La Citadelle, named after the ruin of a fortress at its crest.

BELOW:
old meets new.

A museum well worth calling into is **The Blue Penny Museum Ⓒ** (open Mon–Sat 10am–5pm; tel: 210 8176; admission fee). Home to a rich collection of national treasures, it exhibits fine art, old maps and sections on philately and postal history, coins, paper money, postcards and photography. Many items were formerly in the possession of private collectors.

Place d'Armes

If you cross by the subway just in front of the Tourist Office you reach the **Place d'Armes Ⓓ**, where you'll be greeted by the most famous landmark of the city, the bronze statue of Bertrand François Mahé de Labourdonnais. He arrived in 1735 as the newly appointed French governor-general of the Mascarene Islands and went about transforming shambolic Port Louis into a thriving sea port and commercial centre.

Some local people seem to enjoy having a chat beneath the royal palms that line the square, but the constant buzz of cars around the edge does not make the Place d'Armes a peaceful place. At the top stands **Government House**, the official centre of government. It started life as a ramshackle wooden hut, was enlarged by Labourdonnais in 1738 and later embellished by the British. In the courtyard, secured by wrought-iron gates, is a rather severe marble statue

Reminder of a colonial past.

BELOW: multi-coloured Hindu temple, one of many on the island.

of Queen Victoria, shaded in summer by brilliant red flamboyant trees. Beyond it stands a statue of Sir William Stevenson, British governor from 1857 to 1863. To the right, on the corner of Chaussée, the old Treasury Buildings (1883) are not in a good state, but provide good cover if you get caught in a downpour.

Along La Chaussée is the Mauritius Institute, home of the **Natural History Museum** ❸ (open Mon–Wed and Fri). The museum is an apology for what was once a priceless collection of flora and fauna and you may be disappointed with the displays which include a stuffed dodo sealed inside a dirty cabinet, some giant Aldabra tortoise, shell collections, stuffed Mascarene Island birds and a weary looking shark strung up on the rafters. It is tempting to drop a note in the Suggestion Box by the exit proposing that they start again from scratch. The **Company Gardens** next door could do with some attention too, and tends to be a haunt of prostitutes – though it is quite busy at lunchtime, when city workers take a break beneath giant banyans and bottle palms. The Kentucky Fried Chicken attracts more regular custom.

A walk up Intendance Street

A quick stroll south from Place d'Armes along Intendance Street takes you past the rest of the city's other main historic buildings. First is the **Municipal Theatre**, which was built in 1822 and is the oldest theatre in the Indian Ocean. If it is open during the day, ask the caretaker to show you the beautiful painted dome and crystal chandeliers. During the 1930s, the citizens of Port Louis were entertained to old favourites like *Madame Butterfly* brought to them by visiting troupes from France. The theatre had virtually shut down by the 1950s but re-opened in 1994 after a massive face-lift. Seats now sell fast for modern jazz gigs,

operas and plays, but it's also the hot spot for weddings and prestigious functions when big shots get invited by moneyed Mauritians.

Opposite the theatre, cobbled Rue du Vieux Conseil leads to the **Museum of Photography** (opening hours vary; entrance fee; tel: 211 1705), where you'll find one of the island's oldest displays of cameras and prints, which includes daguerreotypes as well as photographs of colonial Mauritius. All these have been collected by photographer Tristan de Breville, who fights a constant financial battle to keep his museum open.

Heading east, you reach the austere **St Louis Cathedral**. The original French church was reduced to rubble by cyclones in the 1800s. It was rebuilt twice before the present version was consecrated in 1932. To the left is the **Episcopal Palace**, a fine 19th-century colonnaded mansion. The other important church in the city is **St James Cathedral**, nearby in Poudrière Street, which looms over gardens shaded by palm trees and tumbling bougainvillaea. It was once a gunpowder store and prison under the French, before the British turned it into a church, and also saw service as a refuge centre when Port Louisiens would abandon their wooden houses on the approach of a cyclone for the security of its 3-metre (10-ft) walls.

From these two places of worship, it is only a short diversion to the gambling den of the **Champ de Mars** (also known as the Hippodrome), cradled by the Moka mountains at the eastern edge of the city. Once the training ground for French soldiers, today it is the venue of the Independence Day celebrations on 12 March – and the nation's most popular sport: horse racing. An invitation to the members enclosure on classic race days, like the Gold Cup or the Maiden Cup, should not be refused; you get a bird's eye view of the paddock, free rein

Map on page 104

TIP

At the Café du Vieux Conseil, virtually opposite the Museum of Photography, you can enjoy a drink or snack, shaded by trees and away from the bustle of the city streets. It is open in the daytime only.

BELOW: from May to November, Saturday is race day.

A MAURITIAN NATIONAL PASTIME

In Mauritius, it is said that there are three seasons – summer, winter and the racing season. The Mauritius Turf Club, the second oldest in the southern hemisphere, was founded by Colonel Draper in 1812. He had friends in high places on both sides of the divide and, being a passionate punter, thought it only gentlemanly to bring the French and English together in an atmosphere of leisure.

Today, most horses come from South Africa and Australia and are trained in one of the island's eight stables. Race meetings are held every Saturday afternoon from the first week in May to the end of November. Spirits run high, with screams of "Allez, allez!" following the horses as they gallop round the course. Music is played between races as punters press round Chinese bookies to place their bets or collect their winnings, and food sellers do a roaring trade.

Many Mauritians are well versed in the international race scene. They follow the progress of individual horses closely and the use of starting stalls, photo-finish systems and adherence to Newmarket disciplines attracts jockeys from all over the world. There are even professional gamblers who try to make a living from picking a winner; most of them will have a "hot tip", but remember, despite what some may tell you, there is no such thing as a "dead cert".

of all facilities which include bars and comfortable terraces and an unmissable opportunity to rub shoulders with those in the know. On non-race days, joggers replace the horses.

Following the spice trail

If there is one place that no one should miss in Port Louis, it is the covered **Central Market**  (open daily, known as the Bazar Central in Creole), which occupies two blocks just north of Place d'Armes. Traders from all continents have converged here for nearly 150 years, and today Indian, Chinese and Creole traders stand shoulder to shoulder selling their wares. Along the main thoroughfare through the market a few stalls sell t-shirts, baskets and spices packaged for tourists, but the real heart of the market is inside.

Follow the locals wending their way through the dimly lit halls, picking out the best from the mounds of tropical fruit and vegetables, or picking up herbal remedies guaranteed to cure everything from diarrhoea to diabetes. You can pick up spicy pancakes *(dal puris)*, curry-filled *samousas*, and other popular Mauritian snacks for just a few rupees: perfect for a cheap mid-morning snack or light lunch.Those with a more sensitive constitution may want to avoid them, though. You should probably also steer clear of *bombli*, the dried salt fish with a stench that defies description.

Philatelic passions

BELOW: fresh produce for sale at the Central Market.

After the bustle of the market, you can find solace in the calm of the **Postal Museum** (open Mon–Fri 9am–4pm, Sat till 11.30am), which lies across the busy road from the waterfront entrance of the market. This small but delightful museum contains 19th-century postal equipment such as telegraph and stamp-vending machines and a fine collection of stamps, postal stationery, original artwork and printing plates. For serious collectors there are stock books, stamp albums, mounts, magnifying glasses and tweezers and first day covers and commemorative sets of stamps, such as the 400th anniversary of the Dutch landing which was issued in 1999.

A short walk north alongside the busy road takes you to the gardens of the **Aapravasi Ghat**. Once known as the Immigration Depot or Coolie Ghat, it housed the first Indian immigrants who were brought here before being farmed out to the sugar estates. Look for the 11 bronze murals showing scenes of immigrant life, including one depicting a pair of hands breaking free from chains. A poem dedicated to the Unknown Immigrant recalls how "He… turned stone into green fields of gold", a reference to sugar cane.

The Chinese Quarter

The **Chinese Quarter** , encompassed in several streets to the east of the market, is the most colourful part of the city with its specialist food and spice shops and herbal remedy (ayurvedic) stores. There are plenty of eating houses called hotels, too, where fast cheap meals, such as the ubiquitous noodles *(mines)* can be slurped from bowls. A variety of snacks such as *gâteaux piments*, crispy *samousas* or the more unusual combination of fresh pineapples with hot red chilli sauce, are also sold from mobile food wagons on street corners.

The **Amicale Casino**, on the corner of Royal Street and Anquetil Street, used to attract Chinese hopefuls trying their luck on games like Fan Tan, Dai Siu (Big Small) or Pai Koo (Chinese dominoes), but rioters reduced the building to a heap of ruins in an arson attack in 1999 during which seven people lost their lives and at the time of writing there are no plans to re-open it.

The **Jummah Mosque** Ⓚ in Royal Street is open to tourists only at certain times, but one of its most striking features are the beautifully carved teak doors and the ornate decorations of the outer walls. Built in around 1853 for the growing Muslim community and subsequently enlarged, it is the island's most impressive mosque. Plaine Verte, the Muslim Quarter to the north of Port Louis, is home to the annual Ghoon festival, but other than its small tea houses and tumbledown textile shops, has little to interest the visitor.

Symbols of authority

The only reason for going to **The Citadel (La Citadelle)** Ⓛ, also known as Fort Adelaide (open daily 9am–4pm, Sat till noon), is the panoramic views of the city's amphitheatre of mountains, the Champ de Mars race course and the harbour. The basalt fort was named after Queen Adelaide, wife of William IV, and must rank as Port Louis' greatest white elephant. Unloved and unwanted, with just a few small shops selling local arts and crafts, it never seems to wake from its apathy even when the silence is broken by the babble of tourists.

The Chinese temple at the foot of The Citadel on the corner of Generosity and Justice Streets is rather drab, too. A better example of a Chinese temple is **Kwan**

Map on page 104

The Jummah Mosque.

BELOW: the lively Chinese quarter.

Map on page 104

There aren't too many green spaces in Port Louis but you could join the locals at the Robert Edward Hart Gardens, south-west of the Caudan waterfront, where you'll find a rather incongruous statue of Lenin's head.

BELOW:
Government House.
RIGHT:
preparing leaves for weaving, Domaine Les Pailles.

Tee Pagoda, the oldest in town, which sits on the roundabout south of the Caudan Waterfront, dedicated to the Chinese warrior god who fought for justice. Bank notes at the entrance of the temple are deposited by the faithful and burnt at funerals and memorial services as "burial money".

For some Mauritian quirkiness, wander down to **Line Barracks ⓜ** *(caserne)*, home of the Mauritian Police Force, which contains fine examples of 18th-century colonial architecture. Inside, look out for the petrified dodo and for learner drivers taking their test. See the prison dubbed "Alcatraz" and the Golden Gates at the main entrance which caused a stir because they cost a fortune. Nearby is an incongruous blue bathroom-tiled archway marked "Gateway of Discipline" which lead to the cops' car park.

Around Port Louis

The **Church and Shrine of Père Laval** at Sainte-Croix in the foothills of Long Mountain to the northeast is only a 10-minute drive from the city centre. Père Laval arrived as a missionary in 1841 and was soon revered for his work with the poor. When he died in 1864 his body was buried at Sainte-Croix and became the object of pilgrimage. Many Mauritians still believe in his special healing powers and every day hundreds of people of all faiths file past the stone sarcophagus that contains his remains, topped by an effigy framed with flowers, and pray for the sick. He was beatified by the Catholic Church in 1979 and is one step away from being canonised, so that it won't be long before Mauritius has its very own patron saint. An annual pilgrimage to the church takes place during the nights of 7 and 8 September. The curate's residence nearby is a superb example of colonial architecture.

On the approach, its location in the suburbs about 10 minutes' drive south of the city centre (but well signposted off the motorway) seems unpromising, but **Domaine Les Pailles** (open daily 10am–5.30pm; entrance fee; tel: 212 4225) does, in fact, provide an effective escape from the brouhaha of the capital. Some people go only for the restaurants (of which there are five), but there are also 1,200 hectares (3,000 acres) of grounds to explore. The most popular attraction, particularly for children, is the one-hour guided tour (by mini-train or horse-drawn carriage) which aims to inform visitors about the production of sugar, rum and other local products. The tour goes through a working reconstruction of an early sugar factory and rum distillery, as well as a spice garden and mask museum, with, of course, the ubiquitous sega show at the end. Children can also go pony trekking or splash about in the outdoor pool, while adults can can go on a two-hour jeep safari which runs along 11 km (7 miles) of winding mountain tracks spotting wild stag, monkeys and hare on the way – though the vegetation is the main attraction really.

Breathtaking views of Port Louis can be had from the peaceful setting of the Marie Reine de la Paix monument on the flanks of **Signal Mountain**, southwest of the city. In 1989 this place of pilgrimage swelled as thousands of islanders gathered for mass held by Pope John Paul. ❑

THE NORTH

The beach-lined north coast is the most popular on Mauritius, and has the island's only proper resort town, Grand Baie. Only one thing can lure people away from the sea: the Botanical Gardens

Map on page 114

Port Louis

Most visitors to Mauritius head for the hotels north of **Port Louis ❶**. Tourism is well established between the resorts of Trou aux Biches and Grand Baie, which act as bookends to one of the loveliest stretches of beach on the island, with an unbroken chain of powder-white beaches and gentle, crystal lagoons. Hotels, guest houses and private bungalows are plentiful in this area, and more hotels are also sprouting up in the less accessible areas between Trou aux Biches and Port Louis. The coast's best-kept beaches are attached to hotels and reserved mainly for residents' use, but if you want to mix with the locals the public beaches at Trou aux Biches, Mont Choisy and Pereybère are lively, particularly at weekends.

Away from the coast, the sugar-swathed lands of the north are not as scenic as the mountainous interior of the south, but the flat terrain, broken up by the gentlest of hills, is ideal for cycling, and there's something exciting about getting lost in the maze of sugar cane fields and asking for directions – only to get the reply back in Kreol, French, English or a combination of all three.

LEFT: lounging by the pool, Cap Malheureux.
BELOW: Grand Baie basket seller.

Tombs, turtles and shipwrecks

The fastest route to the northern beaches is to take the motorway – either straight to Grand Baie or Trou aux Biches, or to the turn-off for the resorts further south – but if you are in no hurry, you could opt for the longer coastal route.

Just beyond the city suburbs is **Roche Bois ❷**, where the mass of bright red headstones in the Chinese Cemetery, the colour of good luck, bear witness to the island's Sino-Mauritian population. But Roche Bois is also a poor Creole suburb and a byword for poverty on the island. In 1999, one of its sons, a Creole singer called Kaya, was arrested for smoking cannabis at a pro-pot public demonstration and next day died in a police cell.

In 1615, four Dutch East India ships were swept on to the reef during a cyclone and sunk at nearby **Baie du Tombeau (Bay of Tombs) ❸**. Everyone died, including the Dutch Admiral Pieter Both who was on his way to Holland after a spell as the governor of the Company. The sleepy village of Baie du Tombeau lies on the bay's southern flank, apparently turning its back on the world, and blocking its lovely, deserted beach from view. Access to the beach is not easy, but if you persist look out for the ruin of an old French fort partially hidden in shrubbery nearby.

You link up again with the Grand Baie road at the crossroads near **Arsenal** (named after a French ammunition store nearby), where you can also turn inland towards the Pamplemousses Botanical Gardens *(see page 120)*.

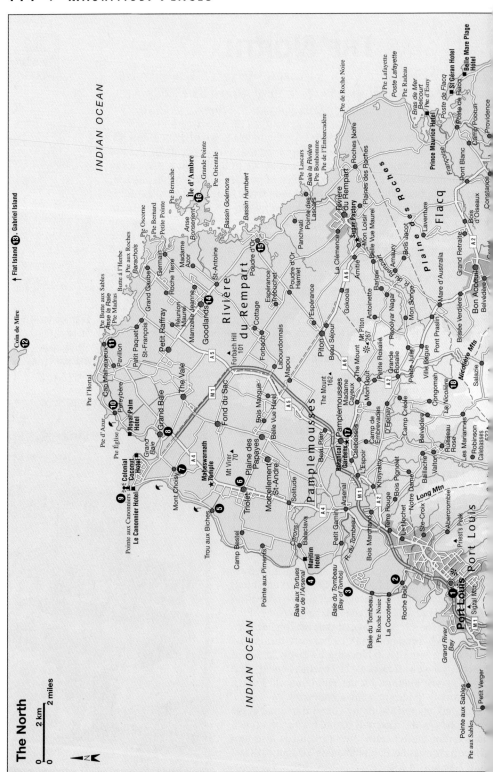

Beyond the tiny community of **Balaclava**, reached through sugar fields on he B41, is an area that is fast being developed – though passers-by will see othing but the entrances to private drives leading to hotels such as the Planta- ion, Oberoi and Maritim. These neighbouring hotels flank the banks of the River Citrons, which enters the estuary forming the **Baie aux Tortues (Turtle Bay) ④**, lso known as Baie de l'Arsenal. The Maritim Hotel occupies grounds which ormed part of a French arsenal at nearby **Moulin à Poudre**, where ammunition or ships was supplied for expeditions to India.

Although hotel development is strictly monitored, some locals fear that the ncrease in the number of hotels in this previously undiscovered area may nreaten the bay, which is reputed to contain 90 percent of live coral. From ìrand Baie, you can take a trip on the *Isla Mauritia (see tip, page 116)*, which rops anchor at Baie aux Tortues, and snorkel in the same clear waters in which reat armies of turtles once swam or ride up the River Citrons.

The road finally hits the coast at **Pointe aux Piments**, where filaos rustle in ¡entle breezes and life chugs on slow and unhurried on the beaches. If you can :ave the pristine paradise fronting the Victoria or Plaza Beach Resort hotels, nen take a stroll outside and surrender to the magic of a Mauritius sunset and /atch wellie-booted fishermen wading in a shallow lagoon.

The Hindu goddess Durga on her mount.

rou aux Biches

'he small resort of **Trou aux Biches ⑤**, with its gently shelving sands and eep blue lagoon, is a mecca for beach-lovers. It is much more sedate than its orthern neighbour, Grand Baie, particularly midweek when you can glimpse napshots of how life used to be, and still is in parts of this former fishing vil- ıge. At the start of the 3-km (2-mile) beach, beside ıe fish landing station, fishermen huddle beneath asuarina trees gabbling in Kreol. Here you'll find a ouple of restaurants and Chez Popo's supermarket /here you can hire bikes and, if self-catering, pick ı a wide range of essentials.

BELOW:
the Maheswarnath
Temple is the
island's largest
Hindu shrine.

The hotels all have facilities for waterskiing, wind- ırfing, diving and snorkelling, and will also arrange ıiling and glass-bottom boat trips. At weekends the ranquillity of the lagoon is broken by the roar of an ıcreasing number of speed boats, but the beach remains retreat for relaxation and beach games. Old boys on icycles sell freshly caught fish (and will skin and gut ıem for you) and touts sell seashells, pareos and model ɔats, keeping you amused with gentle banter. Look out ɔr the the toothless fruit lady called Madonna, who's a ɔcal celebrity. Her skill at chopping pineapples with ɪr razor-sharp machete is a spectacle in itself.

riolet and Mont Choisy

riolet ⑥ can claim to be the largest and longest (and ɛrhaps plainest) village on the island. It has played a vely part in Mauritian political life since Indepen- ɛnce, and is the constituency of Mauritius' first Prime Iinister. The village also has the highest population of ıdo-Mauritians, and is home to the biggest Hindu mple in Mauritius (just inland from Trou aux Biches ɔlice station). Built in 1857, the **Maheswarnath**

TIP

You can book a full-day cruise with the *Isla Mauritia* from Yacht Charters at Grand Baie (tel: 263 8395). The price includes a barbecue lunch at Anse des Filaos where you get serenaded and "sega'd" by the crew. The fine old sailing ship was built in 1852 in Mallorca.

Temple complex is a kaleidoscope of colour and sits beside an enormous banyan tree where a placard welcomes all pilgrims. The caretaker usually volunteers to act as a guide (and expects a tip).

At weekends and holidays it seems that everyone from the area toddles off to **Mont Choisy ⑦** beach where turquoise seas meet a long strip of sugar-soft sand backed by a forest of casuarina trees. Matronly Indo-Mauritian mums make for the shade and unpack pots of rice and curry from great baskets *(tentes)* around which families gather to eat. Children play on a former landing strip, now a grassy football pitch, where a monument celebrates the first ever flight made by French pilots from Mauritius to Réunion in 1933. Midweek, Mont Choisy is a perfect spot for a quiet dip in the warm lagoon or a trip in a glass-bottom boat.

The Creole Cote d'Azur

Grand Baie ⑧ is the island's hub of tourism, where not only hotels and restaurants, but also bars, clubs and designer shops, are strung around a huge horseshoe-shaped bay. Dubbed the "Creole Cote d'Azur" and, by Mauritian standards, brash, busy and boisterous, Grand Baie's development from a tiny fishing village to a holiday haven has not dealt a fatal blow to the village atmosphere even though many of the small shops have become supermarkets. Popular with local residents, many of whom have second homes here, as well as with independent and package tourists, Grand Baie is the only real resort in Mauritius offering a plethora of places to eat and drink not attached to hotels. You can also book tours to all parts of the country from here, including Rodrigues, find self-catering accommodation and hire a car through tour operators, such as Mauritours and many other smaller travel agents.

BELOW:
ferrying tourists to the *Isla Mauritia.*

Most activity centres around **Sunset Boulevard**, a modern waterside shopping mall (closed Sun) opposite a cluster of supermarkets, restaurants and fast food stalls. You'll find a centre for big game fishing on the waterfront and facilities to book undersea walks, undersea safaris and parascending trips over the lagoon. The bay, which at times is crowded with small pleasure craft and catamarans, has no decent bathing beach, but for peace and relaxation take a short stroll to the soft wide sands of La Cuvette public beach to the north of the bay, which has modern facilities including showers, toilets and changing cubicles. Just beyond the black basalt rocks to the right of the beach is the luxurious **Royal Palm Hotel** but be aware that casual beach strollers are not welcome unless they have a reservation for lunch or dinner. Alternatively, try the small shopping and leisure complex of Kapu Kai (tel: 269 1400) on the coast road, where lazy days in the swimming pool with magnificent views of Grand Baie can be enjoyed.

Grand Baie has more nightclubs *(boites de nuit)* than any other resort on the island (which draws quite a few local prostitutes to the area). For a spot of balmy nightlife try Banana Bar for drinks and live music or let your hair down at the disco inside Le Sports Café, which attracts a trendy, young crowd.

Pointe aux Canonniers

Enormous flamboyant trees, emblazoned with deep red flowers in summer, flank the road leading to **Pointe aux Canonniers** ❾, a beach-belted headland at the northern end of Grand Baie which was once used as a garrison by the French and later turned into a quarantine station by the British. Eighteenth-century cannons and a ruined 19th-century lighthouse watch over the reefs (which have caused the doom of dozens of ships) from the gardens of **Le**

Map on page 114

Undersea walks can be booked through tour operators and hotels.

BELOW:
Le Canonnier Hotel.

Canonnier Hotel; this spot affords great views of Coin de Mire island off the northern tip of the island *(see page 119)*.

Hotels and shady villas house tourists and locals attracted by the tranquillity of the area. At the opposite tip of the headland from Le Canonnier is the **Colonial Coconut Hotel**, built around a colonial-style bungalow, complete with planters' chairs and faded pictures, overlooking a small swimming pool *(see Travel Tips)*.

Pereybère

Just 2 km (1 mile) to the north, **Pereybère** ⑩ seems to be merging with Grand Baie. But the pace of life is much slower, providing a foil to the sometimes brash atmosphere of its sister resort as well as cheaper day-to-day living. Traditionally a holiday retreat for the Chinese community, Pereybère is changing rapidly to accommodate increasing numbers of foreign self-caterers, as well as holidaymakers from Grand Baie who come for a change of scene, and to stretch out on the lovely casuarina-fringed beach or snorkel in the lagoon.

A smaller version of Mont Choisy *(see page 116)*, Pereybère is swamped at weekends by islanders, who come to picnic, chat under the trees, swim, go for glass-bottom boat trips, and maybe even round off the day with an impromptu sega party. Food stalls sell hot snacks, drinks and fresh fruit (conveniently cut up into small pieces and sold in bags), and, if you're lucky, there'll be an ice cream van, too. Away from the beach, there's a *boutik* for basic shopping and simple restaurants that serve slap-up meals at knockdown prices. And if you're after a pareo, the tree-lined catwalks along the main road offer plenty of choice; prices are lower than those offered both by shops and beach hawkers.

Unspoilt coasts and sugar lands

Taking on the appearance of a country lane lined with casuarinas shading shallow bays and rocky coves, the coast road swings east to **Cap Malheureux** ⑪, 6 km (4 miles) beyond Pereybère. This, the island's most northern point, probably got its name – Cape of Misfortune – from the number of ships that foundered here. Nothing much goes on in this tranquil beauty spot, though if you get there around 4pm you will see the village wake up momentarily when fishermen bring in their catch to sell to islanders congregating beside the striking red-roofed church. There is a small beach where local kids play, just one restaurant, a general store and petrol station.

A 5-km (3-mile) drive east through sugar cane emerges at the sparkling white beaches of **Grand Gaube,** where the luxurious Legends Hotel overlooks the curvaceous bay, or enjoy tasty snacks at Paul et Virginie Hotel a short stroll northwards.

Offshore islands

Coin de Mire, Flat Island (Île Plate) and Gabriel Island (Îlot Gabriel) all make good day trips. Depending on weather conditions, you can have a fun day out sailing around the islands, being pampered by experienced crew. Full-day tours accommodating 20 to 30 passengers with lunch in the luxury catamaran cruiser

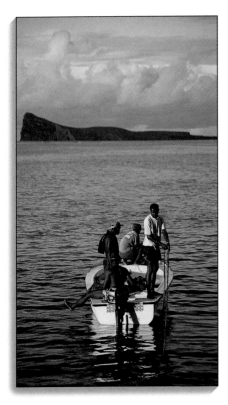

Le Pacha, leave from Verandah Bungalow Village Hotel in Grand Baie. It drops anchor in sheltered bays with plenty of opportunity for snorkelling, swimming and sunbathing on deck. Other operators in Grand Baie lay on similar tours.

Coin de Mire ⓬, the closest island to the shore, is composed of layers of crumbling volcanic sandstone, making landing impossible. Getting on to **Flat Island** ⓭ is worth the effort, just to pad along the lovely beaches ringed by coral reef. The same coral reef encircles neighbouring **Gabriel Island**. These last two islands once served as quarantine stations for immigrants during the cholera epidemic of 1856 which nearly wiped out the population of Port Louis. Picnic parties to Flat Island are popular and you can spend the whole day exploring the little pathways which meander round its lighthouse and cemetery.

You need permission to land on Round and Serpent islands, 24 km (15 miles) north of Mauritius, which are both designated nature reserves; but they are difficult to land on anyway because of their sheer cliffs. **Round Island (Île Ronde)** is home to many endangered species, including the rare telfair skink, two species of snake and the *paille-en-queue* – the tropic bird that graces the tail fins of Air Mauritius planes. **Serpent Island (Île aux Serpents)** is a bird sanctuary, but there are no snakes. And in case you were wondering, **Pigeon House Rock (Le Pigeonnier)**, north of Flat Island, doesn't have any pigeons either.

Ships are the theme

From Grand Gaube the road finally draws you away from the coast and swings south to **Goodlands** ⓮. The streets in this densely populated town are usually heaving with people, who frequent the high street shops and the daily **market**. Goodlands is also home to the largest model sailing ship factory in Mauritius,

Map on page 114

The "Rolls-Royce" of model ships are made at Goodlands.

BELOW: hot Sundays in Pereybère are good for business.

In 1872 traveller
Nicholas Pike
dismissed the idea
that Poudre d'Or
(Golden Powder)
was named after its
sands or deposits of
gold. He claimed the
name came from the
sugar grown in the
district. Between
June and December
you can see cane
being crushed a few
miles south at Mon
Loisir Sugar Factory
(guided tours; tel:
412 7699), near
Rivière du Rempart.

BELOW:
the Lily Pond at
Pamplemousses.

Historic Marine (open Mon–Fri 8am–5pm, Sat–Sun 8am–noon; guided tours entrance fee; tel: 283 9304). There is a large showroom downstairs (with many wooden objects other than ships), while upstairs you can watch the craftsmen patiently working on these mini masterpieces (weekdays only).

The road southeast of Goodlands hits the coast at **Poudre d'Or** , an appealing village where you can linger on the headland opposite the reef where, in 1744, the *Saint Geran* foundered in a storm, a tragic incident which inspired French novelist Bernardin de Saint Pierre to pen his famous love story, *Paul and Virginie*. Some objects rescued from the wreck are on display in the Naval Museum in Mahébourg *(see page 128)*. **Île d'Ambre** , an uninhabited island named after the ambergris once found there, is just 30 minutes' boat ride from here, and if you ask around, you should find a local fisherman to take you from the jetty at Poudre d'Or; arrange for them to pick you up later so that you can enjoy the excellent swimming and snorkelling.

The headland marking our boundary between the North and East Coast, is dominated by the wild and windy beaches of **Roches Noires** and **Poste Lafayette** studded with black volcanic rocks. They are often deserted but for men fishing in the shallows or landing their catch from boats. Be careful if you want to swim since the seas can be rough.

Botanic beauties at Pamplemousses

From Poudre d'Or the road heads inland to the **Botanical Gardens**  at Pamplemousses (open daily 6am–6pm) – a 30-minute drive from Port Louis or Grand Baie. They are not in a particularly good state of repair, but are still well worth a visit, the best time being between December and April.

The 25-hectare (62-acre) gardens were renamed the Sir Seewoosagur Ramgoolam Botanical Gardens in 1988 in honour of the late prime minister, but they are still known by everyone as Pamplemousses (French for grapefruit). The village was named after a variety of citrus plant imported from Java by the Dutch in the 17th century, which once grew in the area. Its fruit resembles a large grapefruit known as "bambolmas" in Tamil, thought to be the origin of the French word.

You should allow a couple of hours to explore the maze of palm-lined avenues. Tour operators often combine a visit with a shopping spree to Port Louis and tend to lead groups on lightning-quick tours. The official guides who offer their services to all visitors (in exchange for a tip) will also whisk you around, but they do point out the main attractions and provide interesting nuggets of information about some of the more unusual species; try to collar one of the older guides, who are likely to have worked in the gardens for years and are usually more informative. If you want to explore independently, it's a good idea to buy the guidebook (available at the main entrance), which contains a map as well an authoratitive explanation of the plant species – only some are labelled – and other attractions. There are no refreshment facilities inside the gardens, so stock up on water from the food stalls by the car park.

Wrought-iron gates (exhibited at the 1851 Great Exhibition at London's Crystal Palace) mark the original entrance to the gardens but the main entrance is now by the big car park on the other side. From here, guides will lead you along shaded avenues named after botanists and benefactors and show you trees such as the bastard mahogany *(Andira inermis)*, marmalade box *(Genipa americana)*, chewing gum *(Manilkara achras)* and sausage tree *(Kigelia pinnata)*.

In all, there are about 500 plant species out of which 80 are palms and 40, such as ebony, mahogany and pandanus, are indigenous to the Mascarene Islands. Among the most impressive sights are the **Lotus Pond**, filled with yellow and white flowers, and the huge **Lily Pond**. Half concealed by the floating leaves of the giant Amazon water lily *(Victoria amazonica)* this is everyone's favourite photo opportunity. The flowers of the lily open white, fade to a dusky pink by the end of the second day and then die; the unmistakable flat leaves can reach as much as 1.5 metres (4½ ft) in diameter. The talipot palm is another remarkable species. It waits 40 to 60 years to flower, then promptly dies. Ginger, cloves and cinnamon are among the many spices you can sniff out.

Map on page 114

Mon Plaisir

The gardens' origins go back to 1735, when Mahé de Labourdonnais bought a house in the grounds which he called Mon Plaisir. He developed the area to supply fresh fruit and vegetables for ships calling at Port Louis. In 1768, Mon Plaisir became the residence of the French horticulturist, Pierre Poivre, who planted the seeds for the specimens you see today *(see page 247)*. The present **Chateau Mon Plaisir**, a 19th-century British legacy, was recently rescued from ruin and is used as an administration office.

Near the entrance, a collection of giant Aldabra tortoises happily munch on leaves in between noisy mating sessions. Next to the pen is a reconstruction of an early sugar mill, although there isn't a scrap of sugar cane in sight.

Scenic route to Pieter Both

For one of the most scenic drives in Mauritius – where a foreground of sugar cane is framed by the quirky peaks of the Moka mountains – take the A2 from Pamplemousses towards Centre de Flacq and the east coast. En route you pass **Grand Rosalie**, where the first sugar estate was established in 1743. The plantation house is closed to the public, but you can get an idea of the lay of the land from the nearby **La Nicolière Reservoir** ⓰. The road winds uphill, giving bird's eye views of the luscious landscape, and descends through woods and sleepy villages. If the light is right, stay a while at the welcoming hamlet of **Malenga**, the nearest you'll get to **Pieter Both**, whose pinnacle resembles a man's head perched precariously on cloak-shrouded shoulders. They say that the day the head comes off some great catastrophe will destroy the island but even the worst cyclones of 1892 and 1960 have failed to shift it. From Malenga you can watch the mountain change colour and shape as sun and clouds cast shadows across its face. From here, the B34 joins the motorway at Terre Rouge. ❑

TIP

Those interested in learning more about sugar cultivation and its history should visit L'Aventure du Sucre Museum on the Beau Plan Sugar Estate near Pamplemousses (open daily 9am–5pm; entrance fee; tel: 243 0660, fax: 243 9699).

BELOW: Pieter Both.

THE EAST

The east coast – with its glorious beaches, secluded hotels, sleepy villages and, in the south, mountains – is more isolated than the island's other resort areas, despite the presence of the airport

Map on page 124

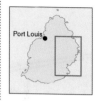
Port Louis

Tourism development has been slow in the east compared to the north and west coasts, though hotel developments are starting to monopolise the white beaches to the north and south of Belle Mare. Some of the island's best hotels are already well established here, including the world-famous Prince Maurice, the St Géran and the Touessrok. There are few local excursions to tempt you away from the beach, and due to the relatively poor road links, access to the north and west coast isn't particularly speedy. If you are eager to do a lot of exploring, it's best not to base yourself on the east coast for your entire stay.

Flat Flacq

The northern area of the east coast lies in the district of **Flacq**, which derives from Groote Vlakte ("Great Plain"), the name given to the area by the Dutch when they arrived in the 17th century. The flat terrain is perfect for the cultivation of sugar, and much of the land is owned by sugar estates, including FUEL (Flacq United Estate Limited), the largest in Mauritius. This is the most rural area in the country, and the vast sugar cane fields are interlined with crops of onions, tomatoes, chillis, peanuts and aubergines grown for local consumption.

When the French arrived they called the main town **Centre de Flacq**, now dominated by a 19th-century British-built District Court House. Apart from a small lively Sunday market (*foire*) and stacks of shops there are few other attractions, but if you want to get around independently, you'll find plenty of buses and taxis to take you to Port Louis, Mahébourg and the east coast villages.

Beautiful Belle Mare

The main concentration of beaches and hotels is around **Belle Mare ❶**, about 10 minutes' drive from Centre de Flacq. There is a better-than-average public beach, backed by casuarina forests where old kilns remain as monuments to the once thriving coral burning industry; from the top of them you get lovely views of coast and cane fields. The public beach is a mere extension of the more pristine, regularly swept ones fronting the nearby **Belle Mare Plage** and the Disneyesque **Coco Beach** resorts.

As you head south, keep an eye out for brightly painted statues of Hindu gods, peeking out of the thick vegetation. The string of hotels continues with **La Residence**, an imposing, plantation-style place, and **Le Palmar**, with its distinctive thatched villas.

Trou d'Eau Douce

Arriving in the village of **Trou d'Eau Douce ❷** ("Hole of Sweet Water") after the string of hotels further north, you may feel jolted back to reality. The

LEFT: sunrise over Belle Mare beach.
BELOW: kayaks and sailboats for hire.

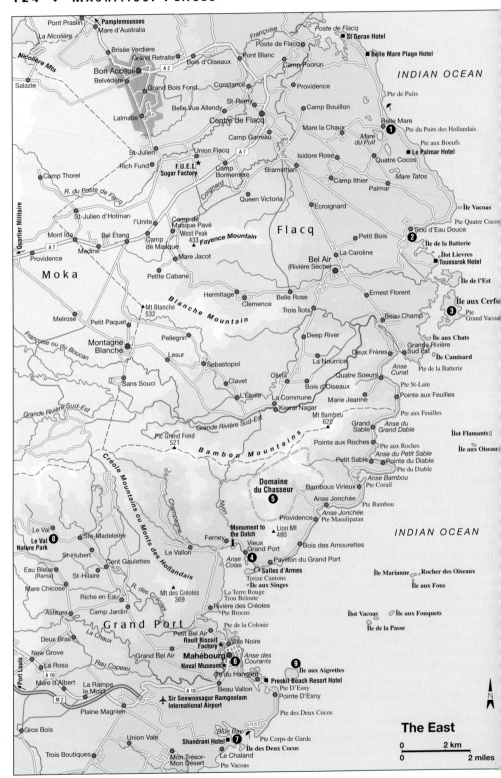

The East

0   2 km

0   2 miles

little village is a maze of narrow streets. Walls of tumbledown dwellings double up as clothes-horses; women wash clothes in the river; fishing boats bob near the shore. Most tourists pass through without stopping, en route to the **Touessrok** or popular Île aux Cerfs, but a few *boutiks* and restaurants have sprung up to try and catch their eye. These friendly, unpretentious places constitute a breath of fresh air if you've been holed up in a resort for a few days.

Map on page 124

Paradise island

The **Île aux Cerfs** ❸ is a long-time favourite with Mauritians and holiday-makers. It is managed by Le Touessrok resort, just south of Trou d'Eau Douce, but it is open to the public (unlike Îlot Mangenie, which is restricted to residents only). If you don't have your own transport you could join one of the full-day excursions (including by catamaran) offered by tour operators in Grand Baie. A couple of companies in Trou d'Eau Douce run a regular ferry service from the waterfront, and local fishermen will also happily take you. The alternative is to park in the free car park inside the grounds of the Touessrok hotel, and jump on the ferry which leaves every 15–30 minutes and takes less than 10 minutes. But for some people chugging across the bay with Creole fishermen is more fun.

Île aux Cerfs' most famous resident is a giant Aldabra tortoise thought to be 200 years old.

The island is covered in 285 hectares (700 acres) of woodland and has lovely beaches and limpid, blue waters. You can swim and snorkel from the shore. A boat-house near the jetty provides equipment for water skiing, windsurfing and boating, and scattered among the trees (and even in the trees) nearby are open-air shops and restaurants. The atmosphere is relaxed, but it can get very crowded. So if you want solitude, there are quieter beaches close by, and enjoyable walks can be made round the island along marked paths. In the trees beyond the jetty is a small Turtle Park.

BELOW: Touessrok diving school – lessons in luxury.

A possible trip from Île aux Cerfs is to the deep estuary of Grande Rivière Sud-Est, the longest river in Mauritius; there is a small settlement of the same name at the river mouth where you can often see bold young islanders diving into the water from the basalt cliffs, hoping to be rewarded with a few tourist rupees.

The Old Dutch Coast Road

The drive from Trou d'Eau Douce south along the B28 or Old Coast Road to Mahébourg is one of the loveliest on the island. Head inland to Bel Air where the road veers towards the coast, hitting the sea at the gorge of **Grande Rivière Sud-Est**. From here, it barely manages to keep a toehold on land as it contrives to avoid the steep foothills of the Bambou Mountains. Fishing hamlets and picturesque villages are scattered along the route.

The **Grand Port** district in the southeastern corner of Mauritius is full of historical connections since this is where the French and Dutch began their colonisation of the island. There are many ruins in the area, some dating from the 17th century, but most are in a poor state of repair. Lying in the shadow of Lion Mountain **Vieux Grand Port** ❹ is of particular historical interest as it was the first base established by the Dutch when they landed on the island in 1598. The original Dutch fort disappeared beneath defences built by the

TIP

To see how essential oils are made from the fragrant yellow ylang ylang flowers, visit the Domaine de Ylang Ylang (open daily; tel: 634 5668), in the foothills near Vieux Grand Port.

French in the 18th century. Now all that remains are a few blackened and disintegrating walls, but in 1997 archaeologists unearthed beakers, pottery, glass and Chinese porcelain from the 17th century. These and other finds are displayed in the adjacent **Fort Frederick Henry Museum** (open Mon–Sat 9am–5pm, Sun 9am–noon), along with a model of the fort, while audio-visual displays explain the history of the Dutch East India Company and its role in Mauritius.

Along the water's edge are the caves of **Salles d'Armes**, where French gentlemen once fought duels. They are best approached by sea with a local fisherman, but you can make your own way by zigzagging through the cane fields at the northern end of Vieux Grand Port village. Further north, the **Bois des Amourettes** was a favourite haunt of French soldiers and their sweethearts. During World War II the British built a naval look-out post but all that remains are some old concrete bunkers poking through the sugar cane on the shore.

Between Vieux Grand Port and Mahébourg, you pass two memorials: one commemorating the first Dutch landing in 1598 and another marking their introduction of sugar in 1639. These memorials sat unnoticed for years, but were spruced up for the royal Dutch visit in 1998, when Mauritius celebrated the 400th anniversary of the Dutch arrival.

Domaine du Chasseur

The private nature reserve of **Domaine du Chasseur** ❺ ("Hunter's Domain"; open daily 9am–5pm; tel: 634 5668) is the unlikely viewpoint from which to survey the theatre of conflict between the French and British navies in 1810, at the Battle of Vieux Grand Port. These days the crashing of cannon is confined to the firing of deer hunters' rifles. Once popular with private hunting parties, the estate

BELOW: cane fields at Domaine du Chasseur.

is now targetting "green" tourists, who wander the 30 km (20 miles) of nature trails that run through forests of spice plants and native trees. Apart from the Javan deer reared in the 160-hectare (400-acre) reserve, you might also spot wild boar, monkey, hare and many endemic species of bird. Mini jeep safaris are also on offer. The Domaine du Chasseur is the most popular on-land attraction on the east coast, and a lot of tour groups are brought here to witness the daily afternoon visit of the endangered Mauritius kestrel, lured by the promise of food. Rustic but not inexpensive hilltop bungalows provide overnight accommodation.

Map on page 124

Mahébourg

Named after the first governor of the Mascarenes, Mahé de Labourdonnais, **Mahébourg** ⑥ (pronounced Ma-y-bourg) lies on the southern shores of the immense Vieux Grand Port Bay. Under the French, Mahébourg was a busy, thriving port which the British later linked by rail (now abandoned) to Port Louis. The names of the neatly laid out grid-style streets reflect the influence of European settlers, and there is a historical feel absent in many Mauritian towns.

These days Mahébourg is a dusty, rather run-down place, crammed with grocers' and fabric stores. Yet it has an appealing, laid-back bustle. The seafront Rue des Hollandais is done no favours by the sprawling presence of the bus station, but this area is the focus of new proposals for a Mauritian-style face-lift; plans for cafés, shops and restaurants are being approved. Multi-coloured pirogues bob around the islet of Mouchoir Rouge ("red hanky island"), while, in the backstreets, life trundles slowly by; women still scrub clothes on the stone sinks at Le Lavoir, the outdoor wash-house off Rue des Hollandais. There is a lively daily market, well worth visiting for exotic fruit, vegetables, herbs and spices.

TIP

The Paranamour Restaurant at the Domaine du Chasseur offers both fine views and excellent food, including venison curry, grilled lobster, roasted wild pig, fresh fish and heart of palm salad.

BELOW: Mahébourg fishmongers.

Naval Museum

Mahébourg's **Naval Museum** (open Mon, Wed, Thurs 9am–4pm; tel: 631 9329), on the southern outskirts of the town is housed in an 18th-century building. Its original owner, Jean de Robillard, turned the house into a hospital where the commanders of the French and British forces who had fought in the Battle of Vieux Grand Port, convalesced side by side.

Now a museum, the house contains an eclectic display of exhibits from the Dutch, French and British periods. Portraits line the walls, among them Prince Maurice of Nassau, Pieter Both, botanist Pierre Poivre and "king of the corsairs", Robert Surcouf, who donated the dagger he seized in 1800 from Captain Rivington of the English ship *Kent* following an attack in the Bay of Bengal. One of the museum's most famous relics is the ship's bell from the ill-fated *St Géran*, which sunk off the northeast coast in 1744. A newspaper cutting recalls the fate of the British steamer, *Trevessa*, which sank hundreds of miles from Mauritius in 1923. The survivors landed at Bel Ombre on the south coast after 25 days in a lifeboat with nothing to eat but ship's biscuits. You can see the remains of the biscuits and the cigarette tin they used to measure water rations. Other exhibits include Mahé de Labourdonnais' four-poster bed and two wooden palanquins in which slaves would carry their masters about.

Around Mahébourg

The approach to **Blue Bay** ❼, south of Mahébourg, isn't promising as you drive past some very poor housing, but Pointe d'Esny is considered a desirable place to live, and high-walled private bungalows dot the coast. En route you pass **Le Preskil Beach Resort** hotel; a nice enough spot, with a small but pleasant beach and views of the mountains, but unless you want easy access to the airport, it's rather an isolated place to stay. The public beach at Blue Bay, however, is worth an excursion. Here, the bluest of calm waters separate the tiny Île des Deux Cocos from the mainland. The sparkling sands backed by casuarina trees beckon sun-seekers to sample what can only be described as true paradise. On the other side of the bay, the **Shandrani** hotel represents the height of luxury (with prices to match). It stands on its own peninsula in 30 hectares (74 acres) of gardens, just 6 km (4 miles) from the airport. On the approach to the Shandrani, a cement dodo marks the spot where, in 1865, an almost intact set of dodo bones was discovered. They were sent to England and pieced together by experts. The complete skeleton is now on show at London's British Museum.

From **Ville Noire**, north across La Chaux river from Mahébourg, signs point the way to the **Rault Biscuit Factory** (open Mon–Fri 9–11am and 1–3pm; entrance fee; tel: 631 9559), where you can take a guided tour to see women baking *biscuits manioc* from the cassava that grows in the nearby valley.

The B7 from Ville Noire runs through cane fields to the village of **Riche en Eau**. The area, literally "rich in water", was home to small family-owned sugar estates, where isolated chimneys, now listed as national monuments, mark the sites of early factories.

The nearby **Le Val Nature Park** ❽ (open Mon–Fri 9am–4pm; tel 627 4545) is supposed to show you how sugar estates have diversified into agricultural activities, but there are no guides and no information provided. However, it is still possible to enjoy the mountain-backed landscapes and bubbling streams where huge plots of watercress and *brède songe* (edible greens) are grown for local use.

Map on page 124

Île aux Aigrettes

Eco-tourism is developing at **Île aux Aigrettes** ❾ (open daily 9am–5pm; tel: 631 2396), a nature reserve that opened to the public in 1998. It's a 20-minute ferry trip from Preskil Beach Resort Hotel *(see Travel Tips)*. A guide from the Mauritius Wildlife Foundation (MWF) leads no more than 20 visitors at a time along marked paths. Look out for bands of pink pigeons *(see page 91)* breeding among flora found nowhere else in the world. The MWF has been active in regenerating the island, its main aim being to re-create a microcosm of the original coastal habitat. During World War II, much of the native forest was cleared to make room for British troops, who installed guns (still in place) as defences against a Japanese invasion. Old hands remember waiting for the enemy which never came. The old generator room has been converted into a museum and if you climb to the rooftop viewing platform panoramic views unfold across the sweeping bay and **Île de la Passe** beyond.

The rare pink pigeon now breeds happily on Île aux Aigrettes.

Among the historic ruins on this islet off Vieux Grand Port are the remains of French defences, an old reservoir and a beautifully preserved 18th-century powder magazine, complete with a harp etched into its wall. This was probably engraved by a home-sick soldier of the 87th Royal Irish Fusiliers, stationed here in the 1830s. Both islets make a wonderful half-day excursion. ❑

BELOW: washday at Rivière des Créoles.

THE SOUTH COAST

The rugged south coast comes as a breath of fresh air for hard-nosed wanderers on the run from the well-trodden shores elsewhere on the island, and can be explored in a day's drive

Map on pages 132–3

T he south has no need to apologise for its lack of tourist amenities. There is ample compensation in the gorgeous scenery and the sense that you are witnessing Mauritius as it used to be. Here, great stretches of rugged basalt cliffs assaulted by strong southeasterly winds lie against a backdrop of hills and undulating sugar fields that are part of century-old plantations. The old estates, built to withstand the southern winds, have survived better here than elsewhere. There are some glorious sandy beaches, particularly in the west, and they are usually completely deserted save for a lone fisherman or two. Right along the southern coast there is scant evidence of the 20th century, let alone the 21st.

Rivers flowing from the central uplands to the ocean have, in many places, prevented coral reefs from gaining a foothold, depriving the area of the gentle lagoons reminiscent of the north, and swimming except from designated beaches can be dangerous. In the west, the Savanne Mountains (which give the district its name) rise steeply from deep coves, relegating the coast road to a narrow strip west of Souillac. The east is flatter. Here, the roads run through cane fields and over bridges spanning rivers and streams, linking shanty villages. Not a lot of tourists pass this way.

If you're driving, the south coast can easily be explored in one leisurely day – less if you're based at one of the hotels on the west coast or on the southeast coast near Mahébourg. If you have a full day to spare, you might even consider making a circular drive by taking in the route through the Black River Gorges National Park (described in The West chapter). Most hotels offer full-day tours of the south coast, which usually include lunch in an old sugar estate house.

LEFT: sugar cane estate worker, with children in tow.
BELOW: braving the waves at windswept Gris Gris.

From beach to sugar lands

Our tour begins at the western end, just south of Le Morne. Here you'll find a quiet rock-strewn beach, where fishermen sit mending their nets and children play among the trees. The first significant hamlet is **Baie du Cap ❶**, typical of many villages along the south coast; there are just a few Chinese-run *boutiks* (and a police station built by a local sugar magnate from a ship that sank offshore in the 19th century).

A short distance beyond lies **Bel Ombre ❷**, where at certain times of year the only vehicles you are likely to encounter are lorries laden with sheaves of sugar cane and minibuses crammed with cane-cutters bound for the sugar factory at St Felix along the coast.

Bel Ombre has long been the heartland of the south coast's sugar industry. Back in 1816, the factory was bought by philanthropic businessman Charles Telfair. Newly arrived from England, he immediately set

Precious eggs of the rare Mauritius kestrel.

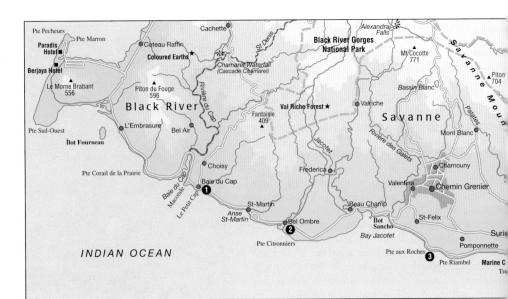

TIP

Information panels in Souillac give scant detail of this former historic port. If you read French, it's worth getting hold of a copy of *Souillac: Village Historique et Cimetière Marin*, which gives a detailed description of the village and its cemetery.

about turning Bel Ombre into a model sugar estate, only to incur the wrath of local slave owners who did not agree with his idea of providing proper food and shelter for slaves.

Bel Ombre factory is closed but if you get permission from the adjacent administrative office, you can take a detour from the coast and drive through the fields along winding uphill tracks. The difficulties of planting, harvesting and irrigation on the 45-degree slopes are soon apparent. You might also spot deer along the track leading to **Val Riche Forest** which contains many fast disappearing indigenous trees growing along the River Jacotet.

One of the best places for a seaside walk is the sandy promontory which lies just across the road from the Bel Ombre factory. Here, sugar cane and banana trees tumble to the water's edge for about 5 km (3 miles) until you reach **Beau Champ**. Behind the beach, pathways meander through fields of beans, chillis and onions.

Driving now through swaying fields of sugar cane, a mile or so east of Beau Champ, the B10 branches inland to **Chemin Grenier**, where a minor road runs north to the water-filled crater of **Bassin Blanc**. Here, with a little patience, you can spot the brilliant green echo parakeet and Mauritius kestrel. (Bassin Blanc is also accessible on foot from the Black River Gorges National Park.)

Beaches white and black

The longest stretch of beaches spreads eastwards for 5 km (3 miles) from **Pointe aux Roches ❸**. Beautifully rugged and totally unspoilt, they are not without their dangers, which probably accounts for the fact that there's just one hotel along this coast. Villas Pointe aux Roches, a complex of self-catering bungalows, stands on a safe crescent of white sand and the restaurant makes a welcome pit stop, but the absence of coral reef at the public beach nearby makes swimming ill-advised. On windy days there are fabulous views of surf beating against the jet-black rocks. Further east, **Pomponnette** is known for treacherous currents, and most locals head for the safe SSR **Public Beach**, just before the peaceful hamlet of **Riambel** (from the Malagasy word meaning "beaches of sunshine").

Souillac

The largest settlement on the south coast is **Souillac ❹**, which lies on an inlet where the rivers Savanne and Patates form an estuary (about 30 minutes' drive from Le Morne on the west coast). At the height of sugar production in the 19th century, steam ships loaded cane from nearby estates and shunted along the coast to Port Louis, but the port fell into decline when road and rail replaced the steamers. In the 1990s, substantial improvements were made to the old port area, prompting the town's designation as a "tourist village". While such a billing owes more to optimism than reality, it is worth stopping off to explore the handful of sights that are scattered around the bay.

On the western side a road turns off to Souillac's **Marine Cemetery**, one of the most beautiful in Mauritius. Who knows what graves were washed out to sea over the years, but in 1957 people reported seeing hundreds of skulls and human bones littering the cemetery as a result of a tidal wave. Meanwhile, constant erosion of the sea wall threatens even more damage to graves, many of which date back to the early 19th century. One of the oldest tombs is that of Thomas Etienne Bolgerd (1748–1818), a Souillac bigwig and owner of 500 slaves who was captured by the British in 1809 and released in exchange for some goats. The most famous member of the d'Unienville family, Baron Marie Claude Antoine Marrier d'Unienville (1766–1831), is also buried here, as is Robert Edward Hart (1891–1954), the country's most celebrated poet and writer.

Next stop is the old **port** area, where the most evident improvement is the restoration of a 200-year-old sugar warehouse, part of which is now occupied by **Le Batelage** restaurant, where tourists on organised trips are often fed and watered. The shady terrace on the quay out front provides good views over the river, now so tranquil after years of inactivity.

Not far from the seafront, a road runs 5 km (3 miles) inland through cane fields to the **Rochester Falls**, which tumble from the Savanne River from a height of 10 metres (33 ft). Constant erosion has fashioned the basalt rock into upright columns, and young Indian boys enjoy scaling the jagged cliffs before diving into the cold fresh water. It's also a great place for a swim. Taxi drivers

Map on pages 132–3

Harvesting the canes.

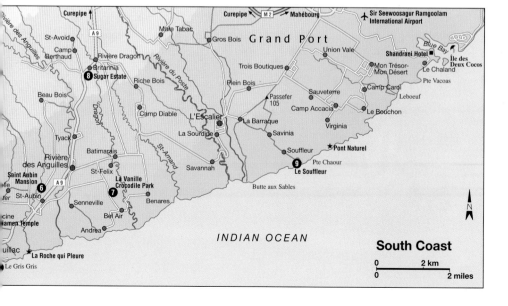

will take you there (and wait to take you back), but you can also hoof it. The track weaves uphill for about 15 minutes before descending to the falls.

On the way, you pass **Terracine**, one of the island's earliest factories dating back to 1820. It closed down in 1947 but the chimney, a national monument, stands as a reminder of its sugar-producing days. Right next to it, the colourful Mariamen Temple, which remains quiet for most of the year, bursts into life in December and January when it is taken over by Tamil fire-walking and body-piercing Cavadee ceremonies.

Gardens, culture and black magic

Heading for the heart of Souillac, the first place of interest is **Telfair Gardens**, just across the road from the bus station. Shaded by gigantic Indian almond trees and banyans, the gardens are a favourite spot among the locals who come here to pass the time of day while kids, quite oblivious to the skull and cross bones signs, swim off the rocky coast. The cemetery is visible across the bay.

From here it is a 10-minute stroll to the site of the **Robert Edward Hart Museum**, the former home of Souillac's most famous son. The half-Irish, half-French poet and writer lived alone in a charming little coral-built bungalow, known as Le Nef ("The Nave"), which contained manuscripts, books and personal belongings. Hart churned out work in English and French and his efforts were recognised in both English and French literary circles with an OBE and a gold medal from the Académie Française. He was obvioiusly inspired by the beauty of his surroundings, and you can understand why when you see the golden beach pounded by ferocious seas at the rear of the house. Sadly the museum was demolished in 2002.

BELOW:
Rochester Falls.

If you continue along the road from Le Nef you reach **Le Gris Gris ❺**, the most southerly point of Mauritius, more like the windswept coast of Scotland than the gentle shores of a tropical island. Some say it is called Gris Gris because black magic (*gris gris* in Kreol) used to be performed here. If you walk along the yawning sandy beach and allow your imagination to run riot, you can pick out the figure of a sorcerer scored out of the rock who appears to be holding a cauldron. Up on the headland, where weather-beaten casuarinas attest to the ferocity of the winds, a 15-minute walk along a small path leads to a rocky outcrop called **La Roche qui Pleure** ("The Crying Rock"), so named because the sea which cascades around it gives the impression that it is weeping. (A monochrome photograph in Le Nef illustrated the uncanny similarity between the silhouette of this rock and the profile of Robert Edward Hart.)

Map on pages 132–3

Packing tea at the Bois Cheri factory.

Saint Aubin and colonial style living

One of the highlights of a south coast tour is a visit to one of the area's colonial homes. Many are off-limits to the public, but the grand residence of **Saint Aubin ❻**, on the A9 5 km (3 miles) northeast of Souillac, can be visited on a group tour organised by the MTTB (tel: 696 3001). The mansion, built in 1870, now belongs to Union Saint Aubin Sugar Estate. You can relax on the broad, shady verandahs overlooking the manicured lawn, enjoy a leisurely lunch in the dining room, take a tour of the vanilla and anthurium plantations, or explore age-old trees in the spacious grounds.

The full-day guided tour includes transport to the **Bois Cheri tea factory**, 10 km (6 miles) inland. Although tea is no longer produced in large quantities, the factory is worth visiting to see how it is processed and packaged. You will

BELOW: plantation house at the Saint Aubin estate.

Map on pages 132–3

TIP

The Hungry Crocodile restaurant in La Vanille Crocodile Park has an interesting menu. If you're not tempted by the idea of crocodile croquettes, you can always opt for a croc-free *croque monsieur*.

BELOW: off to work.
RIGHT: feeding time at La Vanille Crocodile Park.

also be driven to a hilltop tea pavilion overlooking a lake surrounded by neat tea fields. Here, you can sample plain, vanilla- or bergamot-flavoured tea, and go for a stroll on the hillside from where there are magnificent views of the coast.

Another day trip, exclusive to Mauritours (tel: 467 9700), includes a visit to the seaside homes of Franco-Mauritian sugar barons at **Bel Air** and **Andrea**, as well as to the Vanille Crocodile Park *(see below)*. You take morning tea in the palatial parlour at Bel Air, which overlooks a grassy headland on the coast south of the A9, and there's plenty of time to wander around the lush gardens, where exotic birds flit among the coconut palms and vacoas trees, over ponds, mini waterfalls and babbling brooks.

The other seaside bungalow at Andrea opens on to grassy-sloped cliff tops where surf beats on the boulder-strewn mouth of the Rivière des Anguilles. After a tasty, Creole-style lunch, you can work off the calories with a brisk coastal walk along the headland, where deer graze apparently deaf to the sound of the crashing waves below.

Happy snappers

You don't need to be on an organised tour to visit **La Vanille Crocodile Park ❼** (open daily; entrance fee), signposted right off the road running through the large village of **Rivière des Anguilles** (on the banks of the river of the same name). The park occupies a valley that features about the closest thing you'll get to tropical rain forest, which is why Owen Griffiths, an Australian zoologist, chose the area to farm Nile crocodiles. The stud of the estate and four females were brought from Madagascar in 1985, and the mating process produced little critters who grew into man-eating monsters. They are kept in secure enclosures waking only at feeding time to snap mighty jaws with a sickening thud on freshly killed chicken.

A nature trail meanders through the forest, past squads of giant Aldabra tortoises, wide-eyed Mauritian fruit bats, wild boars, macaque monkeys and a host of luminous green geckos and chameleons. (Be sure to douse yourself with plenty of insect repellent before you visit.)

Heading north along the A9, you pass the manicured lawns and pineapple plantations of the **Britannia Sugar Estate ❽**, the south's last significant sugar estate. It is still very active, with a pristine estate village of stone-built homes and a school.

If you are heading towards Mahébourg, you can follow the little-used B8, which branches east from Rivière des Anguilles. About midway, at **L'Escalier**, a road runs south to **Le Souffleur ❾**, a blowhole fashioned in a dramatic outcrop of rock (due to erosion it is now more a cloud of spray than the fierce jet of water that shot skywards 30 years ago). If you walk along the coast you'll get a clear view of the break in the coral reef that allows the sea to rush up against the cliffs. There's also a striking *pont naturel* (natural bridge) which formed when the roof of a sea cave collapsed. Le Souffleur is accessed via the grounds of the Savinia sugar estate, and you need to ask permission to visit the blowhole from the estate office (near the L'Escalier police station). ❏

SUGAR: FROM CANES TO CRYSTALS

Despite rapid developments in the tourism and textile industries, the giant sugar estates are still the country's third biggest employer

Until recently, over 90 percent of the arable land of Mauritius was given over to the cultivation of sugar. With the diversification of agriculture and expansion of the tourism and textile sectors, sugar production is no longer the country's number one earner. Many sugar workers have hung up their overalls and handed in their machetes, opting instead for the more comfortable employment in offices, factories and hotels. Nevertheless, mechanisation has ensured that sugar production continues to play a major role in the economy and there are perks for those who have remained loyal to the industry. Sugar estates provide housing, hospitals and free medical facilities, free school transport and plenty of leisure and sporting activities. Many have scholarship schemes and sponsor the training of workers and their families in technical schools.

Mauritius produces the best unrefined sugar in the world and most of it is exported to the European Union. One important by-product is *bagasse* or cane fibre, which is used to fire boilers in the factory and any excess burned to generate additional electricity for sale to the national grid. Another is molasses, used in the production of vinegar, drugs and perfumes, while cane spirit is used to make rum. Nothing goes to waste; even the scum from the purification process contains essential nutrients which are fed back into the soil, and the long green leaves of the cane are used for animal feed.

▷ **GREEN FIELDS**
Just over half of Mauritius is owned by several giant sugar estates; the rest is shared among 30,000 individual farmers or "planters".

△ **THE NO. 1 RUM**
One by-product of sugar: Green Island, the island's best-selling brand of rum, is made from cane spirit.

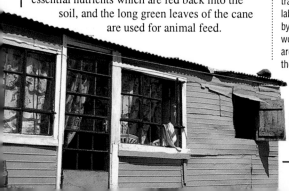

△ **CANE CUTTER**
Although much of the work traditionally undertaken by labourers is now being done by machine, teams of cane workers toiling in the fields are still part and parcel of the Mauritian landscape.

◁ **CUTTER'S HUT**
During the sugar harvest, many cane workers live in houses by the fields, like this one near Mahébourg.

CRUMBLING GIANTS

Sugar cane was introduced to Mauritius by the Dutch who brought it over from Jakarta in 1639. By the time the British came in 1810 thousands of acres had been planted with sugar cane. For generations sugar was the lifeblood of Mauritius. People got rich on it, fought over it and died for it. It wasn't until the 1980s, with the progressive centralisation of the sugar industry, that the number of sugar estates began to dwindle. Of the hundreds of factories that once thrived across the island, only a few are left. But the ruins of the old sites remain, and the chimneys – which have been designated national monuments – are dotted all over the countryside.

To see how the brown sludge from the crushed canes was transformed into sugar crystals, before mechanisation took over, visit the early sugar mill reconstructions at the Royal Botanical Gardens or at the Domaine les Pailles, a ten-minute drive south of the capital.

▽ HARVEST TIME
Between June and December the air is thick with the sweet scent of molasses as cane is cut and loaded into lorries.

△ OX POWER
The first sugar mills used ox-driven crushers to extract the cane juice, but by the mid-19th century, animals had been replaced by machines.

◁ HARD LABOUR
Before the advent of tractors and lorries, cane bundles were transported from the field to the factory on ox-drawn carts.

▽ THE END PRODUCT
After a lengthy purification process, cane juice is transformed into various sugars from fine caster to thick molasses.

THE WEST

In the west, the main attractions are the beaches at Flic en Flac and Le Morne, but inland the mountains of the Black River area provide the best place on the island for hikers and bird-watchers

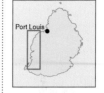

Map on page 142

Soon after leaving the uninspiring suburbs and industrial installations of Port Louis, the quirky angles of the Corps de Garde, Rempart and Trois Mamelles mountains and, in the distance, the solid hammer head of Le Morne Brabant peninsula, stay with you as you travel southwards, offering a range of rewarding views unmatched in other parts of the islands. The A3, which runs the length of the 50-km (30-mile) coast, meanders inland south of the capital, with side roads periodically offering access to the sea, but from Tamarin the road hugs the coast. The glistening beaches of Flic en Flac, Wolmar and Le Morne and their turquoise lagoons remain tantalisingly hidden from view.

Suburban Port Louis and beyond

It is all too easy to speed through the suburbs of Port Louis as you make a bee-line for the obvious attractions of the coast, reachable in about 30 minutes, but there are a few places that might attract your attention along the way.

Heading out of Port Louis along the A1, before the A3 branches off to Flic en Flac, you pass through **Grande Rivière Nord-Ouest**, notable for its iron bridges which span the river of the same name, and for the ruin of an 18th-century hospital. There are splendid views over the river at the point where the B31 leads coastwards to **Pointe aux Sables ❶**. The beach here is mediocre by Mauritius' standards, but attracts a crowd due to its closeness to the capital. Note that the resort has a seedy reputation due to its popularity with local prostitutes; the beach and overall scene is more pleasant at the point than in the village itself.

The B31 links up with the B78 (just before it rejoins the A3), which veers west to **Pointe aux Caves ❷**. A climb to the top of the early 20th-century lighthouse here provides good views of the mountains and coast.

Back on the A3, the road continues southwards bisecting a wide and fertile plain and separating the plateau towns from a picturesque coast of low cliffs. At the busy village of **Bambous ❸**, with flamboyant tree-shaded avenues and pretty dwellings, ask for directions to **St Martin Cemetery**, nestling in cane fields north of the village. Here, 127 identical tombstones are the final reminder of 1,580 Jewish wartime refugees from Eastern Europe. Having been refused entry to Palestine by the British in 1940 because they were considered "illegal immigrants", they were transported to Mauritius. They were well received, but conditions in their refugee camp, where they were kept until the end of the war, were poor. After the war, many started new lives abroad but their families still return to Mauritius to pay their respects to those who never made it back home. There are also some beautiful Tamil tombs in the cemetery.

LEFT: harvesting salt in the Black River estuary.
BELOW: view from Le Morne road.

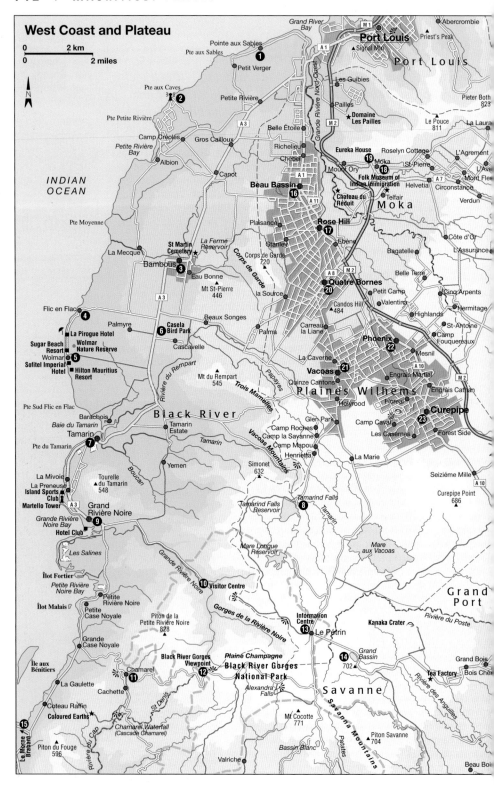

West Coast and Plateau

Flic en Flac

Map on page 142

The name of the village **Flic en Flac** ❹ is Dutch in origin and is thought to derive from "Fried Landt Flaak", meaning "Free and Flat Land"; later, under the influence of the French, this evolved into Flic en Flac. Most visitors don't waste too much time wondering about etymology but head straight for the beach.

Flic en Flac can't pretend to compete with Grand Baie, with its buzz, shops and nightlife, but there are a handful of hotels, a bank and a few shops, as well as a better-than-average choice of restaurants that cater for the growing number of independent, self-catering visitors. It is also within easy reach of Port Louis and the Black River Mountains. For middle-class Mauritians Flic en Flac's proximity to the plateau towns (just a 45-minute bus ride away) is its great asset, and many have built weekend bungalows here.

Thirst-quenching beach snacks.

At the entrance to Flic en Flac is a small clutch of bars and cafés, together with the resort's main hotel, **Villas Caroline**, which overlooks the northern reaches of the enormous beach. Soft, powdery sands shelve into the lagoon, where people windsurf and swim. Further along the main road ubiquitous casuarina trees back the beach, where the sand is packed hard enough for cars to drive on. Sunsets here are often a hypnotic vision of feathered clouds flecked with silvery-peach hues. On weekdays it is quiet, with just a couple of food stalls. But on weekends, the resort springs to life as locals descend on the resort from all around, and at the end of the day, great groups of islanders wait in orderly queues for the homebound bus.

Flic en Flac is a haven for divers, windsurfers and snorkellers. Unlike Grand Baie, no speedboats disturb the waters with wash thrown up from their bows, and the best dive sites in Mauritius lie off this part of the coast *(see page 93)*. One of the best places in Mauritius to learn to dive is the **Pirogue Diving Centre** while more experienced divers will find lots of interesting opportunites at Villas Caroline *(see Travel Tips)*.

BELOW: sailboards for hire on La Pirogue beach.

Less than 2 km (1 mile) south, **Wolmar** ❺ is really an extension of Flic en Flac. The original hamlet has now been completely swamped by a handful of very smart hotels, that include the **Sugar Beach** resort, **La Pirogue** (complete with casino), the **Sofitel Imperial**, the **Hilton Mauritius Resort**, the most luxurious on the west coast, and **Sands Resort Hotel**. These hotels certainly have better facilities than anything you'll find in Flic en Flac.

Just across the road from La Pirogue Hotel is **Wolmar Nature Reserve** (tel: 453 8463). The private estate, previously closed to the public, produces fruit, venison and wild boar for local consumption and hotel restaurants and has some great mountain biking tracks too. Allow two hours for a guided safari tour of the 21-hectare (300-acre) estate or walk with a local guide who points out unusual sights on the way, such as charcoal still being made in traditional kilns, a coral reef lying 500 metres (1,640 ft) inland and the remains of a 250-year-old creole wall. Deep in the heart of the estate deer, wild boar, monkey, hare, giant fruit bats and mongoose roam free. Deer hunting parties, only from June to September, and guided safari tours can be arranged through your hotel.

South to Tamarin

Families with young children might enjoy a visit to **Casela Bird Park** ❻ (open daily 9am–5pm; entrance fee; tel: 452 0693), really a mini-zoo featuring Aldabra tortoise, tiger, lemur and deer as well as 142 species of birds from all over the world, including the local pink pigeon and Mauritius kestrel, both rescued from the endangered list. The 10-hectare (25-acre) park, on the A3 just south of the Flic en Flac turn-off, sits on the flanks of Rempart Mountain and provides wonderful views of the west coast's rolling cane-clothed countryside.

Pressing southwards, the massive mound of Le Morne Brabant appears to rise over Tamarin Mountain, while inland the horizon is dominated by the bulk of Rempart and the Black River mountains. Six kilometres (4 miles) south of Casela you hit the coast and **Tamarin** ❼, named after the tamarind trees introduced by the Dutch. The village, overlooking a tranquil bay, is more relaxed than Flic en Flac, in spite of tourism development, and its cheap pensions provide an alternative base for exploring the southwest. There is a good, unspoilt beach, but the coral reef is subdued by fresh water that flows from the central highlands via the Rempart and Tamarin rivers. In any case, Tamarin is most famous as a surfing centre, and between June and August the waves can reach over 2 metres (6 ft)

The area around Tamarin is one of the west coast's most scenic. In summer the River Tamarin is lined with scarlet-blossomed trees, and at any time of year especially in the late afternoon, there's definitely a romantic feel to the place if you're a photographer this is the best time to capture the reflections of Tamarin Mountain on the river and watch the pencil-thin surf rolling in.

BELOW: high-speed antics.

You should put aside at least half a day (return trip) for the challenging trek to **Tamarind Falls** ❽. Just over 2 km (1 mile) northeast of Tamarin, take the

turning inland signposted Magenta and Yemen. A tarred road leads through the Yemen sugar estate (you can ignore the signs saying "Private Estate" – nobody will bother you) and after less than 2 km (1 mile) a small sign indicates the route to the falls. Park your car here and walk the rest of the way along a rough path that approaches Magenta Dam in the foothills of the Vacoas Mountains. Follow the road from the power station through eucalyptus forests 2 km (1 mile) to the falls, where the river of the same name tumbles over seven stepped cliffs through a deep, narrow gorge.

Though easy to start with, the walk becomes difficult for the last 300 metres (1,000 ft) when you have to negotiate boulders on the river bed. Officially, a forestry department permit is needed, although it is unusual for individual hikers to be asked to produce one. You may prefer to go an organised trek with a guide, in which case permission will have been pre-arranged.

If you want to view the falls the easy way, there is a viewpoint accessible by road from Vacoas in the central plateau *(see page 154)*; you can also hike to the falls from Le Pétrin in the Black River Gorges National Park *(see below)*.

Black River area

Vast rectangular pans, where salt is extracted by solar evaporation, lie alongside the A3 south of Tamarin en route to **Grande Rivière Noire ⑨**, at the estuary of the eponymous river that tumbles through some of the most rugged areas of Mauritius. The Rivière Noire (Black River) area is sparsely populated, with no proper towns, only small villages and hamlets; it is also the poorest region in Mauritius. The people are predominantly Afro-Creole, and you may be lucky enough to come across an impromptu performance of *sega typic*.

During the winter months locals gather the cherry-red fruits of the Chinese guava bush that grows in profusion on the steep-sided slopes of the Black River Gorges. The fruit are great as a Vitamin C-packed snack, while the bushes make a handy hiker's balustrade along the slippery trails.

BELOW: flamboyant tree in full bloom.

MARTELLO TOWERS

Overlooking the public beach of La Preneuse, 2 km (1 mile) or so south of Tamarin, is the best-preserved Martello Tower in Mauritius. The tower is one of five such fortifications that were constructed on the coast of Mauritius by British soldiers in the 19th century; three remain, all on the west coast: one in Pointe aux Sables (see page 141), another at La Harmonie, and one at Les Salines just south of Grande Rivière Noire. The tower at La Preneuse is open as a museum (tel: 493 6648).

The towers were built to withstand gunfire and have walls that are an impressive 3 metres (11 ft) thick on the seaward side. They included a powder magazine and store, living quarters for 20 men and revolving cannons on the roof. They were veritable fortresses, entrance to which could be made only by a ladder that was let down from high up the building, so that attackers would find it almost impossible to enter.

The name comes from Mortella Point in Corsica, where British soldiers first came across such a tower during the French Revolution. Between 1796 and 1815 the British went on to build around 200 Martello Towers in Britain and throughout the Empire – in places as far flung as Bermuda, Ireland and the Ascension Islands.

Life centres around Grande Rivière Noire village, strung out along the A3. It has become popular with tourists, who stop and refresh at the inexpensive restaurants on their way to and from the Black River Gorges. This is also the west coast's centre for deep sea fishing. Between September and March, marlin, sailfish, wahoo, yellow fin tuna and various species of shark migrate to the warm waters around Mauritius *(see page 97)* and feed just beyond the reef where the seabed falls abruptly to a depth of nearly 600 metres (2,000 ft). Trips can be arranged through the **Island Sports Club** and **Hotel Club Centre de Pêche**, a stone's throw from the main road of Grande Rivière Noire. If staying elsewhere, your hotel should also be able to arrange a trip for you.

Black River Gorges Viewpoint.

Black River Gorges National Park

Much of the beauty of the west lies inland, and nowhere more so than in the southwest corner of Mauritius, where the rugged mountains once provided a hideaway for *marrons* (runaway slaves), who lived in isolation, safe in the knowledge that their masters would never find them. The good news for visitors is that these mountains are now easily accessible via the **Black River Gorges National Park**, which was officially opened in 1997 in an attempt to preserve what is left of the island's disappearing native forests. The 6,575-hectare (16,250-acre) park offers something to everyone from dedicated walkers to those who just fancy a scenic drive and a break from the beaches. This green heart of Mauritius is not a place to spot wildlife on a grand scale, but you could spend days tracking down the 150 endemic species of plants and nine endemic species of birds, including pink pigeons and Mauritius kestrels; while you may be lucky enough to spot these two endangered species, you are more likely to see the graceful white tropic bird, cuckoo shrike and Mauritius blackbird.

BELOW: the Chamarel Falls are particularly impressive after heavy rains.

From the west coast you can access the northern area of the park by taking the new road which leaves the A3 just south of Grande Rivière Noire village, near the **Pavillon de Jade Restaurant**, which serves the best Chinese food in the area. This leads through sugar fields to a picnic and parking area just 5 km (3 miles) inland, where a **Visitor Centre ⑩** provides walking maps and information on the condition of the trails. From here you can explore the lower slopes of the park or follow the boulder-strewn Grande Rivière Noire for a strenuous 16-km (10-mile) uphill trek on the "Parakeet" and "Macchabee" trails, which link the Gorges area with the Plaine Champagne.

The other way to get to the Black River Gorges is to drive south from Black River to Grande Case Noyale and then turn inland and upwards to the forested plateau of **Plaine Champagne**, named after the creamy white flowers of the privet that call to mind the white froth of champagne. This route leads to Le Pétrin, the park's other visitors centre *(see page 148)*, but is also better suited to those interested merely in a scenic drive.

Coloured earth at Chamarel

From Grande Case Noyale the road winds steeply through the forested foothills to the village of Chamarel ⑪, offering glorious views down to the coast; if you are heading downhill, be sure to test your brakes beforehand. The Chamarel area is known for its coffee, but the reason most people come here is to see the waterfall and the curious geological phenomenon the village is famous for.

Chamarel Waterfall (Cascade Chamarel) tumbles from the St Denis river into a large crater, and at 83 metres (272 ft) it is the highest waterfall in Mauritius. About 1 km (½ mile) further on are the Chamarel Coloured Earths (open daily 9am–5pm; entrance fee) Geologists are fascinated by this unique rolling landscape of multi-coloured terrain, which is thought to have been caused by the uneven cooling of lava. Interestingly, the colours never fade in spite of torrential downpours and the trampling of thousands of tourists' feet. Now fenced off and beautifully landscaped with viewing platforms and timber walkways, facilities include a children's playground, cafeteria, souvenir shop, giant tortoise pen and toilets. You can buy samples of coloured earth in glass bottles and curiously, even if the different coloured earths are mixed, they will have separated again by the next day.

From the waterfalls, you can continue southwards through sugar cane via a tortuous road to the south coast emerging at Baie du Cap (see page 131), or backtrack to Chamarel village and push eastwards.

Black River Gorges views and walks

The road east of Chamarel running high up across the Plaine Champagne is narrow and lined with scrubby vegetation, offering fleeting chances to admire the scenery. It has no verge and only the occasional stopping place, though there are a couple of designated viewpoints. Most people stop at the Black River Gorges Viewpoint ⓬, where there's usually a snack van and a man selling freshly cut fruit

Map on page 142

TIP

To see Chamarel's seven coloured earths at their best, try to arrive early, and hope for sunshine; otherwise, they can be a disappointing sight.

BELOW: Chamarel's coloured earth.

BELOW:
shrine of Lord
Krishna and Radha
Rani, Grand Bassin.

in the car park – the only source of refreshments for miles. A few miles east, a pot-holed track runs a short way to the **Alexandra Falls**, with shorter views, down to the south coast, and you can hear the falls more than you can see them.

Just east of the Alexandra Falls the road veers suddenly north taking you to **Le Pétrin Information Centre** ⑬, the first port of call for those approaching the Black River Gorges area from the plateau towns and the best place for accessing all areas of the park. Next to the Information Centre, a boardwalk leads to the **Pétrin Native Garden**, a mini showcase of native species, including many medicinal plants. Among the plants is the national flower, the *boucle d'oreille* (earring), and the quirkily named *patte poule piquant* ("prickly chicken legs") used for stomach upsets and liver problems, the *pots de chambre du singe* ("monkey chamber pots") and the umbrella-shaped *bois de natte* tree, often draped with tree ferns, wild orchids and lichens.

Grand Bassin

Located 2 km (1 mile) east of Le Pétrin and surrounded by forests infested with monkeys, the water-filled crater of **Grand Bassin** ⑭ attracts crowds not so much for its natural beauty but for its religious significance. The volcanic crater is known among Hindus as Ganga Talao; legend has it that the lake contains nocturnal fairies, but it was after a Hindu priest dreamed that it was linked to the sacred River Ganges that Grand Bassin became a place of pilgrimage for the annual Maha Shivaratree festival. In February, thousands of Hindus dressed in white walk from all parts of the island and converge on the lakeside to make offerings at the colourful shrines as a sign of devotion to Shiva. It is a strange and eerie place often wrapped in a veil of mist, with the strains of Indian music

and birdsong the only sounds. Bus lanes and vast car parks designed to cope with the February crowds are empty the rest of the year. To see a classic example of a volcanic cone, head 5 km (3 miles) further east through tea fields to **Kanaka Crater**. Only the determined should make the challenging trek to the 180-metre (600-ft) high rim for views into the choked up crater.

Map on page 142

Le Morne Brabant

The peninsula of **Le Morne Brabant** ⓯ is the most westerly point of Mauritius. It is named after the 555-metre (1,820-ft) mountain that rises from its centre. Runaway slaves used Le Morne as a hiding place. In 1835, soldiers were sent here to announce the abolition of slavery, but the slaves, thinking this was just another attempt to hunt them down, are said to have flung themselves to a watery grave.

The isolated spot is now an upmarket tourist area with just four hotels – **Le Paradis**, **Dinarobin Hotel Golf and Spa**, **Berjaya** and **Les Pavillons** – overlooking the idyllic beach. The silence is broken only by the arrival of helicopters whizzing tourists to and from the airport and motorised caddies speeding golfers across an 18-hole golf course; and lagoons fronting the luxury hotels lure waterlovers to try scuba diving, snorkelling, windsurfing and waterskiing and boat trips to the uninhabited Benitiers Island nearby. It seems that even the mountain will not be spared as entrepreneurs, realising its potential as a prime touristic location, vie for land to develop into luxurious accommodation complexes around its lower slopes. But for the moment, the lure of this romantic spot is the 5 km (3 miles) of powdery beach – undoubtedly the best on the island.

Domino Restaurant (on a hillside near the turn-off to the beaches) is ugly but offers great views. There is a public beach at nearby Le Morne village. ❑

Jeeps for hire at Le Morne.

BELOW: fishing trips are organised by the Hôtel Le Paradis.

PLATEAU TOWNS

These heavily populated towns in central Mauritius may not be the stuff of paradise, but for a change of scene from the beach and an insight into the Mauritian lifestyle, they are worth exploring

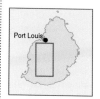

Map on page 142

n the early days of settlement, you had to be mad, bad or indifferent to live in the interior. The area was unexplored and full of runaway slaves who booby-trapped the unwary, but over the years one or two adventurers, such as German wanderer Wilhem Lechenig, settled in the uplands. When the French replaced the vacuum left by the Dutch in 1721 they found Lechenig leading a reclusive life and named the district of Plaines Wilhems after him.

Today, **Plaines Wilhems** contains all the island's significant towns other than Port Louis – that is, Rose Hill-Beau Bassin, Quatre Bornes, Vacoas-Phoenix and Curepipe. With about 30 percent of the population, it is the most densely populated district of Mauritius. The towns grew as a result of several migrations from Port Louis after fire, disease and cyclones sent people scurrying to the healthier uplands. For professional Mauritians, they are desirable places to live, offering better facilities and housing and more shops.

While for Mauritians the plateau towns have a distinct identity, for visitors passing through they tend to merge into one and, in truth, have no immediately obvious appeal. Indeed, most tourists come here only to shop (all tour operators arrange shopping trips). However, anyone interested in discovering the "other" Mauritius should come here. There are pockets of architectural interest and a few minor attractions to seek out, while the cooler climate makes a change from the sultry temperatures of the coast. Getting to (or away from) the plateau towns is easy, either by taking the motorway or the (often traffic-choked) Royal Road (A1). The map of the towns supplied by the Port Louis tourist office is a great help if you want to explore.

LEFT: annual Cavadee gathering at Quatre Bornes. **BELOW:** Sacré Coeur, Rose Hill.

Beau Bassin-Rose Hill

Like Vacoas-Phoenix further south, Beau Bassin and Rose Hill are not so much sister towns as joined towns. Beau Bassin ⑯, the less frenetic of the two, has one or two sights worth visiting. The backstreets contain some beautifully preserved colonial houses. One such is **Le Thabor** (entrance on Swami Sivananda Street) in an area that once attracted the English aristocracy and diplomats, whose love for gracious living, horse-riding and gardening earned it the name of the "English Quarter". Le Thabor, now a pastoral centre for the Catholic Church, has seen some famous faces in its time. During a visit here in 1836, Charles Darwin noted "How pleasant it would be to pass one's life in such quiet abodes". More recently, the Pope dropped in on an official visit in 1989.

In the same street are the **Balfour Gardens** (open daily 6am–6pm; closed Wed), giving wonderful views of the Moka mountains across a ravine to a waterfall which tumbles into the Grande Rivière Nord-Ouest.

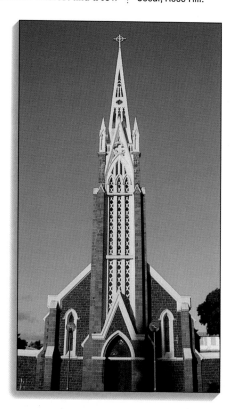

TIP

To get away from the noisy towns head east along the sugar cane-lined Moka road and look for the signpost indicating Le Pouce Mountain, just before Roselyn Cottage. Great walks can be had here and climbing the thumb-shaped peak is not too difficult as long as you go in dry weather.

You may be lucky enough to catch one of the rosy sunsets over Corps de Garde Mountain, which served as a look-out post for runaway slaves and after which **Rose Hill** ⑰ got its name; but you are more likely to remember the concrete, rain-stained office buildings juxtaposed with gaily painted tin-roofed shops and eateries. For a local shopping experience cross the road from the Victorian post office to **Arab Town**, named after the original Muslim traders who gathered here, where Mauritian housewives barter for household goods. Back on the Royal Road, you can pass the time browsing through the jumble of wares, from statues of Hindu gods and Virgin Marys tucked between bottles of shampoo and underwear, to swathes of sari material.

For a taste of local culture visit the **Plaza Theatre** housed in Rose Hill's **Town Hall** (on the right-hand side of the Royal Road, approaching from Port Louis before the town centre) where musicals, plays and shows, performed in all the island's languages, attract a wide and enthusiastic audience *(see Travel Tips)*.

Diversion to Moka

Just north of the A7, less than 4 km (2 miles) east of Rose Hill, is the university town of **Moka** ⑱. Of particular interest is the Mahatma Gandhi Institute, home of the **Folk Museum of Indian Immigration** (open Mon–Fri 9am–3.30pm, Sat 9am–noon; tel: 454 7001), which traces the life and times of the Indian cane workers brought to the island in the mid-19th century.

The president's official residence is in Moka. The magnificent **Le Chateau du Réduit** was built in 1748 as a country residence and retreat for wives and children of the French East India Company in the event of an invasion. Situated on a peninsula isolated by two ravines, the chateau overlooks lawns and

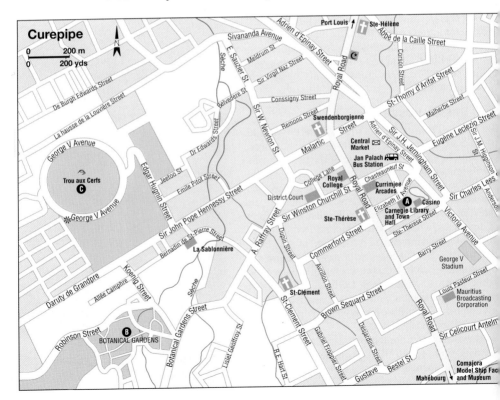

is surrounded by exotic trees and shady pathways. The house is open to the public only twice a year, on specially allocated days in March and October.

Just north of Moka, is the splendid Creole house of **Eureka** ⓭ (open daily 10am–4pm; entrance fee; tel: 433 4951). It was built in 1856 by an Englishman and bought a few years later by the wealthy Franco-Mauritian Leclezio family. Apparently, Henri Leclezio, who devoted his life to restoring the mansion, cried "Eureka" when his bid was accepted at auction. The house and birthplace of many more Leclezios has been known as Eureka ever since. The property comprises two houses and three pavilions. The main house, built of wood, is filled with colonial-style furniture, and the external stone-built kitchen crammed with original Creole cookware. You can easily while away an hour taking tea or lunch on the verandah. A path through the gardens deposits you unexpectedly by a deep ravine. There is usually a guide waiting by the small waterfall and picnic spot if you want to explore further down the ravine.

Map on page 142

Eureka's resident dodo, a familiar friend.

Quatre Bornes

On leaving Rose Hill you enter **Quatre Bornes** ⓴, named after four sugar estates which marked the original boundaries *(bornes)*. To the west rises the Corps de Garde mountain, to the south Candos Hill, a firing range for SMF officers but also a venue for fêtes, cross-country running and other sporting events. In February, the Indian temples on the flanks of Corps de Garde come alive when Tamils undergo a remarkable ritual of body piercing at the most dramatic of festivals, Cavadee *(see page 172)*. There isn't much here to lure tourists from the beach. There's nothing grand about the Grande Route Saint Jean, which slices through town, but wander into the streets behind and you'll find a maze

BELOW: French colonial grandeur at the Eureka Villa.

of bamboo-clad avenues with some lovely old villas set in large gardens. Elsewhere, numerous little restaurants and snack bars provide a taste of local life. On Thursdays and Sundays traders converge for the market or *foire*, where they sell just about everything beneath multi-coloured canopies.

Vacoas-Phoenix

Vacoas and Phoenix, traditionally occupied by ex-pats, diplomats and Franco-Mauritians because of the cooler temperatures, are essentially one big urban sprawl. Other than an animated bus station and market, there seems to be no heart to **Vacoas ㉑**. Older Mauritians muse nostalgically on the "good old days" when the British occupied the land-based communications centre. The old HMS buildings now house the Special Mobile Force headquarters and **museum** (Mon–Fri 9am–4pm), and are worth a visit if you're passing through. Ghoulish crime exhibits from the police forensic unit include pickled human organs with bullet wounds. The building itself is a fine example of colonial architecture: formerly a Scottish presbyterian church and then rum store in Port Louis, it was dismantled stone by stone and rebuilt in its current spot.

Phoenix ㉒ is an industrial area famous for its glass works and food and drinks processing companies, including the **Mauritius Breweries** which produces the local Phoenix Beer.

Curepipe

Curepipe ㉓ is the highest plateau town at 550 metres (1,840 ft), and is traditionally the stronghold of the white Franco-Mauritian community, who live in grand houses hidden behind high hedges in nameless streets around the centre and

Glass-blower at the Glass Gallery in Phoenix.

BELOW: the Trou aux Cerfs crater.

in the suburbs of **Floreal** and **Forest Side**. Curepipe has the dubious distinction of having the highest rainfall on the island, and on rainy days, which is most of the time, the buildings look depressingly grey. The town's most attractive public buildings are clustered in a compound on Elizabeth Avenue near the market. Of most interest are the 1920s **Carnegie Library**  and the impressive Creole-style **Town Hall**, which overlooks a statue of *Paul et Virginie*, central characters of the 18th-century romance inspired by a shipwreck off the Île d'Ambre.

Most people come to Curepipe to shop. **Currimjee Arcades** (on the corner of Royal Road and Chasteauneuf St), is not particularly large, but has a few good clothes shops. **La Sablonnière**, in Pope Hennessy Street, a classic example of colonial architecture complete with miniature Eiffel Tower, has been turned into a shopping emporium. The high-ceilinged rooms echo with the chatter of tourists who arrive daily, deposited by taxis and tour coaches, to buy "duty free" oriental carpets, objets d'art and furnishings. For serious shopping you'd do better to go to Floreal and Forest Side.

Most of the model ships you see on sale all over town are made at the **Comajora** factory in La Brasserie Road at Forest Side (open Mon–Fri 8am–5pm; tel: 676 5388). The private museum next door (open daily 8am–5pm) has a collection of nearly 100 boats. The owner, an authority on sailing history, will be only too pleased to give you a tour.

The **Botanical Gardens** , in the west of town, are not as big or impressive as the Pamplemousses gardens, but are perfect for a quiet stroll.

The most famous local attraction is **Trou aux Cerfs** , a 300-metre (980-ft) diameter crater. Formed as a result of volcanic activity millions of years ago, it is now choked with silt, water and dense vegetation. The crater is a 15-minute walk or a short taxi drive from the centre of town. The view stretches beyond the blanket of buildings to the spectacular mountains which, so far at least, have remained untouched by developers.

The new **Floreal Textile Museum** (Floreal Square; Mon–Fri 9am– 5pm, Sat 9.30am–1pm; entrance fee; tel: 638 8016) traces the development of Mauritius' textile industry, which has become one of the country's biggest employers. It's a modern, interactive museum where you can have fun feeling fabrics and guessing what they are, even try out your knitting skills. A shopping complex below the museum sells quality garments made from raw imported materials such as cashmere, cotton and silk.

Heading south

The plateau towns are a good starting point for a drive south through the Black River Gorges National Park. Either take the B3 from Quatre Bornes south through Glen Park and La Marie to Le Pétrin, or the B70 from Curepipe to La Marie where you turn left for Le Pétrin. If you don't have time to go all the way, you can get a taste of the area by driving to the **Tamarind Falls** *(see page 144)*. There is a viewpoint accessible from the road running south from Vacoas (also easily reached from Curepipe via La Marie). Beyond the village of **Henrietta**, the road ends at a car park, from where it is a 15-minute stroll through sugar cane to the viewpoint. ❏

Maps:
Area 142
Town 152

Curepipe's origins go back to the 18th century. The popular theory is that it was the half-way point where soldiers and travellers crossing the island would stop to rest and clean or "cure" their pipes.

BELOW:
star-crossed lovers,
Paul et Virginie.

RODRIGUES

This island is remote, laid-back and rather neglected. Its beauty lies in its simplicity and, though it may not be able to compete on the tropical beach front, its marine environment is hard to beat

Map on page 158

Rodrigues

Mauritius

Hidden in a lagoon almost twice its size, Rodrigues is the smallest of the Mascarene trio. Lying 560 km (350 miles) east of Mauritius and shaped like a plump fish, the island is just 18 km (11 miles) long and 8 km (5 miles) wide. A hilly ridge runs along its length from which a series of steep valleys extend to narrow coastal flatlands. The appeal of Rodrigues, only now opening up to tourism, lies in its rugged and simple beauty. There are stunning coves and deserted beaches. You can fish in shallow lagoons, dive and snorkel the reefs and enjoy magnificent walks through casuarina forests. The people are warm and welcoming; in spite of being cut off from the rest of the world, they survive with a cheerfulness born of optimism.

Rodrigues welcomes visitors who are unbothered about swift service and five-star trappings. Currently, the island has just four hotels and a handful of guest houses. Tourists from Réunion and Mauritius come here on 3- or 5- day packages which include the flight and half board accommodation. Those who have more time to spare can take a cabin on the *Mauritius Pride* which sails to Rodrigues once a fortnight *(see Travel Tips)*.

A pint-sized capital

Rodrigues was occupied by the French in 1726 who established a tiny settlement at **Port Mathurin ❶**. They imported slaves from Mozambique and Madagascar and settlers from French-occupied Mauritius, increasing the population to just over 100 in 1804. Nobody bothered much about Port Mathurin until the British got round to some town planning in 1864 and laid out the present town in grid style, naming many streets after surveyors and civil servants.

At last count, Port Mathurin numbered 5,390 inhabitants. The capital may be bereft of monuments, but a wander round will give you a taste of Mascarene Island life at its most leisurely. A good place to start is the jetty where a memorial stands to Rodriguan volunteers who fought in both World Wars. It's worth hauling yourself out of bed early for the **Saturday market** in Fishermen Lane. Many of the islanders set off from their villages in the hills at midnight to be on time to set up stalls (trading starts at around 6am) or to be the first to bargain for the best fruit and vegetables. By 10am most people have packed up and gone home. Parts of the market are given over to touristy knick-knacks, such as baskets and wallets, made from woven vacoas leaves, but bottles of home-grown chilli and chutneys and fruit and vegetables sell like hot cakes.

There is no tourist strip as such and most shops, no more than corrugated iron shacks with handwritten

LEFT: the *Mauritius Pride* docking at Port Mathurin.
BELOW: walking the pet pig.

*Baskets for sale
at Port Mathurin
market.*

nameplates nailed to the door, are concentrated in the block bounded by Duncan, Jenner and Morrison Streets. A few shops in Douglas Street sell more unusual gifts and lethal home-bottled chillis, but for a great range of island handicrafts call at the **Craft-Aid Workshop** (Mon–Fri 8am–3pm; Sat 8am– noon; tel: 831 1766) at Camp du Roi at the back of town. Craft-Aid employs 30 disabled people who make and sell original souvenirs. An apiary also produces the clear and distinctly flavoured Rodriguan honey. The workshop is a tourist attraction in its own right and tour operators feature it on every itinerary of Port Mathurin.

The main artery of the town is Jenner Street, one block back from the waterfront, which starts from the island's only petrol station to the west and continues over the Winston Churchill Bridge to the bus terminus to the east. At the western end of Jenner Street, tucked between shops, is the tiny six-minareted **Noor-ud-Deen Mosque**, built for the few descendants of the first Muslims who arrived in 1907 as textile merchants. Also in Jenner Street, hidden by white walls, is the **Island Secretary's Residence** (1873), the last vestige of British colonialism. It's not open to the public but you can peer through the gates and see the wide verandah shaded by a gnarled Indian almond tree.

A short stroll east leads to the Anglican **Saint Barnabas Church**, shaded by gardens and trees. Most Rodriguans are devout Catholics and the little **Saint Coeur de Marie Church** in Ricard Street sees a regular congregation. Crossing the **Winston Churchill Bridge** over the River Cascade you stumble across the spot where Rodrigues' first settlers, led by François Leguat, set up camp in 1691.

Further up river towards Fond La Digue, the latanier huts of the 1940s once occupied by "women of easy virtue", have been replaced by Port Mathurin's only hotel, the delightful Creole-style, **Escale Vacances**, set in a deep-wooded

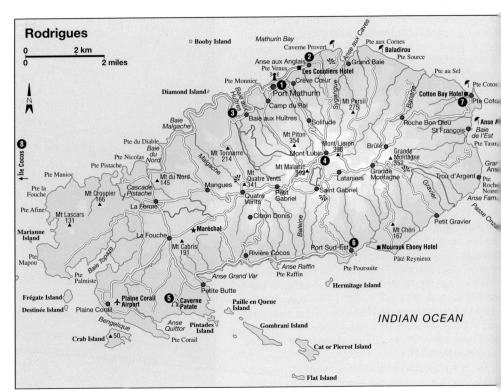

valley overlooking the river. There are some lovely walks from here (some uphill) along jungly boulder-strewn tracks – sturdy shoes are advisable.

Map on page 158

Around Port Mathurin

In 1761 a British fleet arrived and camped on a strip of beach at **Anse aux Anglais ❷** (English Bay) east of Port Mathurin and meeting with little opposition from the handful of French inhabitants, stayed for six months. The Englishness of Rodrigues was compounded in 1901 when cablemen from the Eastern Telegraph Company (later Cable & Wireless) laid a submarine telegraph cable linking the island with Mauritius thus completing the line of communication between Australia and Europe. The cablemen lived in quarters at nearby Point Venus. There are good views across Port Mathurin from the headland where French and British astronomers recorded the Transit of Venus in 1761 and 1874.

A cluster of small guest houses and **Les Cocotiers Hotel** overlook the beach at Anse aux Anglais and at low tide the lagoon is a favourite haunt of groups of fisherwomen, known as *piqueuses ourites*, who make a living spearing octopus which they hang out to dry in the sun. A stiff uphill climb from Anse aux Anglais via the tranquil beachside bungalows of well-to-do Rodriguans and Mauritians at Caverne Provert, leads to a fairly flat area where acacia trees border the road. From the headland are resplendent views over **Grand Baie**. You can follow the road up from Grand Baie beach until it peters out to a narrow uphill track towards the sweeping deserted beach at **Baladirou**. A less strenuous way of getting there is to take a 40-minute boat ride along the coast from Port Mathurin.

Just 2 km (1 mile) west of Port Mathurin is **Baie aux Huitres ❸** (Oyster Bay), an enormous bay surrounded by hills and thick casuarina forest. For the best views, drive up to **Allée Tamarin**, a hamlet at the back of the bay.

Inland from Port Mathurin

Port Mathurin's bus station is a boon for independent travellers and a handy location to start a journey inland, around fearsome hairpin bends, to the spine of the island where little villages overlook the north and south lagoons.

You can jump on a bus, thumb a lift or drive yourself to the Meteorological Station on the wind-swept **Pointe Canon** for panoramic views over Port Mathurin and the lagoon. Here a cannon, erected by British troops during World War II, points out to sea and is oddly juxtaposed beside a white statue of the Virgin Mary, La Reine de Rodrigues. If you're around on 1 May, the approach road and hills are a riot of colour with islanders trekking towards the statue to celebrate Labour Day.

The forest at **Solitude** is 2 km (1 mile) south of Port Mathurin on the Mont Lubin road. Bounded by deep valleys and thick with eucalyptus trees, the forest also has small copses of jamrosa and mango trees which provide food for the Rodriguan fruit bats that swoop down to feed on them at dusk.

Mont Lubin ❹, a busy little village of tumble-down shops, gives the impression of being at the top

The next Transit of Venus (movement of the planet across the sun) is expected on 16 June 2004. For anyone interested in astronomy, Rodrigues is not a bad place to observe this phenomenon, which only occurs twice a century.

BELOW: hanging the octopus out to dry.

of the island, but the highest point is actually nearby Mont Limon at 398 metres (1,289 ft). Most visitors drop in at the **Women's Handicraft Centre** to watch women weaving baskets from vacoas leaves and perhaps buy one of the finished articles on display, before making their way to Pointe Coton and the beautifully isolated beaches of the east *(see below)*.

Heading westwards on the Mont Lubin road, it's worth making a detour to Rodrigues' biggest church at **St Gabriel**. The church was built by locals in 1939 under difficult conditions. Specially trained donkeys carried most of the sand from the coast to the heights of St Gabriel and voluntary helpers, including women and children, brought cement, lime, blocks of coral, corrugated iron and timber up narrow mountain paths. It can be visited anytime, but for a splash of colour, music and singing, get there in time for 9am mass on Sunday.

The 5-km (3-mile) stretch of twisting road between the hamlets of Petit Gabriel, Quatre Vents and Mangues, is peppered with glimpses of translucent blue lagoons and scenes of rural life.

The next main settlement after Mangues is the large and noisy village of **La Ferme** which has a small stadium where the Pope held mass during his visit to Rodrigues in 1989. You need to pass through La Ferme to reach **Cascade Pistache** (2 km/1 mile west of the village), an enormous crater hewn out of granite surrounded by grassy hills. The waterfall which tumbles into Rivière Pistache is particularly beautiful after heavy rains. Alternatively, take the newly opened road northwards from La Ferme to Baie du Nord for a scenic 9-km (5-mile) coastal drive back to Port Mathurin passing isolated homesteads, swathed in poinsettias, hibiscus and marigolds, and causeways filled with mangroves at Baie Malgache.

BELOW: exploring the rocky maze of the Caverne Patate.

VOYAGES AND ADVENTURES

The first settlers on Rodrigues were a band of Huguenots (all men) led by François Leguat. Fleeing religious persecution in France, they set sail from Holland in search of their own island paradise. Travellers' tales drew them to the Mascarene archipelago and, in 1691, they landed on the uninhabited island of Rodrigues. They lived for the next two years on "very wholesome and luxurious foods which never caused the least sickness".

During his stay, François Leguat wrote the island's first guide book, *Voyages and Adventures*, a classic tome documenting the island's unique flora and fauna. In it he describes how the beaches were covered with tortoises weighing over 300 lb (136 kg) so that he literally used their shells as stepping stones to reach the sea. He and his companions lived happily alongside dugongs, crabs and oysters, listening to the excited chatter of thousands of birds, including the now extinct solitaire, a bird similar to the Mauritian dodo *(see page 67)*.

But the island paradise was missing one thing – women. The lack of female company proved too great a burden to bear, so they left the island for Dutch-occupied Mauritius. The tragic irony is that as soon as they landed they were arrested as spies and imprisoned on a tiny island.

In search of the solitaire

For an invigorating walk (not for the faint-hearted or claustrophobic) through dark passages studded with stalagmites and stalactites, head for the coral caves in the southwest corner of the island at **Caverne Patate ❺**. The caves, some 18 metres (60 ft) below ground, have fascinated naturalists ever since the first official exploration in 1786 when bones, believed to be those of the dodo, were found by a French captain. Later searches by British naturalists in 1894 led to more bone discoveries and comparisons with earlier findings proved that they belonged to the solitaire, described by François Leguat back in 1691. According to early accounts the caves contain "superb petrifications of an infinite variety of shapes all different from each other", but modern visitors can, depending on their imagination, discern carved rock lookalikes of Winston Churchill and the Great Wall of China. You need a permit to visit the caves and to avoid bureaucracy the easiest way is to go with a tour guide from Port Mathurin. Arm yourself with your own torch and wear strong, sturdy shoes.

How these shapes were fashioned remains a Rodriguan mystery but you are sure to be entertained by the government watchman, who delivers an exaggerated account of how two Britons took the wrong path and never returned. When you complete the 550-yard (500-metre) circuit and emerge at the exit, locals stand waiting to sell coral-carved solitaires as a reminder of the experience.

The south

The 6-km (3½-mile) journey from Mont Lubin to Port Sud-Est must rank as the most beautiful in the entire island. The road snakes its way down hillsides, twisting and turning along a series of hairpin bends each giving way to vistas of

Map on page 158

Monument to the solitaire, the dodo's long extinct cousin.

BELOW: cycling the scenic route to Port Sud-Est.

Map
on page
158

the lagoons around Port Sud-Est, dotted with small coral atolls. Your journey's end is the **Mourouk Ebony Hotel** *(see Travel Tips)* sitting atop a gentle cliff and as isolated as Rodrigues itself. It has good diving facilities and a boat-house. The nearest shop, a crimson red shack, sells basics such as bread, water, boiled sweets and cigarettes and the nearest village is at Songes where little cyclone-proof houses are scattered on the hillsides like dominoes.

Were it not for fishing, life around **Port Sud-Est** ❻ would grind to a halt. As it is, it's pretty inert except in the mornings, when fishermen wade out to the lagoon to retrieve cages they've left out for a couple of days, which have hopefully trapped lobster, prawn and crab. Now and again they venture out in pirogues and an opportunity to go out with them (for a small fee) should not be missed.

Other attractions around Port Sud-Est include dreamy walks along sparsely covered hills to the pretty beach of **Petit Gravier** and the drive to the quarry at **Plaine Corail** (a little further away, where workmen remove coral slabs from the cliffs and plains to saw into building blocks).

Pointe Coton and the east

Cotton Bay Hotel ❼ overlooks the island's best swimming beach and is flanked by low coral cliffs. The hotel, popular with holidaymakers and honeymooners, makes a comfortable base for walks to **Roche Bon Dieu**, a sandstone outcrop said to have fallen from heaven. For more superb beaches you could pant your way south along cliff-top pathways to **Anse Ally**, **Saint François** and **Baie de l'Est**. The walk veers inland from here into the protected forest at **Tasman**. The area is fenced off to prevent grazing cattle from eating young shoots, but the watchman will let you in. The pathway, bounded by great forests of casuarina trees and acacias, runs parallel to the coast, crossing a plateau of dead coral where massive white rollers pound the reef. From here the paths rise and dip into the lovely coves and bays of **Grand Anse**, **Trou d'Argent** and **Anse Bouteille** before linking up to Port Sud-Est. Looking out to sea from this the most easterly point of Rodrigues, the nearest landfall is the western coast of Australia 5,500 km (3,400 miles) away.

Sleepy lagoon islands

Don't miss out on a trip to **Île Cocos** ❽ (11 km/ 7 miles from Port Mathurin) the last refuge of the fody and brush warbler, which have virtually disappeared from Rodrigues. This idyllic island, one of 18 floating inside the lagoon, promises an all too short experience of desert island living. Soft-spoken fishermen ferry you to sugary white beaches where the only resident, a government watchman, leads a Robinson Crusoe existence in a large bungalow. You can camp out for the day beneath the trees. To visit the island you need a permit from the Central Administration Office in Port Mathurin, which most tour operators will arrange for you *(see Travel Tips)*.

Fishermen from Port Sud-Est make trips to equally beautiful **Cat Island**, ideal for swimming and snorkelling, and **Hermitage Island**, one of the most picturesque of all Rodrigues' satellite islands. ❏

RÉUNION

This may be a Gallic outpost, but you won't find scenery or a local culture like this in France

Réunion, born three million years ago as a result of an undersea volcanic eruption, consists of two great volcanic mountain masses. The oldest, in the northwest, covers two-thirds of the total area of the island and rises to form the Piton des Neiges which, at 3,000 metres (10,000 ft) is the highest peak in the Mascarenes. Over time, the Piton des Neiges, an extinct volcano, collapsed and eroded to form three caldera-like valleys or cirques.

Réunion has its share of popular beaches, but the biggest thrill for tourists is taking in the beauty of the verdant cirques and the eerie landscape of the volcano. The island cannot compete with Mauritius in terms of beaches and luxury hotels, but it has many more conventional sightseeing opportunities in the shape of museums, sugar factories, and well-preserved colonial and creole architecture. Many people come just for the adventure sports, which are the big thing here – from trekking, mountain-biking and horse-riding, to kayaking, canyoning and paragliding.

Eighty percent of Réunion's visitors are French. They see the island as an extension of the motherland and feel comfortable with the left-hand drive Renaults and Peugeots, the smooth roads, the out-of-town hypermarkets, and the bistros and boulevards. They feel at home in the Novotels and mountain gîtes and can even bring their dogs with them, and of course everyone speaks French.

The tropical warmth and breathtaking scenery are intoxicating and the Réunionnais are an attractive, gentle people. A fascinating melange of Malagasy, European, Chinese and Indian, they are taking inspiration from their counterparts in Mauritius and rediscovering their heritage.

Réunion remains a well-kept secret in the English-speaking world and, for the discerning traveller, in many ways it is the most fascinating of the Mascarene trio. ❏

PRECEDING PAGES: breathtaking sights: up in the clouds of the Commerson Crater; down by the wave-beaten, rugged coast.
LEFT: aerial view of marshland near St Paul.

THE RÉUNIONNAIS

The melting-pot phenomenon is seen more clearly in Réunion than anywhere else in the Western Indian Ocean

The culture and people of Réunion can be defined in one word – *metissage*. The overriding importance of the French language and culture throughout most of the island's history has meant that religious and ethnic differences were always subordinate to the notion of integration with the mother country. The assimiliationist tendency which characterised the period from 1946 to 1981 hindered the emergence of a separate Réunionnais identity but today the inhabitants happily juggle several identities and recent years have seen a cultural and religious resurgence among Réunionnais of Tamil, Muslim and other non-Christian minorities.

The foundations of society

The first inhabitants of Réunion were a few exiled Frenchmen and a handful of Malagasy. The birth of their Franco-Malagasy children heralded the beginning of a process of ethnic mixing which has always characterised Réunionnais society.

In the 17th century, more settlers arrived in dribs and drabs from Europe and Asia and pirates relocated to what was then Bourbon from their old haunts in Madagascar. With the development of coffee cultivation, and the importation of slaves from East Africa and Madagascar, 18th-century Bourbon became a society where blacks outnumbered whites. During this period the Kreol language was in its formative stage. Some whites, however, became pauperised as the subdivision of landholdings between siblings forced the less fortunate to the higher regions, to farm the inhospitable terrain of Les Hauts. In 1830 land concessions were made for Salazie, and in 1840 for Cilaos, but Mafate, the largest of the cirques, was still too difficult to access.

The 19th century saw the arrival of sugar cane culture in Réunion – Charles Desbassyns introduced the first steam powered machinery

LEFT: "Petit blanc" from Salazie.
RIGHT: Bois Rouge Tamil Temple, St-André.

– and other *grands blancs* or powerful white families joined them to form the island's plantocracy. By mid-century cane had become the island's principal crop. On 20 December 1848 slavery was abolished, and many of the new freemen established themselves in Les Hauts as blacksmiths and charcoal makers. Among

the indentured workers subsequently imported to Réunion were Malagasy, Indians and Chinese. A few Comorians and Yemenis were also brought.

Towards the end of the 19th century, free immigrants began to arrive from Cantonese and Hakka speaking regions of China. They gravitated into hawking and shopkeeping in the north and south of the island respectively, establishing community networks for themselves and schools for their children. Traders arrived from Gujarat and Bombay over the same period. This last wave of chiefly commercial immigrants adopted a dualistic pattern of socialisation: absorbing one culture while retaining another. To this day, these communities are perhaps the most self-enclosed and distinctive within a largely integrationist culture.

Social realities

Today, almost three quarters of Réunion society is composed of *métis* – persons of mixed origins. There are few signs of racial antagonism although a few white families still wield an economic influence disproportionate to their numbers. They are the remnants of the large landowning class, some of whom

> **PRICK UP YOUR EARS**
>
> The term *z'oreilles* (lit. ears), used for the French living on Réunion, is said to originate from the habit new arrivals had of cupping their hand behind their ear as they attempted to understand the Kreol language.

have moved into banking and import/export businesses. Their numbers have been swelled by professionals and senior civil servants, including many recent arrivals from France. Their luxury homes are in the best quarters of St-Denis and St-Pierre, and they keep holiday villas in cool Cilaos or Hell-Bourg for the summer, and often have a beach-house at St-Gilles which they use in winter.

The less well off whites, or *petits blancs*, who have been living in Les Hauts for generations, have evolved into a tight-knit but distinctive community. Their attachment to the traditional agricultural and handicraft occupations of their forebears, their small stature, characteristic facial

features and eyes of a particular shade of blue, make them highly visible. There is perhaps a greater social gulf between these country dwellers and the urban professionals of St-Denis than between the whites and *métis* of the capital who inhabit the same cultural space.

The Réunionnais today are differentiated less by colour than by creed. The descendants of Indian traders, most of whom are Muslims, are known as *z'arabes*. Almost a quarter of all Réunionnais are of South Indian descent. Their forebears were mostly Tamil-speaking Hindus. Freed from the enforced Catholicism of the colonial period, many Tamils are rediscovering their religious roots. This group are also called Malabars. The largely Catholic Chinese of Réunion are increasingly intermarrying, and may not be a distinctive community for much longer.

The newest constituent of society are the *z'oreilles* or metropolitan French, who help to run the modern state as bureaucrats, teachers and the like. The status of Réunion as a *département* of France means that any EU national can apply to work and live on the island, just as the Réunionnais have the right to travel to, work and stay in France. The plum posts occupied by the *z'oreilles* sometimes provoke resentment among the Réunionnais, just as the metropolitains occasionally give vent to less than charitable assessments of the laid-back approach of the islanders.

Despite the preponderance in Réunion of individuals of mixed ethnicity, the African origins of a significant proportion of the population are clearly evident. Descendants of these Afro-Creoles are sometimes known as *cafres* (from the Arab *kafir* or heathen), but it is a term that can cause offence.

Society as a whole is characterised by dependence: the population is young – almost half are below the age of 25 – and unemployment in Réunion has been as high as 40 percent. A significant proportion of the population relies on social security payments from France. The evident disparities between the haves and have nots have created latent tensions which occasionally erupt: in February 1991 riots in Chaudron, a run-down suburb of the capital, brought these social problems into sharp relief.

Many of these problems are structural – the high living standards which the French have fostered in Réunion mean that entrepreneurship of the kind that has given neighbouring Mauritius a dynamic economy is untenable in a society where wage rates price the islanders out of the market. The political relationship with France is scarcely questioned and is presumably sufficiently important to the French to make the prospect of jettisoning what is unquestionably a financial burden unthinkable. But as long as this is the case, Réunion has little prospect of becoming an economically viable entity.

Culturally, Réunion and surrounding islands benefit greatly from its membership of the Francophone world. Sophisticated media links bring French television into every home and reinforce the commonality of the French–Creole diaspora through the diffusion of French Caribbean rhythms and style.

Culture and religion

Hindu beliefs and practices on Réunion date from the settlement of plantation labourers of Indian origin who built small temples near the sugar estates, some of which can still be seen. The goddesses Draupadi, Mariammen and Kalimai are celebrated in annual festivals, and several Hindu temples in Réunion regroup all three. The monkey-god Hanuman used to be celebrated with an annual dance through the streets led by a devotee painted in bright colours known as the *jacot* (monkey). Traditional funeral rites, or *samblani*, continue to be performed by Tamils.

The older generation of Chinese in Réunion still celebrate their own rites of passage, and a number of pagodas have been built by them in Réunion. Ancestor worship is practised on small altars in the home, and the pagoda at St-Pierre is used by Hakkas for honouring the souls of the dead in an annual ceremony. Distinctive Chinese tombs can be found in several of the island's cemeteries.

There are 13 mosques on the island, the oldest of which dates from 1905. Most Muslims here regularly attend Friday prayers and practise fasting during the month of Ramadan.

LEFT: Cilaos garden in bloom.
RIGHT: shrines to St-Expédit crop up in the most out-of-the-way places.

Many also pay *zakat* (tithes) to the mosque. Most women of Islamic faith in Réunion wear Western dress, although a minority have adopted the veil.

The African and Malagasy cultural heritage is omnipresent – in the faces, music, language and place names of the island. The *maloya* is a former dance of slaves, and many Kreol words derive from "bantu" and other languages associated with East Africa. Malagasy place names in Réunion are particularly evocative. Cilaos means "the place where cowards do not go" and Cimendef, at Mafate, is so called after a Malagasy who escaped –

DANCING THE MALOYA

The variant of the sega music that has survived into present-day Réunion is known as the *maloya*. This slow, sensual rhythm resembles the *sega typic* of Mauritius and the *moutya* of Seychelles while retaining a distinctively Réunionnais flavour. Immersed as they are in La Francophonie, the people of Réunion have developed almost as much of a liking for the zouk music of the French Caribbean as for their indigenous sega beat.

As a result, the Réunionnais are adept at the intricate dance routines of zouk, have developed their own zouk tunes, and are gradually introducing these to their neighbours in the region.

the name means "he who cannot be a slave". A few families of Malagasy origin continue to practise traditional funeral rites, known as *velasa*, and ancestor worship.

Superstitions and the occult

For many years, the practice of non-Christian religions was frowned on in Réunion and, partly as a result of this, some Hindu traditions have been absorbed into Christian celebrations. The cult of Mariammen, for example, is often assimilated with worship of the Virgin Mary, while Krishna's birthday is associated with that of Jesus Christ. The veneration of St-Expédit

(nominally Catholic, but not recognised by the Vatican) is symbolic of the confluence of religious practices found in Réunion, for the saint is also identified as a manifestation of Kali.

Catholicism itself has developed a particular style in Réunion where Christians visit shrines such as that of the Black Virgin at Notre Dame de la Salette to honour a promise made in exchange for a request exacted, in a striking resemblance to Hindu practices. This is just one of hundreds of Virgin shrines scattered around the island, always bedecked in flowers and *remerciements* (thank you notes).

Chinese Catholics continue to adhere to Buddhist rituals in the home, and to venerate their ancestors in the colourful pagodas dotted around the island.

Many folk practices and superstitions brought by immigrants have survived the centuries of French acculturation. Hindus believe that prayers made to specific gods and goddesses can cure certain diseases, while Muslims trace some forms of illness to possession by evil spirits, or *djinns*. The word for an Indian sorcerer is *pusari* in Réunion, and given that Tamil priests are known as *pujaris*, this suggests a cross-over of religious and magical practices. A sorcerer of Malagasy origin is called an *ombiasy*.

Formulas for casting black magic spells have circulated in Réunion for many years. *Petit Albert*, the collection of magic spells imported to the region from Europe, and the brand of African black magic known as *gris gris* in the islands, still have many practitioners.

The belief in wandering, troubled souls is also very common in Réunion and may originate in the Malagasy concept of the *matoatoa*. Persons who have died of the plague or of other epidemic diseases are believed to be possessed of special powers and cemeteries in St-Denis and at the port where such graves are found are frequented by believers at auspicious times.

Public holidays and festivals

The first Hindu festival of the year, Pandyale, takes place in early January when fire-walking ceremonies are held. Cavadee, the spectacular body-piercing festival, takes place in January/February, when fire-walking is also part of the proceedings. Mariammen, a goddess associated with Tamils, is honoured by them in May each year. Kali's festival in August is marked by the sacrifice of cockerels and goats. Chinese New Year is also celebrated in Réunion, in February/March, and in September the mid-autumn festival provides an opportunity to taste moon cake. The Muslim trader families, or *z'arabes* celebrate Eid ul Fitr, and Eid ul Kebir, when animal sacrifices are made. Some rituals are grounded in very real, local fears: on 15 August each year pilgrims go to the shrine of the Virgin at Parasol, Ste-Rose to pray that there will be no volcanic eruption. The abolition of slavery in 1848 is commemorated annually by a public holiday on 20 December. ❏

LEFT: preparations for the Hindu festival of Cavadee.

Cases Creoles

The architectural heritage of the Indian Ocean islands is fast disappearing, as the once ubiquitous delightful wooden homes with their long verandahs are being replaced by modern concrete buildings that have little of their predecessors' appeal. So do take the opportunity of your visit to appreciate the charm and ingenuity of the remaining colonial homes, from the humble *case creole* to the grandiose plantation house.

The design of the typical *case creole* dates from the 18th century when settlers employed marine carpenters to build their houses from local wood. The *bardeaux* or shingle roof, still a feature of many creole houses, and the plank-lined outer walls were clearly inspired by boats. Local weather conditions also played an important role in the development of building styles. The triangular and porch roofs were designed to protect houses from heavy tropical rains, while the *varangue*, or verandah, was spacious and airy to combat the humidity and heat of the tropics and formed an extension of the main living quarters. The inhabitants added their own decorative touches which over time have given the creole house its distinctive style. The designs of the *lambrequins*, mantles which help to shield the house from the elements, often have a unique motif which was the owner's cultural trademark. One of the finest examples of a typical *case creole*, complete with a type of garden extension known as a *guetali*, can be seen at Villa Folio, in Hell-Bourg *(see page 228)*.

In the 18th century when the island port was the centre of commerce, wealthy merchants built more grandiose versions of the *case creole*, and enclosed them within ornate railings. Some of these stylish and historic houses can still be seen in the backstreets of Port Louis and in Rue de Paris in St-Denis. As the middle classes moved to new residential areas, Creole architecture became more refined and was complemented by elegant lawns and gardens. The towns of the Mauritian central plateau, from Rose Hill to Curepipe, are still dotted with the well-maintained former residences of prosperous 19th-century colonists.

The most impressive of the island residences are the grand homes built by the sugar barons and planters of valued export crops such as vanilla and spices. The plantation houses, with their turrets, columns and balustrades, manage to harmonise the classic features of creole design with the evident pretensions of their owners. The verandahs are enclosed by colonnades and extend around the house, on two or three sides. The delicate lacework *lambrequins* above the numerous windows alleviate the solemnity of these 18th- and early 19th- century châteaux. Most are still privately owned, but visitors to Mauritius can take a guided tour of the Maison Eureka in Moka, to see how the plantocracy really lived, or dine at stately St Aubin in the south. Holidaymakers in Mahé, Seychelles, can stay la La Residence Bougainville, which has been converted into

a guest house with sea view, or at the Chateau St Cloud on La Digue, a vanilla plantation house dating from the Napoleonic period.

The seats of government of the French administrators, much enlarged and restored over succeeding years, particularly Le Reduit (the Mauritian president's official residence), retain the simple beauty of colonial architecture, while providing an appropriately stately venue for visiting dignitaries. At the other end of the scale, look out for the quaint stone post offices which the British built in Mauritius and Seychelles. One enduring and endearing feature of the insular landscape is the creole corner shop, with its gaily coloured walls, hand-painted hoardings and corrugated roof.   ❏

RIGHT: with its red corrugated roof, white wooden walls and decorative window, this Hell-Bourg house is a typical example of a *case creole*.

RÉUNION CUISINE

French cuisine is the norm at most hotels and restaurants, and Chinese, Indian and Italian food is on offer in the bigger centres, but traditional home cooking is creole

The food may appear to have a strongly French influence – *café au lait* and croissants for breakfast, *croque monsieur* (toasted cheese and ham sandwich) for lunch and *bouillabaisse* (fish stew) for supper are all standard fare. Nevertheless, even in Réunion creole cuisine rules. Its absence from the bars and bistros of St-Denis or St-Gilles-les-Bains may send you searching, but head for the Cirques and you'll find locals living on *carris* (mild curries), most emphatically for carnivores, white rice or yellow rice (cooked with saffron), pulses (red or white haricot beans, lentils or peas) and a multitude of *rougailles*

(the hot and spicy tomato and vegetable chutney known as *chatini* in Mauritius) and *achards* (sun dried pickles).

Meat curries are usually made with chicken, beef or pork, but one of the tastiest curries you'll find on a menu is goat massala. The meat is cooked very slowly in a rich flavoursome sauce and melts in the mouth. Fish and seafood are also curried, octopus and prawn being favourite ingredients.

Versatile vegetables

Vegetarians are well catered for in the local markets which are stocked with an enormous variety of fresh fruit and vegetables. However, ordering a vegetarian meal in a creole restaurant is a little more tricky. Meat or fish features are central to many main dishes, but a number of starters and accompaniments are vegetable based. Vegetable or lentil *carris* are common fare and *salade de palmiste* (heart of palm) appears on most menus, but check before ordering any other salads, as pieces of meat or fish are often thrown in. *Tarte bredes chou chou*, a creamy pie made from spinach-like greens on a crusty pastry base, is a filling alternative.

Chou chou (also known as christophine) is a very versatile vegetable, which tastes a bit like courgette. There are over 100 varieties. It is added to cakes, jams and curries, served au gratin, as *bredes chou chou* (the edible tops), or just plain boiled. The plant stems can be split and dried and used to make woven handicrafts.

Vanilla

Réunion is one on the world's leading producers of vanilla and it plays an important role in the island's cuisine. You'll find vanilla thrown into sweet and savoury sauces, added to tea and coffee and rum-based liqueurs such as Pause Café. If you're interested to see how it is grown and processed, visit the Bras-Panon factory *(see page 206)*.

Home cooking

For a taste of real Réunionnais cuisine, track down a *ferme auberge* (farm inn) where you could try traditional offerings cooked by enthusiastic home chefs. A typical tourist menu at around €15 might consist of a set number of courses such as *gratin chouchou* for starters, followed by a sumptuous fish curry or duck in vanilla sauce and finished off with *parfait chocolat* – also with vanilla sauce. One of the best *ferme auberges* is at Chemin Rivière du Mat (tel: 0262 51 53 76), run by Madame Eva Annibal, but booking is essential.

Snacks and sweets

There's no shortage of mobile food stalls along the popular west coast beaches selling filled baguettes and sweet and savoury Breton-style *crêpes* (pancakes). Look out for *patisseries*, *croissanteries* and even "sandwicheries" at out

of town hypermarkets such as Continent where you can take your pick from some mouth-watering displays of creole snacks; *bonbon piments* (crunchy chilli cakes), vegetable or meat *samousas*, *brinjals* (aubergine fritters) are piled high and sold cheap.

Rum punch or wine

Relics of Réunion's culinary past are found in drinks of all kinds. *Rhum arrangée*, literally, "arranged rum", is a mind-blowing concoction of rum and fruit which is left for months to macerate and mature in a mixture of spices. Marginally easier on the brain cells is *punch*

creole, usually rum based, made from a range of fruits and berries, cane syrup and juice.

Grapes have always been grown in Cilaos and the region is the only wine-producing area in Réunion where some good table wines are made from the Cot, Pinot Noir and Chenin grapes. In 1991 a small group of vine-growers formed Le Chai de Cilaos Cooperative which markets and exports the wines to France, but if you're in Cilaos then drop in for a wine-tasting session. The dry white wine goes well with grilled fish and cheese, the smooth sweet white is an excellent dessert wine and the full-bodied red from the Cot grape, makes an excellent accompaniment to red meat. ❏

LEFT: locals stock up on fresh home-grown produce at St Paul's seafront market.
RIGHT: food stall selling creole snacks.

VOLCANIC HABITATS

With large swathes of virgin rainforests still remaining, Réunion's dramatic volcanic terrain provides refuge for a wide variety of wildlife

The high rugged mountains and deeply chasmed gorges of Réunion have ensured that, unlike on the other Mascarenes, much of the island's original forests still exist and are in good condition. Nevertheless, this hasn't stopped the demise of some spectacular wildlife, namely, as with Mauritius and Rodrigues, the giant tortoise, flightless birds and gaudy parrots.

Réunion once had a bird that was thought to be a white dodo or solitaire but recent discoveries have revealed that this creature, which was about the size of a turkey, was a flightless ibis. In the 17th century, before the advent of travel guides and bird books, the names of birds were not fixed and were sometimes used to indicate a complete species, hence the term dodo came to be used for any flightless bird.

Other birds lost to Réunion have been the crested starling, called the huppe, which was last seen in the middle of the 19th century, and a beautiful russet brown parrot with a lilac head that died out in the late 18th century. It is believed that these creatures' habitats had mainly been in the lowland rainforests, which had fallen under the settlers' axes for coffee, cotton and spice plantations.

In the cooking pot

But, considering the amount of high altitude rainforest Réunion has, it has long puzzled naturalists why the island should have lost its equivalent to the pink pigeon, kestrel, echo parakeet *(see page 91)*, forest fody and fruit bat, the latter of which can be found in great numbers on the other Mascarenes. However, it has been suggested that extinction rates are higher on French-owned islands because much of the wildlife is heavily hunted for the cooking pot! Today, the best place to see specimens and models of Réunion's extinct wildlife is in the Natural History Museum at St-Denis *(see page 199)*.

Newcomers to Réunion

Many species of mammals were brought to the island by settlers mainly for food, including wild boar, lemurs, squirrels and hares, but most have died out, although not the boar. The Javan deer which arrived in 1761 had already been shot out by 1793. Regrettably,

they were reintroduced in the 1980s to Plaine des Chicots and Bébour. They feed on the saplings of native trees, preventing natural regeneration of the forest.

One of the most interesting of the introduced mammals is the tenrec *(Tenrec ecaudatus)*, a hedgehog-like insectivore which comes from Madagascar. Brought over for the dinner table, it is still on the menu in some rural areas, although many meet their end flattened on the road. The female produces huge litters, the record being 34 young in one litter. Apparently only one egg has to be fertilised, which then divides repeatedly so all the young are the same sex and genetically identical.

LEFT: deep in the rainforest interior.
RIGHT: yellow-streaked tenrec.

The Indian house shrew, a large omniverous mammal that can also be found on Mauritius and Rodrigues, is common over much of the island and preys on reptiles and invertebrates. Apart from the rats and feral cats, similar to the spotted tabby African wildcat, there are few mammals on Réunion and none that are indigenous.

Island birds

Despite the rats that steal birds' eggs and the cats that have catching birds down to a fine art, there are large numbers of native birds which should be easy to spot, especially in Roche Écrite or the Forêt de Bébour. The stonechat,

Réunion is most famous for two threatened species of endemic petrels, the Barau's petrel *(Pterodroma baraui)* and the black petrel *(Pterodroma atterima)*. The former was only discovered in 1963 and its nest sites found a few years ago in the high cliffs of Piton de Neiges. The nesting sites of the black petrel have yet to be discovered. The Barau's petrel can be seen over the beach at St-Gilles in the late afternoon and in the cirques and mountains as they fly in to roost. They are a wonderful sight to watch wheeling around the cliffs of Cilaos in the evening. Sometimes the young will fly into buildings on the coast on their way home.

or *tec-tec* (the exact sound of its call) is the most common, appearing everywhere except the low coastal areas of the north and west. You are more likely to see a paradise flycatcher – known locally as the *vierge* because it has a purple head and is believed to have seen the Virgin Mary – in Réunion than in Mauritius. The same goes for the island's black bulbul *(merle)* and two species of white-eye.

The Mascarene cave swiftlet lives here too and can often be seen feasting on clouds of flying insects. However, the swallow is quite rare keeping to the lowland east of the island, and Cilaos. The bird you are least likely to see is the rare Réunion cuckoo-shrike *(tuit-tuit)*, which hides in the forest of Plaine des Chicots above St-Denis.

Soaring or gliding over forests and in the cirques, the Réunion harrier or *papangue* is the largest and most spectacular bird on the island. A bird of prey with a wingspan of more than a metre (3 ft), the adult male is stunning in its grey, white and black plumage; the females are brown. They have a varying diet of tenrecs, rats, birds and invertebrates.

Escaped cage birds

Many of the pretty perching birds that you will see around the gardens are descendants of common cage birds that have escaped from captivity and are relative newcomers. These include the yellow village weaver birds, waxbills, spice finches, the beautiful yellow green-singing finch and the not-so-pretty mynah bird.

The gentle cooing sounds are provided by the small grey confiding barred ground dove and the Madagascar turtle dove, which was thought to have come from Madagascar but sub-fossil bones have since been found proving that it is native. The bright red Madagascar fody can be seen everywhere.

Fortunately for the game birds, the mongoose has never been introduced to the island, so three species of quail, two partridge, wild chickens and a button quail, thought to be a native, all live in relative peace.

Important seabirds

As well as the Barau's petrel and black petrel, Réunion is home to Audubon's shearwater, a small black and white seabird that nests in the cliffs and feeds on fish and squid and several small colonies of wedge-tailed shearwater.

Keep an eye open in the cirques, gorges and around cliffs for the spectacular white-tailed tropic bird *(paille-en-queue)*, which has a long, streaming tail and is the island's national bird. Petite Île, just off the south coast and Réunion's only satellite island, has a breeding population of at least 300 pairs of common noddies and up to 300 non-breeding lesser noddies, who have recently been joined by a fairy tern.

Colourful geckos

Apart from the many nocturnal house geckos that you see darting about the gardens and houses, the island has two brightly coloured

red stripes down each side, its distribution has been split by lava flows from the volcano, creating different races of the same species. You can sometimes spot them lurking around the tourist kiosks up there.

The beautiful green, blue and red panther chameleon from Madagascar is the only introduced species that is protected; it can be found around St-Paul.

Tamarinds and orchids

Cultivated land bearing sugar cane reaches as high as 800 metres (2,600 ft) above sea level, then gives way to verdant mixed forest which

endemic day geckos which are worth looking out for. Funnily enough, the only place you will see the stunning green, red and white Manapy day gecko is on a walk through Manapany on the south coast. There you will see them all over the place, basking on banana leaves, scuttling up coconut palms and the pandanus, or screw pine. The Réunion day gecko, however, is a much more difficult species to find as it lives high up in the forests of the northeast and east. A blue-green colour with

becomes a dwarf heath as you move up to the higher elevations. There are more than 60,000 hectares (148,000 acres) of natural forest on the island, looked after by the Office National des Forêts (ONF), and the endemic tamarind of the acacia family, alongside an island bamboo called the *calumet*, is quite a common sight. Epiphytes, including a wide variety of orchids (seven of which are unique to Réunion), and ferns grow in abundance on trees that lend their physical support.

Some of the introduced plants are a menace, such as the goyavier from Brazil, which runs rampant in the forest undergrowth. But its guava-like red berries are rich in vitamin C. ❑

LEFT: Réunion's national bird, the white-tailed tropic bird, is easily distinguished by its two long tail plumes.
RIGHT: wild lupins at Mafate.

ISLAND OF ADVENTURES

The spectacular landscape of Réunion is punctuated by trails, craters, peaks, rivers, forests and waterfalls, tailor-made for a vast array of outdoor pursuits

Experiencing the great spectacle of the interior uplands of Réunion can take as little or as much effort as you choose. Whether you take it easy and fly across the island in a helicopter, take a stroll along a nature trail, or prefer the challenge of hiking along a Grand Randonnée *(see pages 186–87)*, or testing your nerve abseiling down a waterfall or paragliding off a mountain ridge, you will discover mystery in its isolation, magic in its inaccessibility and power in its grandeur.

The cirques, mountains and plains providing the magnificent terrain for such activities were formed at different stages of the island's volcanic development over many thousands of years. Originally the Piton des Neiges (3,609 metres/11,840 ft) was the summit of a massive volcanic dome which collapsed around it and then was eroded to form the three great amphitheatres of gorges, waterfalls and ridges known as the cirques – perfect for canyoning, white-water rafting, rock climbing, hang-gliding and paragliding.

Les Hautes-Plaines, comprising the Plaine-des-Palmistes and the Plaine-des-Cafres, form an open landscape of forests and pastureland between the extinct volcanic landscape and the active Piton de la Fournaise. They are criss-crossed with mountain-bike tracks, hiking paths and horse-riding trails. The higher Plaine-des-Cafres is the gateway to the volcano *(see pages 217–21)*.

Be prepared

The best time to take on any arduous, lengthy activity, such as hiking, horse-trekking or mountain biking, is during the cooler and drier months of May to November when mountain temperatures hover between 12°C (54°F) and 18°C (64°F) during the day but can drop to near zero at night. The Maison de la Montagne will give you a general update of weather conditions which can change very rapidly, or if you

understand French, you can phone the meteorological office *(see Travel Tips, page 378)*.

It's important that you are aware of your own level of fitness and stamina before starting any activity and stick to rules of basic safety. Helicopters frequently survey the cirques and should you be injured or in trouble you can send a dis-

tress signal by raising both arms in a V shape. During 2002, scores of people, mostly suffering from broken bones or twisted ankles, were rescued in the cirques.

For overnight stays en route, there are several types of accommodation ranging from *gîtes de montagne* (mountain huts or lodges), to *chambres d'hôtes* (B & B) and youth hostels. Campsites are rare, but there are a number of *abris* (shelters) on trekking routes. The shelters consist of only a roof so you need your own tent and sleeping bag.

Many of them provide meals and at several of the *chambres d'hôtes*, a *table d'hôte* is offered when all the guests sit down to a meal

LEFT: paragliding off a mountain ridge.
RIGHT: negotiating the rapids.

together with the host. Reservations must be made in advance for all accommodation through Maison de la Montagne *(see box below)*. There is usually a grocer's shop *(épicerie)* in the villages *(îlets)* scattered around the interior, selling a basic range of foods, but not in all of them.

Up, up and away

The cirques and mountains are an awesome sight, especially from the top, and you can experience the sensation of flying between the peaks in a helicopter *(see page 220)* or smaller still, in a microlight. One or two people can fly in a microlight round a choice of the cirques, Piton des Neiges, or the volcano. Bookings can be made through Felix ULM Run (tel: 0262 45 58 38) or Les Passagers du Vent (tel: 0262 42 95 95), both to the north of Le Port, before St Paul.

To fly like a bird with only the rush of wind in your ears has to be one of the greatest thrills especially over, within and around such dramatic scenery as Réunion's. The best hang-gliding and paragliding spots are Piton Maïdo on the edge of the wild and secluded Cirque de Mafate, from the top of Piton des Neiges and the Hauts de St-Paul, where protected from the strong winds, the conditions are perfect for

MAISON DE LA MONTAGNE

Whether you spend a day or a week in the cirques and mountains, Maison de la Montagne, which has centres in St-Denis and Cilaos *(see Travel Tips, page 390)*, can assist you with whatever you would like to do. Knowledgeable, English-speaking staff will advise on hiking routes, can arrange mountain accommodation and provide guides if necessary. They can also organise horse-trekking trips, canyoning, mountain biking, hang-gliding and many other mountain sports, and stock the Institut Géographique National's 1:25,000 scale maps (4401 RT to 4406 RT), and the ONF's walking guides.

To ensure safety in the mountains, the organisation has drawn up the *Ten Commandments of the Crafty Papangue*:

● Never venture alone in the mountains.
● You must be fit to take full advantage of the mountains.
● For peace of mind, arrange your tour through La Maison de la Montagne.
● Good shoes, warm and waterproof clothing ensure comfort.
● To avoid accidents never take unmarked paths.
● If you do get lost, stay calm.
● Know the distress signal – arms held up in a V.
● Never leave a wounded person alone. Wait for help.
● If you don't know the mountains, take a guide.
● Always keep the mountains litter free.

beginners, too. Contact Azurtech (tel: 0262 34 91 89) in St Leu, and Parapente Réunion (tel: 0262 24 87 84) in St-Leu, which also offers training sessions.

Rivers wild

Streams cascading over ridges and waterfalls powering off the mountains provide ideal conditions for the hair-raising sport of canyoning. For daredevils only, in a well padded wetsuit, canyoning means abseiling down waterfalls and torrents in the heights of the cirques. Try Îlet Fleurs Jaunes and

ADRENALINE RUSH

Réunion's dramatic chasms are an ideal bungee backdrop. Bungee jumping is available from October to April and costs around €28 per jump (tel: 0262 24 77 34).

Mountain bike challenges

Seven large areas of the island's magnificent interior have been devoted to mountain biking (VTT), and marked tracks, approved by the French Cycling Federation, total nearly 700 km (435 miles). These areas each with their own steep challenges and beautiful views include Maïdo, Entre-Deux, Cilaos, two at Hautes-Plaines, St-Philippe and Ste-Rose. Suitable bikes can be hired from companies such as Rando Bike (tel: 0262 59 15 88) and VTT Réunion (tel: 0262 38 01 97).

Îlets du Bois Rouge in the Cirque de Cilaos or Trois Cascades. As the slopes become less steep rivers, such as the Rivière des Roches, provide exciting conditions for kayaking, and there are plenty of rapids, such as those of the Rivière des Marsouins for white-water rafting. Companies specialising in river sports are Austral Aventure (tel: 0262 32 40 29) in St-Gilles-les-Hauts and Kalanoro (tel: 0262 50 74 75) in Bras-Panon. These companies will organise mountain climbing expeditions as well.

LEFT AND RIGHT: more adventurous ways to explore Réunion's heights and depths – canyoning, mountain biking or horse-trekking.

Trekking on horseback

Viewing the beauty of Réunion at your own pace from the back of a horse has to be an enriching experience – for an hour, one day or for several days, with tent and meals included in the price. With Ferme Equestre du Grand-Etang (*see pages 222–23*) you can ride a three-day circuit through the Forêt de Bébour- Bélouve (tel: 0262 50 90 03), and with Centre Equestre Alti-Mérens (tel: 0262 59 18 84) you can go on a two-day ride to the volcano. The horses in Réunion are the gentle Mérens breed brought over from the Pyrénées in France on which even a beginner will feel at ease. (*For more details on adventure sports, see Travel Tips pages 390–92.*) ❏

Hiking along the Grandes Randonnées

Réunion is a walker's paradise, in spite of what novelist Walter Besant had to say about it when he walked to the Piton des Neiges in 1863. His tramp in the tropics may have been "a time of bruisings, and barkings of the skin, of tearings and scratchings, of dirt, discomfort and disaster", but today there are more than 1,000 km (620 miles) of well-marked trails across the island, mostly maintained by the Office National des

Forêts (ONF) and ranging from an hour's easy walk to a challenging week-long hike.

There are several organisations that will help you plan your route, book accommodation in advance and provide guides, the main one being Maison de la Montagne *(see page 184)*. Maham (tel: 0262 47 82 82) in Hell-Bourg *(see page 228)* provides a package tour with guide, meals and accommodation that includes seven days of hikes of varying levels. If you are not familiar with the island, hiring a local *guide-pei* (native guide) through the tourist office is a good idea. Not only will you be in safe hands but they enjoy sharing their in-depth knowledge of their native land. On the other hand, a good locally available book is

Topo-Guide, "a trekkers' bible" which covers eight one-day walks along the Grandes Randonnées (GR R1 and GR R2), of varying levels illustrated by extracts from the IGN maps.

The opening of GR R1 in 1979 makes trekking less hazardous than in Besant's days. The 60-km (37-mile) trail encircles Piton des Neiges through the three cirques of Salazie, Cilaos and Mafate. No visit would be complete without spending at least one night in the cirques, if only to wake at sunrise and gaze upon deep mysterious valleys clothed in magnificent forests. The air is clear and sharp and rouses even the weariest walker to experience a world of soaring, spectacular peaks.

The 150-km (93-mile) GR R2 crosses the island from the north to southeast. It starts from La Providence just outside St-Denis, links with the GR R1 at Marla in the Cirque de Mafate, and continues through diverse landscapes of rugged mountains, fertile plains, volcano and humid forest to St-Philippe. The following are some ideas for hikes that take in the Grandes Randonnées and last from half a day to as long as you would like.

La Roche Écrite. One of the most popular walks starting from St-Denis, it takes you south to La Roche Écrite (2,277 metres/7,470 ft). The trail passes through Réunion's various stages of vegetation from humid lowlands and tamarind forests with an abundance of rich flora to the almost denuded summit of La Roche Écrite itself.

If you're on limited time, the return trip can be done in one full day, but overnighting at the *gîte* at Plaine-des-Chicots will enable you to wake early to complete the final ascent to the ramparts of La Roche Écrite where you can experience the best views of Réunion's two highest mountains, Piton des Neiges (3,609 metres/11,840 ft) and Le Gros Morne (2,991 metres/9,813 ft) and the cirques of Mafate and Salazie to the right and left.

Most people drive inland from St-Denis on the D42 to Le Brûlé and park in the car park at Mamode Camp, about 5 km (3 miles) along the Route Forestière (RF1). From here the trail is clearly signposted rising gently through forests of cryptomeria and eucalyptus and lush areas of wild flowers and fruits and endemic bamboo *(Nastus borbonicas)*. Continue southwards, crossing two ravines surrounded by forests of mixed evergreens or *bois de couleurs* and tamarinds to reach the *gîte* at Plaine-des-Chicots, where you can stop for the night. From here it is another 1½-hour trek southwards to La Roche Écrite through landscape that changes to a plateau of lichen and moss.

You'll pass two intersections on the way but you should ignore both and keep to the marked path; the first on the right after about 45 minutes leads to La Mare aux Cerfs, a small watering hole noted for dawn sightings of Réunion's deer, which you could make a detour to on the way back. The second leads to Caverne Soldats. Continue on for another 25 minutes to La Roche Écrite.

Mafate. The most isolated of the cirques, no roads penetrate its rim. Mafate is wild and peaceful only disturbed by the sound of the odd helicopter coming in for a closer look. But there are plenty of trails criss-crossing the cirque that offer a challenging choice, from a simple, but not so interesting, three-hour walk along the Rivière des Galets to more difficult day-long walks. Alternatively, you can stay in Mafate trekking from *îlet* to *îlet* and overnighting in mountain *gîtes*.

The *îlet* of Dos d'Ane on the D1 is a handy starting point for a couple of days of trekking along the GR R2. This trail descends steeply for two hours taking you down to the Rivière des Galets, which flows from the slopes of Le Gros Morne through a huge valley of *bois de couleurs* and meets the ocean at Le Port on the northwest coast. The trail crosses the river several times before it forks off to the left, leading to the *îlet* of Aurère, a good two-hour climb. Here you can stay at M Georget Boyer's *gîte* (tel: 0262 55 02 33) – basic, but breakfast and an evening meal are provided.

The next day you can do a four-hour hike to Le Belier on the edge of the Cirque de Salazie along either the Scout path, or the shorter, but more dramatic, direct path. This descends to the bottom of a ravine before climbing up to the top of the Grand Rein ridge, then down again and along the Route Forestière for the last leg.

Grand Place, past the turn off to Aurère, is a good *îlet* to make your base for a few nights if you would like to spend several days exploring Mafate, as many of the trails pass through here.

Salazie. Hell-Bourg (*see pages 228–29*) at the end of the D48 has plenty of places to stay and is where you can start a hike to the Piton des Neiges, lasting about 5½ hours. The Gîte de la Caverne Dufour offers basic but hospitable dormitory-style accommodation at the foot of the mountain. From there it is a 1½-hour climb to the top, best started before dawn before the clouds descend.

LEFT: spoilt for choice.
RIGHT: walkers at Grand Étang.

Starting from Hell-Bourg, the trail climbs steeply to the Terre Plate, a wooded plateau where trails turn off to Manouilh, mineral springs on the edge of cliffs, and lead through woods of cryptomeria. You join the GR R1 towards the Piton des Neiges, skirting the edge of the Forêt de Bébour and crossing heathland, called *les branles*, until you reach the *gîte*.

Cilaos. The GR R1 winds and climbs its way west from Cilaos to Marla in the Cirque de Mafate. The six-hour hike goes via the Cascade de Bois Rouge and Col du Taïbit (2,082 metres/6,831 ft). If you want to try to do it in a day, start from the trailhead on the Îlet à Cordes road, 6 km (4 miles) west of, and accessible by bus from, Cilaos. Alternatively,

you can do a round walk to the Cascade de Bois Rouge in around two hours.

The volcano. Starting at Pas de Bellecombe or from the RF5, an alternative to climbing the Piton des Neiges (*see pages 217–21*) is to follow the GR R2 along the southern ridge (l'Enclos) of the volcano to the Nez Coupé du Tremblet. This five-hour hike, which passes through the magnificent Plaine des Sables (*see page 219*), has been graded as not too difficult but you could just go halfway by returning at Foc-Foc where the trail forks. Here the main section of the GR R2 continues steeply, and is slippery in parts, down through dense and humid forest to Basse Vallée on the south coast – at least a seven-hour hike. ❑

PITON DE LA FOURNAISE: "PEAK OF THE FURNACE"

In 1801, explorer Bory de St Vincent described the volcano as "immense, tumultuous, bloody and majestic". He was inspired by it, but many feared it

▷ SOME LIKE IT HOT
Any volcanologist will tell you that all live volcanoes, no matter how predictable, should be treated with caution and respect.

Piton de la Fournaise, a "Hawaiian-type" shield volcano, is one of the most active on earth. It has erupted at least 153 times since 1640. In 1778, it added notably to the size of the island by pouring millions of tonnes of lava into the sea; in 1786 the explosion was so loud that it was heard in Mauritius; the following year "the sky turned red and the ocean turned into a boiling cauldron as fire met water".

Piton de la Fournaise has two main craters. The highest one, Bory, has been inactive since 1791, while the active Dolomieu manages, for most of the time, to confine its eruptions within the enclosure. On 8 April 1977 the islanders witnessed the sheer power of their volcano when for five days the Dolomieu spewed red fire from its molten heart. Lava rolled down the mountainside destroying 20 houses and a petrol station at Ste-Rose on the east coast, only to stop just before the doorstep of a church and harden into a black mass.

Then on 20 March 1986 the Dolomieu crater exploded again, spitting out great gobs of lava which flowed at the rate of 100,000 cubic metres (353,100 cubic ft) per hour reaching temperatures of up to 1,160°C (2,120°F). The lava flow trickled down to the coast, sizzling as it sank into the sea, extending the island's land mass by several hectares.

On 9 March 1998, yet another spectacular eruption, this time lasting for 196 days – the longest in the 20th century – caused panic and excitement as blood-red fire fountains turned into rivers of lava. They flowed down to the Tremblet area only to peter out beside a shrine to St-Expédit on the RN2, 7 km (4 miles) north of Pointe de Tremblet *(see pages 207–8).*

△ COASTAL EXTENSION
Pointe de la Table was where the lava flow from the 1986 eruption came to rest, extending the east coast here by several hectares.

△ CIRQUE DE CILAOS
Stream cutting through volcanic basaltic rocks en route to the Cirque de Cilaos, visible in the distance.

◁ VOLCANO FACTS
Find out everything about volcanoes and see footage of recent explosions at the Maison du Volcan in Bourg-Murat.

FOUNTAINS AND RIVERS OF FIRE

Like the volcanoes of Hawaii, Piton de la Fournaise is a shield volcano. It produces spectacular fire fountains and churns out rivers of basalt lava which flow over great distances. Because the lava is so fluid it trickles easily downhill without piling up, which explains why shield volcanoes are not steep. Around the Piton de la Fournaise you'll find two types of solidified lava flow which have been given Hawaiian names: *pahoehoe* (pronounced pa-hoy-hoy) and *aa* (ah-ah). *Pahoehoe*, which looks like coils of rope, is smooth and easy to walk on. This type of lava cools slowly and remains viscous for a while, allowing the gases to ooze through a steadily solidifying "plastic" skin. In contrast, *aa* flows quickly and solidifies into sharp angular chunks of lava called scoria which can ruin your shoes.

DRAMATIC SEAS
ust south of L'Etang-Salé les ains, the RN1 cuts through jagged expanse of black va rock with views of ashing waves and water ts, known as *souffleurs*.

LUNAR LANDSCAPES
he area around the volcano d following the lava flows wn to the coast is an eerie oonscape of twisted basalt rmations – a truly triguing facet of the island.

◁ **SOLIDIFIED LAVA FLOW**
A river of lava runs through the Grand Brulé forest and into the sea.

▷ **OUR LADY OF LAVA**
In 1977, the volcano disgorged its molten lava into the coastal village of Ste-Rose, miraculously coming to a halt at the doorstep of the village church.

PLACES

A detailed guide to Réunion, with principal sites
clearly cross-referenced by number to the maps

If you've just flown in from Mauritius, the contrast in landscapes comes as a shock, confounding the idea of being on yet another Indian Ocean island. Instead of the low-lying fields and long stretches of beach that characterise the latter, you'll find awesome volcanic craters, rugged coastlines and lush gorges. Roland Garros, as modern as any airport in "la métropole", as the mainland is called, fully complements the Gallic spirit of the capital, St-Denis, with its brusque, business-like beat and traffic-packed boulevards. Apart from some attractive, tumbledown buildings and a couple of interesting art collections, however, there is not much to see or do here. Most people head straight for the west coast between St-Paul and St-Pierre where all the beaches are, but no trip to Réunion would be complete without a visit to the volcano and at least one of the cirques.

Thanks to the good roads, getting around is easy, either in a hire car or on the comfortable public buses. A smooth coastal highway goes all the way around the island and it's possible, though not necessarily advisable, to get round the island in a day. The stretch of road that runs between St-Denis and St-Paul, known as the Corniche, cuts a coastal route round powerful mountains towards the fashionable beaches of St-Gilles-les-Bains, but it is often choked with commuting cars. If you're not in a hurry you can take the high road that runs along the ridge. It's slower and more winding, but fantastically picturesque.

St-Gilles-les Bains, the self-styled "St-Tropez of the Indian Ocean", is a buzzing resort on the west coast. It's a good place to base yourself if you want to be by the sea, with plenty of bars and restaurants and all the facilities you need for watersports, but it does get crowded. At the far end of the island's western beach stretch is St-Pierre, one of Réunion's most pleasant towns and another good base, being within easy reach of the southeast coast and about an hour from Piton de la Fournaise.

The east coast areas around the town of St-André and the sleepy corner of St-Philippe are often neglected, but deserve more than a brief stop to explore the inland forests, volcanic wastelands, rugged seascapes and walking trails.

There's no doubt that the island's greatest assets lie inland. At the heart of the country you'll find mysterious mountains, jagged peaks and gorges, rivers and waterfalls, extinct craters, isolated villages and a temperamental volcano. For an altogether different experience, Hell-Bourg at the eastern edge of the Cirque de Salazie is a popular base for trekkers and adventurers. It is the starting point of the Piton des Neiges climb, and has some of the best-preserved creole architecture on the island. ❑

PRECEDING PAGES: locals on the beach at St-Gilles-les-Bains.
LEFT: sailing tours office in the port of St-Gilles-les-Bains.

ST-DENIS

Map on page 196

Sometimes called "Paris of the Indian Ocean", St-Denis is more like a provincial capital. Many people come just to gather information, but it's worth pausing to look at the lovely creole architecture

When French governor Regnault founded St-Denis in 1669, he chose a sheltered spot on the uninhabited north coast. Life for the first 77 inhabitants was dull and, save for the odd pirate or two who dropped by, fairly uneventful. Even when the headquarters of the French East India Company was transferred from the old capital, St-Paul, in 1738, the town still had little going for it, in spite of a hundredfold increase in population. Successive governors tried to turn the new capital into a maritime and military base, but it ended up as neither, and by the late 1950s the infrastructure was so poor that even tourists had a job finding a place to stay.

St-Denis

All that's changed, and St-Denis has transformed itself into a reasonably sophisticated capital of 140,000 people, and these days offers much that you'd expect from any major town in metropolitan France. The difference, of course, is the tropical setting. Splendid creole homes, sometimes ramshackle, often with grand wrought-iron gates and lush gardens, are one of the chief attractions to casual visitors. And while the restaurants may look typically French, you'll find *carri* (curry) and unfamiliar vegetables such as *chou chou* on the menu; and the dozens of small creole eateries offer all the local delicacies such as *samousas* and *bonbons piments* (fritters).

LEFT: La Préfécture.
BELOW: filigree woodwork is a feature of creole houses.

Spending a day in St-Denis will give you plenty of time to stroll the streets, visit the major sights, and to look accommodation in the interior if you need to. But two words of warning: St-Denis is not a cheap city, and there are better things to do and see elsewhere. If you want to base yourself on the coast, you would do better to plump for St-Gilles, Boucan-Canot or St-Pierre.

The waterfront

Your first glimpse of St-Denis will most likely be from the air. The plane descends into Roland Garros Airport 11 km (7 miles) east of the city, sweeping past dark mountains which must have struck awe into the hearts of the early settlers. Hemmed between the Rivière des Pluies and the Rivière St-Denis, the city spreads upwards on to the flanks of La Montagne where modern apartment blocks and luxurious houses have replaced the shanty town of the 1950s.

A good place to start is at the shaded waterfront promenade known as the **Barachois Ⓐ**. The area, once an inlet for unloading ships, had an adjustable jetty affixed to the shore by a set of iron chains which was raised or lowered above the sea to allow passengers to disembark; according to the writer T. V. Bulpin, they had to leap upon it with some display of acrobatics, with the thought of sharks if they slipped". The contraption was rendered useless during cyclones, and the iron pier which later replaced it was equally ineffec-

To order a bottle of the local Bourbon beer ask the barman for "un dodo".

tual; so the inlet was eventually filled in and planted with palm trees. Nine cannons face out to sea, placed there to symbolise St-Denis' supposed days as a military base. They are among Réunion's many coastal cannons that were either salvaged from shipwrecks or bought for decorative purposes by various governors.

Le Barachois is as chic as St-Denis gets, overlooked from across the busy Boulevard Gabriel Macé by Hôtel St-Denis and a handful of cafés and restaurants. Several former French East India Company warehouses survive here, in Place Sarda Garriga, with their facades still intact. One houses the town's oldest restaurant, the **Roland Garros** *(see Travel Tips)*, named after the famous aviator who was born in the capital. In another warehouse, on the other side of Hôtel St-Denis, is **La Maison de la Montagne**, where you can ask for advice, plan walking itineraries, book *gîtes* and so on. The huge relief model of Réunion on the wall conveys the island's dramatic topography, and provides plenty of inspiration to explore the cirques and volcanoes. You can buy IGN walking maps, books, crafts and a lot more at the **Caze de la Montagne** next door.

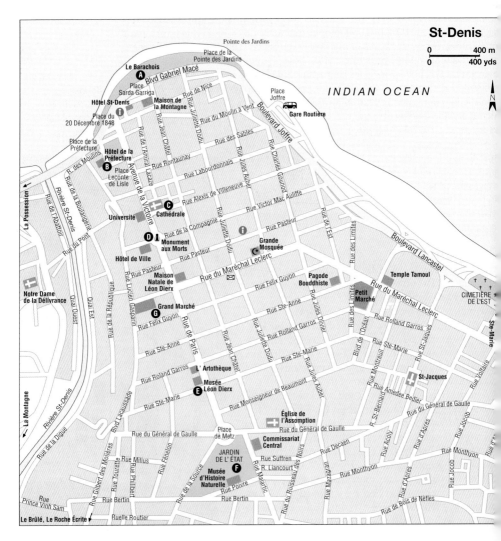

An architectural tour

A walk inland, south along Avenue de la Victoire, leads to some of the city's finest buildings. First is **Hôtel de la Préfecture** , an attractive colonial mansion overlooking pretty gardens. It began as a humble coffee warehouse, grew into the headquarters of the French East India Company and later became the official governor's residence. In 1942 it was occupied by Free French Forces, who arrived to rid the island of its Vichy sympathisers, closely followed by General de Gaulle. Later visitors included Giscard d'Estaing and Jacques Chirac. The Préfecture is closed to the public.

In the adjacent square, now used as a car park, a **statue of Mahé de Labourdonnais** stares solemnly out to sea. It was here that important announcements from the motherland were made, including the abolition of slavery in 1848. Labourdonnais is best remembered in Réunion for treating the island as a rather forgotten satellite when he was governor of the Mascarene Islands.

Three blocks beyond, past an uncharacteristically unobtrusive branch of McDonald's in a converted warehouse, is the 19th-century **Cathédrale** . It has some interesting bas-reliefs of St-Denis, but is not a beautiful building. The square out front, with its vast, twisted trees and 19th-century iron fountain, is more attractive.

As you head south, on the right in quick succession are several more notable colonial buildings, including the **Université**, built in 1759, but the best old buildings are still to come. The towering **Monument aux Morts** , which commemorates the death of over 1,000 Réunionnais who fought in World War I, marks the start of **Rue de Paris**, lined with some of the capital's grandest creole homes. Poet and landscape artist, Leon Dierx (1841–1912), was

Map
on page
196

In 1913 Roland Garros (1888–1918) became the first pilot to fly across the Mediterranean. Taken prisoner during World War I he escaped only to die in action a month before it ended. His statue stands outside the Hôtel St-Denis in Place Sarda Garriga.

BELOW: St-Denis Cathédrale in 1832.

TIP

Parking is not normally problematic in St-Denis. You may be lucky enough to find a space in Place Sarda Garriga. There is also a car park by the Grand Marché on Rue du Maréchal Leclerc, where you can park for one hour for free. There are also spaces by the Jardin de l'Etat.

BELOW: *Jeune femme au divan* by Berthe Marisot (1841–95).

born in one of them, and the **Musée de Leon Dierx ⓔ** (open Tues–Sun 9am–5pm; entrance fee; tel: 0262 20 24 82), in a fine colonnaded mansion just up the road, displays his work alongside original sculptures and engravings of rather more famous artists such as Cézanne, Gauguin, Renoir and Picasso, as well as work by other Réunionnais artists. Unfortunately, the museum earns money by lending its best works to foreign museums, but there is normally at least one Gauguin or Picasso piece on show. Next door, in another superbly restored 19th-century villa, regular exhibitions of modern art are held in the former Maison Mas, now **L'Artothèque** (open Tues–Sun).

A lesson in natural history

Rue de Paris ends at Place de Metz and the **Jardin de l'État ⓕ**. A golden age blossomed under botanist Nicolas Bréon, who came to Réunion in 1817 with a collection of European trees. From his continued expeditions to far flung places, he brought back the seeds with which to produce one of the most interesting botanical collections in the Indian Ocean. Two busts of green-fingered giants attest to the gardens' importance; Pierre Poivre who founded the Pamplemousses botanical gardens in Mauritius *(see page 120)* and Réunion-born botanist, Joseph Hubert, who brought back some useful spices from his travels. Labels cater to those interested in plants, while shady benches, the small café and space for *boules* are the main attraction for most locals.

The centrepiece of the gardens is the **Musée d'Histoire Naturelle** (Natural History Museum; open Mon–Sat 10am–5pm; entrance fee; tel: 0262 20 02 19), in the former Palais Législatif. The themed sections inside show how fauna survived before the arrival of humans, how it suffered under them and the mea-

sures that can be taken to protect already threatened species. Upstairs, a separate room devoted to Madagascar includes displays of stuffed lemurs. Centre stage is a moulded replica of a stuffed coelacanth, a prehistoric fish known only in fossil form until 1938, when a living specimen was caught off the Comoro islands. Other exhibits include stuffed specimens of the island's fauna, and reconstructed skeletons of extinct Mascarene birds, notably the solitaires of Réunion and Rodrigues, and the dodo.

Map on page 196

Shops and temples

Rue du Maréchal Leclerc is the centre of the shopping scene in St-Denis – though this isn't saying much. Most popular among visitors is the **Grand Marché ⊙** (open daily) at the street's western end, on the corner of Rue Lucien-Gasparin. This craft market caters mainly to tourists and lacks the buzz of most tropical markets, including the Petit Marché further east *(see below)*. But don't let this stop you trying to bargain with the traders, many of whose prices deserve to be reduced. You can't miss the tablecloths which are draped above many stalls, while down below you'll find *tentes* – shopping bags made from the dried leaves of the vacoas tree – t-shirts and crafts mostly from Madagascar.

East of Rue de Paris, the Rue du Maréchal Leclerc is partially pedestrianised and lined with shops catering to the everyday needs of the local people. Nestled among the shops, near the corner of Rue Jules Auber, is the **Grande Mosquée** (open daily 9am–noon, 2–4pm); the minaret is easier to locate than the entrance. For fruit and vegetables, people head east to the **Petit Marché**, at the end of Rue Ste-Anne. Just opposite the market is the **Chinese pagoda** (Pagode Bouddhiste) and on the other side of the market is the Tamil **Kalikambal Temple** (Temple

The Three Graces in the Jardin de l'État.

BELOW: the Natural History Museum, set in lovely grounds.

Map on page 196

TIP

Golfers can enjoy the mountain views and a challenging enough course at the Colorado leisure park. For information and reservations, tel: 0262 23 79 50.

BELOW: bird-of-paradise flower.
RIGHT: tending the gardens.

Tamoul), a madly colourful confection with lovely bas-reliefs of deities. To complete the religious medley, visit the 19th-century gothic **Church of St Jacques**, in the street of the same name nearby, just off Rue du Maréchal Leclerc.

You could take a detour to the seafront **Cimetière de l'Est** (Eastern Cemetery) about 3 km (2 miles) east of the Barachois, with early tombs and the communal graves of the thousands who died during the Spanish Flu epidemic of 1919. In a separate section are the unmarked graves of sentenced men, including one belonging to a Mr Zett, who was decapitated in Salazie in the early 1900s for taking part in an orgy of rape and pillage. Right-thinking citizens of the day, afraid that his soul would rise again to terrorise the population, ensured it wouldn't by sending his head to St-Denis.

Heading back to the waterfront from Rue du Maréchal Leclerc, you'll see some delightful creole homes along **Rue Juliette Dodu** and nearby streets. There are several restaurants and hotels in this area, too, including on Rue Pasteur, which also has the city's main **tourist office** (between Rue Dodu and Rue Auber).

Into the hills

If you have time for just one excursion from St-Denis, take a drive along the **Route de La Montagne**, a well-signposted road southwest of the capital on the D41. With enough switchbacks to make you dizzy, this scenic route gives a taster of Réunion's winding roads as well as panoramic views of the city. About 15 minutes along the route is the **Jardin de Cedrillon** (48 Route des Palmiers, La Montagne; entrance fee; tel: 0262 23 63 28), a garden with over 300 varieties of orchid, a profusion of variously coloured anthuriums and a garden of medicinal plants and spices. Don't worry about the huge but harmless armour-plated spiders (*nephila inorata*), known locally as the 'bib', spinning fine silky webs in the greenhouses. If they get too close for comfort, you can always sit outside surrounded by bird-of-paradise flowers and admire the views over St-Denis. The garden is in private hands and it is necessary to book a tour (minimum of 4 people) at the tourist office in St-Denis. The 1½-hour tours are in French, but an English interpreter can normally be arranged.

Of more popular appeal is the enormous outdoor leisure park at **Colorado**, just beyond La Montagne and about 30 minutes by car from St-Denis. The park gets busy with local picnickers at weekends, but also offers a range of activities from walking, mountain biking, horse-riding, tennis and even golf (9-hole).

For a wilder experience, you should head south along the D42 to the mountain village of **Le Brûlé**, from where you can explore the surrounding cryptomeria forests. A well-marked trail runs 4 km (2½ miles) – about 30 minutes – southwest to the lovely waterfalls of **Cascade Maniquet**.

A more challenging 18-km (11-mile) trek leads southwards from Le Brûlé to the 2,277-metre (7,468-ft) peak of **La Roche Écrite** for spectacular views of the Cirque de Mafate *(see page 225)*; allow a full day for this excursion starting from the car park at Camp Mamode (see IGN 1:25,000 4402RT Map St-Denis, Cirques de Mafate et de Salazie). ❑

St-Denis

Aérop
la Réu
Roland (

Pointe du Gouffre Les Brises
Ruisseau Blanc La Montagne Le Chaudron
La Grande Chaloupe Colorado Bellepierre
N1
Pointe de la St-Bernard Rivière St-Denis
Ravine à Malheur Le Dix-Septième St-François La Bretagne Ri
des
Pointe des Galets Le Camp Magloire Le Brûlé Piton Moka
La Ravine à Malheur Morne de Patates Fontaine
Le Port La Possession St-François 950
Belle Vue L'Espéranc
les-Ha
Ste-Thérèse Cascade Cascade
Pointe de la La Mare Maniquet du Chaudron
Rivière des Galets Ilet Lautret
Piton la Rivière St-Denis
des Galets Rivière des Galets
Baie de St-Paul La Plaine Dos-d'Âne
Le Bout de l'Étang Savannah Mon Repos Ilet Nourry Plaine des Plain
Le Bois de Nèfles Les Deux Bras Chicots
St-Paul 23 Le Ruisseau La Roche Écrite
Cimetière Marin Grande Fontaine Ilet Fougères 2277 Mare
Cap la Houssaye Bois Rouge Aurère CIRQUE à Mar
Cap Boucan Canot N1 Ilet à Malheur Grand-Ilet Vieille
Boucan Grotte des Le Guillaume Cayenne CIRQUE
Pointe des Aigrettes 21 Canot Premiers Français Le Bélier
L'Eperon Le Bernica Ilet des Orangers Ilet à Bourse DE Piton d'Ench
St-Gilles-les-Bains 20 Musée St-Gilles- Grand Place DE 1352
Cap des Chameaux de Villèle 22 les-Hauts Les Palmistes Ilet à Vidc
Villa Bourbon Villèle Roche Plate Ilet Cimendal SALAZIE
Jardin d'Eden Tan Rouge Piton Maïdo La Nouvelle Hell-E
L'Ermitage 2203 MAFATE Le Gros Morne
Hermitage-les-Bains La Saline 3013 Piton des Nei
La Saline-les-Hauts 3070
La Saline les Bains Le Barrage Marla Le Grand Bénare
Pointe des Trois Bassins Les Trois Bassins 2896 Ilets de
Le Bois de Nèfles St-Paul Ilet Fleurs Jaunes Bois Rouge
Conservatoire Botanique CIRQUE
Jardin de Mascarin Le Petit
Les Colimaçons La Chaloupe St-Leu Le Piton Rouge Cilaos Matarum
Bras Mouton 2401 DE Mare Sèche
Pointe des Châteaux 1190
Ferme Corail St-Christophe or Ilets du Bras Ilet à Cordes
Élevage de Tortues La Fontaine Étang-les-Hauts de St-Paul CILAOS
St-Leu 19 Le Cap Camélias Palmiste
Le Cap Lelièvre L'Étang St-Leu Peter Both Rouge
1190 La Fenêtre 1837
Grand Fond Le Pavillon
Stella Matutina les Hauts
Pointe au Sel ou Stella Le Plate Ilet Auréli
Pointe de Bretagne Les Makes 1392 Dijo
Le Gouffre Le Piton St-Leu Le Tan Rouge 17 Le Petit Serree
Le Portail La Le Grand Serré
Souffleur Les Canaux
Pointe du Portail N1 Les Bananes
Les Avirons Le Piton Rouge Entre-Deux Le Br
Bois Blanc Le Maniron Le Gol les Hauts de Po
Pointe des Avirons Les Canots Le Quatorz
18 L'Étang-Salé- Bellevue La Mare
L'Étang-Salé-les-Bains les-Hauts La Rivière Les Troisième
Pointe de l'Étang Salé Croc Nature Roche Maigre Les Quatre
Le Gouffre Park Le Camp du Gol Le Ouaki Cents
La Ravine Le Tam
St-Louis 16 des Cabris Condé
Exotica Les Cocos La Vallée Le
Pierrefonds Mon Caprice
N1
Caserne Basse Terre Bassi
Aerodrome les Hauts
de Pierrefonds Les Casernes
La Ravine Blanche St-Pierre
Pointe de la Ravine Blanche 15 Terre
Terre Sainte N2
Pointe du Parc La

INDIAN OCEAN

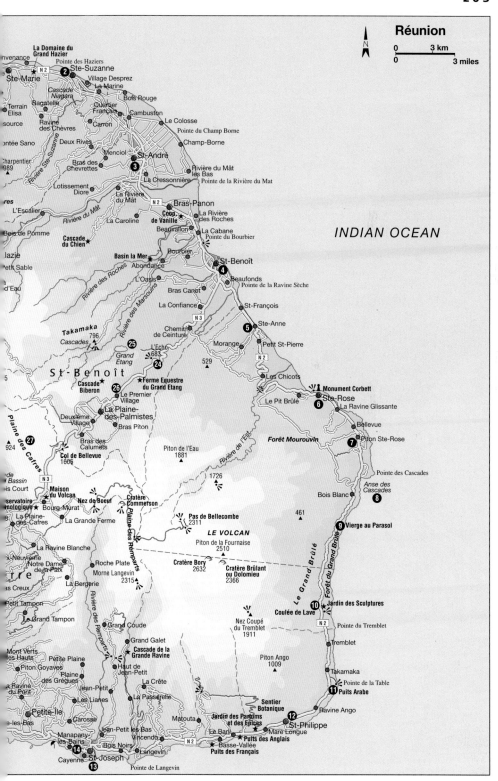

Réunion

0   3 km
0   3 miles

La Domaine du
Grand Hazier
nvenance   Pointe des Haziers
  N 2   ② Ste-Suzanne
Ste-Marie   Village Desprez
         Cascade   La Marine
         Niagara   Bois Rouge
Terrain Bagatelle   Quartier
Elisa   Français Cambuston
source   Ravine   Carron   Le Colosse
         des Chèvres   Pointe du Champ Borne
ontée Sano Deux Rives   Champ-Borne
                 Menciol
harpentier   Bras des   St-André
989   Chevrettes ③
                          Rivière du Mât
Lotissement   La Cressonnière les Bas
Diore   Pointe de la Rivière du Mat
res   La Rivière
L'Escalier   du Mât   **N 2** Bras-Panon
         Rivière du Mât   Coop. La Rivière
      La Caroline de Vanille des Roches
Bois de Pomme   Beauvallon La Cabane
         Cascade   Pointe du Bourbier
lazie   du Chien
lazie   Basin la Mer Bourbier
etit Sable   Abondance   St-Benoît
a   Rivière des Marsouins ④
d'Eau   L'Oasis   Beaufonds
              Bras Canot   Pointe de la Ravine Sèche
         La Confiance   St-François
Takamaka   **N 3**   Ste-Anne
796   Chemin
Cascades   de Ceinture ⑤
         ㉕ L'Echo   Morange   Petit St-Pierre
      Grand 683
      Etang ㉔   529   **N 2**
S t - B e n o î t   Les Chicots
      Cascade★   ⚡ Monument Corbett
      Biberon ㉖ Le Premier   Ste-Rose
               Village   Le Pit Brûlé ⑥
Deuxième La Plaine-   La Ravine Glissante
Village   des-Palmistes
              Bras Piton   Bellevue
㉗   Bras des   Forêt Mourouvin ⑦ Piton Ste-Rose
924   Calumets
      Col de Bellevue   Piton de l'Eau
      1606   1881
de   Pointe des Cascades
Bassin **N 3**   Anse des
s Court Maison   1726   Cascades
servatoire du Volcan Nez de Boeuf Cratère Bois Blanc
nologique★ Bourg-Murat Commerson   ⑧
La Plaine- La Grande Ferme Pas de Bellecombe 461 ⑨ Vierge au Parasol
des-Cafres   2311
         LE VOLCAN
La Ravine Blanche Piton de la Fournaise
X-Neuvième   2510
Notre Dame Roche Plate Cratère Bory
de la Paix Morne Langevin 2632 Cratère Brûlant
s Creux La Bergerie 2315   ou Dolomieu
Petit Tampon   2366   ⑩ Jardin des Sculptures
Le Grand Tampon Grand Coude Nez Coupé Coulée de Lave **N 2** Pointe du Tremblet
Mont Verts   du Tremblet   Tremblet
es Hauts Petite Plaine Grand Galet 1911
Piton Goyaves Cascade de la Piton Ango Takamaka
Plaine   Grande Ravine   1009
des Grègues Haut de   Pointe de la Table
a Ravine Jean-Petit La Crête   ⑪ Puits Arabe
du Pont Jean-Petit La Passerelle
      Les Lianes   Sentier
Petite-Ile   Botanique Ravine Ango
e-les-Bas Carosse   ⑫
      Jean-Petit les Bas Jardin des Parfums St-Philippe
Manapany- Vincendo et des Epices Mare Longue
les-Bains   La Bari Puits des Anglais
⑭ Bois Noirs Langevin **N 2** Basse-Vallée
Cayenne St-Joseph   Puits des Français
⑬   Pointe de Langevin

INDIAN OCEAN

THE COAST

Discover the extremes of Réunion's coast on the Route Nationale, from sugar fields and volcanic wastes in the east to coral-fringed beaches in the west, with a handful of interesting towns in between

Map on pages 202–3

There's little doubt that Réunion's main attractions lie inland. Compared to the lush interior, the coastal area is dry and scrubby, particularly in the west and south, but it does have a handful of interesting towns and a few stretches of sandy beach. You can drive around Réunion's 207 km (128 miles) of coast in a day thanks to one well-asphalted road, the Route Nationale (RN1), but it is worth spending at least two or three days exploring. Most of the towns have decent accommodation and tourist offices, and several are natural gateways to the cirques and other inland excursions.

The most popular coastal stretch is on the west coast between St-Paul and St-Pierre where all the beaches are, but don't neglect the area around the eastern town of St-André and the southeast corner around the sleepy hideout of St-Philippe, whose inland forest, volcanic wastelands, rugged seascapes and walking trails deserve more than a brief stop.

Driving along the Route Nationale is reasonably straightforward, though it's perfectly possible to tour the coast on one of Réunion's comfortable public buses *(see Travel Tips)*. There are stretches of dual carriageway, but this often reduces to single lane traffic through towns, when impatient local drivers tend to hang on your tail desperate to pass. If you are planning to drive through St-Denis, try to avoid travelling between 8am and 10am when the road into and out of the capital is clogged up with commuter traffic.

LEFT: La Corniche, France's most expensive stretch of road.
BELOW: catch of the day.

On the sugar and spice trail

The gently sloping plains east of **St-Denis ❶** were transformed into vast sugar plantations during the colonial era, and cane still smothers the area today. The other legacy of those early entrepreneurs are the grand houses that they built for themselves. One such is **La Domaine du Grand Hazier** (open for pre-booked guided tours only; tel: 0262 52 32 81; entrance fee), just 3 km (2 miles) west of **Ste-Suzanne ❷**, which was opened to the public in 1998. Concealed at the end of a palm-lined road, the 18th-century mansion contains original furniture and paintings and is surrounded by lush vegetable gardens and orchards.

Sugar production boomed in Réunion between 1815 and 1832, but when slavery was abolished in 1848 plantation owners had to source labour from India. Waves of immigrants arrived as contract workers, and today many of their descendants still live in the area between Ste-Suzanne and St-André. Some of these work at the sugar factory at **Bois Rouge**, where an old plantation house survives, too (open for guided tours only during the sugar season – Aug to Nov. Tours can be arranged on 0262 58 59 74. Several temples nearby catered to the spiritual needs of the

Réunion is one of the world's leading producers of vanilla.

Indian sugar workers, including an impressive **Tamil temple** tucked away in the fields beside the Rivière St-Jean, just west of Bois Rouge, and three others nearby at **Le Colosse** on the coast.

Quartier Français, just south of Bois Rouge, was home to Réunion's first settlers, back in 1656, and to one of the oldest sugar factories, which once formed part of the vast Kerveguen sugar empire. The factory, in Avenue Raymond-Verges, closed in 1981 but is worth visiting for the finely preserved chimney.

St-André ❸, 10 km (6 miles) from Ste-Suzanne and about 30 minutes' drive from St-Denis, is the gateway to the Cirque de Salazie *(see page 227)*. It is a pleasant enough town, with a buzzing main street and a couple of interesting sights. Foremost among these is **La Maison de la Vanille**, in Rue de la Gare one block north of the main street (open Tues–Sun 9am–5.30pm; guided tour only; entrance fee; tel: 0262 46 00 14), where you can follow the stages of production of the precious vanilla pod; the plantation produces pods in sufficient quantities not only to stock its own shop but also to export. The tours are informative, and the shop sells vanilla-flavoured everything. The **Vanilla Cooperative** (tel: 0262 51 70 12) in nearby Bras-Panon also offers tours of its factory and grounds.

On the ocean side of the Route Nationale, you can take Chemin Lagorgue to the coast. At the seafront turn right for **Champ-Borne**, where you can see the remains of a 19th-century church, seriously damaged by Cyclone Jenny in 1962 when huge waves swept inland and partially destroyed the cemetery.

From St-Benoît to Ste-Rose

The next bead in the necklace of coastal towns, **St-Benoît ❹**, is of scant interest unless you like ghost stories. The ghost of local mayor, Louis Brune

(1847–1905), whose mausoleum is behind the town's 19th-century church, is said to wander through the town. For many people, St-Benoît simply marks the Route Nationale's junction with the N3, which heads up to the high plains and volcano (see page 217). If all you want is a taste of the interior, you could take the D53 which runs 15 km (10 miles) along the course of the **Rivière des Marsouins** to Takamaka and the lovely **Cascade de l'Arc-en-Ciel** (and hydro-electric complex).

Map on pages 202–3

Ste-Anne ❺, 5 km (3 miles) beyond St-Benoît, would seem an unlikely place to feature in a film if it weren't for its church, whose intricate, baroque-style stonework must have appealed to François Truffaut; he used it in *La Sirène du Mississippi* (1968), starring Catherine Deneuve and Jean-Paul Belmondo. The church dates from the 19th century, but the extraordinary carving was done in the first half of the 20th century by a group of Tamil craftsmen.

From Ste-Anne the road winds inland to the foothills of the volcano, crosses the 1893 suspension bridge over the Rivière de l'Est, and then descends to the small fishing town of **Ste-Rose** ❻. In 1809, British men o' war tested the town's defences just before they took the island from the French; on the waterfront here is a monument to Commodore Corbett, second-in-command of the British fleet, who died in one of the skirmishes. Ste-Rose is constantly under threat from the volcano which, in April 1977, twice disgorged its molten lava into the next village of **Piton Ste-Rose** ❼, destroying some 20 houses. People watched entranced as the lava flowed around the church, now known as **Notre Dame des Laves**, without destroying it, and instead hardened to form a thick black girdle – still visible today – around the building. Newspaper cuttings inside the church reveal that some villagers saw their lucky escape as "God's miracle". Local artist, Guy Lefèvre, made the stained-glass windows.

For the calm and quiet of a spectacular seascape, follow the signs south from Piton Ste-Rose for 3 km (2 miles) to the turn-off for **Anse des Cascades** ❽. Here, waterfalls tumble from towering cliffs into a shaded bay where fishermen sell their catch on the jetty. The secluded restaurant makes a perfect lunch stop and at weekends the cool forests of coconut trees are popular with picnickers.

Volcanic wasteland

By far the most dramatic coastal scenery of Réunion can be seen along the next stretch of road to St-Philippe, as the RN2 negotiates the southeast corner of the island, skirting an immense volcanic ravine known as **Le Grand Brûlé**, formed by the lava flow from Piton de la Fournaise and Les Grandes Pentes (the steep slopes). Every now and then, barren wastes of solidified lava indicate the progress of previous eruptions. Just inside the ravine, soon after **Bois Blanc**, you'll see the flower-bedecked shrine of the **Vierge au Parasol** ❾ by the side of the road. This was erected by a 19th-century landowner who believed that it would protect his vanilla plantation from the fury of the volcano. The Virgin was clearly unimpressed because when the mighty volcano blew he lost the lot.

There are several red shrines to St-Expédit (see page 208) in the area. One lies right beside a **lava**

TIP

About 2 km (1 mile) south of Ste-Suzanne is the 30-metre (98-ft) Cascade Niagara, a mini version of the Niagara Falls and a good place for a dip. Go midweek unless you are happy to share the pool with plenty of locals, for whom this is a popular picnic place.

BELOW: Vierge au Parasol – the Virgin with the Umbrella.

flow **⑩** *(coulée de lave)* which cut off the RN2 in 1998 turning the area into an instant tourist hot spot. The nearby **Jardin des Sculptures** features phallic symbols fashioned in cement and volcanic scorie by local sculptor, J. C. Mayo.

If you stay on the coast road you'll be treated to more moonscapes of hardened black lava at **Puits Arabe ⑪**, where information boards (in French) describe the sequence of events which resulted in the evacuation of 500 people as lava flowed in four stages between 19 and 30 March in 1986, coating the slopes of **Takamaka** above the village before stabilising itself just 300 metres (980 ft) from the road. You can scramble for 200 metres (650 ft) over the solidified lava to **Pointe de la Table**, where another lava flow from the same eruption extended the island by 25 hectares (62 acres) into the sea, or opt for a lengthier 5-km (3-mile) trek northwards towards **Tremblet**, crossing cliffs where an 18th-century lava flow gives a good example of the structures of cooling.

St-Philippe to St-Joseph

Rugged, ragged and fierce best describes the south coast, where screw pines torn by warm winds watch over wild seas beating against black basalt cliffs. The sleepy little town of **St-Philippe ⑫** is a good place to break after your journey through the volcanic wastelands of the east coast and stock up on supplies if you need to. It has some interesting examples of creole architecture and, in addition to a helpful tourist office, there are roadside eateries that provide ready-packed baguettes and other snacks – perfect fodder to take on a walk up into the hills.

West of town, tracks head inland from Mare Longue, Le Baril, Basse-Vallée and Langevin, some of them running all the way up the flanks of the volcano. If you aren't keen on the idea of a major hike, the forest inland from **Mare**

ISLAND SAINT: ST-EXPÉDIT

St-Expédit is a relative newcomer to the world of sainthood and probably reached such heights more through folklore than by holy deeds. He started out as a Roman soldier, was made a martyr for his Christian beliefs and was revered in Germany and France for his power to produce fast solutions. In the 1930s, those powers were put to the test when a Réunionnais woman keen to leave Marseilles prayed that a boat would appear to take her home. Whether or not it was thanks to convenient sailing schedules, she soon arrived clutching a statue of St-Expédit, and his reputation for prompt action spread.

In the 1960s, blood-red shrines to St-Expédit appeared in cemeteries and caves, along the roadsides and beside statues of the Virgin Mary. Viewed with suspicion by the Catholic clergy, St-Expédit has achieved cult status because many locals call upon him to do good or harm.

The biggest shrine is at Mare Longue at St-Philippe in the south, but there are over 300 elsewhere which contain burned-down candles, flowers, fruit or cigarettes as inducements to expedite a problem or to thank him for his intervention. Some contain beheaded statues, presumably the work of unhappy locals, but most bizarre are the shrines draped in underwear.

ongue, just west of St-Philippe, is easy to explore. Here, the forest spreads over 0 hectares (173 acres) and includes pandanus and casuarina trees entwined 'ith vanilla creepers, mixed evergreens *(bois de couleurs)* and tall edible palms. are plants can be seen along the Sentier Botanique, but if you have more time, sk the St-Philippe tourist office (Rue Leconte-Delisle; tel: 0262 37 10 43) to rganise a visit to the **Jardin des Parfums et des Epices**, where orchids, moss nd ferns grow wild among aromatic plants.

At **Basse-Vallée** tiny creole houses in flower-filled gardens cram the roadside ke cardboard cut-outs from a children's story book. A couple of kilometres east 'ong the route nationale is **Hôtel Le Baril**, the only place to stay along this :mote coast. It is flanked by two lava wells, Puits des Anglais and Puits des rançais. The story goes that one of them contains a treasure chest watched over y the spirit of a dead slave, but which one may be a matter for Anglo-French ebate. Try asking the boss at the hotel; he claims to know the answer.

There's not much to see at the next town of **St-Joseph ⓭**, but it is the start-ıg-point for a challenging trek up the gorgeous valley of the **Rivière des .emparts** – the river which flows through the town and whose source is 30 km ა9 miles) north at **Nez de Boeuf** *(see page 218)*. Experienced hikers only iould try this two-day uphill trek along the Rivière des Remparts. The path om St-Joseph traverses some of Réunion's original lowland forest before the ınal, tough climb up to the Nez de Boeuf. Along the way there's a *table d'hôte* ı the isolated hamlet of **Roche Plate** en route (19 km/12 miles) provides ıeals and overnight accommodation (book ahead: tel 0262 59 13 94).

If you want views without the effort, a road runs halfway up the valley, on ɛ eastern side, to **Grand Coude**.

Map on pages 202–3

BELOW: solidified lava flow.

Between May and December you can see (and smell) the vetiver plant, which grows around St-Joseph. The essential oil of the vetiver is used in the perfumery industry, and the leaves can also be dried to make thatched roofs. You can buy bundles of vetiver in some markets, which, if placed among your clothes, give off a pleasant aroma.

BELOW: locals moor their boats at Bassin de Radoub.

The pebble beach at **Manapany-les-Bains** , 3 km (2 miles) west of St Joseph, and the sandy beach at Grande Anse, beyond, are often dangerous due t the fierce currents, but there are natural pools among the rocks where it is saf to swim. If you want to treat yourself to some fine creole and sea food, try **L Cap Méchant** at Basse-Vallée. Although pricey, this is one of the best restauran on the island, and also offers spectacular sea views. You'll get more great view as you head west over the impressive Manapany ravine en route to St-Pierr

Forgotten St-Pierre

St-Pierre , which lies on a wide coastal plain at the mouth of the Rivièr d'Abord, is the largest settlement in the south, with 55,000 inhabitants. It one of Réunion's most pleasant towns, and makes a good base, being we placed for reaching the southeast coast, just 45 minutes' drive from St-Gille les-Bains on the west coast, and about an hour from Piton de la Fournaise.

The town sometimes receives the full fury of cyclones raging in from the India Ocean; in 1990, Cyclone Firinga left it nearly in ruins, but a face-lift ensued: a ne port was built and an airport at Pierrefonds opened nearby, bringing in a fresh wav of tourists, mainly from Mauritius. St-Pierre's waterfront restaurants, late-nigh bars and discos, choice of hotels and adequate (but windy) beach attract islande from as far away as St-Denis. The port is packed with fishing boats and pleasu craft and is fun to stroll around; on one side is the pretty **Bassin de Radoub** a small creek where boats were careened in the 19th century which is now a hi toric monument. Just behind it is the old railway station which houses the touri office (open Mon– Fri 8.30am–5.15pm, Sat 9am–3.45pm), and trendy **Café de Gare** *(see Travel Tips)*. If you haven't time to sit down, there is normally a clu

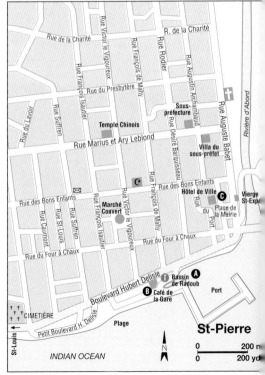

St-Pierre

er of snack vans beyond the car park, selling drinks, fried snacks and filled
aguettes. There are several restaurants on the other side of the seafront Boulevard
Iubert Delisle, directly opposite the port.

It is worth having a quick stroll around the town. The restored **Hôtel de Ville ☉**,
former East India Company building, is a fine example of colonial architec-
ire, and further west on Rue Victor le Vigoureux you'll find a very attractive
narket – an unusual circular structure. The Marine Cemetery, at the western end
f Boulevard Hubert Delisle is a lovely flower-filled cemetery, which contains
ne grave of Sitarane one of Réunion's most notorious bandits, said to have
runk the blood of his murdered victims. Each night, offerings of cigarettes
nd headless black cocks or fruits and flowers are left as an inducement to
itarane to bring mishap, misfortune or even worse to enemies. Nocturnal visits
re for the courageous.

Six kilometres (4 miles) west of St-Pierre, inland along the D26 towards
ntre-Deux, are the quirky gardens of **Exotica** (open Mon–Sat 9am–5pm;
ntrance fee; tel: 0262 35 65 45), which children at least should enjoy. Winding
athways are lined with cacti and curious papier mâché creatures, from
inosaurs and dragons to giraffe and giant frogs. There's a hothouse of anthuri-
ms and orchids, entered through the belly of an enormous stone gorilla.

St-Louis ⑯, the next town along, is the starting-point of the winding RN5 to
ne Cirque de Cilaos *(see page 229)*. However, for a glimpse of the cirque with-
ut the long drive, you could take the D20 which runs 12 km (7½ miles) inland
om St-Louis to **Les Makes ⑰**. This tiny village, situated at 1,000 metres
,280 ft), is home to **L'Observatoire** (18 rue Georges Bizet; tel: 0262 37 86 83;
pen daily 10.30am–2.30pm; entrance fee), where you can study the stars on a

Maps:
Area 202
City 210

TIP

In St-Pierre there is
plenty of room to park
under the trees right
next to the old railway
station.

BELOW:
picnic en famille.

guided tour, or attend a special night show. Ten kilometres (6 miles) beyond L Makes, along the wildly twisting RF14, you'll come to **La Fenêtre**, a natur window on to Cilaos cirque. If you arrive before the mid-morning mists yc should get glorious views.

Take the high road

If you've experienced the white beaches and lagoons of Mauritius you ma find Réunion's coast disappointing. The beaches are clean but small and get s crowded at weekends that you may wonder if it's worth the bother. Mid-wee however, the beaches are a delight, and at any time of the week there are se eral tourist attractions inland that are well worth a visit.

L'Etang-Salé-les-Bains ⓲ marks the beginning of the west coast beac stretch, but it is very quiet, with just a couple of hotels and restaurants, and tl 5-km (3-mile) black sand beach is not particularly picturesque. If you hav children, you could take them 2 km (1 mile) up the hill to the **Croc Natu Park** (open daily 9.30am–5.30pm; entrance fee; tel: 0262 91 40 41) in L'Etan Salé-les-Hauts. In addition to the 180 Nile crocodiles (brought from Mad gascar), there are farm animals, duck ponds and peacocks, as well as a mod Réunion village, complete with town hall, post office and church. A tour of tl park takes about an hour; there is a snack bar and a shop.

The 2-km (1-mile) trip south along the coast road from L'Etang-Salé-les-Bain to **Le Gouffre** is likely to be of more universal appeal. Here, you can witness tl ferocity of the Indian Ocean as the waves crash against the basalt cliffs. Tl RN1 slices through jagged black lava rock close to the shore for the next 22 k (13½ miles) to St-Leu. You'll pass a couple of laybys on the way where you ca stop for spectacular views of *souffleurs* (blowhole where, if the the sea is rough enough, tall jets of wat spurt through the rocky crevices. For a different pe spective, consider taking the high road (the D1 between L'Etang-Salé and St-Leu via **Les Aviron** Known as the Allée des Flamboyans, this is a deligh ful route and also offers lovely views of the coas Keep your eyes on the road, however, as it twists an turns and local drivers like to move at speed. Ju before you rejoin the RN1, you'll pass the Stel Matutina museum *(see below).*

Surfers' spot

The town of **St-Leu** ⓳ witnessed a slave revolt i 1811, survived a cholera epidemic in 1859, and ha been hit by several devastating cyclones, but othe wise life here is reasonably uneventful and easygoin The large, black-sand beach accommodates the wee end crowds reasonably well. When the conditions a right, surfers flock here to ride what are reputed to t some of the best waves in the Indian Ocean. The be spot is near the mouth of the **Ravine des Colimaçon** north of the town centre. In addition to the beach the are several attractions in the vicinity of St-Leu, so it worth devoting at least a half day to the town.

The church of **Notre Dame de la Salette** was bui in the town in honour of the Virgin who the Réunio nais believe saved the lives of the people of St-Le

Map on pages 202–3

hen the 1859 cholera epidemic swept the island. Every September, there is a estival in her honour, which culminates in a pilgrimage to the church.

About 4 km (2½ miles) south of St-Leu along the Avirons road is **Stella Matutina** (open Tues–Sun 9.30am–5.30pm; entrance fee; tel: 0262 34 16 24), former sugar factory and now a fascinating museum devoted to the history of ugar production and agriculture on the island. If you aren't interested in all he machinery, you can take refuge in the history room hung with original maps nd oil paintings of sugar barons. Set in a sloping meadow opposite is an Ostrich Farm (open daily 9am–6pm; entrance fee; tel: 0262 34 00 05).

At the **Ferme Corail** (open daily 9am–6pm; entrance fee; tel: 0262 34 81 10), km (1 mile) north of St-Leu on the RN1, thousands of hawksbill and green ea turtles at varying stages of maturity, live in tanks. The farm claims to be a tudy and observation centre, concentrating on breeding and feeding habits, but he shop sells tinned turtle soup and turtle meat as well as a range of souvenirs nade from turtle leather; remember that your home country may well prohibit he import of turtle products.

Virtually opposite the Ferme Corail, the D12 runs uphill to Les Colimaçons nd the **Conservatoire Botanique Jardin de Mascarin** (open Tues–Sun am–5pm; entrance fee; tel: 0262 24 92 27). This magnificent outdoor museum, hich contains 4,000 botanical species, offers an insight into Réunion's remark-ble flora and is landscaped into themed gardens of rare indigenous and endemic lants, plants introduced by early settlers, a collection of palm trees, an orchard f local fruits and an eye-popping enclosure of cacti. But the pièce de résistance the 19th-century villa, fully restored and filled with colonial furniture. You can lso visit the stables, hunting lodge and the old family kitchen, which now erves as a cafeteria. Next door to the gardens is the hurch of Les Colimaçons, which offers spectacular ews over the reef-fringed coastline.

To reach St-Gilles-les-Bains, you can choose etween the winding inland route via St-Gilles-les auts (and the fascinating Musée de Villèle: *see elow*), and the faster coastal route.

A visit to the Ostrich Farm near St-Leu is fun for kids.

he beach stretch

t-Gilles-les-Bains ㉔, dubbed the "St-Tropez of the dian Ocean", is the hub of Réunion's holiday scene, tracting hordes of local and French holidaymakers. his is the best place on the island in which to soak up e sun, enjoy all the pleasure of the sea, or just lie back d recover from a hard mountain trek. If that's all too date, then plenty of canyoning and paragliding oper-ors are on hand to book that jump of a lifetime down éunion's ravines and gorges. At night, the restaurants, rs and clubs that line – and spill on to – Rue General Gaulle come alive. The cast of characters from old-shioned hippies to trendy young locals are attracted the blend of gallic chic and creole insouciance that zes from the restaurants and bars.

One reason St-Gilles' broad, sloping beach is so pop-ar is that it has white, albeit rather coarse, sand. The cus of activity is north of the Ravine St-Gilles; it is re that most people gather to watch the sunset, some-ing of a local tradition. South of the ravine, the beach

BELOW: heading for the beach.

is not so nice but more peaceful – backed by holiday homes and pensions rather than loud bars and restaurants. The port in the mouth of the ravine is scattered with boats belonging to game fishing and scuba diving operators. Half a dozen game fishing boats depart on day trips to hook blue marlin, sailfish, tuna and sea bream October to May is the best time. If you're a first-time diver, enquire at Bleu Marine Réunion (tel: 0262 24 22 00), which also offers special packages for children.

If you have a car, park first and then walk to the beach, which is hidden from view by the shops and restaurants along Rue General de Gaulle. Parking is not always easy, though. There are a couple of small car parks on Rue General de Gaulle, but they are often full. A good place is the patch of ground just before the bridge crosses the ravine.

Loulou's bakery is a local institution.

Just five minutes' drive north of St-Gilles-les-Bains, **Boucan Canot** ㉑ is smaller and more laid back resort than its neighbour. Unlike in St-Gilles, most of Boucan Canot's cafés and restaurants are by the beach, so it's easier to potter off for a drink or snack in between stints on the sand. The sandy beach is clean but small, and can get crowded at weekends. Drivers should note that the main drag is one-way (north to south), and that the only place to park is either at the north or south end of the seafront.

A glimpse of times past

The **Musée de Villèle** ㉒ (open daily except Mon 9.30am–noon, 2–5pm; guided tour; tel: 0262 55 64 10) in St-Gilles-les-Hauts is the former family seat of the Desbassyns dynasty. Built in 1787, the house's most famous resident was Madame Desbassayns, a coffee and sugar baron and notorious matriarch, who is said to have inflicted horrific punishments on her slaves. The colonial mansion

ow houses memorabilia and family portraits, maps of slave ship routes and ne French East India furniture. The slave hospital in the grounds was established ot out of altruism but to conform to the law. Madame Desbassyns, who died in 846, is buried in Chapelle Pointue, next to the ruins of the estate's sugar mill.

On the RN1 at Hermitage-les-Bains, just south of St-Gilles-les-Bains, the **Jardin 'Eden** (open Tues–Sun 10am–6pm; entrance fee; tel: 0262 33 83 16) is another asis of calm away from the beach. Here, you can wander through orchards of fruit ees and spices, learn how to cure a hangover with medicinal plants, or settle for ome mysticism in the mini rice field surrounding the Zen garden.

t-Paul: the old capital

t-Paul ㉓ is a pleasant town less than 30 minutes' drive from St-Denis and well orth visiting. It is the island's original capital, and many historical buildings urvive, such as the Hotel de Lassays, now a fire-station, and Grand Cour, the bandoned home of the Desbassyns dynasty on the Route Royale. There are ves- ges of the old French East India Company, too, including the town hall, built in 767. But most holidaymakers come to St-Paul not for an historical tour, nor to lie n its long, black-sand beach, but to visit the **seafront market** held on Friday fternoon and Saturday morning. The crowd that flocks here is a lively mix of ourists searching for crafts, spices, baskets and other souvenirs and locals buying uit and veg, fish and other fresh produce. Numerous stalls and vans sell tasty nacks. Towards the end of the day, bands start playing, and people gather in the eachside bars to watch the sun disappear into the sea.

Don't miss the **Cimetière Marin**, set in a stunning position right by the beach ust south of the centre. Here lies the body of the Mascarenes' most notorious irate, Olivier Le Vasseur, alias La Buse ("The Buz- ard"), who was hung in St-Paul in 1730 *(see page 46)*. His grave, bang opposite the entrance, is marked y a simple skull and crossbones crudely etched on a asalt cross, and is apparently still visited by followers. resumably, they would not like the theory that La use's body isn't actually buried there – based on the ct that the cemetery did not exist in 1730.

a Corniche

ne 14-km (9-mile) stretch of the Route Nationale from -Paul to St-Denis is the busiest stretch of road in the lascarenes. Known as **La Corniche**, it's a dramatic de as you whizz beneath cliffs and through tunnels ly metres from the sea. The road converges over two rrow bridges as it crosses the enormous estuary of the ivière des Galets, by-passes **Le Port** and emerges at **a Possession**, where Governor Pronis took posses- on of Réunion in 1642, before continuing to St-Denis. ne piece that hugs the cliffs between St-Denis and Possession is said to be France's most expensive retch of road. It runs along the old railway line and the e place you can stop is at **La Grande Chaloupe**, te of one of Réunion's original railway stations. The il service stopped in 1963, but a Scafader 030T is eserved in the small **museum** (open daily 9am–5pm) remind you of the heavy locomotives which plied e southern route from St-Denis to St-Pierre. ❑

Map on pages 202–3

TIP

The road between Boucan-Canot and St-Paul is sandwiched between cliffs and the sea as it rounds Cap la Houssaye: it is sometimes closed in rough weather.

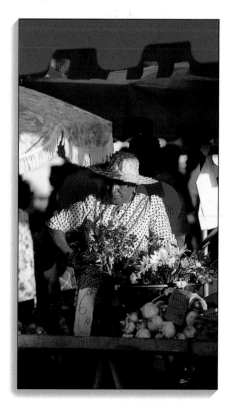

BELOW: waiting for customers at the St-Paul market.

VOLCANO AND HIGH PLAINS

Map on page 218

When Piton de la Fournaise trembles, both fear and excitement lure many to witness the great natural phenomenon. Most of the time, however, the volcano is an awesome but peaceful sight

St-Denis

The Piton de la Fournaise is one of the most active volcanoes on the planet; it has erupted at least 153 times since 1690 (the last eruption was in 2002), and the lava flows have left trails of destruction. For modern visitors, however, getting a close-up view of the smouldering volcano is reasonably safe and easy to do, provided, of course, that you stick to the marked route.

Born on the flanks of an extinct volcano called Piton des Neiges, between 500,000 and 600,000 years ago, Piton de la Fournaise, a twin shield volcano known to volcanologists as the Hawaiian type, rises to 2,632 metres (8,630 ft). It is surrounded by a horseshoe-shaped lava cliff enclosure, called Enclos Fouqué, which is 10 km (6 miles) in diameter and has two craters; the higher one, Bory, has been inactive since 1791, while the active Dolomieu manages, for most of the time, to confine its eruption within the enclosure.

Reaching for the top

Each year some 200,000 visitors make the journey up above the clouds to the top of the volcano. Most people drive to **Pas de Bellecombe Ⓐ**. Perched on the edge of the canyon-like Enclos Fouqué, it is a natural platform for spectacular views of Piton de la Fournaise across a wild and barren moonscape. Irrespective of whether you join an organised tour or make your own way, you should aim to reach the caldera before 10am, when cloud often descends to mask the volcano's wild beauty. But don't despair if you can't see a thing on the way up – or even when you reach the top. The area is subject to sudden climate changes which can go from swirling cloud and mist and sharp drops in temperature, to clear vistas across crisp blue skies. For this reason, you should also go equipped for all weathers. Good walking shoes are essential, and it can be chilly, so wear long trousers, take a jumper and don't leave your hotel without a waterproof.

The gateway to Piton de la Fournaise is **Bourg-Murat Ⓑ**, on the RN3, the only cross-island route, which links St-Pierre in the south and St-Benoît in the north. The journey from the two coasts takes about 40 minutes and an hour respectively. More a large village than a town, Bourg-Murat is home to the **Observatoire Volcanologique**, set up in 1979, from where eruptions can be viewed in complete safety. High-tech equipment records seismic activity so that these days the islanders have plenty of notice of an eruption. Bear in mind, however, that there was only a 45-minute warning of an eruption – albeit small – inside the Enclos Fouqué on 19 July 1999. If you're in Réunion to witness such a spectacle, expect to find droves of enthusiasts and experts jostling for the best positions with cameramen and reporters.

LEFT: Piton de la Fournaise…
BELOW: …"peak of blazing fire".

Bourg-Murat's other main attraction is the futuristic building of the **Maison du Volcan** (open Tues–Sun 9.30am–5.30pm; entrance fee; tel: 0262 59 00 26). Opened in 1991, this fascinating museum owes much of its collection to French husband and wife volcanologists, Maurice and Katia Krafft. Even if your French is not up to scratch, you can still learn about volcanoes through interactive video screens and a ten-minute film. There's also an art gallery, an exhibition on extra-terrestrial volcanoes, and recordings of Piton de la Fournaise eruptions.

The **Boutique du Volcan** next door sells all sorts of volcanic knick-knacks, from lumps of lava to posters, books and t-shirts commemorating particular eruptions. For a bite to eat the best place is the nearby **Auberge du Volcan**, which serves tasty creole curries.

For 20 years Maria and Maurice Krafft travelled the world filming and recording the eruptions of 170 volcanoes, and through scientific research papers they contributed to our understanding of how volcanoes work. They died in 1991 while watching an eruption of Mont Unzen in Japan.

Volcanic views

Most people are too eager to get to the top to even pause in Bourg-Murat on the way up. From here, it's 23 km (14 miles) and about 40 minutes' drive up to Pas de Bellecombe, but what an interesting route. The RF5 – or "Route du Volcan" – which heads east from Bourg-Murat, becomes gradually more winding as you leave the town behind and head ever upwards, sweeping through pine woods, dairy farms, small villages and alpine meadows. The road is not in mint condition but is paved for most of the way.

As you get higher, you will enjoy new, and often astonishing, views at every turn. Some of the best of these are at established viewpoints. (However keen you are to reach the top, if the sky is clear on the way up, don't resist the temptation to stop, as you never know when the clouds are going to roll in). The first of these, 7 km (4 miles) from Pas de Bellecombe, is at **Nez de Boeuf C**

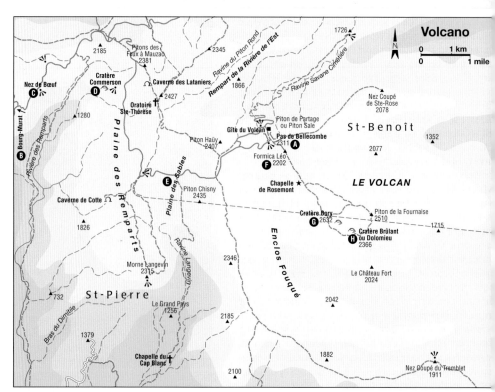

(2,070 metres/6,973 ft) from where there are absolutely staggering views of the huge ravine of **Rivière des Remparts**. From these heights, the river appears as a thin pencil line flowing southwards to St-Joseph. A challenging Grande Randonnée (GR) trail runs along the banks of the river from the coast and links up with the RF5 just beyond the Nez de Boeuf viewpoint; the 30 km (19 miles) trek is rather easier north to south than vice versa.

Map on page 218

Next stop is **Cratère Commerson ❹**, where an observation platform perches over a 120-metre (380-ft) deep crater, a few paces from the road. The extinct crater, named after French botanist, Phillibert Commerson, who discovered it by accident in 1771, is a dramatic sight. Most breathtaking of all, however, are the views across the crater's 200-metre (650-ft) diameter towards the jagged ridge of Cilaos cirque.

However, the view that is likely to remain etched on your memory for longest is the one from the top of the Rempart des Sables ridge where the road begins its dramatic descent into the **Plaine des Sables ❺**. An information board describes the landscape that spreads below you – an utter wilderness of raw beauty and incredible wide-angle views of corroded lava ground by the elements into fine black gravel and restrained by massive mountain ramparts and distant peaks. As the road descends across the eerie reddish-brown landscape, pockmarked with bizarre rock formations, the only signs of life are sparse bushes of gorse, heather and lichen and a trail of moving cars, before it climbs briefly to end at the parking area at Pas de Bellecombe. The track across the Plaine des Sables is unpaved but smooth and easy to follow; even so, drive slowly to avoid skidding, and be particularly careful in wet conditions.

A walk around earth's fire

Pas de Bellecombe is also the starting point of several walking routes to and around Piton de la Fournaise. In an unmanned shelter by the car park a few displays provide information on the geology and fauna and flora of the area. Most useful, however, is the relief model of the volcano which shows the routes (and distances) of the various walking trails. You don't really need a map for the more well-trodden circuits, such as Pas de Bellecombe to Cratère Dolomieu, but for more involved trekking you should invest in the IGN 1:25,000 series map 4406RT Piton de la Fournaise. You can buy this at the Maison de la Montagne in St-Denis, or pick it up at the Maison du Volcan in Bourg-Murat.

There is also a list of rules for walkers. The most important ones to heed are a) don't go alone, b) tell someone where you have gone and c) take water and food. The only refreshments and toilets in this remote spot are found at the **Gîte du Volcan**, about ten minutes' walk along a path from the car park. If you're driving, the track to the *gîte* branches left off the main track just before you reach the car park.

For the full experience you should consider doing the 13-km (8-mile) circuit, a "medium" classified trek, which takes about four and a half hours. (Alternatively, you could choose to do just part of the route; for example, the return walk to Formica Léo takes

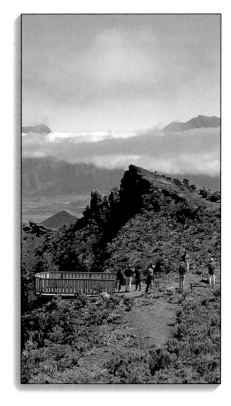

BELOW: spectacular views across Commerson crater.

BELOW: eerie moonscape of the Plaine des Sables.

about 40 minutes). Make sure you pack some energy-giving snacks and plenty of water. Provided you don't wander off the marked paths, heed the danger warning signs and wear the right clothes, you can't go wrong.

A stepped pathway winds its way down the 200-metre (650-ft) cliff to the bottom. On the way down take a good look at the plants that grow on the cliff face – beyond there is nothing but layers of lava from across the ages decorated with splodges of white paint that mark the entire route. The first landmark on the volcanic floor is the rather undramatic scoria cone of **Formica Léo ❻**. From here the path continues about 2 km (1 mile) to **Chapelle de Rosemont**, a hollow volcanic mound which looks like a small cathedral complete with a door and window – hence the name. This is a good place to rest and decide which of the two available paths you want to take. For the more strenuous route take the right-hand fork which will lead you directly up a steep slope to the extinct 2,632-metre (8,636-ft) high **Cratère Bory ❼**. Caution should be taken on the potentially unstable paths. The left-hand fork takes you to an easier route that snakes gently northwards along the contours of the volcano to **La Soufrière** (2,530 metres/8,300 ft), the northern wall of the active **Cratère Dolomieu ❽**; you can normally smell sulphur emissions here. There is another choice of routes here: one carries on along the rim of both Dolomieu and Bory before heading back to Pas de Bellecombe; the other, shorter route cuts across straight to Cratère Bory.

There is a whole series of other walks to do. One of the easiest is the 9-km (5-mile) walk north along the rim from Pas de Bellecombe to **Nez Coupé de St-Rose** and back. Another is the 8-km (5-mile) circular route from the Rempart des Sables to **Morne Langevin**; you should allow about three hours for this relatively easy but scenic route.

A BIRD'S-EYE VIEW

Réunion's scenery is awe-inspiring whatever angle you look at it from, but the aerial views you get from a helicopter of Piton de la Fournaise, and the Cirque de Salazie and Cirque de Mafate *(see following chapter)*, are hard to beat. These tours may be expensive, but they are worth every euro. Pilots fly in and out of deep ravines and hover precariously over isolated hamlets and the cirques, allowing plenty of time for photographs, before heading east to the volcano.

Depending on weather conditions helicopters, seating up to eight passengers, take off at 7am, 8.15am and 9.30am. The price includes transfer from your hotel, individual headphones and commentary (in French), but you should try to book at least 72 hours in advance since these flights are extremely popular.

Héli-Réunion (tel: 24 00 00) operates 25-minute flights exclusively to the volcano from Roland Garros airport, St-Gilles-les-Bains and Pierrefonds (just west of St-Pierre) for around €130 per person. Individual tailor-made trips, which are ideal for professional photographers, can be organised through Felix ULM (Base ULM de Cambaie, St Paul; tel: 0262 45 58 38) in specially equipped two-seater microlights.

Among the other much longer routes you could opt for, are treks along sections of the Grande Randonnée R2 which crosses the island (IGN 1:25,000 series map 4406RT Piton de la Fournaise). One of these follows the southern edge of the volcano to **Nez Coupé du Tremblet** before descending to Pointe du Tremblet on the east coast. Another heads south from Pas de Bellecombe on the GR2, across the so-called Plateau de Foc Foc to link up with the **Vallée Heureuse** and the Gîte de Basse Vallée, before continuing all the way to the town of Basse Vallée on the coast.

Map on pages 202/3, 218

Not so plain plains

The High Plains (Hautes Plaines) that separate Piton de la Fournaise and the three cirques may lack volcano-style drama but are still well worth exploring. Centred around La Plaine-des-Palmistes (named after the palm trees that no longer grow there) and La Plaine-des-Cafres in the west, these upland areas reveal magnificent mist-enshrouded forests, waterfalls, lakes and mountains, too: in short, perfect terrain for tranquil walks, scenic drives and more active pursuits such as horse-riding and mountain biking. The route described below runs in a north-south direction from the coast. A number of villages on the way, such as Le Vingt-Troisieme (23rd) and Le Dix-Neuvieme (19th), have been named unimaginatively after their distance in kilometres from the sea, but at least they're handy landmarks.

From St-Benoît, the RN3 meanders through sugar cane fields before hitting a series of switchbacks that lead to a viewpoint at **L'Echo ㉔**, which offers fine views north towards the coast and the ocean. Before the road winds up to L'Echo, about 12 km (8 miles) from St-Benoît, a track runs 6 km (4 miles) west

Gorse, heather and lichen are the only plants to sprout from the black earth.

BELOW: at the rim of the Formica Léo.

to **Grand-Etang** ㉕, a lake in a most stunning spot at the foot of an awesome ridge. To prolong the pleasure, you can follow the path right around the shores of the lake; there's a waterfall just off the path near the southern shore.

Beyond L'Echo you hit La Plaine-des-Palmistes, a popular holiday retreat, particularly in January and February. Even so, the area remains a comparatively untouched agricultural heartland where the red-berried goyavier fruit has become so important that every summer there is a festival in its honour. Attractive wooden houses are very characteristic of this area; you'll see them featured on postcards and posters. **Le Premier Village** ㉖, 20 km (12 miles) from St Benoît, is centre of operations, and is often referred to as **La Plaine-des-Palmistes**. You may want to stop here to make use of the tourist office in Rue de la République, which can supply details of accommodation and walks, ranging from gentle to strenuous, in and around the forests of Bébour *(see opposite)*.

Mountain gîtes dotted around the interior provide basic accommodation for walkers, but book in advance.

Horse-riding and forest-walking

To the northeast of Le Premier Village, a dozen gentle Merens horses wait at the **Ferme Equestre du Grand Etang** (RN3 Pont-Payet; tel: 0262 50 90 03), to take even the most inexperienced rider for a pleasant half-day's trek. A morning with Rico Nourro, a former farmer who turned his love of the outdoors into a going concern, should not be missed. His enthusiasm is infectious as he leads groups of riders along rocky narrow pathways to the stunning lake of Grand Etang where the horses take a break and splash about in the cool water. The trek takes you along a nature trail, passing through a garden of traditional medicinal herbs and citrus orchards where you can help yourself to fruit without getting out of the saddle. Rico believes in giving all his clients a hands-on experience,

BELOW: hosing down the horses after a day's trek.

so you'll be expected to prepare the horses before the ride and hose them down afterwards. Four-day rides to the volcano can also be arranged.

For a gentle 2-km (1-mile) walk, take the marked path from Le Premier Village which passes through boulder-filled streams, leading to the 240-metre (787-ft) high **Biberon** waterfall. There are a number of longer hikes through the **Forêt de Bébour**, noted for the endemic tree, *tamarin des hauts (Acacia heterophylla)* which contrast in height and huge girth with the indigenous *bois de couleurs* or mixed evergreens and imported cryptomerias. For an in-depth look at this forest which merges with the silvery tamarind forests of **Bélouve** and the rain-soaked gorge of Takamaka to the north, you'll need to spend a full day exploring the numerous trails and spend the night at the Gîte de Bélouve, about a 2-hour trek to the east of Hell-Bourg in Salazie cirque (be sure to book well in advance through La Maison de la Montagne in St-Denis). Serious trekkers should equip themselves with the IGN 1:25000, no 4405RT map.

Cross-country road

To see La-Plaine-des-Palmiste's luxuriant vegetation head southwards along the RN3, stopping after a 6-km (4-mile) upward sinuous drive to a parking-cum-picnic viewpoint called **Col de Bellevue**. Continuing southwards along the RN3, the road straightens across **Plaine des Cafres** ㉗, once the hideout of runaway slaves, where the pasturelands, dairy farms and cattle give it an alpine feel. Although the area has less charm than La Plaine-des-Palmistes, there are some memorable walks and a range of *chambres d'hôtes* and restaurants dotted along the RN3 to neighbouring Le Tampon. As you enter La Plaine-des-Cafres from Col de Bellevue, look out for the pretty flower-bedecked shrine to St-Expédit which looks strangely isolated as it stares across countryside towards Piton des Neiges. It's one of many dedicated to the Roman soldier *(see page 208)* who died for his beliefs, but this one is distinctly religious, unlike the dozens of his other red-daubed shrines which are often linked to black magic.

There's a lovely 5-km (3-mile) walk which goes from the village church of La Plaine-des-Cafres (also known as Le Vingt-Troisieme or 23rd) north to Bois Court and the waterfalls of Grand Bassin. They tumble into a deep gorge where three rivers – the Bras Sec, Bras de Suzanne and Bras des Roches Noires – meet along the southeastern foothills of the Cilaos cirque. Another possibility is to take a pleasant 9-km (5-mile) drive along the D36 from Le Vingt Quatrieme (24th) through Notre Dame de la Paix to the picnic area, where you can explore the surrounding forests and botanical paths overlooking the Rivière des Remparts.

The tortuous RN3 then descends to Le Tampon (from the Malagasy word *tampony* meaning "peak") to St-Pierre on the coast. Since 1830, when the land was bought by Gabriel de Kerveguen and developed into a sugar-growing area, Le Tampon has remained primarily agricultural. It also used to be the centre of a thriving geranium growing area, but in spite of Réunion essential oil being the best in the world for the perfume industry, production has fallen to 10 tonnes per year compared with 165 tonnes back in 1962. ❏

Map on pages 202-3

TIP

Tourist offices in the Hautes Plaines area are: Domaine des Tourelles, Rue de la République, Plaine-des-Palmistes (tel: 51 39 92) or Bourg Murat, 213 RN3, Plaines-des-Cafres. (tel: 59 08 92). Mon–Fri 9am–6pm, Sat, Sun and public holidays 10am–5pm; closed Tues.

BELOW: tree ferns in the Bébour Forest.

THE CIRQUES

Map on page 226

Only one road penetrates the cirques of Salazie and Cilaos, and you need a helicopter for Mafate. But the footpaths that festoon the dramatic landscape make this a paradise for walkers

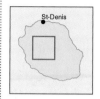

The spectacular natural showpieces of Mafate, Salazie and Cilaos are huge caldera-like valleys that radiate north, east and southwest in a clover leaf pattern, with the extinct volcano of Piton des Neiges at its centre. The three cirques became the home of runaway slaves *(marrons)* in the mid-18th century and later by impoverished white settlers *(petit blancs)*, who came up from the coast a century later. Here, they discovered awesome landscapes of jagged peaks, verdant gorges, rivers and waterfalls. As you take in the almost Dantesque panorama, it is hard not to wonder how those first slaves and settlers ever survived in such an environment.

By far the easiest of the cirques to get to, if you're on limited time, is the waterfall-strewn cirque of Salazie. Rains brought in by the southeast tradewinds ensure that the area is lush and green all year round, unlike Mafate, which is much drier. Unsurprisingly, Salazie is the most visited of the cirques and in the tourist season can get quite busy. If you're staying on the west coast, Cilaos appears deceptively close, but the drive from St-Louis is slow-going, and you should allow up to one and a half hours to negotiate the narrow and tortuous RN5. Whichever cirque you choose, weather conditions are very changeable, so so prepared for both sun and rain. Finally, make sure that you take enough euros with you as there are no banks in the cirques, although most restaurants and hotels in Cilaos and Salazie accept major credit cards.

LEFT: Salazie waterfalls.
BELOW: bungalow nestling in a ravine.

The lost world of Mafate

With no cars, no roads and no large shops, the **Cirque de Mafate** is a happy escape from the maelstrom of the outside world. Runaway slaves knew that their masters would have a very hard job getting there, and even today tourists face similar difficulties. The cirque's few hundred inhabitants live in a dozen scattered hamlets *(îlets)* linked by paths and tracks, and everyone, including the postman, walks.

Mafate is the least populated and least accessible of all the cirques, unless you take one of the dozens of hiking trails of the Grand Randonnée *(see pages 86–7)*. If you're on limited time, you can take a helicopter ride over hamlets and dizzying ravines before landing for an al fresco curry at La Nouvelle. Flights with Heli-Réunion *(see page 220)* leave every day from the heliport at Hermitage-les-Bains, near St-Gilles.

La Nouvelle ❶ is the most populated hamlet, with 130 inhabitants and three grocery stores, and has become the self-styled "capital" of Mafate, relying on tourism, small-scale cattle farming on Plaine des Tamarins, and geranium oil production, though the number of distilleries has dwindled over the years. It well worth the effort to trek as far as **Marla**,

Geraniums were first brought from South Africa in around 1870 and became an economic lifesaver for the petits blancs, who made a living cultivating them for essential oil.

Mafate's highest hamlet, if only to overnight in a *gîte* and wake early to catch the spectacular cloudless views. An alternative – and comparatively easy – route for trekkers is from Grand-Ilet in Salazie cirque *(see page 227)*.

If you're not a trekker, then you can still admire Mafate from its western rim at **Piton Maido ❷**, sometimes known simply as Le Maido. It is worth making an early start in order to arrive before clouds descend between 10 and 11am. From St-Paul or St-Gilles, you should allow up to two hours to drive the winding 25-km (16-mile) road to the top. The route takes you through the geranium-growing area of **Petite France**, and past numerous picnic places. A stunning panorama spreads before you at the Maido **viewpoint**, at 2,203 metres (7,222 ft). Looking from left to right you can see the peaks of La Roche Écrite (2,277 metres/7,469 ft), Le Cimendef (2,226 metres/7,301 ft) and Le Morne de Fourche (2,195 metres/7,200 ft) which separate the Salazie and Mafate cirques. The peaks of Le Gros Morne (3,013 metres/9,882 ft) and the Piton des Neiges (3,070 metres/10,070 ft) rise from the Salazie range of mountains mark

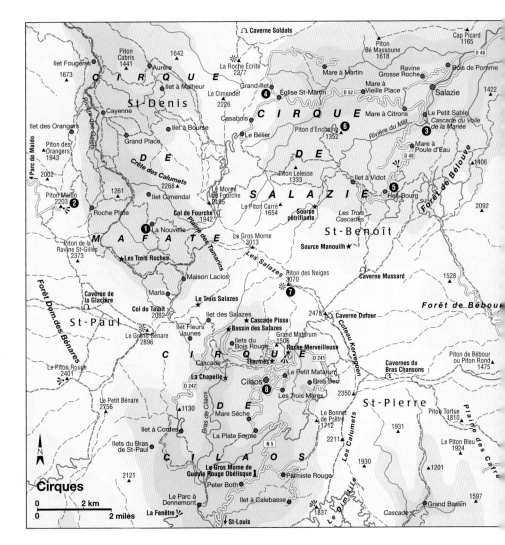

Cirques

0 ___ 2 km
0 ___ 2 miles

Map on page 226

ing the centre of the three cirques. To the south, Col du Taibit (2,082 metres/ 6,832 ft) and the peak of Le Grand Bénare (2,896 metres/9,499 ft) divide Mafate and Cilaos cirques, providing another stunning spectacle. You can hike along the rim of the cirque to Le Grand Bénare, but it's tough going, and you'll need to allow 6–7 hours to do the return trip.

For gentler walking, or a place to keep the kids happy, stop at **Parc du Maido** (open daily 9am–5pm; entrance fee; tel: 0262 32 52 52), a recreational centre about 15 minutes downhill from the viewpoint. You can go mountain biking or pony trekking through the tamarind forests, which are dotted with picnic sites, or stay put and try your hand at archery.

Easygoing Salazie

The name Salazie comes from the Malagasy word *salazane*, which means a 'stake" or "post", and probably stems from the three peaks of Le Gros Morne, which stand like sentries at the far southwestern corner of the cirque. The first European settler, a certain Monsieur Cazeau, lived in a home-made hut and made a name for himself by surviving on nothing but pumpkins during a 43-day period of rain. "When it rains at Salazie," noted one visitor in 1863, "it does rain…in a steady, business-like European way."

The ultimate high – paragliding over the Cirque de Mafate.

It still rains in Salazie, making it the most verdant of the cirques. These days the 25 villages carry on the farming traditions introduced in the 1840s, growing watercress, tobacco, coffee beans, apples and an abundance of *chou chou*. The lime green, pear-shaped vegetable *(see page 177)* is fêted each May in a three-day carnival which attracts many visitors to the colourful stalls groaning with local produce. It's a jolly affair with local music groups and a Miss Chou Chou contest.

BELOW: the cirques are strewn with isolated hamlets.

It does not take long, having left St-André behind on the coast, to get a taste of Salazie, as you enter the luxuriant, tree-clad gorge of Rivière du Mât, where soaring peaks and dozens of pencil-thin waterfalls fill the space above you. Some of the latter are mere trickles of water – but not the **Voile de la Mariée ❸** or "Bride's Veil", which positively cascades into the Rivière du Mât just beyond the village of Salazie. If you're driving take advantage of the handful of stopping places along the route to admire the scenery safely. The road is winding but mostly flat as far as Salazie; after that the climb is virtually continuous. There isn't much to Salazie, though it has a few shops and places to eat, and also a tourist office (in the *mairie*). For an on the hoof breakfast, you can pick up freshly baked brioches, croissants and pastries at the *boulangerie* in rue Père Boiteau.

Close to the Voile de la Mariée, the D52 branches off west and snakes for 34 km (21 miles) through the heart of the cirque to **Grand-Ilet ❹**, a hamlet overshadowed by the peak of La Roche Écrite. This is a base for treks into Mafate cirque, and has a handful of cheap *chambres d'hôtes*. Most walks kick off from **Le Bélier**, a hamlet 3 km (2 miles) south of Grand-Ilet (accessible by road), and follow the GR1 and GR2; one route penetrates south into Cilaos cirques *(for details on long treks, see pages 186–7)*. Alternatively, you can carry straight on to Hell-Bourg, a 30-minute

Decorative open-fronted extensions, known as guetalis, *are a common feature of traditional creole houses.*

winding drive above Salazie. There are two stunning viewpoints worth stopping at – one at **Mare à Poule d'Eau**, and the other at **Le Point du Jour**, just at the entrance of Hell-Bourg, at 892 metres (2,926 ft). La Roche Écrite is right in front of you and you can see Le Bélier up in the hills to the left.

Delightful Hell-Bourg

Hell-Bourg ❺ – named after a certain Governor de Hell rather than the domain of sinners – is a slow-paced, delightful village and a pleasant place in which to spend a couple of days. There are several things to see inside and just outside the town, and walkers can join up with the GR1 here, too. To cater for the steady flow of visitors, Hell-Bourg has a handful of small hotels, and there are a few small food shops and restaurants on the main street, **Rue Général de Gaulle** as well as a helpful tourist office (tel: 0262 47 89 89).

There are some lovely creole houses in Hell-Bourg, some of them brightly painted and with luxuriant gardens shaded by bamboo, orange trees and ferns like parasols. Note in particular the decorative little kiosks known as *guetalis*; strategically placed at the edge of gardens overlooking the street, they allowed the occupants to watch passers-by without being seen themselves. The name comes from the French verb *guetter*, which means "to watch out for" or "look at".

For a close look at a traditional home, visit **Villa Folio** (open 9am–11.30am 2–5pm for guided tours; entrance fee; tel: 0262 47 80 98), almost hidden among its lush gardens opposite the church in rue Amiral Lacaze. Built in 1870, the tiny villa belongs to Jean-François Folio, a descendant of Réunion's earliest settlers. The house is typical of the times and offers a rare insight into creole life, when much of one's time was spent on the verandah. The two small

BELOW: the picturesque cemetery at Hell-Bourg.

pavilions at the back used to be the kitchen and servants' quarters and a *guetali* which served as a reception area for friends who'd drop by for drinks made from the local rum and spices. The house contains original furniture, including a 19th-century English four-poster bed complete with canopy – hijacked, so the story goes, from an East India ship by corsairs

The discovery of medicinal springs near Hell-Bourg, in 1831, drew the sick to its healing waters for over a century. A landslide in 1948 reduced them to ruins, which you can see today by taking a pleasant 15-minute walk west of the defunct Hotel des Salazes (a former military hospital) in Chemin du Cimetière

Some of the casualties of the landslide were buried in the **Cemetery**, at the north end of Chemin du Cimetière. This is perhaps the most picturesque cemetery on the island, framed by luxuriant bamboo and verdant cliffs behind. Hidden among the graves of settlers, soldiers and aristocrats is a grey mound of rock with a simple iron cross. It is said to contain the headless corpse of a Mr Zett, a bandit and rapist, who terrorised the neighbourhood in the early 1900s. To ensure he would not rise again in one piece he was decapitated and his head despatched to St-Denis Glasses of rum and cigarettes are sometimes placed around the grave to appease what's left of him.

If you'd rather hook a trout than a lost soul, follow the signs to **Parc Piscicole d'Hell-Bourg** (open daily

8am–6pm), near the Relais des Cimes Hotel. This freshwater trout farm provides bait and line, and you can have your catch cooked to order in the restaurant. For more active pursuits head for the waterfalls at **Les Trois Cascades**, about 1 km (½ mile) south of Hell-Bourg, which provide ideal conditions for canyoning. And if hanging on a rope in a wet-suit in the thundering crash of a waterfall doesn't set your pulse racing, have a go at white-water rafting and career at break-neck speed to a calm lagoon.

For the best views of Salazie cirque, head northwest out of town along the D48 towards **Ilet à Vidot**. Rising to 1,352 metres (4,436 ft) from the centre of the cirque is the hump-shaped **Piton d'Enchaing ❻**. You can follow a very challenging section of the GR1 to the peak either from Hell-Bourg or Ilet à Vidot, but take plenty of supplies. You'll need to allow at least five hours to go there and back from Hell-Bourg. A more popular trek is south to the top of **Piton des Neiges ❼**. The best option is to stay overnight at the Gîte de la Caverne Dufour, and then head on up to the summit first thing, before the clouds have descended *(see page 187).*

Cirque de Cilaos

Cilaos is named after a runaway slave called Tsilaos, from the Malagasy *tsy aosana*, meaning "the place one never leaves" – and you probably won't want to after you've negotiated the 262 hairpin bends along the RN5, the only access road from St-Louis on the south coast. Following the course of the Rivière Bras de Cilaos, the RN5 climbs steadily to the entrance to the cirque at **Le Pavillon**. Early travellers were confined to palanquins as the only means of transport to continue their journey beyond Le Pavillon, along narrow roads which at each twist and turn open up new vistas of cloud-capped mountains and isolated villages dotted along the deep ravines.

The town of **Cilaos ❽**, at 1,220 metres (4,000 ft) is similar in many ways to the French alpine resort of Chamonix, its twin town. It's an excellent starting point for hikes and walks, with a few things to entertain you in the town itself.

Cilaos' 6,000 inhabitants are mainly the descendants of 19th-century settlers from Normandy and Brittany, who dreamed up evocative names for the peaks which surrounded them, including Les Trois Dents de Salazes (Salazie's Three Teeth) or Le Bonnet de Prêtre (The Priest's Bonnet). These days, the local people make a living through tourism and farming, though the area is also known for its embroidery, wine and lentils.

In **Rue Père Boiteau** in the town centre there are some beautifully restored bijou creole houses; notable examples include a pink and grey house called Soledad, across the road from the Stamm pharmacy; the salmon-pink, 80-year-old restaurant called Chez Noé (which serves good goat massala curry); and Cilaos' oldest house, painted in blue and white.

Hotel des Thermes in Route des Thermes is worth staying at just to witness the sunrise as it casts hauntingly beautiful shadows and colours over the ramparts of the cirque. It's Cilaos' oldest, most upmarket and quirkiest hotel (currently closed for a major refurbishment, it re-opens in 2004). It was built in 1935 to

Map on page 226

BELOW:
the spa resort of Cilaos, also a good base for hikers.

The Cilaos red is a sweetish, full-bodied table wine made from the Cot grape.

BELOW:
threshing lentils.

accommodate guests visiting the thermal springs nearby.

Ever since **thermal springs** *(thermes)* were discovered in 1819 by a goathunter, Cilaos has been a health resort attracting the sick and infirm, who would make the long journey up from the coast. In 1948, a cyclone destroyed the springs but the **Etablissement Thermal d'Irenée-Accot** is still active (Route de Bras-Sec; tel: 0262 31 72 27; open daily 8am–noon, 2–5pm; closed Wed pm and in June). Whether you've got digestive problems, rheumatism or arthritis, the waters from the same thermal springs can help put it right. If you're after sheer indulgence, or a restorative after a long trek, treat yourself to a sauna or massage, have a work-out in the gym and then flake out in the jacuzzi.

The best places to buy the local wine are Cilaos and nearby Bras Sec. Locals sell cheap bottles of Cilaos wine along the roadside, but it is often of inferior quality. Export-quality wine produced and bottled under hygienic conditions can be bought at the **Chaie de Cilaos** in Bras Sec (34 Rue des Glycines; tel: 0262 31 79 69; open Mon–Fri 9am–noon, 1.30–4pm; entrance fee), where you can also learn about local wine-making methods and enjoy a wine-tasting session. Modern methods using stainless steel vats are used, but the process of pressing, fermenting and bottling in makeshift cellars hasn't changed in years.

Many of the area's skilled embroiderers work from home and are concentrated in **Palmiste Rouge**, south of Cilaos on the CD240, but a handful come to work at the **Maison de la Broderie** (Mon–Sat 9am–noon, 2–5pm, Sun 9am–noon; entrance fee; tel: 0262 31 77 48) in Rue des Ecoles, which was founded in 1953 by the sisters of Notre-Dame-des-Neiges. Many of the designs originated in Brittany, but today workers struggle to keep up traditional procedures and patterns *(see Travel Tips)*.

Stretching your legs

The tourist office is at 2 Rue Mac-Auliffe (open daily 8.30am–12.30pm, 1.30–5.30pm, Sun and public hols: 9am–1pm; tel: 0262 31 71 71), in the same building as the Cilaos branch of La Maison de la Montagne. Here you'll find every map and walking plan imaginable and details of accommodation and adventure sports available in the cirques, as well as a huge relief map of the whole island. And if you have ever wondered what a palanquin looks like, there's an original one on display.

One of the most straightforward walks from Cilaos, for which you need four hours for the return trip, turn left at the Hotel des Thermes and follow the signs north to **Roche Merveilleuse**. (It is also possible to drive, along the RF11.) No real effort is needed to climb the rock and the views from the summit are great. From left to right you will see the village of Bras Sec, perched on a plateau overlooking the cirque, followed by Palmiste Rouge and Ilet à Cordes, where the best lentils are grown. Access to the Roche Merveilleuse is through the **Forêt du Grand Matarum**, noted for the local tamarinds-des-hauts, Japanese crypto-merias and Réunion's only oak trees. Marked paths weave through the forest.

For a more ambitious hike, head west to Marla in the cirque of Mafate *(see page 187)*, which is more easily reached from Cilaos than anywhere else. Other possible walks from the town are along the GR2 to Bras Sec and beyond to Palmiste Rouge.

In the area around the hamlets of **Îlet Fleurs Jaunes** and **Îlets du Bois Rouge** canyoning is the latest craze. The sport is enough to scare the pants off you as you abseil off cliffs into water-filled gorges, but at least a guide goes with you, and life jackets, harnesses, helmets and jump suits are provided. ❑

Map on page 226

BELOW: freshly painted houses and flower-filled gardens give Cilaos an alpine feel.

SEYCHELLES

The islands' reputation as a tropical paradise is well earned

and preserving the environment is a crucial concern

The Seychelles islands are the oldest ocean islands on earth. A micro-continent, isolated millions of years ago, evolving its own flora and fauna, from which man, and indeed all land mammals, were absent. Seychelles' human history began just a few hundred years ago. In 1609 a small landing party of English sailors made the first recorded landing in Seychelles. They had left England in March the year before, and sailed past the Cape, through the Mozambique channel, calling in at the Comores and Pemba, north of Zanzibar. They stumbled upon Seychelles by accident, but were glad they did. The boatswain, one Mr Jones, declared the islands "an earthly Paradise".

Seychellois are proud of their spectacular country, and happy to share it with visitors. They have a certain reserve on first acquaintance, but when relaxed are incredibly warm and generous. They love to talk, make music and create delicious creole dishes, and throw open their homes and the bounty of their table to those they come to know.

This is a young nation, dealing with the inevitable problems a small and isolated island population faces when struggling to keep up with the outside world. The characteristic "mañana" syndrome is in some conflict with the need to modernise and perform to the standards of a faster, busier world beyond the coral beaches.

But it's precisely this relaxed attitude to life that appeals to visitors who come here in search of a stress-free environment and unrivalled natural beauty. If all you want out of your holiday is sun, sea and sand, there are other, cheaper tropical destinations. But if you are prepared to pay extra to enjoy unique flora and fauna and loll on some of the best beaches in the world, look no further. Many changes to the landscape have occurred since 1609, but there are so many beauty spots that still fit Bo's'n Jones' definition of "an earthly Paradise". ❑

PRECEDING PAGES: gaily painted wood, a splash of Seychelles colour to take home; St Pierre Islet, off Praslin; red-footed boobies on Cosmoledo, in the Outer Islands. **LEFT:** local fisherman, Mahé.

THE ORIGIN OF SEYCHELLES

An Indian Ocean Atlantis, Seychelles has the oldest
and only granitic ocean islands in the world

The Seychelles islands can be divided into five main groups: the granitic islands, the Amirantes, the Alphonse Group, the Farquhar Group and the Aldabra Group. The 40 islands that make up the granitic group are the world's only ocean islands built from the stuff of continents. All other isolated ocean islands

are made up of coralline or volcanic rocks, both of which have grown out of the ocean. The main islands of Seychelles are different. Their rocks have never been completely submerged. They were formed from material ejected from deep within the fabric of the earth some 750 million years ago, perhaps in a frozen, lifeless wasteland close to the South Pole.

For millennia, the rocks of Seychelles were a part of Pangaea, the ancient super-continent that once encompassed all the world's land masses. Some 200 million years ago, the forces of continental drift tore Pangaea apart. It split into Laurasia (modern Europe, Asia and North America) to the north and Gondwanaland

(South America, Africa, Antarctica, Australasia and the Indian subcontinent) to the south. Seychelles at this time lay near the point where Madagascar, India and Africa were linked.

As the process of continental drift continued, about 125 million years ago, Madagascar, Seychelles and India broke away as one land mass. Madagascar became an island around 90 million years ago, drifting away with its own unique assemblage of wildlife. Then 65 million years ago, Seychelles drifted from the western coast of India.

It may not be pure coincidence that the birth of the world's only oceanic fragments of continental rock coincided with the death of dinosaurs. There are many dinosaur extinction theories. Many scientists believe that their disappearance was caused by the earth's collision with a comet that struck the Yucatan Peninsula in Mexico, sending shock waves through the globe and triggering volcanic activity at the opposite side of the earth. A second theory suggests that a vast comet broke up on entering the earth's atmosphere, major fragments of which hit the Yucatan and 12 hours later, as the earth turned, struck the Indian ocean. Other scientists believe that extinction was not instantaneous, but the result of an extensive period of volcanic activity in western India, close to the point where Seychelles was once attached to the subcontinent.

Isolated in mid-ocean, this new micro-continent was one land mass, covering an area of around 300,000 sq km (116,000 sq miles) – roughly the size of Britain and Ireland combined. Today, all that remains are the peaks of the highest mountains. The combined forces of erosion, sea level change and the sheer weight of coral growth (forming what geologists term a carbonate platform) have submerged all but 250 sq km (100 sq miles) of granite, less than one thousandth of its original extent, creating the archipelago we see today.

Though superficially similar to the other granitic islands, Silhouette and North Island are younger and made up largely of a type of volcanic rock called syenite. Silhouette was born rapidly and dramatically, the result of an eruption which probably occurred on land. Limited outcrops above the surface today make it difficult to determine with certainty, but it is probable that the volcano's crater lies southeast of La Passe, now almost entirely eroded away and submerged. This volcano erupted many times and Silhouette may have towered 3,000 metres (10,000 ft) or more at one time. At Pointe Zeng Zeng, you can see the only volcanic ash above sea level in Seychelles, while fingers of basalt reach out from the island to Mahé and can be seen at Glacis and elsewhere.

The Amirantes is a linear chain of coral islands and atolls that rise no more than 3 metres (10 ft) above sea level. Volcanoes once rose out of the ocean, but as they died and were reclaimed by the sea, coral growth maintained contact with the surface. Farquhar Atoll, south of Seychelles, must also have witnessed volcanic activity at one time. It is believed that while the granitic group was a micro-continent, Farquhar may have been a nano-continent (a tiny fragment of continent).

Aldabra, Assumption, Cosmoledo and Astove in the southwestern corner of Seychelles are different again. These islands of the Aldabra group

On the edge of the Seychelles Bank lie the much younger islands of Bird and Denis, thought to have emerged about 4,000 years ago when the sea level dropped as a result of a change in ocean currents. These currents stirred the waters causing a shift in the average local sea levels. Mahé's sea level, for example, is now 5 metres (16 ft) below the level in southern India. It is thought that the sea level change that revealed Bird and Denis exposed the Amirantes group at the same time.

are raised coral islands. In fact Aldabra is the largest raised atoll in the world. Unlike the usual low-lying coral atolls, they rise to up to 8 metres (27 ft) above sea level. This appears to go against the conventional wisdom that the volcanic basement of coral atolls is contracting and sinking. However, it may not be so much that the land has risen, rather that the sea level has fallen.

The cycle continues today. The biggest fear is that global warming and the rise in sea levels may spell disaster for low-lying coral islands. Signs of beach erosion can be seen throughout Seychelles and nowhere more than in the coral islands, which could disappear if present trends continue. ❑

LEFT: Aldabra channel.
ABOVE: geologists are still trying to work out the precise origins of Farquhar Atoll.

Decisive Dates

EARLY DISCOVERERS

851 Arab traders probably visit Seychelles. An Arab manuscript of this date refers to the "high island" beyond the Maldives.

961 Arab charts drawn up on which Seychelles referred to as Zarin (Sisters).

1502 On its way to India via Mozambique, Vasco da Gama's expedition sights the outer islands, which later became known as the Amirantes.

1609 A ship from the English East India Company trading fleet visits Mahé, making the first recorded

landing. Nevertheless, Seychelles remains un-occupied for more than 100 years.

Late 17th century Piracy is rife in the area. Pirates probably use Seychelles as a base.

FRENCH POSSESSION

1742–90 Seychelles' strategic position on the route to India arouses French and British interest. The French establish a settlement.

1742 Lazare Picault leads an expedition to chart the islands northeast of Madagascar, reporting to Mahé de Labourdonnais, the French governor of nearby Mauritius.

1744 Picault returns to Seychelles to collect more information and names the main island Mahé.

1756 Nicholas Morphey claims Mahé for France.

1770 A settlement is created on Ste Anne island.

1771 Pierre Poivre establishes a spice garden on Mahé.

1778 A 15-man garrison is established at L'Etablissement du Roi (later Victoria).

1786 The colony now comprises 24 military personnel, five civilians and 122 slaves. Its income is derived from provisioning ships. A legal system is introduced.

1790 In the wake of the French Revolution, the Seychelles settlers create a Colonial Assembly to run the colony.

THE WAR YEARS

1794–1803 Anglo-French rivalry in the region makes life difficult for the tiny colony. Seychelles becomes a haven for French corsairs. The pragmatism and smooth tongue of Commandant de Quinssy ensures Seychelles actually profits from the Napoleonic wars.

1794 First capitulation signed by de Quincy. In all, it is renewed seven times.

1801 French political deportees arrive.

1803 Population 215 white residents, 86 coloured and 1,820 slaves. Cash crops include cotton, maize, sugar and rice.

BRITISH CONTROL

1815–1901 Somewhat reluctantly, Britain assumes control of Seychelles. Still subservient to Mauritius, the colony declines until the arrival of liberated Africans boosts the economy.

1815 Seychelles ceded to Britain by Treaty of Paris.

1818 The population of 7,500 prospers from the cultivation of cotton.

1822 Price of cotton falls. Many planters return to Mauritius.

1835 Slavery is abolished.

1840 The population reaches 5,400. The first coconut plantations are established.

1841 L'Etablissement is renamed Victoria.

1860s Coconut oil is almost the sole export.

1861 Arrival of first of 2,500 liberated Africans.

1862 An avalanche of mud lands on Victoria. At least 70 people are killed.

1875 Ex-Sultan of Perak arrives, first of many political prisoners exiled here by Britain.

1880 General Gordon visits and suggests Seychelles was the Garden of Eden.

1891 Vanilla becoming an important cash crop. Other exports include copra and cloves.

1901 The population reaches 19,000.

INDEPENDENCE

1903–71 Seychelles emerges into the modern world with the building of an International Airport, and independence from Britain.

1903 Seychelles becomes a separate Crown Colony under its first governor, Sweet-Escott.

1906 A fall in the price of vanilla rocks the economy. Coconut products again dominate the market.

1908 Cinnamon exports increase.

1914–18 World War I causes hardship in Seychelles due to isolation from shipping. Seychelles Pioneer Corps serve in East Africa.

1921 The population reaches 24,500.

1926 Electricity and telephone services installed.

1937 Creation of the League of Coloured Peoples to lobby for plantation workers.

1939 Creation of the Seychelles Taxpayers Association, which represented employers.

1939–45 World War II. Seychelles used as a refuelling base for flying boats and warships. Seychelles Pioneer Corps again serves with British forces.

1951 The population reaches 34,000.

1963 America begins the construction of a satellite tracking station on Mahé.

1964 Creation of two new political parties, the Seychelles People's United Party (led by Albert René, demanding independence) and the Seychelles Democratic Party (led by James Mancham, wanting closer links with Britain).

1965 Creation of a new British colony, called British Indian Ocean Territory, consisting of several islands from the Seychelles group.

1967 Universal adult suffrage is introduced.

1970 First Constitutional Conference discusses the future of Seychelles. A legislative assembly is created.

1971 Completion of the International Airport and commencement of regular flights. Tourism is now the most important component of the economy.

THE MODERN AGE

1976–99 Politically troubled times in the 1970s and 1980s bring violence to Seychelles, but stability returns in the 1990s.

1976 Seychelles declared an independent republic. A coalition government formed in which

---

LEFT: *Portolan Atlas of Africa and the Indian Ocean,* mid-16th century.

RIGHT: Campaign poster of René during the presidential elections.

James Mancham becomes president and Albert René prime minister.

1977 Mancham overthrown in a coup which establishes René as president of a socialist government.

1979 A new constitution makes Seychelles a single party system, led by the Seychelles People's Progressive Front.

1981 A mercenary force led by Colonel "Mad Mike" Hoare attempts to seize control of the country, and fails.

1982 A mutiny in the Seychelles army is put down by Tanzanian troops.

1984 René is elected for second term of office.

1989 René elected for third term.

1992 Return to a multi-party system. Mancham, back from exile in London, is reconciled with René.

1993 A new constitution is adopted. René and his SPPF party are elected back into power.

1998 In a three-way contest, René is re-elected. Mancham's Democratic Party is forced into third place by the United Opposition (later renamed the Seychelles National Party or SNP).

2001 René wins snap presidential elections held in August.

2002 In elections to the National Assembly, René's SPPF takes 24 seats and SNP win 11 seats. Mancham's DP fails to win a single seat.

2003 René names James Michel as his successor.

BIRTH OF AN ISLAND NATION

Quincy and René, the historic heavyweights of Seychelles, were key to its transformation from deserted paradise to modern independent state

We can only speculate as to early human history in Seychelles. Polynesians, who eventually settled on Madagascar, may have lingered here around the 3rd and 2nd centuries BC. It is likely that Arab traders plying the Indian Ocean in around the 9th century knew of the islands' existence. A manuscript dated AD 851, written by an Arab merchant, refers to the Maldives and higher islands beyond them, possibly Seychelles. Evidence also suggests that long before European discovery of the islands Arabs were trading the legendary coco de mer nuts, found only in Seychelles *(see page 320)*. Because of the mystery surrounding their origin, the nuts were highly sought after. No shrewd trader would reveal the source of supply of such a rare and valuable commodity. To keep the myth alive the Arabs claimed they found them washed ashore in the Maldives, but as the nuts are not buoyant in saltwater, this is unlikely.

The first Europeans

The early history of Seychelles is a story of people passing through. In 1502, Vasco da Gama, on his way to India via East Africa, sighted the outer islands which became known as the Amirantes, but the Portuguese made no attempt to colonise them. Later in the 16th century, the inner granitic islands began to appear on Portuguese charts as the "Seven Sisters".

The British were next on the scene. In 1609 the *Ascension*, one of the ships from a trading fleet of the English East India Company on its way to India, got lost in a storm. Its crew sighted "high land" and headed for it, anchoring "as in a pond". They found plentiful fresh water, fish, coconuts, birds, turtles and giant tortoises with which to replenish their stores. The ship's captain reported the bounty they had found, but the British took no action and Seychelles was to remain unoccupied for more than a hundred years.

By the end of the 17th century, piracy in the Indian Ocean was rife. Pirates fleeing from the Caribbean, whose waters were by this time heavily policed, based themselves in Madagascar. From here they preyed upon vessels plying the Red Sea and the Gulf, probably using islands as a hiding place and refreshment stop.

EARTHLY PARADISE

On 19 January 1609, the *Ascension*, a merchant vessel under the command of the English captain Alexander Sharpeigh, was separated from the fleet by a storm and anchored off Mahé. On board was one John Jourdain, an agent sent by the East India Company to trade and negotiate in India. He wrote an enthusiastic account of the "earthly paradise" they had happened upon. His is the first known written description of Seychelles:

"it is very good refreshing place for wood, water, coker nutts, fish and fowle, without any feare or danger, except the allagartes: for you cannot discerne that ever any people had bene there before us."

LEFT: an Arab boat navigating on the Indian Ocean.
RIGHT: Vasco da Gama.

French occupation

It wasn't until 1710 that the French occupied Île de France (as Mauritius was then known), but the colony quickly grew in importance. In 1735 an energetic administrator, Bertrand François Mahé de Labourdonnais was appointed. His brief was to protect the French sea route to India. Labourdonnais, himself a sailor, turned his attention to making a speedier passage from Île de France to India and in 1742 he commissioned Lazare Picault to lead an expedition to chart the islands northeast of Madagascar. On 21 November 1742 the *Elisabeth* and the *Charles* anchored off Mahé at

Anse Boileau (not Baie Lazare, later mistakenly named as Picault's landing place). They found a land of plenty. In fact, Picault's first name for the island was Île d'Abondonce.

Picault's mapping was poor, so in 1744 he was sent back on a second mission, this time anchoring off the northeast coast near present-day Victoria. He renamed the main island Mahé, and the archipelago the Îles de la Bourdonnais. He had high hopes for the islands, but his plans for settlement were thwarted. The colonial war between England and France had reached India. Labourdonnais was called away to fight a campaign and the islands were once

LAYING THE HERCULEAN TRAIL

Olivier Le Vasseur, also known as La Buse (the Buzzard) was a notorious French pirate operating in the early 18th century. For a number of years, he teamed up with fellow brigands from Britain, Edward England and Charles Taylor. Together they cruised the Indian Ocean and terrorised European merchant ships. Their most lucrative haul came from a royal Portuguese ship, which they plundered as she lay helpless in the harbour of Réunion. The booty taken included the "Fiery Cross of Goa". Encrusted with diamonds, rubies and emeralds, it took three men to lift it. Le Vasseur kept this magnificent piece of treasure for himself. He was finally captured by the French authorities and on 7

July 1730 was taken to Mauritius and hung. The story goes that just before they put the noose around his neck, he threw a sheaf of documents into the crowd crying, "Find my treasure, who can!" The search for this priceless cross has continued ever since.

Most famous of the treasure hunters was Reginald Cruise-Wilkins, who dedicated his life to the quest. He was convinced the treasure was buried on Mahé and that Le Vasseur had laid a series of traps and clues based on the labours of Hercules. He died without finding the treasure, but his sons have continued the diggings, some of which may still be seen by the shore at Bel Ombre.

more forgotten. It wasn't until 1756 that the authorities on Île de France decided to take possession of the islands before the British did. Two ships were sent to claim them, commanded by Corneille Nicholas Morphey.

After a thorough investigation of Mahé and the surrounding islands, Morphey raised the French flag and took possession for his king and the French East India Company on 1 November 1756, to hearty cries of "long live the king" and nine shots from the ships' cannon. He renamed the largest island Île de Séchelles (the name later used for the island group, when the largest granitic island reverted to the name of Mahé).

The end of the Seven Years' War, France's loss of Canada and its reduced status in India, accelerated the decline of the French East India Company. The settlements of Île de France and Seychelles, formerly controlled by the Company, now came under direct royal authority and in 1768, during a commercial expedition for the collection of timber and tortoises, French sovereignty was extended to cover all the islands of the granitic group. But the French were in no hurry to settle Seychelles. A colony there could not pay for itself, and would be costly to maintain. Then, in 1769, the navigators Rochon and Grenier proved that a faster route to India could safely be taken via Seychelles and the importance of its strategic position began to be realised.

Frenchman Brayer du Barré (died 1777) was given royal permission to run a settlement in Seychelles at his own expense. He decided that the best place to begin a colony was the little island of St Anne, off the northeast coast of Mahé. On 12 August 1770, with 15 white colonists, seven slaves, five Indians and one negress on board, Du Barré's ship, the *Télémaque*, set sail from Île de France and landed on the island 14 days later.

Du Barré himself did not join the expedition, but stayed in Île de France seeking funds, but his appeals for help to Île de France and Versailles fell on deaf ears. In desperation, he went to Seychelles to try and rescue the situation, but to no avail. A ruined man, he left for India and died there shortly afterwards. By August 1772, Du

Barré's people had abandoned St Anne and moved to Mahé or returned home.

Cinnamon, nutmeg and cloves

The intendant of Île de France at this time was Pierre Poivre (1719–86), a man of ideas. Determined to break the Dutch monopoly of the lucrative spice trade, he thought Mahé would be perfect for spice cultivation. He had obtained seedlings of nutmeg and clove, and 10,000 nutmeg seeds, but his attempts to propagate them on Île de France and Bourbon (later Réunion) met with little success. So, in 1771, Poivre sent former soldier Antoine Gillot to

LEFT: *A Fleet of East Indiamen at Sea*, by Nicholas Pocock (1741–1821).
RIGHT: Mahé de Labourdonnais.

Mahé to supervise the creation of a spice garden. Gillot chose Anse Royale, on the southeast coast as the site, and set about establishing the "Jardin du Roi" which was planted with nutmeg, clove, cinnamon and pepper.

When British ships were sighted around Seychelles, the French authorities were spurred into action and despatched a garrison from Île de France under the command of Lieutenant de Romainville. They built the Établissement du Roi (Royal Settlement) on the site of modern Victoria. Gillot was nominally in charge of the civilian colonists, but had no real authority over them. So Île de France sent as replacement a man of stronger mettle, Jean Baptiste Philogène de Malavois. He drew up 30 decrees which protected the timber and tortoises. In future, only sound farming techniques and careful husbanding of resources would be tolerated. He assumed command of the settlement in 1788.

In 1790, as a result of the French Revolution, the settlers declared independence from the other French colonies and formed a Colonial Assembly. They drew up their own constitution and decided that land in Seychelles should only go to the children of existing colonists, who should be able to dispose of the colony's produce as they chose, not as Île de France dic-

THE LOST KING OF FRANCE

An intriguing anecdote concerns the mysterious figure of Pierre Louis Poiret. Late in 1804, a boy of 19 years old came to Poivre Island, having been brought from France by a Monsieur Aimé, who treated him with great respect. Aimé continued to Mahé, where he presented secret letters to Quincy, the commandant. After working the cotton gin on Poivre, Poiret came to Mahé. He was given land at Cap Ternay and Grand Anse and slaves to help him farm it.

An aloof man, respected by his fellow planters, he led a largely unremarkable life. Then he suddenly declared he was actually Louis XVII, heir to the French throne. He said that, after the execution of his parents, he had been placed in the care of a cobbler, Simon Poiret. Later, Royalists smuggled him out of Paris in a box of hay, and brought him out to Seychelles. In his later years, he wrote repeatedly to Charles X of France, whom he said was his uncle. Interestingly, the names he gave all his four sons began with Louis, and the names of his five daughters with Marie.

Official history records that the crown prince Louis died of tuberculosis in 1795. His heart was removed and preserved in a crystal urn. This was opened in December 1999, DNA extracted and compared to that of Marie-Antoinette and living relatives. Sadly for romantics, it proved the official version to be correct.

tated. But independence did not last long. Enthusiasm for the Revolution began to wane, not least because revolutionary theory supported the abolition of slavery, which the colonists wholeheartedly opposed, believing that without slave labour, they could not survive. Eventually they agreed to hand over control to a commandant.

The war years

In 1794, Jean-Baptiste Queau de Quinssy (1748–1827), whose name was later anglicised to Quincy, took command of the colony. A wily man, he used skill and expediency to steer Seychelles through the years of war ahead.

Seychelles became a haven for French corsairs (pirates carrying *lettres de marque* from the French authorities entitling them to prey on British enemy ships). Quincy hoped this might go unnoticed, but in 1794 a squadron of three English ships arrived. They were well armed and in no mood for resistance. The British commodore, Henry Newcome, asked for help with his wounded, many of whom were French prisoners, but Quincy refused.

This resistance meant little in practical terms and was but a gesture. Quincy knew he was powerless and Newcome gave him an hour in which to surrender. There were only 20 colonists on the French side "capable of carrying arms". Newcome had almost 13,000 men. Quincy had eight cannons, Newcome had 166. In all, Quincy made seven capitulations to the English. While they were in port, he flew the English flag, but as soon as their ships were out of sight he raised the tricolour. The strategy worked. In effect, Seychelles remained neutral, supplying both British and French ships. The islanders avoided conflict and the colony flourished.

This was not an end to Quincy's problems, however. To his dismay, on 11 July 1801 the French frigate *Chiffonne* arrived with a cargo of notorious French prisoners sent into exile by Napoleon and Quincy was warned that there were more on the way. Together, these deportees would outnumber the local population. Were this not enough, the British ship

HMS *Sybille* arrived soon after. Quincy had no choice but to try to defend the *Chiffonne*, but after a brief battle, she was taken. Captain Adam of the *Sybille* demanded to know why Quincy had interfered, in contravention of his capitulation terms. With characteristic guile and charm, the commandant managed to talk his way out of the difficulty, and even persuaded Adam to let Seychelles vessels fly a flag bearing the words "Seychelles Capitulation", allowing them to pass through the British blockade of Mauritius unmolested.

Although confrontation with the British may have been avoided, the problem of deportees,

whom the Seychellois feared, still remained. As political prisoners they refused to work and talked of liberty and equality within hearing of the slaves. Quincy was afraid that the slaves and deportees might join forces and revolt. So he transported a number of them to the small island of Frégate and wrote to the Île de France authorities pleading for assistance with the rest. In the long run, however, his fears proved unfounded as very few of the deportees ended up staying: 33 were redeported to the Comores, six stowed away aboard visiting ships, and a number of others were taken to Île de France. Only a few of the most peaceable settled down in Seychelles.

FAR LEFT: plan of the "Jardin du Roi".
LEFT: the aptly named Pierre Poivre (Peter Pepper), introduced spices to Seychelles.
RIGHT: stamp commemorating the bicentenary of the French Revolution (1789–1989).

British control

The colony entered the 19th century with a population of 215 whites, 86 free blacks and 1,820 slaves. The war raged on, but the British were fast gaining the upper hand. They tightened the blockade on the French Indian Ocean colonies. Réunion surrendered, followed in December 1810 by Île de France, which they renamed Mauritius. In April 1811, Captain Beaver arrived in Seychelles on the *Nisus* to announce that while the preferential terms of Quincy's capitulation could stand, Seychelles must recognise the terms of the Mauritian surrender. Beaver left behind a royal marine, Lieu-

of the Peace and remained a respected figure in the colony until his death in 1827.

The British allowed customary French practices to remain in place. The administrator may have been British, reporting to London, but he governed according to French rules.

The colonists had two main grievances with their new masters. One was their dependence on Mauritius. The other was the abolition of slavery in 1835. The plantations were already in decline, their soil exhausted by years of cultivation and a lack of investment. The plantocracy believed they could not farm without slave labour. Some planters took their slaves and left.

tenant Sullivan, to monitor the Seychelles situation, but there was little Sullivan could do to stop the settlers continuing to provision French frigates and slavers. The British had outlawed the slave trade and Sullivan, later given the title of Civil Agent, played cat and mouse with the pro-slaver colonists. Once, acting on a tip-off, Sullivan was rowed over to Praslin and confiscated a cargo of newly landed slaves. It was but a small triumph among many frustrations, and Sullivan, complaining that the Seychellois had "no sense of honour, shame or honesty", resigned. In 1814, the first civilian administrator of the British regime, Edward Madge, arrived. Quincy was kept on as Justice

The liberated slaves had no land, and most squatted on the estates they had tended in bondage, working sporadically to keep themselves from starvation. It was a poor sort of freedom, and the colony entered a period of stagnation. There were no exports, and no money to pay for new infrastructure. The situation was only improved when planters realised they could grow coconuts with less labour and more profit than the traditional crops of cotton, sugar, rice and maize.

The British took their anti-slavery stance seriously, and operated patrols along the East African coast, raiding Arab dhows transporting slaves to the Middle East. Slaves liberated south of the Equator were brought to Seychelles and apprenticed to plantation owners. It was these ex-slaves who saved the economy as they were a source of cheap labour. They worked the land in return for rations and low wages. Over a period of thirteen years from 1861, around 2,400 men, women and children were brought to Seychelles.

The main settlement on Mahé (named Victoria in 1841, to mark the marriage of Queen Victoria and Prince Albert) began to grow and prosper. Licences granted in 1879 give us some idea of the range of businesses in the town; there was a druggist, two auctioneers, five retailers, four liquor stores, a notary, an attorney, a jeweller and a watchmaker.

> ### DISASTER STRIKES
>
> On 12 October 1862, Mahé was hit by a storm. Torrential rain and strong winds caused an avalanche of mud and rocks to fall on Victoria, killing more than 70 people and devastating the town.

more liberal flow of funds was ensured by the Colonial Development Act, but it was a time of economic depression; the price of copra was falling and so were wages. Workers petitioned the government about their poor working conditions and the burden of tax they had to bear. Governor Sir Arthur Grimble instigated some reforms, exempting lower income groups from taxation.

He was keen to create model housing and distribute smallholdings for the landless. Sadly, many of his reforms were not

Crown colony

Seychelles yearned to be a colony in its own right, not an appendage of Mauritius and the authorities in the mother colony supported this desire. Sir Arthur Gordon, the Mauritian governor, sent a petition on their behalf to London. Concessions were made, but Seychelles did not become a separate Crown Colony until 1903, when its first governor, Sir Ernest Bickham Sweet-Escott, took office. Befitting its new status, the colony acquired a botanical gardens, and a clock tower in the heart of Victoria.

World War I brought great hardship to the islands. Ships could not bring in essential goods, nor take away exports. Wages fell and prices soared. Many turned to crime and the prisons were bursting. Joining the Seychelles Labour Contingent formed during the war, seemed to offer an escape, but it was no easy option. The 800-strong force was sent to East Africa. After just five months, so many had died from dysentery, malaria and beriberi that the depleted corps was sent home. In all, 335 men died.

By the end of World War I, the population of Seychelles, which was around 24,000, was feeling neglected by Whitehall. There was agitation from the newly formed Planters Association for greater representation in the governance of Seychelles affairs. After 1929 a

LEFT: the British Invasion, 1810.
RIGHT: the Botanical Gardens in Victoria, *circa* 1930.

> ### A GILDED CAGE
>
> The British saw Seychelles as a useful place to exile political prisoners. Over the years, it became a home to prisoners from Zanzibar, Egypt, Cyprus and Palestine. The first in the line of exiles was the Sultan of Perak who arrived in 1875 after his implication in the murder of the British Resident there. Like many exiles who followed, he settled well into Seychelles life and became fond of the islands. Perhaps the most famous exile was Archbishop Makarios, who arrived in 1956. He too fell in love with his prison. "When our ship leaves harbour," he wrote, "we shall take with us many good and kindly memories of the Seychelles... may God bless them all."

approved before World War II had broken out, and everything was put on hold.

The Planters Association lobbied for the rich white land owners, but those who worked for them had no voice. In 1937, the League of Coloured Peoples was formed to demand a minimum wage, a wage tribunal and free health care for all.

World War II caused more distress in the colony and led to political change. In 1939, the Seychelles' first political party, the Taxpayers Association, was formed, but it was entirely concerned with protecting the interests of the plantocracy. A British governor described it as

Britain was cool on the idea of integration, while opinion in Seychelles appeared to be split. In 1967, universal adult suffrage was introduced and at the first election each party gained three seats, with Mancham claiming victory through the support of an independent. Subsequent elections in 1970 and 1974 gave Mancham a small majority in votes, but a large one in seats, through the "first past the post" voting system.

Meanwhile, Britain's lack of enthusiasm for integration convinced Mancham to join René in calling for independence. In 1975, a coalition was forged between the two rivals.

"the embodiment of every reactionary force in Seychelles". After the war, literate property owners were granted the vote; just 2,000 in a population of 36,000. At the first elections in 1948, most of those elected to the Legislative Council were predictably members of the Planters and Taxpayers Associations.

It was not until 1964 that any new political movements were created. In that year, the socialist Seychelles People's United Party (SPUP) was formed. Led by France Albert René, they campaigned for autonomy. By contrast, James Mancham's Seychelles Democratic Party (SDP), created the same year, wanted to retain its close links with Britain.

Independence

Independence was declared on 29 June 1976. James Mancham became the first president of the Republic of Seychelles and René his prime minister. Less than one year later, on 5 June 1977, while Mancham was in London to attend the Commonwealth Conference, René's supporters staged a coup. New elections were called in 1979 with René as the sole candidate. A one-party socialist state was established and the SPUP changed its name to the Seychelles People's Progressive Front (SPPF).

René used Seychelles' strategic importance to play America and Russia off against each other, while remaining non-aligned, obtaining substantial help from both superpowers without having to commit himself to either.

There were several attempts to oust René by force. The most dramatic of these took place in November 1981, when 50 mercenaries arrived on a Royal Air Swazi flight, posing as a charitable organisation bringing toys for local orphaned children. Beneath the toys, however, hidden in secret compartments of their luggage were guns and ammunition. The mercenaries were led by "Mad Mike" Hoare, whose previous exploits had included installing Mobutu as president of Zaire. They passed undetected through customs, until an official discovered a bunch of bananas in the case of a French tourist, the only non-mercenary on the plane. The importation of fresh fruit into Seychelles is illegal and the customs officers decided to give the luggage of the last two passengers a more thorough check. On discovery of a gun, all hell broke out. The mercenaries took over the airport and after a shoot-out escaped to South Africa in a hijacked plane, where they were promptly arrested. Mancham maintained that the plot had nothing to do with him, and commented wryly that the coup "had been foiled by a bunch of bananas".

Mancham remained in exile in London for 15 years. In 1992, with the resumption of multi-party democracy, he returned and rivalry between the DP, as it was now known, and the SPPF resumed. In 1993 the first multi-party presidential election since independence in 1976 was held. But it was René who triumphed with 59 percent of the votes cast.

Meanwhile, a third force was emerging. At the 1998 elections, the Seychelles National Party (SNP) gained more votes than the DP, but still fell short of the number of votes cast for the SPPF. Once again René was elected president of the Seychelles Republic. René managed to get re-elected again for a third time at a snap presidential elections held in August 2001. Mancham and his DP party declined to stand at this election but Wavel Ramkalawan of the SNP doubled his share of the vote. At the next National Assembly elections in December 2002, SPPF took 22 seats, while SNP took 11. Mancham's DP, however, received just 3 percent of the vote and was wiped out. In 2003, René announced that James Michel would be his successor as

leader of the SPPF and President of Seychelles.

Just as Quincy had done centuries earlier, Albert René used craft and guile to steer a course through the changes taking place in the world. Both have left their indelible marks as they led their small country through times of great change.

Seychelles today

Modern-day Seychelles is a middle income country with low unemployment and a good standard of living. Tourism (which has been carefully planned to avoid overcrowding and environmental damage) and tuna fishing, industries virtually non-existent a generation ago,

dominate the economy. With such a small population, the benefits of these sources of income have been profound. The traditional agricultural way of life is now just a distant memory of the older generation. Old habits such as washing clothes in streams and walking with heavy burdens on the head are disappearing, replaced by the use of washing machines and cars.

The future remains uncertain, with an economy based on two industries which can be fickle. A severe shortage of foreign exchange also clouds the horizon and the government has struggled to balance its budget. Nevertheless, Seychelles is a prosperous nation and appears destined to remain so. ❑

LEFT: Victoria clock tower in 1856.
RIGHT: pro-Mancham election poster.

THE SEYCHELLOIS

Descended from African slaves, French settlers, British colonists and Asian immigrants, the Seychellois are an intriguing people

The Seychellois could be called a "new" people. They have a short history, having existed as a separate entity for only around a hundred years, fused more closely since independence in 1976, while facing the difficulties of a small island state embarking upon nationhood. They are heartening proof that people of differing ethnic backgrounds can live together in peace.

Origins

From the time the first settlers arrived little more than 200 years ago, the Seychelles have been a melting pot. The French colonists, who had sought their fortunes in Mauritius and Réunion before arriving in Seychelles, brought with them slaves of both African and Indian origin and the process of racial intermingling began almost immediately. Pierre Hangard, probably the colony's first permanent settler, was an emigrant from Mauritius, who came to Seychelles with five slaves. He does not appear to have married, but did have a daughter by Annette, one of his slaves. He freed Annette and gave her a property at Bel Ombre. His daughter later married a Frenchman who owned one of the finest properties on Mahé. It was a scenario that was to be repeated again and again in the history of Seychelles; and there in a nutshell is the origin of the Seychellois. The colonial government census grouped people by ethnic origin until 1911, when it was decided that this was no longer possible. This bureaucratic decision can perhaps be seen as the date of birth of the Seychellois people.

Although slaves came, in the main, from eastern Africa, some were from Madagascar but only a few came from India. The largest influx of Indians came much later, along with the Chinese. They arrived during the 19th century working as road labourers or setting themselves up as traders. They brought with them their reli-

gions and customs, which they have retained. But the largest cultural influences are African and French. Despite the British takeover in the 19th century, few Britons settled in Seychelles, and the colonial government was slow to change French laws and institutions or the use of French in public life. Indeed, the British were reluctant

rulers, initially attempting to persuade France to retain the islands in exchange for French possessions in India, without success. French social customs were already well entrenched. Britain retained the same Frenchman as governor and did little to change the French way of life. The British did contest the influence of the Roman Catholic church as opposed to Anglicanism, but this was the faith which won the heart of the Seychellois.

Seychellois today

The modern Seychellois, particularly the young, look more to Europe than to Africa or Asia. Men are likely to follow the fortunes of

PRECEDING PAGES: schoolchildren, Côte d'Or.
LEFT: Praslin family gathering.
RIGHT: artist, Colbert Nourrice, in his Mahé studio.

Manchester United, and girls to wear Western clothes. They dance to British pop music and aspire to Western values. This is not the third world, but a middle income country where few go hungry. Prices in the shops may be high, but the ocean is full of fish and fruit is plentiful. There is no apparent tension between tourist and local. They may display a certain reserve, which sometimes comes across as indifference or surliness, but when barriers are broken down, visitors soon learn that the Seychellois can be among the most kind and friendly people you could ever hope to meet. Top on the list given by many visitors of reasons to return to Seychelles, apart from the obvious natural beauty of the country, is the friendliness of its people.

Language

When the early French planters were trying to communicate with slaves, who often spoke only their own tribal languages, they used a simplifed form of French, interspersed with words they picked up from their slaves' conversations. In this way, Kreol evolved. Since it is based on a form of French spoken in the 18th century, it retains many archaic and dialect words rarely heard in modern French. Over

A MULTILINGUAL SOCIETY

Seychelles has three official languages: Kreol, English and French. The Seychellois seem to have an innate ability to pick up languages quickly, not surprising perhaps in view of the nation's history. Most speak Kreol and English and happily drift from one to another when in conversation. These are the languages you are most likely to hear on the streets, though some of the longer-established families do make a point of speaking French in the home and amongst themselves.

Seychelles Kreol evolved from a mixture of influences. Though largely based on French, it has many African, Malagasy and Arab words, as well as an increasing number of English words. Terms used at football matches, a popular sport, are English, not French. A good goal kick, for example becomes a *zoli goal kick*.

The most noticeable features of Kreol are a very simple grammar, the extensive use of the letter "z" (for example, *les oiseaux*, French for birds, becomes *zwazo*), and the use of "k" instead of "c".

While English is spoken in hotels, shops and offices, a few words of Kreol are useful away from tourist sites and Victoria, particularly when talking to older Seychellois. If you can speak a bit of French, you should have no trouble understanding basic Kreol.

time, Mauritius, Réunion and Seychelles developed their own accents and patterns of speech. Today, despite the inevitable local differences, all the islanders can generally understand each other's forms of Kreol. *(For more information on language, see page 23 and the box on page 258. A list of useful Kreol words and phrases appears on page 376.)*

Religion

Most Seychellois are Roman Catholics. Going to church is a social event, as well as a spiritual occasion, and the opportunity to get dressed up. The women compete in their colourful outfits,

Pentecostals and Jehovah's Witnesses. In Victoria, there is a Hindu temple and an Islamic mosque, while in recent years, the Bahai faith has become quite popular.

Family relationships

The Seychellois have a relaxed approach to marriage. It is common practice for couples to *kantmenm zot an menage*, in other words live together informally, often producing large families. It is not unusual for a man to drift away (a practice known as *marse marse*), set up a new relationship and father other children. Often, in later years, the wanderer returns to

while older men wear long-sleeved white shirts as a mark of respect. You won't see anyone in shorts or skimpy beachwear which are considered disrespectful. First holy communion is a major landmark in the life of a young Seychellois, and it is not unusual to see processions of little girls in frothy white lace dresses and formally attired little boys arriving at the cathedral in Victoria.

Other Christian sects are also represented, including Anglicans, Seventh Day Adventists,

LEFT: bicycles are an efficient form of transport for girls-about-town and policemen on the beat.
RIGHT: old couple outside their creole home.

an earlier partner, to end his days in a more committed relationship. The reunited couple may even go so far as to have an elaborate and expensive wedding, with their children as pageboys and bridesmaids.

Many households are extended families consisting of a mother with her children, usually including a daughter or two with their children, maybe even a granddaughter with hers. Children in such households tend to grow up with a great respect for their mothers, but less for their errant fathers, perhaps reflected in the traditional mourning period for parents: 18 to 24 months for a mother, nine to twelve months for a father.

Exorcising ghosts

Like the Malagasy, the Seychellois have a healthy respect for ghosts and departed spirits, and death is treated very seriously. Modern Seychellois are perhaps no more superstitious than other peoples, but old traditions originating in Africa and Madagascar are still, to some extent, followed alongside Catholic rites. People still hold vigils at home for deceased loved ones, laying the body out in the best room of the house, withe the head pointing towards the mountains and the feet towards the sea. In flickering candlelight, a solemn procession of visitors, family, acquaintances and the idly curious pass by the open coffin and sprinkle the body with holy water. The closest family and friends spend the whole night beside the body, but they certainly don't sit in silence. They play cards or dominoes, and make as much noise as possible to scare evil spirits away from their loved one and prevent them from stealing the body and turning it into a *dandosya* or zombie.

Funerals have always had a huge turn out, though sleek black hearses have now replaced the traditional handcarts that once conveyed the dead to church. A long trail of mourners follows the coffin and buses are often hired to bring the many guests to church.

GHOSTS AND SUPERSTITIONS

The Seychellois revel in a good ghost story. Certain islands are said to be haunted: Ste Anne by a cruel French woman who had a slave girl beaten to death; Long Island by a Creole girl who drowned her child; Moyenne by an eccentric Englishwoman who lived there with her dogs.

They are also renowned for their superstitions and sayings linked with good and bad luck, death and evil. It is said, for example, that bad luck will follow if you sweep the house after sunset; that a kestrel found roosting in the eaves of your house is a portent of death in the family; and that an unfamiliar call or voice in the dark should go unanswered – it could be a zombie.

Gris gris

For generations, this blend of folklore, black magic and traditional medicine played an important part in people's day to day lives. Black magicians were once quite influential people and the power of *gris gris* was greatly feared by the Roman Catholic church and by colonial administrators, who tried to stamp it out. It certainly still goes on, but like so many traditions, it is losing the hold on people's lives it once had.

ABOVE LEFT: harvesting cinnamon.
ABOVE: "beating" an octopus.
RIGHT: playing the makalopo.

The traditional theory is that *gris gris* came with the slaves from Africa or Madagascar, but some experts claim that European beliefs in witchcraft also found their way into its practices. Two books on magic written in 1800 that came here from Europe were particularly influential. The spells and potions described in them became absorbed in local magic customs.

A *gris gris* "practitioner", known as a *bonnonm* or *bonnfanm dibwa* (man or woman of the woods), supposedly has the power to protect you from the evil eye, help you in your career or love life, or get revenge on your enemies. He or she might provide a love potion, a protective talisman or small package with bits of cooked food, iron, even urine and hair; or they might foretell your future using playing cards, tea leaves or by casting pebbles on a table.

A sound knowledge of herbal medicine is often combined with these more spurious talents, and the Seychelles flora is a veritable medicine chest. Seychellois were using the Madagascar periwinkle medicinally long before Western scientists used it in the treatment of childhood leukemia with spectacular results. Tea made from lemon grass to settle the stomach, *tokmarya* for sore throats, *montosyel* for hernias and *bred mouroung* leaves for liver complaints are just a few items from the herbalist's store cupboard.

Gris gris is taken most seriously by older people, but younger people will certainly resort to a *bonnonm*, especially for the love potions. It is still a sensitive and secretive subject. Unless you were inquisitive and went out of your way to seek it out, it's unlikely that you'll see any evidence of its existence.

African rhythms

Seychellois love to dance. Nowadays, it is most likely to be in a club to modern music, but traditional music is far from dead. The most commonly seen dance is the sega. In Seychelles, the sega is a flirtatious, light-hearted dance, less smoulderingly sexy than its Mauritian counterpart, the *sega typic (see page 79)*. In fact, it is often performed by school children in dance competitions. It's not as easy as it looks. There is a definite knack to it and you need flexible hips. The men wear a long-sleeved white shirt, long black trousers and a colourful cumberbund, with perhaps a straw hat. The women are

TRADITIONAL INSTRUMENTS

Sadly, the traditional instruments that once plucked out the rhythms and tunes for the sega and *moutya* dancers are no longer commonplace. These simply constructed instruments were introduced to Seychelles by the African and Malagasy slaves, who made them with whatever raw materials they could find.

There are several stringed instruments, or zithers. The *zez* has one string and its sound box is a hollow dried out gourd. The string is plucked to produce music. The *bonm* is similar, but the string is attached to a wooden bow with a gourd on the end and played with a thin stick. The *mouloumpa* is a cross between a wind and a string

instrument. It is made of a piece of bamboo with strings on the outside that the player plucks and blows down at the same time.

The most unusual of all these instruments is the *makalapo*. It is made of a string attached at one end to a sheet of tin half buried in the ground, and to a flexible stick a few feet away at the other. Notes are produced by plucking the string and their tone is varied by manipulating the stick to tighten or slacken the string.

For percussion there are the skin drums, the *tam tam* and tambour, and the *kaskavel*, which is a small container filled with seeds or grit and shaken.

dressed in long, full, swirling skirts. Bare feet are *de rigueur*. Although the movements are swaying and lascivious, dancers do not touch.

The *moutya* is more erotic and is unique to Seychelles. Invented by the slaves as a secret escape from the drudgery of plantation life, it was performed late at night in the forest. Colonial governors and bishops were outraged by its sexiness and tried to ban it (as they had tried to ban *gris gris*). A description of a *moutya* from the 1930s reveals the attitude of the authorities: "As soon as these drums are beaten with rhythmic measure the men and women dance back to back, occasionally turning round

Both the sega and the *moutya* were of African origin, but from their European forebears, the Seychellois took the *kanmtole*, a dance tradition still very much alive. *Kanmtole* refers to a whole set of dances modified from their formal origins in the courts of France: the *lavals* (waltz), *ekosez* (Scottish jig), *mazok* (mazurka), *polka*, *kontredans* (similar to a Scottish reel), *berlin* and *pas-dikat*. No doubt the transition to Seychelles livened many of them up. A *kanmtole* band must have at least a fiddle and a triangle, but can also include banjos, accordions and a drum. The most important band member is the *komandan*, who

and facing each other while making suggestive signs. Compared to the *moutya*, the notorious *danse de ventre* [belly dance] is as innocent of offence as… a children's Christmas party."

The dance begins with the men chanting, either a known song or an improvised one – usually a bawdy tale or a taunt aimed at a rival in love. In the old days, this would also have been an opportunity for slaves to vent their anger against the plantation owners. In due course, the drums begin the beat and the men approach the women of their choice, arms outstretched. The partners dance back to back with sensuous, shuffling movements, but again, never touch.

shouts instructions to the dancers in time with the music, in much the same way as a caller in a barn dance.

The dance shows laid on by the bigger hotels tend to revolve around sega. Only the more "serious" cultural shows will include *moutya*, a more sombre dance which doesn't lend itself so well to the glitz of a tourist spectacle. *Kanmtole* nights are often advertised. They are usually held at smaller hotels, local social centres or restaurants, and anyone going along would certainly be made welcome. ❑

ABOVE: the sega dances performed in hotels are modernised versions of the traditional dance.

An arts tour

In the short time since the arrival of tourism, there has been an explosion in the arts and crafts output of Seychelles. Though the roots of the industry are not deep, they are uniquely Seychellois, drawing their inspiration from the dazzling colours and pristine nature of the environment. A tour of the numerous small art studios is a pleasant diversion from the beach and an opportunity to view paintings, prints, batiks and ornaments with little pressure to buy and, frequently, an opportunity to meet the artists themselves.

A good place to begin an arts tour of Mahé is the capital, Victoria, where there is no shortage of craft shops *(see page 291)*. South of the capital on the east coast, the Craft Village is an essential port of call. At the entrance is **Maison Coco**, a shop dedicated to the coconut palm, housed in a building made out of palm products. The range of goods includes leaves woven into bags and baskets, while the fibre that swathes the shoots, known as *tami*, is used to make various items including decorative stuffed fish, or wrappings for soaps perfumed with vanilla. The nut itself is used for napkin rings, candleholders, cups and trinket pots. Coconut oil is used to perfume soaps and bath oils. Inside the village, **The Natural Art Gallery** features works by local painters, including Barbara Jenson, Elizabeth Ragauin, Elizabeth Rouillon who specialises in detailed watercolours of plants, etchings and vivid watercolours by George Camille, and prints by Christine Harter of local scenes. Nearby is the studio of **Colbert Nourrice**, one of the most innovative of Seychellois artists. His abstract works are a narrative on canvas, telling small anecdotes from his life and experiences almost in comic strip form. One of his favourite themes is the local folklore character, Soungoula, a tricky customer, always full of mischief.

Gerard Devoud has two art galleries, one on the east coast at Les Mamelles and one on the west opposite the entrance to Plantation Club. He uses light and colour broken into "bits", creating mosaic-like landscapes and village scenes, using predominately watercolours.

The west coast of Mahé is the location for the studios of two of Seychelles most famous creative geniuses, artist **Michael Adams** and sculptor **Tom Bowers** *(see page 297)*. **Donald Adelaide** is

another artist based on the west coast. He produces bright, piecemeal images of the island and island life, mostly in watercolour. He has a studio near Harvey's Café *(see page 296)*, where he sells prints and originals.

At the Plantation Club Hotel is **The Yellow Gallery**, studio of Italian-born Antonio Filippin. Wood is his favourite working material, combined at times with granite and coral. The abstract works are quite large. In his gallery, he also exhibits the work of other local artists.

Ron Gerlach's Batik Studio is situated directly on Beau Vallon beach. Using authentic batik processes, he produces beach robes, shirts and

pareos in a range of attractive colours to his own, unique designs. A Ron Gerlach pareo is unmistakable. Many of them feature elegant, stylised, swooping tropic birds against delicate pastel backgrounds.

Away from Mahé, inevitably, art studios are fewer and some are merely outlets for artists based on Mahé. However, **Galerie des Arts** at Anse Volbert on Praslin is worthy of special mention. It is the best art gallery on the island, its displays including the art of Christine Harter and the superb photographic work of Paul Turcotte. On La Digue, **Barbara Jensen Studio** at La Passe is worth visiting to see this artist's bold colourful acrylics and watercolours. ❏

RIGHT: one of George Camille's vivid creations.

PRESERVING NATURE

The natural history of Seychelles echoes the ancient land link between Africa and Asia; much of it is still preserved in relatively pristine condition

Islands are laboratories of evolution. Nature's experiments have been going on for a longer period in Seychelles than in any other group of ocean islands, so it is no surprise that such a unique assemblage of flora and fauna should have evolved here. The roots of some species can be traced back to Africa, Madagascar, Asia and even to Australasia, originating from a time when all these land masses were linked in the supercontinent of Gondwanaland, before continental drift cast them apart.

Bats, tortoises and turtles

Seychelles was isolated in mid-ocean long before mammals appeared on earth. No mammals ever reached here by natural means except for those with the power of flight, namely the bat. Of the two endemic species, the sheath-tailed bat and the Seychelles fruit bat, the latter is by far the most common. It is one of the few creatures to have benefited from the arrival of humans and the consequent proliferation of fruit trees. Not so beneficial from the bats' point of view is the culinary speciality, curried fruit bat, a local favourite which often pops up on restaurant menus. Despite the Seychellois' taste for them, however, bats remain very common and their noisy squabbling in the trees at night is one of the islands' characteristic sounds.

With no mammals for competition, Seychelles became the last Kingdom of Reptiles. The estuarine crocodile was an early casualty of human settlement, but the giant tortoise still thrives. Aldabra has the world's largest population with around 100,000 animals. Giant tortoises occupied islands across the Indo-Pacific for millions of years, safe from the mammals that came to dominate the continents. Their waterproof exoskeletons, their ability to survive for weeks without food and the female's inbuilt mechanism for storing sperm made them ideal candidates for ocean transport. The luckier ones

that had been swept away by the tide from the shores of the mainland were washed up on remote tropical islands. This happened rarely enough for unique island races to evolve. Sadly, most of these are now extinct, victims of human exploitation. It was thought the granitic island species had suffered the same fate until the

PROTECTED AREAS

Literally 1,000 miles (1,600 km) from anywhere – India to the north, Africa to the west, Sri Lanka to the east and Madagascar to the south – the Seychelles islands were uninhabited until the late 18th century. While the natural beauty of other Indian Ocean islands was gradually decimated, that of the Seychelles has been preserved. There are many protected areas where nature lovers can marvel at unspoilt flora, fauna and marine life: the Morne Seychellois National Park, Mahé; the Vallée de Mai, Praslin; the Veuve Reserve, La Digue; and special reserves on the islands of Cousin, Aride and Aldabra.

LEFT: giant tortoise on Aldabra.
RIGHT: the Seychelles black paradise flycatcher is easily identified by its long black tail.

recent discovery of some unusual tortoises. DNA tests were carried out on these strange-looking creatures with exciting results that pointed to not just one, but two surviving species, Arnold's tortoise and Seychelles tortoise. A conservation project has been established on Silhouette to breed both species to ensure their survival.

Another conservation programme is run on Curieuse where Aldabra giant tortoises are bred. There are also feral populations on Frégate and Cousin, while many are kept in pens in hotel or

CALL OF THE WILD

The call of the male Aldabra tortoise is said to be the loudest noise in the reptile kingdom. It is, in fact, a seduction technique – the actual mating is a silent affair.

nised that live turtles have a higher value enhancing the reputation of the country while encouraging eco-tourism. The sale of all tortoiseshell products is now banned.

Two species now breed here – the hawksbill turtle and the green turtle. Remarkably, the granitic islands are the only place in the world where hawksbill turtles come up to breed in the daytime. Green turtles occasionally nest in the granitic islands but their stronghold is Aldabra where around 2,500 females haul them-

restaurant gardens at the Botanical Gardens and elsewhere so there are plenty of opportunities to see this lovable Seychelles symbol. Once it was traditional to present a baby tortoise to a newborn girl and raise the animal as a family pet until the girl grew up and married. The tortoise would then be slaughtered at the wedding feast. This tradition has died out, though many Seychellois still keep a few lumbering giants as pets.

Likewise, the future of turtles is slowly brightening. In the past they were slaughtered mainly for their "tortoiseshell" which was converted into jewellery and other trinkets for sale to tourists. Thankfully, the authorities recog-

selves ashore each year to breed. In the past, they were heavily exploited for their meat and, although poaching still poses a threat, they have escaped the near total extermination suffered elsewhere. Aldabra is one of the few places on earth where turtles, classed as among the most endangered of creatures under the Convention on International Trade in Endangered Species (CITES), are actually increasing in number.

Unique reptiles

For sheer quantity of reptiles, there is nowhere quite like the seabird islands of Seychelles, particularly Cousin, Cousine and Aride which have a greater concentration of these beasts than anywhere else on earth. It is partly thanks to the seabirds themselves that the lizards survive in such large numbers. They feed on eggs or chicks left carelessly unguarded or a catch that has been dropped. Most reptile species found here are unique to Seychelles including the Seychelles skink, Wright's skink and several species of green gecko.

One of the characteristics of ocean islands is the absence of amphibians. Once again, Seychelles is an exception to the rule. The islands support 13 amphibian species in all, 12 of which are unique to Seychelles; one of these was described for the first time in 2002. Among the

Land and seabirds

The lure of birdwatching in Seychelles is not the number of species. You may see more varieties in a single day in East Africa than in a lifetime in Seychelles. Also, island birds tend to be less colourful than their continental cousins. However, what they lack in variety and spectacular plumage they more than make up for in their rarity value.

Successful programmes have been implemented to restore the fortunes of two of the rarest birds in the world, the Seychelles warbler and Seychelles magpie-robin. Programmes are also underway to study, protect and reverse

frog species is the minuscule pygmy piping frog. Though difficult to spot, its high pitched squeak is often the only sound to be heard in the higher hills. Another species, the croaking carrycot frog, has evolved the surprising habit of carrying its tadpoles on its back. Amazingly, the only other places frogs do this are New Zealand and tropical South America – opposite ends of the former super-continent.

LEFT: Cousin warden counting turtle eggs.
ABOVE: a pygmy piping frog – a candidate for the title of the world's smallest frog.
RIGHT: the Seychelles green gecko is unusually active in the daytime.

the historical decline of other species. This includes probably the most beautiful of the endemic birds of Seychelles, the Seychelles black paradise flycatcher. It is the symbol of La Digue, where a special nature reserve has been established for it. The male is staggeringly beautiful with its shiny black plumage and ridiculously long tail feathers. Though less eccentric the female is also an attractive bird, chestnut above, white below with a black head.

The enigmatic Seychelles scops owl occurs only on Mahé, its population concentrated in the Morne Seychellois National Park, while the white eye survives on Mahé, Conception and Frégate. Both are among the rarest birds in the world. Praslin, too, has its own special bird, the Seychelles black parrot. Its piercing whistle is often the only sound echoing around the Vallée de Mai. One of the world's smallest birds of prey, and the only bird of prey in the granitics, is the Seychelles kestrel. It is found mainly on Mahé with smaller numbers on Praslin and elsewhere, often announcing its presence with its far-reaching 'ti-ti-ti-ti' cry (its name in Kreol is *katiti*). The Seychelles fody (*tok tok* in Kreol) survives on five islands including Aride and Cousin, the easiest places to spot it.

More common, but also unique to the granitic islands, are the Seychelles blue pigeon, Seychelles cave swiftlet, Seychelles bulbul and Seychelles sunbird. Even the laziest of bird-watchers can spot them, possibly in their hotel grounds, but certainly in Victoria's Botanical Gardens in the early morning or late afternoon.

Aldabra Atoll is particularly rich in avifauna. The unique forms of this World Heritage Site include the last surviving flightless bird of the Indian Ocean, the Aldabra rail. Aldabra is also famous for its seabird colonies including the world's second largest colony of frigatebirds. Closer to the main islands, there are more spectacular seabird colonies notably Aride (ten breeding species), Cousin (seven breeding

SAVED FROM EXTINCTION

Conservation success stories are few and far between but Seychelles boasts more than its fair share. Take the humble Seychelles warbler. By 1960, it stood on the threshold of annihilation. An international appeal was launched and in 1968 Cousin was placed under the protection of the Royal Society for Nature Conservation and BirdLife. The warblers thrived. By the 1980s numbers reached around 350. However, it was too early to take the species off the critical list so long as they remained confined to one island where a local disaster might threaten their survival. In 1988, 29 birds were transferred to Aride. It was hoped they might settle to breed around the usual time in January. The birds had other ideas. With virtually unlimited space and food supply they bred year-round and by 1999 there were almost 2,000 birds. With a smaller colony also established on Cousine, the species is now one of the few to be taken off the Red Data list of endangered species.

The Seychelles magpie-robin is now receiving similar treatment. Once widespread in the granitic islands, its tame and confiding behaviour meant it fell victim to man and introduced predators. Down to fewer than 20 birds on Frégate, a BirdLife recovery programme was launched. Cousin, Aride and Cousine now host breeding populations and numbers have increased to over 100 birds.

species) and Bird Island, named in honour of its million plus sooty terns that return to breed annually between April and October. The attraction here is the sheer number of birds competing for every inch of space.

Yet the Seychelles species list contains far more visiting birds than breeding ones, most of which turn up between October and December.

Plant life

The large-scale deforestation that laid bare almost every tropical island during the age of exploration did not pass Seychelles by altogether, but unlike most islands, the scars have healed. Although virgin forest is now confined to the higher areas of Mahé and Silhouette, and the Vallée de Mai on Praslin, there are no large expanses of wasteland, no vast areas of cultivation or big sugar cane plantations. Seychelles is like one gigantic botanical garden.

Today, there are well over 1,000 species of plants in the granitic Seychelles. About 250 occur naturally of which around 75 are unique to the islands. Symbols of the tropics such as bougainvillaea, frangipani and hibiscus appear in almost every garden. The colourful flame tree and fruit trees such as breadfruit and jackfruit are common. Coconuts, once confined to the beach crest, have been planted in huge numbers further inland. In the coral islands, as with the birds, there is a much smaller variety of species, but again Aldabra is an exception. Here, a remarkably diverse flora includes about 40 endemics.

Some of the endemic plants of Seychelles are so rare they are only found in a few remote locations, such as the *bwa d fer* and *bwa d nat* trees, once prized for shipbuilding. The jellyfish tree has apparently always been rare, but still clings to survival on a few Mahé hilltops. The insect-eating Seychelles pitcher plant, though not so rare, can be elusive until you know where to search. Other unique plants are more common including the beautiful wild vanilla, its leafless stems climbing over bushes.

No one can fail to notice the majestic palms of Seychelles. There are six species unique to the granitics including the fabled coco de mer, confined to Praslin and Curieuse. The female

tree has the largest seed in the world, a double nut with an uncanny resemblance to the female pelvis complete with pubic hair. The enormous catkin of the male tree also has to be seen to be believed! Certainly, some male and female toilets in Seychelles that choose the nut and the catkin as symbols to tell them apart leave no visitor in any doubt as to which is which.

For those able to drag themselves away from the beaches, there are several well-marked trails where many of the plants of Seychelles can be seen. More sedentary visitors may take a trip to Victoria's Botanical Gardens, while a visit to Vallée de Mai is virtually mandatory for any

visitor to Praslin. However, such is the profusion of life in the hot and humid tropical climate of Seychelles, that even a stroll round a hotel garden can be very rewarding.

It is fortuitous that so much of the flora and fauna of Seychelles has survived to a more enlightened age in which their intrinsic value is appreciated. This is partly due to the fact that when compared to most other places in the world, Seychelles was settled comparatively recently. Thankfully, the government was quick to recognise how essential it was to protect its country's natural assets. Today, more than 40 percent of its land mass is given some form of legal protection. ❑

LEFT: fairy terns mating on Bird Island.
RIGHT: *Bwa zanget* found on Aldabra, one of Seychelles' many rare endemic plants.

UNDERWATER WORLD

Exploring the shallow waters of the Indian Ocean, where coral reefs support
hundreds of species of spectacular fish, is like swimming in a giant exotic aquarium

The islands of the Seychelles provide visitors with access to some of the best protected ocean areas in the world. Seychelles has had a long history of conservation and has had marine reserves for over 30 years with the St Anne Marine National Park being the first protected marine area in the region.

This enlightened and far-sighted approach has paid dividends in terms of the range and abundance of marine life found. Because spear-fishing and other destructive fishing techniques commonly used in other island states have long been banned, visitors are impressed to find that fish species that are normally shy and elusive are easy to find and apparently visitor friendly.

Exploring the deep

Most hotels and resorts rent out snorkelling equipment (though the quality varies) or you can buy your own from one of the dive centres which sell masks, snorkels and fins at very reasonable prices. A number of tour operators and some private companies offer snorkelling excursions by boat to favourite spots such as St Anne Marine National Park, Bay Ternay Marine Reserve and St Pierre in Curieuse Marine Park. These trips may be for a half or full day and many include lunch at one of the renowned creole restaurants to be found on the smaller islands.

For scuba divers, Seychelles has long been an established world class diving destination both in terms of diving conditions and professionally run diving operations. Most diving centres belong to the Association of Professional Divers, Seychelles (APDS) which sets additional standards for the operation and provision of diving services. Their members also support a number of marine related environmental and conservation projects such as the Whale Shark Monitoring Programme run locally by the Marine Conservation Society of

Seychelles and the Shark Research Institute, Seychelles. For those who have never tried diving, the shallow waters and rich coral reefs around Seychelles islands provide the perfect opportunity to learn, combining safe and enjoyable diving conditions with world class diving instruction.

GENTLE GIANTS

The largest fish in all the oceans is the whale shark, found around the coastal waters of Seychelles. This harmless plankton feeder can grow to a length of 18 metres (59 ft) and weigh over 25 tonnes. Until recently, these sharks were not regularly hunted; now however, there is a big demand from the Far Eastern restaurant trade, particularly for their fins. Little is known of this impressive fish except that, like many sharks, it is extremely slow growing. Several treaties recognise the need to protect sharks, but international co-operation is lacking. In November 2002, a proposal to list whale sharks in CITES' Appendix II was narrowly defeated due to opposition led by Japan.

LEFT: the striking emperor angelfish
RIGHT: filming a whale shark, the ocean's biggest fish.

Learners and pros

APDS centres offering the PADI programme introduce complete beginners to scuba diving, starting with a tutorial and confined water skill session prior to the first shallow open water dive. They all offer four-day courses culminating in the internationally recognised PADI Open Water Diver certificate. For already qualified divers they also offer a number of advanced and supervisory courses right through to those aspiring to become Dive Instructors. There are dive centres on Mahé,

NATURE'S CURE

If you are unlucky enough to tread on a sea urchin, rub papaya on to the wound: the juice of the fruit contains an enzyme that helps dissolve the spines.

Praslin and La Digue as well as on the outer island of Desroches.

Diving is possible all year round with the calmest sea conditions being in March, April and May and then in October and November. Visitors hoping for the thrill of diving with a whale shark should consider July and August or November and December. October/ November is also the period when the APDS hosts the annual Indian Ocean underwater festival, SUBIOS, where some of the world's top underwater photographers,

CLEANING SERVICES

Apart from moray eels and octopuses, the gaps and crevices in the granite rocks house animals that would happily feature on the moray's diet sheet, especially crabs, shrimps and lobsters, but one group most closely associated with the moray is the brightly coloured cleaner shrimp. This little creature performs a valuable service not just for morays but for many fish species, cleaning parasites off skin, scales and even from between their teeth. The shrimp's bright red and white banding and long white antennae act as an advertisement for their cleaning services and seem to guarantee that they will not be eaten in return for their skilled services.

Another creature offering cleaning services to reef inhabitants is the little striped cleaner wrasse whose vertical black and blue stripes are easily identified. Wrasse are very territorial and set up shop by particular rocks or coral heads where they bob and weave in a characteristic display to attract business. The careful observer will be able to see these little fish working away deep inside the mouths or gills of larger reef fish in apparent security.

Closer to the shore, meanwhile, the long sausage-shaped sea cucumbers scattered across the shallow sands keep the seabed clean, as they feed on detritus and algae in the sand's surface layer.

film makers and conservationists present a programme of films and lectures to visitors and residents.

Seychelles seascape

Whether you're an experienced or first-time diver, Seychelles has so much to offer in terms of diving attractions. The unique granite rock formation of the northerly island group, known as the Inner Islands, creates submarine conditions that are much more varied than might be expected, supporting a prodigious variety of marine life. The diversity is further broadened by the coral atolls to the south which include Aldabra, the world's largest raised coral atoll and a designated UNESCO world heritage site.

The water temperature, which is somewhere between 26 and 30°C (79–86°F), promotes the prolific growth of sponges, corals and invertebrates which paint the granite walls and canyons in a kaleidoscope of colours. The underwater terrain of the Inner Islands is a mirror image of the landscape above the surface characterised by dramatic granite formations. The rocks and boulders form natural gullies and crevices that are prime real estate for many marine creatures. A common inhabitant of these nooks and crannies is the moray eel, a species with an undeserved notoriety. Its reputation stems mainly from the habit of greeting visitors with its toothy jaws gaping in an apparently threatening manner. But appearances are deceptive. These eels live quiet lives, bobbing about harmlessly in their crevices. There is little water flow and so they have to gulp water over their gills in order to breathe, hence the gaping jaws. Morays are successful hunters of fish, crabs and snails, but have little interest in bigger fare.

Another crevice inhabitant occasionally found around the reef during the day is the octopus. This, the most highly developed of all the molluscs, is an extremely active predator, feeding mainly at night on other molluscs, crabs and small fish, catching prey with the muscular suckers lined along its eight arms. The octopus is also the master of disguise, especially the marbled octopus commonly found on the granitic reefs. Its skin has special cells which allow it to change colour and alter its texture.

LEFT: preparing for the plunge.
RIGHT: the moray eel's impressive dentition keeps unwanted visitors at bay.

Distinctive fish

Visitors to Seychelles are always impressed by the sheer volume of fish encountered. The brightly coloured butterfly and angelfish are often the most apparent but with a little practice you can become familiar with the extreme body shapes of some species. The elongated cylindrical forms of the trumpet fish and flutemouths are an easy first step; however, discerning between the two can take patience – the trumpet has a fan-like tail and is generally seen in several colour forms on the coral reef while the flutemouth is normally seen just below the water's surface and has a whip-like tail.

Another easy to distinguish group are box fish and pufferfish, the former having angular cube-like bodies with apparently undersized fins while the puffers resemble deflated tropical fruit swimming over the reef – they only "puff" up if harrassed or cornered. Both these groups have teeth sharp enough to cut through coral that can deliver a deep and painful bite if tormented.

Lionfish and their cousins the scorpionfish are also fairly easy to identify; lionfish by their dramatic array of long feather- or whip-like spines on their back and side fins; scorpionfish by their camouflaged and bottom dwelling habit. The problem with scorpionfish is actually finding them to begin with.

Once the odd-shaped fish species have been identified you're still left with a bewildering array of "fish" shaped fish. Of the reef dwellers, the majority belong to the parrotfish or wrasse families. Parrotfish come in a huge range of sizes and colours but all exhibit the characteristic horny coral cutting beak, like that of a real parrot. Wrasse, an equally large group, have no such distinguishing characteristics. Keen divers and snorkellers should invest in a fish spotter's guide to identify fish beyond this level.

> ## SEX CHANGE
> Some fish have the ability to change sex; parrotfish, anthias and wrasse start as females and can become males as needed.

along the reef's perimeter. Keen underwater photographers home in on these fans as they support their own array of co-inhabitants ranging from small cowry shells and spider crabs to their own specialised, if somewhat small predator. The long-nosed hawkfish uses the fan corals as a look-out point from which to capture the small crustaceans on which it feeds.

Big fish

The other attraction of these remote island spots is the chance to encounter larger fish and pelagic species such as shark, barracuda and tuna. Diving and snorkelling along the vertical walls of some islands almost guarantees the sighting of the dog tooth tuna, a real warrior of the deep. These large powerful fish swim with a slightly open mouth proudly displaying a set of canine-like teeth; their large black eyes seem to follow your every move.

As there is comparitively little fishing here, the marine eco-systems in the outer regions are under less pressure and should have more abundant marine life. Here the food chain supports a larger number of predators and on many reefs the various species of grouper such as the rare potato cod, are typically abundant here. These large fish can grow to well over 1 metre (3 ft) in length and are characterised by large black potato-like blotches on their grey bodies; the species has a reputation for being aggressive which may or may not be deserved; however, any fish of this size should be treated with respect.

Outer island terrain

Visitors to the Outer Islands will notice a distinct difference in the underwater terrain to that of the Inner Islands. These islands and atolls are either large sandbanks, such as Bird Island and African Banks, or coral atolls such as Aldabra. The coralline islands often have dramatic walls which plunge from the surface into deep water and thus have a very different range of inhabitants. The deeper sections of these walls are characterised by intricate gorgonian fan corals which are supported by a springy backbone of horn-like material. They grow at right angles to the current so that they can filter out food particles from the water as it runs

Turtle spotting

Turtles are another common sight on the Outer Islands. While hawksbill turtles are the predominant species of the Inner Islands, as you travel south the green turtle becomes more common. Green turtles are generally larger then their sharp-billed cousins and have a broader head and less pronounced bill. A third species, the loggerhead turtle, is rarely seen and while it seems to have a blend of characteristics from the other two species it can normally be recognised from its massive head, large eyes and immensely thick and powerful beak which is much more heavy duty than either of the common species. ❏

LEFT: male stoplight parrotfish.

Top Dive Sites

There are numerous world class dive sites in Seychelles. The following are the top Inner Island sites as rated by resident divers. Apart from Ave Maria on Praslin, most of these are suitable for more experienced divers. However, the list is by no means comprehensive. The dive centres on Mahé, Praslin and La Digue include many more interesting sites in their programme, suitable for novices and experienced divers alike. *(For more information on diving and dive sites in the Inner Islands, see Travel Tips.)*

Shark Bank

A granite massif with a depth of between 20 and 35 metres (65–115 ft); this outcrop between northwest Mahé and Silhouette island is a focal point for schooling fish and predators. The rocks are especially renowned for sightings of large marbled stingrays. A deep site which can have strong currents, it is suitable for experienced divers.

L'Îlot

This classic granite island lies off the northwestern tip of Mahé. Thanks to its position at the confluence of the east and west coast currents, its waters support a plethora of marine life. It is one of the few Inner Island sites with good soft coral formations and good schooling fish opportunities. Although the maximum depth is only 23 metres (75 ft), currents and patchy visibility mean that in adverse conditions divers need to have suitable experience.

Brissare Rocks

A granite massif 5 km (3 miles) off the northeast coast of Mahé, this site attracts many schools of fish including a resident school of six-line snappers and a family of Napoleon wrasses. With depths of down to 20 metres (65 ft) this site is suitable for all but novice divers.

The Wreck of the Ennerdale

The remains of this stricken tanker lie 8 km (5 miles) off the northeast coast of Mahé at a depth of 30 metres (98 ft). Due to the distance from shore and its exposed position, the wreck is not often visited and so hosts good marine life. The structures are encrusted with corals and inver-

RIGHT: there are some excellent sites for schooling fish around Seychelles.

tebrates but over the passage of time metal fatigue and corrosion are beginning to compact some sections of the wreck. When conditions are good, this is an excellent dive for experienced divers, with schooling fish, shark and ray prospects.

Marianne

The southern tip of Marianne Island is a rarely visited site. The terrain of jagged granite rocks and giant boulders offers refuge for many large fish and it is the seasonal home for a group of grey reef sharks which, for some unknown reason, are all female. An exciting dive to 27 metres (88 ft) with or without the sharks for experienced divers.

Ave Maria

Praslin's version of L'Îlot; this granite group is renowned for a broad range of fish species as well as regular shark and stingray sightings. With a maximum depth of 26 metres (85 ft), in good conditions this site is suitable for all divers.

The Outer Islands

Outer Island sites have not been included here as this area would need a whole chapter to do it justice. The Desroches Drop is one of the best-known sites *(see page 345)*, but anyone lucky enough to experience diving off Alphonse, Astove, Cosmoledo and Aldabra will find the richness of marine life incomparable. ❑

FISHING

Fish and fishing are dear to the souls of all Seychellois. That's hardly surprising:
they're surrounded by some of the richest fishing grounds in the world

Fish is the staple diet of all Seychellois and, indeed, quite a few tourists. The bounty of the Indian Ocean includes a tremendous variety of fish, excellent for both sport fishing and the dinner table. There are many game fishing boats to serve the tourist industry, equipped with the finest fishing gear around. Fly-fishing

is a relatively new sport in Seychelles, following the discovery of unexploited grounds, described by specialists as among the best in the world. Indeed, Seychelles holds world records for both fly-fishing and game fishing.

Big game fishing

The majority of game fishing boats operate out of Mahé. However, with the growth of tourism on Praslin and La Digue, these islands also have a number of good boats available. Each of the resorts on Silhouette, Frégate, Bird, Denis (a popular venue for serious big game fishermen), Desroches and Alphonse also have boats. Most charter boats fish exclusively by trolling (draw-

ing bait through the water with rod and line), as this is the best way to catch the finest game fish. Tag and release is favoured by some operators and, if you believe in promoting this technique, it is as well to discuss it in advance.

The quality of fishing will depend partly on weather conditions, but the best fishing grounds are at the drop off at the edge of the Seychelles Plateau (up to 32 km/20 miles offshore), within easy reach of all the granitic islands: bigeye tuna, dogfish tuna and yellow fin tuna all inhabit the edge of the Seychelles Bank; sailfish are commonly caught in waters between Mahé and Silhouette; dorado can be caught over the Bank in season; and barracuda, jobfish *(zob)*, even sharks are sometimes caught on trolling lures.

Though some fish – tuna and bonito, for example – can be caught all year round, others come and go according to the season. The best time of year for catching sailfish is during the southeast monsoon, from June onwards. Though dorado can be caught all year round it is most commonly seen between January and September. Kingfish, also known as wahoo, are most plentiful from January to March, and trevally *(karang)* from November to December. Huge marlin weighing in at 150 kg (330 lb) or more can be caught year round, including blue, striped and black marlin, but they are encountered far less frequently than sailfish.

Bear in mind that sea conditions can be rough during the southeast monsoon (June to September). Larger boats afford a more stable platform from which to fish, but unless you are sharing the cost with other people, this can be costly: the bigger the boat the bigger the expense.

For the real enthusiast, liveaboard charters are available and may be customised to take into account both the needs of the fisherman and family members who may have other priorities such as exploring the islands.

For more details on liveaboard charters and game fishing specialists see Travel Tips.

LEFT: yellow fin tuna fighting a losing battle.
RIGHT: landing "the big one".

Fly-fishing in St François

Seychelles offers world-class fly-fishing, primarily for bonefish and trevally. A few may be caught at Denis Island, but the best place by far is in the St François lagoon, which can be reached via the nearby Alphonse Island Resort (*see page 347*). St François is a natural reservoir which remains virtually unexploited. The hotel is trying to keep it that way by restricting numbers to a maximum of 12 fishermen per day. Hooks are barbless and all fish caught are released. Anglers are transported to the lagoon on two mother boats then transferred to flat boats (two fishermen per boat) which, depending on the state of tide, can travel throughout the lagoon, even in shallow water.

It is nothing remarkable for a reasonably good fly-fisherman to catch more than 50 fish in a day, while beginners can catch as many as 20. The average bonefish caught here weighs 2–3 kg (5–7 lb) though they can weigh up to 7 kg (15 lb). Not surprisingly, St François has claimed several world records.

Other fish caught here in the traditional way include small hammerhead shark, lemon shark, bigeye and barracuda. In 2002, fly-fishing operators at Alphonse became the first in the world to pioneer a technique for catching milkfish, a fearsome fighting fish despite its innocuous name.

Bottom fishing

Bottom fishing may lack the excitement of the chase involved in game and fly-fishing, but if it's dinner you're after, fishing with lines, lead weight and natural bait is a great way to get it. Local fishermen traditionally fish by this technique, baiting lines with crabs, shellfish, squid, mackerel or other fresh fish, and using two or three hooks. The most sought-after of the 200 or so species of fish that can be caught on lines include red snapper *(bourzwa)* and grouper *(vye)*. They feature on menus in most of the major hotels and restaurants, and are among the tastiest fish you can eat here.

Apart from in the Marine National Parks, where fishing is prohibited, you can fish almost anywhere. Enquire locally about renting a little boat and if you don't have your own equipment, you should be able to pick up what you need in Victoria. If in doubt, ask a local fisherman for advice. ❑

CREOLE CUISINE

Seychelles cuisine is a product of its history and geography, rooted firmly in the riches of the sea and the spices of the tropics

With the exception of the family pig, a clutter of chickens kept behind the house and the occasional few cattle, there has never been a tradition of rearing livestock in Seychelles because of the limited land available. Meat was only served on special occasions. The ocean has always been the main supplier. Little has changed. Today, the Seychellois are among the biggest per capita consumers of fish in the world.

Fish and shellfish

Seychellois love fish; but not just any old fish. They have such a bounty of marine life around their islands that they can afford to be choosy. For example, the meaty tuna known locally as bonito can make a delicious curry, but most Seychellois look down on it as inferior and feed it to their dogs. They love the firm, white, flaky flesh of the *bourzwa* or red snapper, which is left whole but scored with long slits on both sides which are stuffed with ginger, garlic, chilli, onions and other spices. It is then wrapped in banana leaf (for purists) or tin foil and cooked over charcoal. Many Seychellois consider the finest meat from a red snapper is to be found in the head, and make good use of it in fish soup. Mackerel is also grilled in a parcel over hot coals, or on bamboo skewers, and drizzled with freshly squeezed lime to keep the flesh moist. *Zob* (another type of snapper) and *karang* (trevally) are served as steaks.

Parrotfish is put into fish stews, or battered for a Seychelles slant on the British favourite, fish and chips. Steaks of tuna, kingfish and swordfish are marinated in oil and spices then grilled on the barbecue. Shark meat is grated with garlic, ginger, *bilimbi* (a sour fruit), lime, onions and turmeric, then stir fried until it looks like yellow desiccated coconut. This dish is known as shark chutney. Sailfish is cut wafer

LEFT: food served up at the higher-class hotels is often an eclectic mix of local fish, home-grown produce and imported ingredients.
RIGHT: Fish is a menu staple.

thin and smoked, to produce a delicacy every bit as good as smoked salmon, delicious on crusty bread with salad.

Shellfish are also popular in Seychellois cuisine. The favourites are *tektek* and *palourd*. *Tekteks* are winkle-like shells collected fresh from the sandy beaches and put into soup. It is

not uncommon, even on busy Beau Vallon beach, to see a Seychellois woman, often assisted by a couple of her young children, stooped over the sand at the point where the waves lap the shore. As the water recedes it uncovers the *tektek*, which quickly burrow out of sight pursued by a darting hand.

By contrast, *palourds* are found on muddy shores such as in the estuarine area north of Victoria's Inter-Island Quay. They are similar to cockles and delicious when cooked in herbs and garlic butter. The superb local prawns offered in most restaurants are a relatively new addition to the local diet. Prawns do not occur naturally in sufficient numbers around Seychelles to be worth harvesting. However, there is now a farm on Coetivy Island producing both for the local and export markets. The prawns are excellent, particularly the large ones, grilled in garlic butter, in a traditional Seychellois curry or in sweet and sour sauce.

Hot and spicy

Indian and Chinese cuisines have not influenced Seychellois cooking so strongly as in the Mascarenes. Most restaurants specialise in creole cooking and seafood. However, one Indian dish Seychelles has taken and made very much its own, is curry. A Seychelles curry (usually

fish, but also, commonly, chicken, pork, goat or beef) is simply crammed with flavours, and is hot! An exception to this rule is the *kari koko zourit* a mild octopus curry with creamy coconut milk. How they get the octopus so tender is kept a closely guarded secret by some; others will happily confess the secret is to cook your octopus in a pressure cooker. Whatever the truth, when cooked properly, it comes out more tender than chicken, melting in the mouth.

Spicy local sausages figure in a local speciality, sausage and lentil stew. Although there are *tenrecs* on the islands (small mammals similar to hedgehogs in appearance), originally introduced from Madagascar as food, Seychellois no longer eat them. They occasionally eat fruit bat, caught by hanging nets close to the fruit trees where the animals feed.

As for accompaniments, be warned, Seychellois love their chillies hot. The tiny chillis are the hottest. To the average Western palette a single seed can set the mouth on fire, yet Seychellois think nothing of eating them whole or ladling copious amounts of the minced chilli in vinegar that comes separately in a little dish, onto their meal.

Vegetables and salads

Rice (plain, white, boiled) is the staple, but you will occasionally be offered breadfruit, a versatile potato-like "fruit" served up as crispy chips, boiled and mashed, or stewed in coconut milk and sugar to make a gooey dessert. Best of all is baked breadfruit, the perfect complement to any beach barbecue. It is put whole among the burning coals until black on the outside and tender on the inside, then cut into piping hot slices and served with melted butter. Local legend has it that if you eat breadfruit, you'll be sure to return to Seychelles.

There is not a great deal of variety in the vegetable department. It is not easy to grow them in Seychelles due to the limited amount of flat land and the relatively poor soil. Exceptions include aubergines (usually served as deep fried fritters), watercress and the tasty spinach-like *bredes*. Avocados are abundant in season and salads are more than just the token lettuce leaf. Any true creole spread will come with a range of so-called chutneys – finely grated pawpaw, mango or *fisiter* (golden apple) with onion, lime juice and pepper. They make a refreshing and cooling addition to a spicy meal.

CONSIGNED TO HISTORY

Seabird eggs were once of great importance to the Seychellois, simply because the annual bounty of eggs was a welcome variation to an otherwise monotonous diet. Egg exploitation is now controlled, in an attempt to ensure the survival of the sooty tern colonies, but a seabird egg omelette is still considered a delicacy.

Turtles and tortoises were also eaten on special occasions. Traditionally, a baby tortoise was bought on the birth of a daughter and kept until the girl's wedding day, when it would be eaten at the wedding breakfast. This practice is now illegal. Both the giant tortoise and the turtle are protected species.

Starters on a creole menu usually include octopus salad, raw fish marinated in lime juice, and *palmis* salad. It became known as millionaire's salad, because the whole tree had to be sacrificed to obtain the shoot. Conservation legislation now protects this unique majestic palm and, today, the salad is made with the living shoot of the coconut palm, which grows all over Seychelles, chopped into thin slices.

Banana feast

More often than not the dessert choice is limited to local ice creams or fruit salad. Occasionally the fruit salad will come with coconut

if fresh juice is available. Try passion fruit juice or lime with a pinch of salt and sugar to taste. *Sitronel*, a kind of tea made from lemon grass, is also refreshing.

You are unlikely to be offered any of the local alcoholic brews with your meal but these are a part of local culture. *Kalou* (or toddy) is made from coconut sap which ferments quickly and naturally, and makes the ideal lazy man's tipple. *Baka* is a rum-like drink made from fermented sugar cane juice (a far cry from Bacardi). The most lethal of the local firewaters is *Lapire* made from almost anything which will ferment when mixed with sugar. ❑

nougat (caramelised coconut) or coconut milk. There are 25 species of banana in Seychelles, ranging from the foot-long *sen zak*, used to make crisps, to the sweet stubby *mil*, which is extremely sweet and crops up in the fruit bowl, or comes flambéed or stewed in *ladob*.

Drinks

There are plenty of fruit juices, soft drinks, locally brewed beers and imported (expensive) wines available. At restaurants, it pays to ask

LEFT: grating coconut.
RIGHT: a young girl carries bananas straight from the plantation to market.

CRACKING COCONUTS

Many a tourist works up a sweat trying to crack a coconut found at the roadside by hurling it against a rock or attacking it with a small penknife. Forget it, it doesn't work. To remove the thick fibrous husk that protects the nut, most Seychellois have a sharpened spike stuck in the ground. The husk of the coconut is impaled on this and worked loose. It takes an islander a few seconds, but for the novice a little practice is required.

On some excursions you may be offered *koko tann*, a green coconut with the top lopped off so you can drink the milk (refreshing, but an acquired taste). The thin jelly-like flesh of the unformed nut is also delicious.

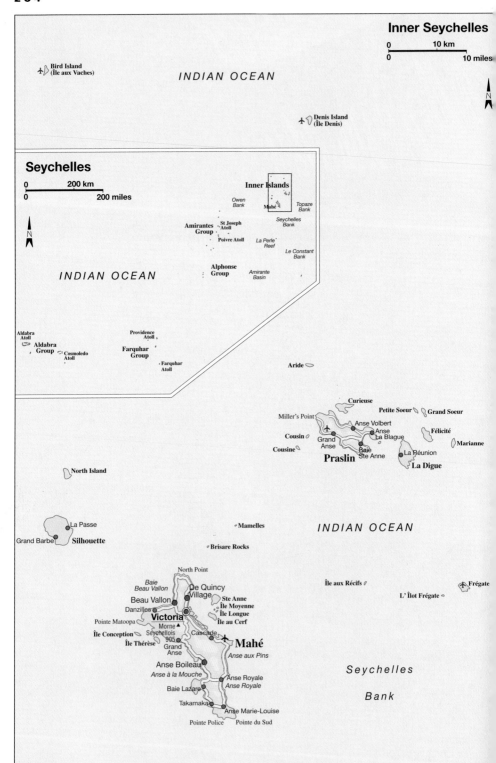

PLACES

A detailed guide to Seychelles, with principal sites clearly cross-referenced by number to the maps

To plan the perfect Seychelles holiday, you have to get three things right: the time of year (make sure you know beforehand when and where the monsoons hit); the quality of hotel (in the past, these have not enjoyed a great reputation, but there have been great improvements in recent years); and, last but not least, the choice of island.

Each of the many Seychelles islands that now welcomes overseas tourists has its own special attractions. Most tourists flying into Mahé head straight for their final destination, without taking time to explore the main island. It may be more commercial and developed than its fellow granitic islands, but beyond the tiny capital of Victoria, Mahé has some spectacular beaches and forests of its own to discover, with the added advantage of art and cultural attractions.

However, if you only have time to visit one island, Praslin is the one. Apart from its beaches bordered with granite boulders, the other main attraction is the Vallée de Mai, a magnificent dense palm forest – home of the unique coco de mer and its notorious love nut – which could well have inspired the set designers of *Jurassic Park*. Praslin also makes a perfect island-hopping base: Cousin, Curieuse, St Pierre, La Digue and Aride are all just a short boat ride away.

Laid-back La Digue can be visited on a day-trip from Praslin, but to take in the spectacular coastline – a favourite location for fashion shoots – and explore the inland trails by bike or on an ox-cart, a couple of days here would be well spent.

Even quieter than La Digue, Silhouette and North are the least-known of the Inner Islands. Seemingly stuck in a timewarp, Silhouette is a paradise for walkers. There are no roads but plenty of paths – not all well-trodden – that cut through the tangled and mountainous interior. In 2003, a new ecotourism resort opened on North Island, and it is hoped that the luxury resort will draw a new wave of environmentally conscious tourists.

Frégate, the most remote and exclusive granitic island, is privately owned. At around £1,000 (US$1,500) a night, for most of us it remains the stuff of dreams.

The coral islands of Bird, Denis, Desroches and Alphonse, a relative newcomer, are perfect for getting away from it all. Each island has its own luxury resort, but has been developed to carefully preserve the environment. With facilities for sailing, diving, snorkelling, deep-sea fishing and bird-watching among other activities, there's plenty on offer for those who want to do more than just dream the days away lounging by crystal waters. ❑

PRECEDING PAGES: traditional creole house on La Digue.

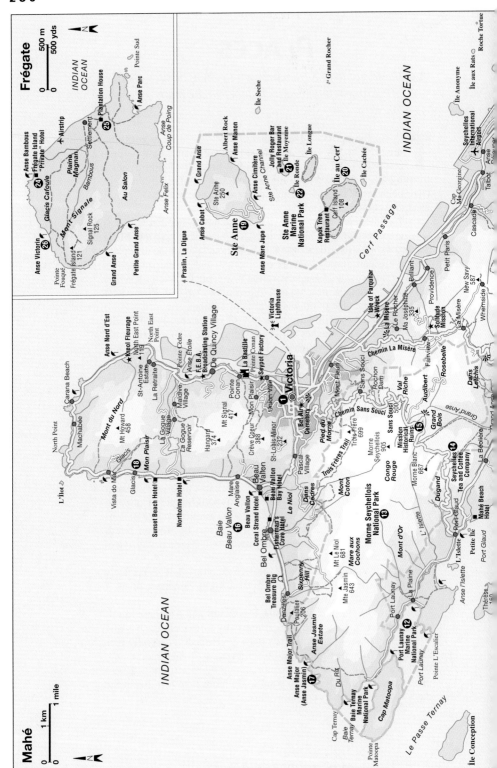

Mahé

0 ___ 1 km
0 ___ 1 mile

N

INDIAN OCEAN

North Point

L'Îlot

Carana Beach

Vista do Mar

Machabée

Glacis

Mont du Nord

Mt Howard 458

La Gogue Village

La Gogue Reservoir

Sunset Beach Hotel

Northolme Hotel

Baie Beau Vallon

Beau Vallon

Beau Vallon Bay Hotel

Coral Strand Hotel

Fisherman's Cove Hotel

Bel Ombre

Bel Ombre Treasure Dig

Danzilles

Pellaie 206

Sixpenny Hill

Mte Jasmin 643

Mt Le Niol 681

Mare aux Cochons

Anse Major Trail

Anse Jasmin Estate

Anse Major (Anse Jasmin)

Du Riz

Baie Ternay Marine National Park

Cap Ternay

Baie Ternay

Pointe Matoopa

Cap Matoopa

Le Passe Ternay

Île Conception

Mon Plaisir

Mare Anglaise

Le Niol

Dans Cèdres

Morne Seychellois National Park

Mont d'Or

La Plaine

Port Launay

Port Launay Marine National Park

Port Launay

Pointe L'Escalier

Anse l'Islette

Thérèse 160

L'Islette

Petite Île

Port Glaud

Port Glaud

Anse du Est

St-Antoine Estate

La Retraite

Maldive Village

Mt Signal 417

Mon Plaisir

Crève Coeur 388

St-Louis Minor 232

Pascal Village

Kreol Fleurage

North East Point

Pointe Cèdre

Anse Étoile

Pointe Conan

F.E.B.A. Broadcasting Station

De Quincy Village

La Bastille

Pointe Conan

Union Vale

Seypot Factory

Victoria

Bel Air Cemetery

Pied du Morne

Mont Fleuri

Trois-Frère 699

Mont Seychellois 905

Morne Blanc 667

Trois Frères Trail

Mont Coton

Congo Rouge

Morne Seychellois National Park

Dugand

Pascal Village

Sans Souci

Mission Historical Ruins

Chemin Sans Souci

Grand Bois

Seychelles Tea and Coffee Company

Mahé Beach Hotel

Port Glaud

Victoria Lighthouse

Isle of Farquhar Wreck

La Misère

Chemin La Misère

Pochon Dam

Val Riche

Sans Souci

Audibert

Rosebelle

Fairview

Dans Letchis

Grand'Anse

INDIAN OCEAN

Solitude Mission

Ma Josephine 335

Le Rochel

Brillant

Petit Panis

Providence

New Savy 587

Whemside

La Misère

Cap Ste-Georginel

Cascade

Talbot

Cerf Passage

Kapok Tree Restaurant

Cerf Island 108

Île au Cerf

Île Cachée

Ste Anne Marine National Park

Ste Anne 250

Ste Anne Channel

Anse Cimetière

Île Moyenne

La Ronde

Jolly Roger Bar and Restaurant

Albert Rock

Anse Manon

Grand Anse

Anse Cabot

Ste Anne

Anse Mare Jupe

Praslin, La Digue

Île Seche

Île Longue

Seychelles International Airport

Anse

Roche Tortue

Île Anonyme

Île aux Rats

1º Grand Rocher

Frégate

0 ___ 500 m
0 ___ 500 yds

N

INDIAN OCEAN

Pointe Sud

Anse Parc

Plantation House

Anse Bambous

Frégate Island "Private" Hotel

Airstrip

Settlement

Plaine Magnan

Glacis Cafoule

Mont Signale

Bambous

Au Salon

Anse Coup de Poing

Anse Felix

Signal Rock 125

Frégate Island 121

Anse Victorin

Pointe Fouque

Grand Anse

Petite Grand Anse

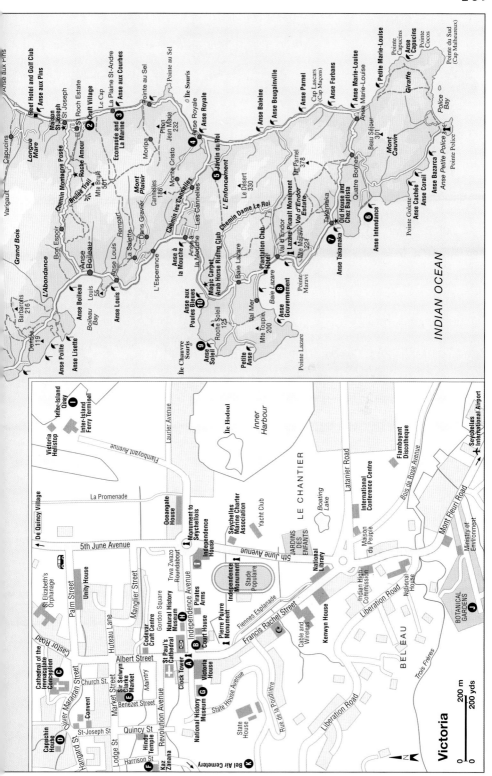

MAHÉ AND SATELLITES

Map on pages 286–7

Away from the spread of the capital, Victoria, there is breathtaking beauty around the coast and, in the mountains, another mysterious world in the rainforest awaiting exploration

Mahé is the largest and most densely populated island in Seychelles, home to 90 percent of Seychellois. The instinct of many visitors soon after touching down at the International Airport is to rush away to Praslin, La Digue or even further afield to discover the real Seychelles. This is a mistake. Of course the capital, Victoria, has its fair share of traffic jams and building works, but it's still the sort of place where everyone knows everyone else and where a game of dominoes outside the local shop is a social highlight. Beyond the town, there are plenty of opportunities to leave the paraphernalia of modern life behind, with escape routes down to the beach or up into the mountains.

Mahé covers an area of 154 sq km (59 sq miles) and rises to 905 metres (2,970 ft) above sea level. It is 27 km (17 miles) long and, at its widest, 8 km (5 miles) across, so it can easily be covered by car in a day. There is a good network of roads, both coastal and inland, and a day spent driving round the island in an open jeep or Mini Moke is a great way to start your holiday.

Most of Seychelles' present population of 81,000 live on Mahé, concentrated on the north and east coasts. Land reclamation along the east coast created valuable stretches of flat new terrain for development, and allowed for the building of a straight route from the airport to Victoria, cutting out the many twists and turns of the old coast road. The creation of this "new" land has meant that the vital development of the island's infrastructure has been largely concentrated in the area around the capital, thus limiting its impact on the rest of the island.

Being the largest and highest island, there is an element of grandeur in Mahé's beauty the other islands don't have. The coastal scenery goes from wild granite cliffs where waves crash against massive boulders tumbling into the ocean, to tranquil palm-fringed coves. If jaded by turquoise waters and silver sands, you can escape into the high hills and experience the eerie silence of the remote rain forest. The atmosphere is unforgettable, and one which many tropical islands have long since lost.

VICTORIA

Victoria ➊ is still a tiny capital by modern standards. It lies on the east coast, 8 km (5 miles) north of the airport, bounded by mountains on one side and sea on the other. The town grew up around the natural harbour formed by the sheltering satellite islands of Ste Anne, Moyenne, Ronde, Longue and Cerf. The original settlement was founded in 1778 by the French who built a military base here. In the early days of colonisation the islands, considered remote by the colonial powers, remained sparsely populated and expansion of the settlement was slow. It was known quite simply as

LEFT: tropical landscape by Victorian painter, Marianne North (1830–90).
BELOW: taking fresh chickens home from the market.

L'Établissement (The Settlement) until 1841, when it was named after Queen Victoria. Today, Victoria is the commercial centre of Seychelles and during business hours the streets throng with people and traffic. "Old" Victoria, the area that lies at the foot of the mountains, is built around narrow streets with eccentric pavements that rise over great storm drains one minute, and drop into a gutter the next. Elegant if dilapidated French colonial-style buildings are huddled around them. The modern avenues of "new" Victoria, laid out on the reclaimed land, are more stately, their pavements broad and flat, and lined here and there with attractive garden areas, bright with canna lilies and bougainvillaea.

If you're interested in Seychelles culture and the day-to-day life of its capital, it's worth spending a bit of time here. However, if your top priority is to experience the forests and coasts, half a day in Victoria should be enough.

Victoria's clock tower is a copy of the "Little Ben" tower outside London's Victoria station.

The heart of town

The centre of Victoria is easy to explore and its hub, standing at a central crossroads, is the **Clock Tower ⓐ**. It was built in 1903 both as a memorial to Queen Victoria and to commemorate the establishment of Seychelles as a Crown Colony in its own right. Next to the Clock Tower stands the **Court House ⓑ**, a typical colonial-style building with a fancy ironwork balustrade on the upper storey. The nearby fountain is topped with the replica of a very small bust of Queen Victoria. The original, now in the National History Museum *(see page 292)*, was unveiled in 1900 to mark Queen Victoria's 60th year on the throne.

On the corner of Albert Street and Revolution Avenue is the Anglican cathedral of **St Paul's**, Seychelles' oldest church, consecrated in 1859. A new cathedral, preserving the original tower, was completed here in 2003.

BELOW: transport that's eco-friendly.

Colonial grandeur

The Roman Catholic **Cathedral of the Immaculate Conception ©**, built in the French colonial-style, was completed in 1874, but has had many additions made since. On weekdays the church is quiet, but on Sunday mornings the strains of the organ and choir ring out from the open doorways, and the congregation, dressed in their best, spill out onto the steps. Sunday mass is as much a social occasion as a religious one.

Just down the street from the cathedral is Victoria's most impressive building, **Capuchin House ❶**. Built in 1933 with funds from the Swiss Capuchin order, and designed by one of the monks, it is used as a seminary for priests and brothers, some of whom still teach in the schools.

Morning market

Heading back south towards the town centre, you'll pass the pedestrianised Market Street and the **Sir Selwyn Selwyn Clarke Market ❸**, also known as Victoria Market. Saturday morning is the best time to come here. The fish stalls are the commercial heart of the market, piled with freshly caught barracuda, parrotfish, cordonnier, bonito and kingfish. Produce stalls are stacked with neat pyramids of exotic fruits and seasonal vegetables. Others are laid out with trays of mixed spices, neatly rolled quills of fresh cinnamon bark, packets of turmeric and old jars crammed with small but deadly red and green chillis.

For a bird's eye view of the goings-on, climb the stairs to the upper floor. There are a few craft shops open here, selling the more usual lines in souvenirs.

Cutting through the market, leaving by the side entrance, you come out into a little alley called Benezet Street. Turning left, past the bakery (which does

Map on pages 286–7

"Hellfire" chillis – hot favourites among the Seychellois.

BELOW: waiting for a thirsty customer.

SOUVENIR SHOPPING

Codevar is an artisans' association set up by the government to promote local craftsmanship. One of the best places to pick up gifts and souvenirs is the **Codevar Craft Centre** at **Camion Hall** in Albert Street (named after the old open lorries or *camyons*, used as buses, which used to set out on their routes from this spot). There is a shop on the street front selling pottery, wood-carvings, textiles and various objects made from coconuts and shells. In the arcade **Kreolor** have a wide range of jewellery made out of green snail shell, tiger cowrie and coconut shell in combination with gold, and crafts made from local woods, coconut shell, coconut wood and polished palm seeds. Immediately across the road, the **Sooty Tern** boutique specialises in stained glass work. Round the corner in Revolution Avenue, **Memorabilia** sells a wide range of crafts and books. **Sunstroke Gallery** on Market Street has a range of locally made beachwear, jewellery, hand-printed tablecloths and bed linen. Upstairs there is a gallery of local artwork. **Antigone**, the town's best bookshop, is in Passage des Palmes. **Antik Colony** in the Pirate's Arms building, sells quality souvenirs on colonial themes. On either side of the entrance to the Stadium Car Park are craft kiosks that sell beachwear, t-shirts, coconut crafts and spices.

excellent bread), you'll come back on to Revolution Avenue. If the heat and noise have made you weary, turn right and keep walking until you reach **Kaz Zanana** (Pineapple House), a quiet spot to pause for a bite to eat. The restaurant is on a terrace at the back, overlooking the garden. They serve light meals throughout the day and the best cappuccino and chocolate cake in Seychelles. The rest of the house is made up of small galleries which exhibit paintings and drawings by local artists, most notably George Camille.

Seychelles history

The nearby **National History Museum** (State House Avenue; open Mon–Fri 8.30am–4.30pm, Sat 8.30am–noon, closed Sun; entrance fee) is housed in a pretty colonial building, dating from 1902, with a characteristic ironwork balcony around the second storey. The museum houses a random collection of artefacts which don't help much in the understanding of Seychelles' history, but do have a curiosity value. Displays include traditional costumes, musical instruments, items salvaged from the avalanche and from shipwrecks, and a motley collection of objects associated with local magic or *grigri* which includes playing cards, chicken bones, face powder, herbs, mirrors and tobacco tins. The most important item in the museum is the original **Possession Stone** laid by the French in 1756 when they claimed the islands.

Strolling south

BELOW:
a not-so-busy
day at the market.

The shady **Fiennes Esplanade** which runs alongside Francis Rachel Street, was laid out by a British governor with the splendid name of Sir Eustace Edward Twisleton-Wykeham Fiennes (1918–21). At the start of the esplanade is

a **bust of Pierre Poivre**, the governor of Mauritius who arranged for the first spice plants to be brought to Seychelles for propagation (*see page 247*). A little further on you'll see the renovated colonial-style offices of **Cable and Wireless**, next to the elegant manager's residence, **Kenwyn House**, built in the 1860s.

Map on pages 286–7

East to the quays

East of the Clock Tower, on Independence Avenue, is the **Natural History Museum** ❻ (open Mon–Fri 8.30am–4.30pm, Sat 8.30am–noon, closed Sun), with displays of endemic birds, reef life, tortoises, geology and the skulls of estuarine crocodiles that once lived in the mangrove swamps around Mahé's coast and terrorised the colonists.

Opposite the museum is Victoria's best-known rendezvous, the **Pirates Arms** (open Mon–Sat 9am–midnight, Sun 4–11pm), a large, informal café-bar popular with tourists and locals alike. There is a small arcade of shops beside it, several of which sell curios. A little further down the street on the same side is the **Tourist Office**, a good place for advice and literature on accommodation, excursions and museum opening times. They also have leaflets on walks and trails in Mahé, Praslin and La Digue.

Continuing straight on, past the Trwa Zwazo (three birds) roundabout (named after the sculpture erected in 1978 to celebrate 200 years of human occupation), the first turning on the left is Flamboyant Avenue leading to **Inter-Island Quay** ❶, the departure point for ferries and boats to the islands, and for the fast catamaran to Praslin. The traditional island schooners also ply between Mahé, Praslin and La Digue from this point, and the fleets of the largest charter boat operators are based here. While waiting for your ferry, **Le Marinier** restaurant on the quayside offers a ringside seat of the comings and goings and you're left to linger over your drink for as long as you like. The charter boat marina is at the end of the jetty, near **Victoria Helistop**, the place to go for scenic tours or island transfers by helicopter. Just south of the Trwa Zwazo roundabout, on 5th June Avenue, is the **Marine Charter Association**, the departure point for glass-bottom boat and subsea viewer trips, and for some charter yachts.

Gardens and graves

The walk from the Clock Tower to the **Botanical Gardens** ❶ (open daily 8am–6pm; entrance fee) at the foot of Mont Fleuri takes about 20 minutes. They were laid out in 1901 by a Frenchman, Rivaltz Dupont, who collected many of the plant specimens on his travels. The site he chose was not ideal – the soil was poor and the land scattered with huge boulders – but it was the only affordable piece of land near town. Wandering through this green oasis today, it is hard to imagine the unprepossessing site Dupont was confronted with. The boulders are now an attractive feature, and the bubbling streams that run down either side of the park create a cool, soothing atmosphere.

At the top of the hill the gardens open out onto broad lawns dotted with specimen trees and shrubs. One of the most noticeable is the elephant apple, with fruits

The "Three Birds" sculpture on Freedom Square represents the African, Asian and European elements of Seychelles' heritage.

BELOW: tuna fishing boats.

The cannonball tree in bloom.

like huge, heavy apples that smell of rubber. There are attractive ponds with water lilies and darting dragonflies. The path leading from the ponds takes you past a mighty banyan tree and several drumstick trees that shed remarkable, long, thin fruits. One tree you can't miss, if it is in flower, is the cannonball tree which sheds its leaves when flowering, to reveal bizarre, fleshy coral pink flowers. A number of Aldabra giant tortoises are kept here in a large pen shaded by a coco de mer palm.

The gardens are shady enough to explore at any time of day, but it's best to avoid the heat of the midday sun. Ask at the entrance kiosk for the leaflet which maps out the gardens and names all the plants. There are no refreshment facilities inside the gardens, so it's a good idea to pick up a drink on the way.

On the outskirts of Victoria, at the beginning of the Sans Souci road, is **Bel Air Cemetery** , Seychelles' oldest cemetery. Tombstones lie strewn haphazardly, there are no signposts and no guide, but it is an atmospheric place, nonetheless. Settlers and their slaves were buried here from the earliest times. The more splendid tombs bear the names of illustrious Seychelles' families. According to legend, a young giant was killed by the locals and rumoured to be buried here in the 1870s. The grave of French corsair, Hodoul, is also rumoured to be here.

THE EAST COAST

There are two roads leading out of Victoria that head south towards the airport. For speed and convenience, the new road (Bois de Rose Avenue), is the one to take. But if you're in no hurry, a journey along the narrow, winding, rather chaotic old Mont Fleuri Road (which becomes East Coast Road further along) will tell you far more about Mahé. The buildings that line it are a fascinating jumble of the modern (such as the Pentecostal Assembly on the junction of Mont Fleuri Road and Liberation Road) and the charmingly dilapidated. You can catch glimpses of elegant old planters' homes peeping over high stone walls, identifiable by their steep-pitched roofs, shuttered windows, wide verandahs and high, stone foundations.

The two coast roads recombine at Providence, leading to **Cascade**, a traditional fishing village now dominated not by the fishing industry, but the nearby airport built on reclaimed land. The blessing of the fishing boats here on the feast of St André (November) used to be an important celebration in Seychelles, attracting spectators from all over Mahé. The number of boats is far fewer nowadays, but about half a dozen pirogues, decorated with flags and flowers, still gather here for the annual blessing.

Old plantations

Another 6 km (4 miles) down the coast road, past Anse aux Pins, on the site of a former plantation is the **Craft Village ❷** (Le Village Artisanal) where you can while away a bit of time looking at the workshops and shopping for souvenirs *(see Travel Tips)*. In the middle of the village the old plantation house, dating from 1870, has been furnished in typical colonial style. The cool, dark rooms smell of wax polish and cinnamon, and conjure a picture of the genteel existence once enjoyed by the privileged few. It's easy

to imagine a candlelit social gathering, the ladies in their long dresses frantically fanning themselves and the gentlemen in full evening dress savouring the fine wines imported at great expense from France. **Vye Marmit Restaurant** is a good place to sample local specialities such as fruit bat, octopus, crab and fish.

About 2 km (1 mile) further down the coast is the **Ecomusée and La Marine ❸** (La Marine: open Mon–Fri 7.30am–5pm, Sat 8am–3.30pm. Ecomusée: open Tues–Fri 10am–5pm, Sat–Sun 1–5pm; entrance fee), another restored plantation house and a model boat workshop, where it's fascinating to watch the skill and patience of the craftsmen at work. Each ship requires many hours of work, and the cost of the models (on sale next door) reflects this.

Map
on pages
286–7

Deserted coves

Beyond the Pointe au Sel promontory, **Anse Royale ❹** is the main east coast beach. The sheltered, sandy bay is scattered with giant boulders, dividing the beach into a series of "mini-coves" pretty much deserted on most weekdays. The snorkelling is reasonably good around the offshore islet of Île Souris. The currents between the mainland and the island can be strong, but run parallel to the beach, and it is fairly easy for a confident swimmer to cross them.

Minutely detailed models of old sailing ships are hand-made at La Marine.

Kaz Kreol at the southern end of Anse Royale is an informal restaurant right on the sand, where you can turn up in your swimming costume for lunch.

The King's Garden

Continuing south, the next turning off the main road is Les Cannelles. Sweet Escott Road is a left turning off this road. It was around here, in 1772, that Antoine Gillot, under instruction from the French government, planted a Royal Spice Garden *(see page 248)*, but this is long since overgrown. In its memory, the **Jardin du Roi ❺** ("King's Garden"; open daily 10am–5.30pm; entrance fee) has been established on the hillside above Sweet Escott Road. This renovated spice plantation, based on the former L'Enfoncement Estate, gives you a chance to see many aromatic plants growing (including nutmeg, pepper, cinnamon, vanilla and cloves). There is a walk laid out which you can follow using the printed guide. The small museum in the plantation house has some interesting exhibits, including old prints, maps and photographs of Seychelles, and information on growing and using spices. On Sunday the restaurant serves a popular curry buffet *(see Travel Tips)*.

BELOW:
a colonial house.

THE WEST COAST

The east coast road continues to Anse Marie-Louise where it turns sharply inland and cuts across the southern end of Mahé. At Quatre Bornes, a road leads down to a spectacular bay, **Anse Intendance ❻** where a very exclusive hotel, **The Banyan Tree Resort**, opened in 2001. The long, pristine beach is pounded by crashing breakers, exhilarating to watch as they sweep in with a tremendous roar and a haze of spray. The strong swimmer might enjoy body surfing in the waves, but it's easy to get caught in the rollers and dumped hard on the beach or rocks. As with many of Seychelles

beaches, conditions vary according to the monsoon season. Seas are at their roughest in the southeast monsoon (May to October) and there can be a strong undertow. During the northwest monsoon (October to April) the waves here are still big, but the water is calm enough to swim in. Intendance is a popular picnic spot for Seychellois at weekends and can get quite busy, but the beach is so long there is room for all.

Rejoining the main road at Quatre Bornes and heading west, you'll reach **Anse Takamaka ❼**, the first beach on the west coast road, whose large shady takamaka trees and golden sands entice many tourists and surfers, but currents are strong around here and swimming is dangerous.

Baie Lazare

The road swings northward, staying fairly close to the shore, offering dramatic views at Pointe Maravi of the rocks below before it descends again to **Baie Lazare ❽**. Here, beside the coast there is a **monument** (an anchor on a stone pedestal) commemorating the 250th anniversary of the first recorded French landing on Mahé by Lazare Picault in 1742 (in fact, Picault landed at Anse Boileau). Baie Lazare has a long expanse of beach, though swimming here during the southeast monsoon is not recommended. The best way to explore it is to call in at the **Plantation Club Hotel**, Seychelles' largest hotel. It has a swimming pool which is open to non-residents and a pool bar that serves drinks and snacks. To the rear of the hotel is an attractive marsh, an aspect of the Seychelles' landscape not often seen.

Baie Lazare village, on the hill overlooking the beach, is a typical Seychelles hamlet, centred around the neo-Gothic church of St Francis of Assisi. This is the starting point for the **Chemin Dame Le Roi** forest drive. The winding road leads uphill from **Harvey's Café**, a good place to linger and observe village life, and passes through scattered houses, forest and plantations of pineapple, cassava and sugar cane (mostly grown to make *baka*, a local spirit). This is old Mahé, still firmly fixed in another age, where chickens peck around the washing laid out on the boulders to dry.

Second best bay in the world

Just north of Harvey's Café a road leads on to a western promontory which has three bays. The best of these is **Anse Soleil ❾**, an enchanting small sandy beach, rated the second best "hidden secret" in the world by the German magazine *Reise & Preise*, with good swimming and excellent views. It is rarely busy, except on Sundays, when the simple but very good restaurant is popular with locals. Neighbouring **Petite Anse** is another attractive, sandy cove, about 10 minutes' walk along a shaded track. Reaching **Anse Gouvernement** involves a trickier drive along a narrow track with two raised concrete ramps on which you balance your wheels, while hoping you don't meet any traffic coming the other way. This sandy bay, dotted with massive granite boulders, is wild and windswept during the southeast monsoon, so not good for swimming at this time of year. Weekends apart, it is very quiet and romantic.

TIP

Allow some time to explore the peninsula around Anse Soleil, one of the wildest and most beautiful corners of Mahé.

BELOW: walking the dog Seychelles-style.

Artists' studios

Continuing northward on the coast road, the next place you come to is **Anse aux Poules Bleues** ⑩ where you'll find Michael Adams' Studio (open Mon–Fri 9am–4pm, Sat 9am–noon). The best-known artist in Seychelles, his jungle landscapes are a riot of leaves, stalks and stems, criss-crossing and clashing in every shade. He also takes a wry look at village life. Excellent prints of his work are on sale at the studio, but expensive.

The wide vistas of **Anse à la Mouche** open up as the road curves around the bay. The beach has the usual pristine, white sand and plenty of shade, and the shallow waters are calm all year round, which makes it ideal for children. It's also a good place for beach parties and groups of Seychellois often get together here at weekends. But on weekdays it is usually very quiet. The **Anchor Café** serves drinks, snacks and simple meals at reasonable prices.

Les Cannelles Road at the end of Anse à la Mouche leads inland to Santa Maria and the studio of **Tom Bowers** (signposted on the right as you climb Les Cannelles from the coast). Like so many artists before him, the London-born sculptor visited Seychelles, fell in love with it and settled. He uses resin for his sculptures of local people which are then cast in bronze.

Coastal views

Back on the west coast, the next right turn is Chemin Montagne Posée, not worth the diversion unless you intend to walk the mountain trail near the summit. The following turn-off, just after the unmistakable giant masts of the BBC World Service Relay Station, is La Misère Pass which rejoins the east coast at Mont Fleuri close to Victoria. Cutting across the west side of the

Map on pages 286–7

Tom Bowers' sculptures of local people are sold in limited editions.

BELOW: watching the waves at Takamaka beach.

Souvenirs made from the coconut palm – a versatile resource for artisans.

mountains, this pass is quiet, with few houses and views over the coast. The road falls steeply from here and the views over the east coast and the Inner Islands are spectacular. There is an off-road **viewing point** about 2 km (1 mile) after the summit.

The west coast road continues past **Barbarons Estate** to the bay of **Grand Anse** . This is a majestic, tree-lined beach with fine white sand and granite rocks, but the treacherous offshore currents make it unsuitable for swimming (a governor of Seychelles drowned here in 1962). Nearby is the **Mahé Beach Resort**, departure point for boats to Île Thérèse *(see page 304)*.

The last 5-km (3-mile) section of the west coast road is a narrow stretch which comes to a dead end just before **Baie Ternay**. There is no access beyond this point. The drive is spectacular, passing over a causeway and through a mangrove swamp and, as it climbs, giving marvellous views over the **Port Launay Marine National Park** (formed in 1979 to protect the reef). To reach the secluded beaches of **Port Launay Bay**, pull over in a convenient spot and stroll down to the shore. The snorkelling here is good and reaching the reef is easy over calm waters.

NORTHERN MAHÉ

If you only have a day on Mahé, the first place you should drive to is the Sans Souci road, most of which runs through the Morne Seychellois National Park *(see page 299)*. The circuitous drive from coast to coast takes about an hour and is an ideal way to experience the mood of the mountains; the eerie silence broken only by the distant croaking of frogs and the mighty trees rustling in the cool winds. Even on a clear day, clouds can suddenly settle on the heights or roll

BELOW: tea picker.

MISSION RUINS

The area known in colonial times as Venn's Town is now called Mission. The ruins, dating from 1875, are that of a school built by Anglican missionaries for the children of rescued slaves. Following the abolition of slavery in the colonies, the British ran an anti-slavery patrol in the Indian Ocean. Their main purpose was to intercept Arab dhows transporting captive Africans to the Middle East. Those they managed to save from slavery were not taken back to Africa for fear they would be rounded up again, so they were brought to Seychelles and freed. Their children were given a basic education by the missionaries prior to being apprenticed or sent into service.

Marianne North, an intrepid Victorian traveller and botanical artist, made a trip to Venn's Town in 1883 by mule, and later commented in her diary "...the situation... one of the most magnificent in the world, and the silence of the forest around was only broken by the children's happy voices". Nowadays the only sound here is the rustling of the trees, and perhaps some echoes of the past in the forest – some say the ruins are haunted.

You can see this view for yourself. A short avenue lined with magnificent sangdragon trees leads to the viewing platform, built for the visit of Queen Elizabeth II in 1972.

ıp from the sea enfolding you in a damp chill and a complete silence. There are ıreathtaking views at almost every turn and many places to pull over and enjoy hem. Some of the highest slopes are planted with tea or mahogany trees, but nuch of the vegetation is a wild tangle of forest.

Maps on pages 286–7

Mountain passes and nature trails

The **Morne Seychellois National Park** ⓭ was established as a protected area n the 1970s. If you want to explore the area on foot, there are a number of vell-marked nature trails and mountain walks varying in length and degree of lifficulty *(see page 300)*. Trail guide booklets are available from the Seychelles Tourist Office in Victoria.

Two places are worth a detour on this route. The **Seychelles Tea & Coffee Company** ⓮ (open Mon–Fri 8.30am–noon; guided tours only), makes a ıleasant refreshment stop. Locally grown tea is served here, but the coffee is mported and not high quality. Just after the summit of Morne Blanc the **Mission Historical Ruins and Viewpoint** ⓯ offers one of the most stunning panoramas n Seychelles *(see box opposite)*.

Beau Vallon and around

Mahé's main tourism centre is the bay of **Beau Vallon** ⓰. It might well be Seychelles' busiest beach, but most visitors would not call it crowded. The vater is excellent for bathing, the sand is white and seaweed free, and there is ılenty of shade. It is one of the best places in Seychelles for watersports with acilities for windsurfing, diving, sailing and waterskiing, even parascending nd "sausage" riding, where you, and whoever else is along for the ride, sit

From the peak of Signal Hill, a look-out would keep watch for approaching ships in the days before telegraph and radio communication. Once word was given that a ship was in sight, people would hurry to town to pick up mail and goods ordered from overseas.

BELOW: *baka* for sale – cane spirit that packs a punch.

Nature Walks

The best season for walking is during the cooler, less humid months from June to September. The worst time is at the height of the rains from mid-December to January, when paths are muddy and slippery. Avoid the middle of the day for your trek; early morning and late afternoon are best, remembering that it gets dark around 6.30pm. Do not attempt any walk (except Danzilles to Anse Major) after rain as the path will be dangerous. You will need a solid pair of shoes (trainers with a good grip are fine), a hat, sunglasses, a bottle of water and a snack to enjoy when you reach the top or the end.

Danzilles–Anse Major Walk: An easy one-and-a-half hour walk (this one can be done in flip flops), most of which is within Morne Seychellois National Park. The peaceful walk follows the coast (one of the few coastal stretches in Mahé with no road access) and leads to a small secluded beach. It starts at Auberge Club des Seychelles, at the end of the road from Beau Vallon to Bel Ombre. Here, the road turns into a well-marked path crossing the Danzilles River. Highlights include wonderful views of Beau Vallon and Silhouette Island, and spectacular areas of granitic rock slopes.

La Reserve and Brulée Walk: This is Mahé's answer to Praslin's Vallée de Mai; the island's best area of palm forest, with five of Seychelles' six unique palm species – only the coco de mer is missing. This walk should take about an hour and a half up and another hour back down. The trail begins by the Cable and Wireless station, with a steep climb under mahogany trees. It is signposted but there are a couple of points where you may go wrong, so go with the trail brochure, available at the tourist office, or, better still, take a guide. There are three main vantage points along the way, which offer fabulous views over the west coast and the islands of Île aux Vaches, Thérèse and Conception.

Tea Factory–Morne Blanc Walk: This is a short, sharp climb up to Morne Blanc in the Morne Seychellois National Park. The views from here are breathtaking and the rain forest very spooky. The walk starts at the Tea Company off the Sans Soucis Road and should take about two hours altogether. The trail is marked with dabs of yellow paint on trees. Along the way you will see many of Seychelles' unique plants, but surprisingly few birds. Take care at the summit – the cliff you are standing on is almost vertical and it's a long way down. Return via the same route.

The Congo Rouge Trail: The best mist forest is on this trail which circles the summit of Morne Seychellois. It's a grade 3 walk, taking 3–6 hours, that should never be attempted without a guide as it is easy to get lost.

You may get more enjoyment from your exploration of the mountains with a knowledgeable guide. Basil Beaudouin knows all the trails and can identify most of the 250 indigenous species of plants you may see. He leads walks of varying difficulty lasting from as little as 1–2 hours to as much as 6–8 hours. He is available to meet anyone interested in organising an excursion at the Coral Strand Hotel every Monday at 6pm (see Travel Tips). ❑

LEFT: shady trail lined with sangdragon trees.

stride an inflatable tube towed through the water by a speedboat. The Coral Strand, Beau Vallon Bay and Fisherman's Cove (probably the best in Mahé) are the only hotels on the bay. The poolside bistros of the Beau Vallon Bay and Coral Strand are accessible from the beach.

Map
on pages
286–7

Beau Vallon by night

Beau Vallon is the only beach on Mahé that stays lively in the evenings. The stretch of pedestrianised road between the Coral Strand Hotel and the Pizzeria is particularly busy. Apart from the hotels, there are three main eateries to choose from. During the day the **Boat House** runs game fishing trips to North and Silhouette Islands. The day's catch is barbecued the same evening and served with other creole dishes and salads at a fish fry that kicks off at 7.30 on the dot every night. It's a popular event, so it's best to book and arrive about half an hour early if you can to choose a good table and enjoy a drink before dinner. **La Fontaine** opposite the beach is much quieter and enjoys a romantic setting. On the beach itself, tucked in the northern corner, is the ever-popular **Baobab Pizzeria** which is simple, cheap and quick (at least by local standards).

Baywatch at Beau Vallon.

It is quite safe to stroll up the road to the Boat House, La Fontaine or the Pizzeria, but avoid the areas away from the hotels and restaurants that are not so well lit, as there have been reports of a very few unpleasant incidents in recent years.

There is no road around the northwest coast, but there is a beautiful and easy walk from Danzilles to **Anse Major** ⑰, a charming little beach; sheltered, secluded and good for bathing *(see page 300)*.

BELOW:
we have liftoff.

To the North East Point

North of Beau Vallon is Victoria's "commuter belt", with occasional stunning views to the west of Silhouette and North islands. As the road climbs it passes several spectacular villas clinging to the granite cliffs. You could stop for lunch or afternoon tea at the **Northolme**, Seychelles' oldest hotel, which has tried to retain an old colonial atmosphere. It attracted several famous literary guests including Noel Coward, Somerset Maugham and Ian Fleming.

Just beyond the Northolme Hotel and Vacoa Village is **Glacis** , surrounded by some beautiful scenery. There are a number of hotels and guest houses here, the most exclusive of which is **The Sunset Beach Hotel**, built on a promontory whose beach is open to non-residents *(see Travel Tips)*. The road carries on around the northern tip of the island passing **Machabeé** and **Carana Beach**, a good spot for bathing, though there are no facilities.

The road between **North East Point** and **Pointe Cèdre** runs very close to the beach; sand and waves often blow on to the tarmac. It is a very attractive beach but not ideal for swimming as it's rocky underfoot and a bit too close to the road for comfort. Just before the road curves around Pointe Cèdre to Anse Etoile, look out for **Kreol Fleurage** (open daily 9am–5pm) across the road from the beach on North East Point. This perfumery, founded by a German micro-biologist, manufactures a range of natural perfumes made from 102 local plants.

The Chemin la Gogue from Anse Etoile to Northolme is a pleasant two-hour walk (or a 20-minute drive) across the northernmost peninsula which takes you past **La Gogue Reservoir**, an attractive lake and ideal picnic spot.

Once around Pointe Cèdre, the hillsides to the right and cliffs to the left become more thickly dotted with houses as you approach Victoria's environs.

BELOW:
treasure seekers.

BEL OMBRE TREASURE DIG

In 1949, Reginald Cruise-Wilkins, a Grenadier Guard recuperating from malaria on Mahé, got hold of some documents that he believed belonged to the notorious pirate Olivier Le Vasseur *(see page 246)*. He was convinced that Le Vasseur had laid a trail for would-be treasure seekers involving riddles and puzzles based on astrology, astronomy and mythology. He devoted his life to the quest for the fantastic treasure – gold coins, silver bars, diamonds, silks and the jewel-encrusted regalia of the archbishop of Goa, which included a huge cross studded with rubies, emeralds and diamonds – seized in 1721 from the Portuguese merchant ship, *Virgen de Cabo* en route from India.

Cruise-Wilkins concluded that the clues were based on the twelve labours of Hercules and he was spurred on by a series of proofs that he was on the right track – a pig's jawbone, bits of china, a bull's horn – but found no treasure. One unsolved riddle led him to Bel Ombre where he believed the end of the trail lay in an underwater cavern. He brought in pumps, but to no avail. The treasure was undiscovered when he died in 1977, and though his sons have taken up their father's quest, its location still remains a mystery.

'he most notable building before you reach town is La Bastille, just after Pointe 'onan. This sombre, impressive house was built in the 1930s as a family home. t once housed the Seychelles National Archives (now in the National Library 1 Victoria). The gardens are open to the public (Mon–Fri 9am–4pm). There is collection of traditional medicinal plants, a sugar cane press and a dilapidated 1odel of a traditional creole house. Nothing is labeled, but the staff are friendly nd willing to help.

HE SATELLITE ISLANDS

'he Portuguese called Seychelles the Seven Sisters on their charts because 1ahé stands like a grand elder sister surrounded by her lesser siblings, of which ix lie just off the east coast, encircling Victoria's magnificent natural harbour. 'hese islands lie within the **Ste Anne Marine National Park**, created in 1973. 'he corals are a shadow of their former selves, due in part to siltation from ind reclamation around Victoria, with the effects of the El Niño weather system ind perhaps global warming also implicated. However, the fish life is still rolific and the short journey to the marine park, combined with lunch on one f the charming and peaceful islands which have restaurants, is still a very leasant way to spend a day. Tour operators offer full-day trips by glass-bottom oat or subsea viewer starting from Marine Charter in Victoria *(see page 293)*. 'he subsea viewer gives a superior view, but is completely enclosed and some eople might feel claustrophobic. Either way, you'll have plenty of time to wim or snorkel.

Ste Anne ⑲ is the largest of the islands off Victoria and one of the least xplored. The first Seychelles settlers lived here rather than on Mahé, perhaps ecause of the crocodiles then inhabiting Mahé's xtensive coastal mangrove swamps. Once people egan to settle on Mahé, Ste Anne was largely left 1 peace as a coconut plantation, and since then has een put to various uses. In 1832 a whaling station 'as established here and in World War II the British ad a fuel store here. In the 1980s, Ste Anne was riefly a centre for the National Youth Service, a olitical experiment that was eventually abandoned. hen it became the headquarters of the Marine Parks .uthority (now moved to Baie Ternay on Mahé). oday, it is the site of a new five-star hotel, Ste Anne esort *(see Travel Tips)* opened in September 2002. he hotel controls access to the island.

Île au Cerf ⑳ is a small, low-lying island, mostly overed in coconut palms and scrub, and it is easy to nd trails up the hill if you want to explore inland. 'ou can either come here as part of an excursion rganised by a tour operator, or hire a boat from the 1arine Charter Association. Tourist boats land on 1e sheltered northern coast near **Kapok Tree .estaurant** where lunch is provided. After an xcellent creole meal, you can take a walk along the 1ore, past the homes of some of the 80 or so :sidents, a number of whom commute to Victoria y speedboat. One of Seychelles' most famous :sidents, South African writer Wilbur Smith, used) have a house here.

Map
on pages
286–7

Enjoying the underwater world without getting wet.

BELOW: north coast hideaway haven.

Map on pages 286-7

To stay on Cerf is a wonderful way to experience the tranquillity of life on an island with no roads or shops, secure in the knowledge that all the conveniences of modern life are just a 10-minute boat ride away. The only accommodation is a **Cerf Island Chalets** on the south coast *(see Travel Tips)*. The beach is always sheltered, good for swimming and snorkelling. Guests often hire pedalos to visit the beaches around Cerf, and even get as far as Moyenne, Ronde or Ste Anne.

Île Cachée is a tiny dot off the southeast coast of Cerf. It's possible to wade over to the islet at low tide.

Île Moyenne ㉑ has been owned since 1962 by Brendon Grimshaw, a British former newspaper editor, and is open to tour parties operated by Mason's Travel and TSS in Victoria. Visitors to Moyenne usually question the owner closely on two subjects: the pirate treasure worth £30 million said to be buried somewhere on the island and the ghost of Miss Best, an eccentric Englishwoman who lived on the island with a pack of stray dogs, until she died in 1919.

Moyenne covers just 9 hectares (4 acres) and is easy to explore. Efforts have been made to encourage endemic plants, including coco de mer and Wright's gardenia. A circular trail, which takes no more than an hour at a leisurely pace goes from the **Jolly Roger Bar and Restaurant** near the landing, past the house Miss Best built for her dogs, along the beach at Coral Cove and back past the graveyard, chapel, through Coco de Mer Vale, past the museum (with a small array of items relating to the island and its natural history) and back to the bar. The trees and plants along the way are labelled. Snorkellers should head for the northwest coast and the waters between Moyenne and St Anne Bathers should be happy on the Jolly Roger beach by the landing. The island and its bar-restaurant are open daily.

BELOW: a free ride.
RIGHT: sailboards and catamarans can be hired at most hotels.

You can walk around the tiny **Île Ronde** (Round Island) ㉒ in less than half an hour. There are several small beaches in the northwest, but these are not ideal for swimming, snorkelling or sunbathing; they can be weedy and the water is very shallow for some distance out. The Marine Park's information centre is here and has interesting displays on wildlife. Île Ronde is best known for its excellent restaurant, **Chez Gaby**, housed in old buildings, once part of an isolation camp for women sufferers of leprosy. The menu features creole cuisine and its barbecued tuna steak is a Seychelles legend. After lunch, most people are happy just to relax in the shade of the flame trees by the restaurant.

Île Longue is used as a prison and is out of bounds. Prisoners in their grey uniforms can often be seen making the boat trip to and from Victoria, where they form work details. Longue was a quarantine station in the days when the dreaded smallpox might arrive aboard a ship and spell disaster for the isolated Seychelles' population.

Île Thérèse ㉓ on the west coast is a beautiful island for a day trip. Boats depart from Mahé Beach Resort, though the service has become erratic in recent times. There is a beautiful beach facing Mahé, the shelter of the mainland making swimming here easy. Watersports and snorkelling equipment is available for hire. ❑

FRÉGATE

*Once home to pirates, Frégate is now an exclusive destination
with seven beaches and just one resort, where the emphasis
is on the "private island experience"*

Map on page 286

The most isolated of the granitic islands, Frégate lies 55 km (34 miles) east of Mahé. Covering 3 sq km (1 sq mile) and surrounded by coral reefs, this privately owned island is the kind of place most of us can only dream of staying in. The 15-minute helicopter flight alone costs over £800 (US$1,200). Frégate is very exclusive; most of the guests (limited to 40 at a time) are super rich and come here to hide away in one of the resort's 16 luxury villas.

Pirates' lair

Frégate was christened by the French explorer, Lazare Picault, during his 1744 expedition. He probably named it "Île aux Frégates" after the frigatebirds once present on the island. Among the mysterious ruins found on the island were the walls of a large enclosure, thought to be the remains of a pirate settlement, a lead-lined water conduit and three tombs built of coral. Early residents found a teak mast set in a stone platform at Anse Lesange and in 1812 a gold cross belt and shoulder strap were discovered. In 1838, a visitor from Mauritius reported that golden Spanish coins were frequently found on the beaches. He also described the wreck of a large ship lying offshore. There is no direct evidence that these artefacts were left by pirates; they could just as easily be traces of an Arab trading post. Whatever their origin, these various finds make Frégate one of the few sites of archaeological interest in Seychelles.

In 1802 Frégate became a place of exile. A ship load of Jacobin terrorists, accused of having plotted to assassinate Napoleon, had been sent from France to Seychelles. Quincy, the commandant of Seychelles, suspected several of these deportees of joining forces with the slaves and inciting them to rebellion, and so he sent the ringleader, Louis Sepholet, together with three slaves, to Frégate. They were among the first inhabitants of the island, though they didn't stay long. Later the same year, Sepholet was transported to Anjouan in the Comoros with 35 of the other deportees. They all died there; it is said they were poisoned on the orders of the sultan.

Luxury resort

The only way you can stay on Frégate is as a guest of the hotel **Frégate Island "Private"** ㉔. Opened in 1998, this resort is a celebrity haunt. Pierce Brosnan spent three weeks here before the release of *The World Not Enough*. The design of the spacious villas (almost £1,000/$1,500 a night), strung along the beautiful **Anse Bambous**, was influenced by the architecture of Bali and Thailand. Each one has a living room, large bedroom and two bathrooms with showers inside and out, all linked by a terrace, plus a private garden,

LEFT: a siesta in the shade.
BELOW: a jacuzzi in the sun.

Until recently an endangered species, the magpie-robin now thrives on Frégate.

BELOW: have a drink at the bar or have it brought to your villa.

secluded outdoor jacuzzi with amazing views, and a sundeck with a king-size sunbed. The resort is centred around Frégate House, where the main dining room gymnasium and library are located with a freshwater swimming pool and ba nearby. Facilities for every watersport you can think of are available and the German multi-millionaire owner has also built a marina here for his own private yacht and other boats which can be chartered. In short, Frégate is completely kitted out for the ultimate paradise island experience.

Plantation House

As a result of intense farming, most of the island is now covered with introduced vegetation. The higher hills are dominated by sangdragon woodland among which coffee, breadfruit, banyan, cashew and ylang ylang trees all grow Plantations were laid out on the flat land, and have been regenerated to provide fresh food for the new resort, including pawpaw, banana, cabbage, lettuce and sweet potato. Cattle, pigs and chickens are also reared to provision the hotel The original **Plantation House** ㉕ not far from the airstrip has been restored and now houses a restaurant specialising in creole cuisine.

Wildlife walks

Apart from Cousin, Aride and Cousine, Frégate is the only place where the Sey chelles magpie-robin now survives. This pretty black and white bird had become extinct on the other granitic islands where it was once common. It was perilously close to disappearing from Frégate too but was rescued from extinction by the intervention of BirdLife International. It is now thriving again and new popula tions are being introduced back to the other islands. Other birds hotel guests car

pot here include the Seychelles fody – a sparrow-like endemic species – and the Seychelles blue pigeon, which has a striking red, white and blue plumage. There is a resident conservationist from South Africa available for guided nature walks.

Frégate is also the only home of the giant tenebrionid beetle. When this strange-looking creature was first shown to European entomologists, it was thought to be a hoax specimen made up of bits of different insects. It is a large, flightless beetle, which spends much of its life clinging to the bark of sangdragon trees. Gardiner's gecko, a species of green gecko, is also found only on Frégate.

Each guest is given the use of an electric golf cart to get around, but the best way to experience the diversity of Frégate's flora and fauna is to follow one of the shady tracks that criss-cross the island on foot. Apart from the path that runs around the main plantation, there are three trails that radiate from the Plantation House worth exploring. For the best snorkelling, take the path to the southeast of the island to **Anse Parc**. The walk takes only about 10 minutes. Close to the beach a sign points to the **Pirate's Wall** (where the gold shoulder strap mentioned above was supposedly discovered).

To reach the superb **Anse Victorin ㉖**, considered by some to be one of the finest beaches in the world, start from the Plantation House and take the path that runs inland at an angle from the airstrip. Cross the Bambous River and continue to the coast. At a leisurely pace, the walk takes about 30 minutes.

A third walk along a well-marked track heading inland from the plantation leads due west to **Grand Anse**, another beautiful beach. The hill to your left as you approach the bay, is called Au Salon, where sangdragon trees flourish. To your right is **Signal Rock**, at 125 metres (410 ft) the highest point on the island. The walk to Grand Anse takes about 20 minutes. ❏

Map on page 286

Legend has it that Frégate is haunted by a headless woman. Those islanders less inclined to romanticism say she was invented by one of the island managers anxious to keep outsiders away from his precious fish stocks.

BELOW: scene from Polanski's *Pirates*, filmed on Frégate.

SILHOUETTE AND NORTH

Map on page 312

Though Silhouette and North lie within close proximity of Mahé, they are completely different in character, with a separate geology and an atmosphere akin to the more remote Outer Islands

Silhouette, the third largest island of the granitic group and the fifth largest in Seychelles, lies 20 km (12½ miles) northwest of Mahé. The island's topography and limited development means an exceptional diversity of plants and animals has been preserved. Indeed, conservationists regard Silhouette as one of the most important biodiversity hotspots in the Indian Ocean. The highest of its three main peaks, Mont Dauban, rises to 740 metres (2,430 ft) and is the second highest summit in Seychelles. Although it is bigger than La Digue, Silhouette (which can only be reached by helicopter) is much quieter.

Silhouette has no roads, so its thick virgin forests remain largely untrodden. However, there is plenty to recommend it, not least the fact that it is one of the least known Inner Islands. The beaches on the east coast are sheltered by a coral reef and are perfect for swimming and snorkelling, and the forest trails, while not always easy going, take you through beautiful, dense vegetation. In 1987, the surrounding waters were declared a Marine National Park.

North Island is similar to Silhouette though less mountainous and it has suffered more from forest clearance. However, the current owners are developing the island with eco-tourism in mind and hope to re-introduce much of the endemic flora and fauna.

LEFT: sunset on Silhouette.
BELOW: beachside house.

The Dauban family island

The first recorded sighting of Silhouette was made in 1609 by the crew of the *Ascension*, an English East India Company vessel, yet the island was not settled by Europeans until the early 19th century. It was named after the French minister Etienne de Silhouette, Controller of Finances in 1759. It's a perfect name for the island which appears as a mysterious shadow on the horizon when viewed from Beau Vallon on Mahé.

In the mid-19th century, Silhouette was gradually bought up by a French naval officer, Auguste Dauban, and it remained in the family for over a hundred years. They built a plantation house, cleared several paths across the island and introduced vanilla, cloves and other plants. Many coconuts were planted, often in seemingly inaccessible locations, because land had to be "under coconuts" before it was deemed of any value. Today, most of these paths and crops lie abandoned and much of the forest has recovered. The Dauban era came to an end in the 1970s when the island was sold to a French hotel group who handed it over to the Seychelles government in 1983.

La Passe to Pointe Zeng Zeng

The majority of the island's 135 inhabitants live in and around the main settlement of **La Passe ❶**. Standing close to the harbour is **La Grande Case** (the

Plantation House) the former Dauban family residence. Made up of four wooden buildings – the main house, toilets and bathroom, kitchen and dining room – the layout is typical of an island plantation house. The kitchen was usually built away from the house because of the risk of fire, with the dining room nearby so that the food could be served hot. In the days before air-conditioning was invented, the wide verandah provided the main living space.

NPTS (Nature Protection Trust of Seychelles), an organisation involved in conservation management, has its headquarters at La Passe and an information centre next to the tortoise enclosure. Projects include a captive breeding programme for Seychelles giant tortoises set up to preserve the last surviving animals of the granitic species, Arnold's tortoise and Seychelles tortoise rediscovered 150 years after they had been thought extinct. In 2002, the first baby tortoises hatched. NPTS have also discovered a species of frog new to science, the Seychelles palm frog, found only on Silhouette.

A little south of La Grande Case, along the same track, is a gated enclosure containing the island's small population of **Aldabra tortoises**. Immediately behind the pens is the **Dauban Mausoleum ❷**, a grand, rather incongruous construction surrounded by tall palms, modelled on the Madeleine in Paris. Adjacent to this is a marsh, where grey heron and black-crowned night heron (a recent coloniser) can be seen.

Continuing uphill from the mausoleum, the path leads to **Anse Lascars ❸**. Legend has it that Arabs settled here prior to European settlement and for a long time it was thought that the graves found at Anse Lascars were those of Arab tradesmen who plied the Indian Ocean around the 9th century. However, bones from these graves have since been carbon-dated to around 1800 and are

Among the many pirate legends that echo across the Seychelles is the story of notorious French corsair, Jean Hodoul. It is said he used Silhouette as his lair, hiding his treasure up in the hills.

BELOW: crosses like this one were erected all over Seychelles by early missionaries.

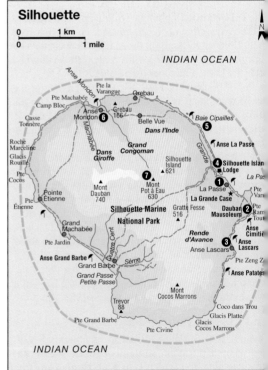

Silhouette

more likely to be the remains of the slaves who were the first occupants of Silhouette, having fled from Mahé in the late 18th century. From here, the path winds uphill to a viewing point at the headland of **Pointe Zeng Zeng**. It then descends to the secluded bay of **Anse Patates** with its mature mangrove swamp and beach crest of windswept sea hibiscus. The walk to Pointe Zeng Zeng from La Passe takes about 20 minutes at a leisurely pace.

Map on page 312

Best of the beaches

The only hotel, **Silhouette Island Lodge** ❹, lies north of the La Passe jetty on **Anse La Passe**, a beautiful sandy beach that stretches northwest of the hotel. Beyond it lies an equally lovely, palm-fringed and deserted beach, **Baie Cipailles** ❺. The path running along the coast between the bays winds through an abandoned coconut plantation and a line of takamaka trees.

At the northern end of Baie Cipailles, there are two paths leading to **Anse Mondon** ❻, a one-house settlement which offers the best snorkelling on Silhouette. The lower path is overgrown and best avoided. The upper path which runs over Belle Vue through thick forest is easier and more scenic. Just before the descent back to the coast, the forest opens up to reveal a spectacular view of Anse Mondon. If landing at Anse Mondon, this walk may be done in reverse. Either way, it takes about two hours.

Insectivorous pitcher plant.

The old path from Anse Mondon to Grande Barbe has all but disappeared so this walk is no longer possible. However, the path connecting La Passe and **Grande Barbe** is well worn. It's about a three and a half hour walk from one side of the island to the either, but you can arrange for your boat to drop you at one side and collect at the other. Once home to many families, Grande Barbe is now a virtual ghost town. A short way inland from the beach, on the coastal plateau, is a marsh. This area is the largest surviving wetland in Seychelles.

BELOW:
Mont Pot à Eau.

Mountain walk

The trek from La Passe to the summit of the magnificent **Mont Pot à Eau** ❼ (630 metres/2,067 ft) takes the best part of a day. It is not for the faint-hearted, and should not be attempted without a guide (obtainable from Silhouette Island Lodge or NPTS): as it is infrequently used, the path is sometimes unclear and is often muddy and slippery due to high rainfall on the mountainside. However, if you enjoy a challenge, it's wonderful walk that takes you through a fascinating mist forest, rich in exotic flora, including the insectivorous pitcher plant that grows on its exposed summit.

North Island

North Island lies 7 km (4½ miles) north of Silhouette and is considerably smaller and less mountainous. Most of the original forest was cut down, but a restoration programme is underway, with plans to replace introduced plantlife with endemic species. There is a beautiful beach on each side of the island, separated by a plateau across the middle and rocky promontories at either end. Day visits from Mahé by helicopter (15 minutes) can be arranged *(see Travel Tips)*. A five-star resort comprising 12 villas opened in 2003. ❑

PRASLIN

*A slower pace of life, glorious beaches and the Vallée de Mai –
a designated World Heritage Site – are three good reasons to
spend some time getting to know Praslin*

Map
on page
316

Praslin is the second largest granitic island of Seychelles and lies 45 km (28 miles) northeast of Mahé. It is much less mountainous, reaching a height of just 367 metres (1,204 ft), and less populated with about 5,500 inhabitants. The hills look rather threadbare after the green profusion of Mahé's mountains, but the sheltered valleys harbour primeval palm forest. Away from the shadows of the forest, there are many superb beaches and hotels. The island's popularity stems from these dreamy stretches of soft white sand and crystal waters, which have been declared the best in the world by many travel writers.

The pace of life is much more leisurely here than on Mahé. There are no towns and very little traffic. Taxis are available, but there is no taxi rank other than at the airport and at Baie Ste Anne jetty. Buses are cheap, but it may involve a long wait at the roadside for one to appear and timetables are flexible. Ask any local when the next bus is due and they will tell you "very soon". This is more a hope than a statement of fact. The best way to explore the island is by car, though getting around by bicycle is a pleasant alternative and there are plenty of trails for those who prefer to explore on foot.

Praslin is connected with Mahé by air and by sea. The flight takes just 15 minutes and Air Seychelles operates services between the two islands throughout the day. The fast catamaran ferry, *Cat Cocos*, departs from the Inter-Island Quay, Victoria, and takes one hour to reach Baie Ste Anne. It is popular with locals, making booking essential at weekends and advisable during the week. The same trip by schooner is cheaper, but takes three hours.

Baie Ste Anne to Anse Lazio

If you are arriving by boat, your first sight of the island will be the pretty **Baie Ste Anne ❶**. It is one of the two "capitals" of Praslin (the other being Grand Anse) and there is some rivalry between them. The village has a few shops, a hospital, a church and a bank, but apart from a couple of self-catering establishments, a boat rental company and a handful of takeaways, tourist facilities here are minimal. Baie Ste Anne is a short drive from the Côte d'Or and the Vallée de Mai, and you can arrange a hire car as soon as you step off the ferry. If you are flying in, it would be best to collect your hire car at the airport for which there is no extra charge.

The coast road running north from the pier forks at the northern end of the bay. The right-hand branch cuts across the headland to the eastern shore at **Anse la Blague ❷**, a beautiful and secluded bay, which is great for snorkelling. There is a snack bar on the beach and for something more substantial **Vanille Restaurant**, on a terrace overlooking the sea, has a

LEFT:
old man "Toto"
with his fish trap.
BELOW: inspecting
a mangrove.

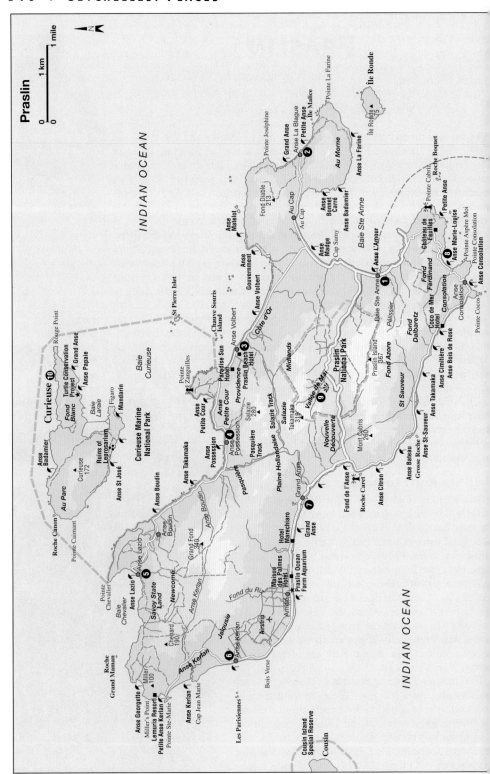

Praslin

0 —— 1 km

0 —— 1 mile

N

INDIAN OCEAN

Rouge Point

Turtle Conservation Project

Curieuse ⑩

Curieuse Marine National Park

Anse Papaie

Grand Anse

Baie Curieuse

Fond Blanc

Baie Laraie

Figaro

Mandarin

Anse Badamier

Au Parc

Curieuse 172

Ruins of Leprosarium

Anse St José

Roche Caiton

Pointe Caimant

Anse Boudin

Anse Takamaka

Anse Possession

Anse ④ Possession

Anse Petite Cour

Pasquière Track

Pasquière

Anse Boudin

Grand Fond 340

Anse Boudin

Anse Lazio

Anse Lazio ⑤

Newcome

Pointe Chevalier

Baie Chevalier

Roche Grand Maman

Miller's Point

Lemuria Resort

Petite Anse Kerlan

Anse Georgette

Anse Kerlan

Pointe Ste-Marie

Cap Jean Marie

Les Parisiennes

Cousin

Cousin Island Special Reserve

Bois Verse

Savoy State Land

Chétard 190

Anse Kerlan

Jalousie

Anse Kerlan

Anse Kerlan ⑥

Airstrip

Amitié

Fond du Riz

Maison des Palmes Hotel

Praslin Ocean Farm Aquarium

Hotel Marechiaro

Grand Anse

Grand Anse ⑦

Plaine Hollandaise

Salazie Track

Salazie 280

Salazie Track

Salazie

Takamaka 319

Takamaka

Nouvelle Découverte

Mont Cabris 260

Fond de l'Anse

Roche Caret

Anse Citron

Anse Bateau

Grosse Roche

Anse St-Sauveur

St Sauveur

Fond Azore

Praslin National Park

Midlands

Providence

Côte d'Or

Vallée de Mai

⑨

Paradise Sun Hotel

Praslin Beach Hotel ③

Anse Volbert

Anse Volbert

Charve Souris Island

Pointe Zanguilles

St Pierre Islet

Anse Gouvernement

Anse Matelot

Au Cap

Au Cap

Fond Diable 213

Anse Madge

Cap Samy

Anse Badamier

Anse Bonnet Carré

Au Morne

Anse La Farine

Pointe La Farine

Baie Ste Anne

Baie Ste Anne

Pélissier

Anse L'Amour

Anse L'Amour ①

Praslin Island 367

Anse Cimetière

Anse Bois de Rose

Anse Takamaka

Coco de Mer Hotel

Fond Dalbaretz

Consolation

Anse Consolation

Pointe Cocos

Fond Ferdinand

Château de Feuilles

Pointe Cabriz

Roche Boquet

Petite Anse

Anse Marie-Louise

⑧

Pointe Aspere Moi

Pointe Consolation

Anse Consolation

Grand Anse

Au La Blague

Petite Anse

Île Malice

②

Pointe Josephine

INDIAN OCEAN

Île Ronde

Île Ronde 75

good reputation. Diving, windsurfing and jet surfing can be arranged by **Bleu Marine**, based at the small hotel here. There is a pleasant walk from the bay which takes you along the shore, past Petite Anse and up a hill towards Anse La Farine. From the top of the hill you can see Île Ronde and La Digue.

The Côte d'Or

The inland road that links Baie Ste Anne to Anse Volbert and the northeast coast passes through casuarina woodland. **Anse Volbert ❸**, also known as Côte d'Or, is the island's main tourism centre. Its long beach is sheltered by Curieuse Island so that swimming is safe all year and there are no large breakers, making it ideal for children. The beach shelves very gradually so you need to walk out a long way to find water deep enough for swimming. The best snorkelling is around the boulders at the northern end of the beach and out towards **Chauve Souris Island**.

While it is by no means over-developed, Anse Volbert is relatively crowded by Seychelles standards. Beside the beach there are several hotels, guest houses, restaurants and souvenir shops, with more restaurants, boat operators and watersports centres strung along the coast road. Several of these organise snorkelling trips to **St Pierre Islet** as well as trips further afield to the islands of Curieuse, Cousin and Aride.

Next stop on the east coast road is **Anse Possession ❹**, a lovely bay with a view of Curieuse Island. It was around here, in 1768, that the first French explorers erected a plaque, claiming possession of the island. A cairn of stones and a flagstaff marked the spot. However, the location was lost. The French blame the English, who visited the island soon after, of deliberately obliterating the spot. The coast north of here, facing Curieuse island, is picturesque, quiet and good for swimming. The road runs through takamaka and casuarina groves and passes the pretty bays of **Anse Takamaka** and **Anse Boudin**. The short excursion from here to the top of Grand Fond (340 metres/1,115 ft) is worthwhile for the view across Praslin and the surrounding islands.

The best beach in the world

After Anse Boudin the road turns inland over the hill to **Anse Lazio ❺**, hailed as "the best beach in the world". The sand here is as fine and soft as caster sugar and is scattered with granite boulders. The swimming is excellent except when the northwesterly winds are at their strongest, mainly around January and February. Snorkelling is best around the rocks and at the two small coves at the northeastern end of the bay. To enjoy the beach at its finest it is best to come early in the morning before the crowds. The **Bonbon Plume**, with its thatched umbrellas laid out across a lawn by the sea, is a wonderful seafood restaurant. But it's not cheap and is the only place to eat here, so it's best to book for lunch, unless you prefer to bring your own picnic.

Exploring the west coast

If you are flying in, you will land on the west side of the island, 3 km (nearly 2 miles) from Grand Anse –

Map on page 316

OPEN 9AM-5PM TEL 232253

Most of Praslin's hotels, restaurants and souvenir shops are concentrated around Côte d'Or.

BELOW: cooling off after a ride.

Praslin is famous for its pink granite; the colour is due to the feldspar in the rock. It is popular in building construction and can be polished like marble.

the other place to pick up a hire car *(see Travel Tips)*. The coast road leading north of the airstrip from Amitié goes through a coconut plantation and farmland, past **Anse Kerlan**  to **Petite Anse Kerlan**, both beautiful sandy beaches framed by granite rocks. The sea can be wild in rough weather, but on calmer days the area is excellent for swimming and snorkelling, though you should always beware of strong currents.

Petite Anse Kerlan is home to the **Lemuria Resort**, an exclusive hotel complex in a spectacular location spread over 36 hectares (90 acres) with three beaches and Seychelles' only 18-hole golf course. Birdwatching in the grounds is excellent but it is necessary to call in advance to arrange access *(see Travel Tips)*. Further north, lying within the grounds of the golf course, is **Anse Georgette**, a wild and remote beach worth exploring.

Back at Amitié, opposite the airstrip by the sea is **Praslin Ocean Farm Aquarium** (open Sun–Fri 8am–6pm; entrance fee), whose main business is the culture of pearls in offshore oyster beds. As a sideline they have set up a series of open concrete aquarium tanks, where you can look at corals, reef fish and invertebrates. The guide is helpful and informative. Within the same complex is a jewellery boutique.

Around Grand Anse

The first settlement south of the airport is **Grand Anse** ❼. It's the largest village on Praslin, but it is far from commercialised and retains a sleepy character. The beach here is good, though often covered in seaweed. There are several small hotels, as well as shops, banks, takeaways and restaurants. The travel agents all have their Praslin offices here. **Scubamania Dive Centre** is based at

BELOW:
the Pagoda at
Coco de Mer Hotel.

he Hotel Marechiaro which, together with Maison des Palmes Hotel, runs boat rips to the small islands around Praslin.

From Grand Anse the coast road continues southward past a series of picuresque bays. The 5-km (3-mile) walk from Fond de l'Anse to Anse Marie-Louise is pleasant and easy with beautiful views. There are a couple of hotels and restaurants en route. This is the best stretch of coastline for deserted beaches, hough not all are good for swimming as the water is shallow except at high tide. The first bay along this road is **Anse Citron**, followed by **Anse Bateau**, which as Les Rochers Restaurant, one of the best on Praslin, at its far end. Sirene Boat Excursions operates from here to islands around Praslin. **Anse Bois de Rose** is noteworthy for the Black Parrot Restaurant *(see Travel Tips)* and **Coco de Mer Hotel**. Rounding Pointe Cocos, Anse Consolation is less ideal for swimming due o the beach rock barrier, but neighbouring **Anse Marie-Louise ❽** is the best bathing beach of all the above and a particularly quiet and picturesque spot. From this bay, the road winds steeply and passes the exclusive **Chateau de Feuilles Hotel and Restaurant** before descending to **Baie Ste Anne**.

A journey back in time

One of Seychelles' greatest natural treasures is the **Vallée de Mai ❾** (open daily 8am–5.30pm; entrance fee, free for children under 12), a primeval forest claimed by General Gordon to be the Garden of Eden. The valley, designated a UNESCO World Heritage Site, occupies the heart of Praslin, mid-way between Grand Anse and Baie Ste Anne. Several well-marked nature trails run through it and the official brochure, available from the entrance kiosk, maps these out quite clearly. It also lists the plants and wildlife you are likely to come across

Map on page 316

Seychelles' rich underwater world makes snorkelling a highlight of any trip.

BELOW: running through the streets of a forest village.

Coco de Mer

When he visited the Vallée de Mai in 1881, the British general, Charles Gordon (of Khartoum fame) was so struck by its natural beauty that he truly believed he had discovered the original Garden of Eden. He concluded that the coco de mer tree *(Lodoicea maldivica)* must be the Tree of Knowledge and its nut the forbidden fruit. His reasoning was that "the heart is said by the scriptures to be the seat of desires and ...the fruit [of the coco de mer] externally represents the heart, while the interior represents the thighs and belly... which I consider to be the true seat of carnal desires". While some might demur as to his Biblical conclusions, few people could argue that the coco de mer nut which grows on the female tree does resemble the thighs and belly of a woman, complete with a strategically placed tuft of hair. The enormous catkin of the male tree is equally suggestive.

The average male coco de mer grows to 15 metres (50 ft) and the average female to 9 metres (30 ft). Each nut weighs somewhere between 18 and 22 kg (40–49 lb), which makes it the heaviest seed in the world. The male tree, which can reach up to 32 metres (105 ft), grows taller because it lives longer, but its height is also thought to facilitate wind pollination. The female tree, on the other hand, which can be heavily laden with more than a dozen nuts, is more susceptible to being felled by high winds. This may be nature's way of ensuring that the trees spread up the steep slopes as well as down the valley.

The pollination of the coco de mer is still a mystery. The wind probably acts as one agent, but the large white slugs often seen feeding on the male flowers and the green geckos common among the trees, may also act as pollen carriers. Legend has it that on stormy nights the male trees uproot themselves and engage in passionate love-making with the female palms. Some say that witnesses to this orgy are certain to die.

The coco de mer palm can live for 200 years or more. In the last survey (1985) the oldest tree was dated at 205 years. Though now confined to Praslin and Curieuse, coco de mer trees may once have been much more common worldwide. During excavations for a new airport in Brussels in the 1980s, skeletons of large tortoises and fossils of nuts similar to the coco de mer were unearthed and dated to about 50 million years ago.

"Love nuts" have been highly prized since their discovery. They fetched such a high price in Europe that they became like gold dust. Today, they are more plentiful and carefully protected. Nuts gathered by the Ministry of Environment are hollowed out to reduce the weight and polished to be sold as souvenirs. Official collection is controlled and each nut is numbered and stamped, and sold with a permit. The fact that they still fetch a high price (a good one costs around 2,000 rupees) has encouraged poaching, so if you are offered a nut without a licence you can be sure it has been acquired illegally and is liable to be confiscated at the airport. ❑

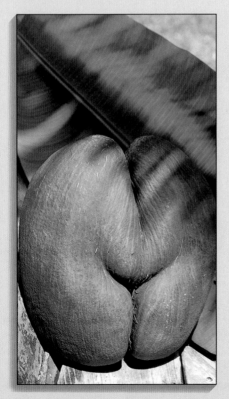

LEFT: some people believed the voluptuous coco de mer nut had aphrodisiac properties.

en route. You can choose between a short tour (about an hour) taking in most of the botanical sites, or a longer circular route which includes a spectacular viewpoint (allow two to three hours).

A visit to the Vallée de Mai is a journey back in time. Dinosaurs would have ambled through prehistoric valleys just like this. It is thought that the coco de mer palm evolved the world's longest leaf stems to keep its leaves out of the reach of herbivorous dinosaurs. Likewise, young palms probably developed spines to protect them from being eaten by the giant tortoises that dominated the eco-system at one time. The enormous leaves of the coco de mer palms tower far above you like green vaulting and the dry leaf-litter that lies like a thick carpet on the forest floor, rustles as geckos scuttle by. Streams can be heard tinkling and the giant leaves clatter in the breeze.

Map on page 316

Primeval palms

About a quarter of the trees in the valley are coco de mer palms *(see opposite)* and almost half the remainder are endemic palms found only in Seychelles. These include the thief palm *(Latannyen fey)*, with its broad, undivided leaves, so called because the first specimen sent to Europe was stolen from Kew Gardens; the millipede palm *(Latannyen milpat)* whose divided leaves are reminiscent of the legs of a millipede; the palmiste *(palmis)*, a splendid, tall palm once the source of the main ingredient for millionaires' salad, so called because an entire tree had to be sacrificed to obtain the edible shoot near its tip (the *palmiste* salad you now see on restaurant menus is made from the shoots of coconut trees, so you can tuck in with a clear conscience); and the Cinderella palm *(Latannyen oban)* a comparatively short tree with a slender trunk.

BELOW: the Vallée de Mai is the home of the Seychelles black parrot.

Map on page 316

Pitted beach rock, Curieuse Island.

Black parrots

You will see few birds inside the valley; they tend to stay above the tree tops. Only the piercing whistle of the black parrot reminds you that they are out there, somewhere. Of all the forest birds, the black parrot is the star attraction. It breeds only on Praslin, nesting in the hollows of rotten coco de mer palms and screwpines (a number of artificial nest boxes have been erected in the valley). Because the vegetation is so dense, black parrots are, in fact, easier to spot outside the valley. In the early morning and late afternoon, they can be seen from the car park, flying in and out of the tall trees on the edge of the valley. They are also commonly seen at sea level where there are suitable feeding trees (such as at Villa Flamboyant, Britannia Restaurant and Coco de Mer Hotel).

There is an Information Centre at the entrance which also sells souvenirs, snacks and drinks. It's a good idea to arrive early to beat the crowds. Take drinks with you, but don't forget to dispose of the rubbish properly. Visitors are also requested to stick to the paths, avoid the temptation of touching the plants, and smoking is strictly forbidden.

A short drive, or a 10-minute walk from the entrance in the direction of Grand Anse will take you to a spectacular **waterfall**.

The Red Island

Just off the north coast of Praslin, **Curieuse Island** ⑩ lies at the centre of a Marine National Park. From the sea, Curieuse is noticeably red, which explains why the island was first known as Île Rouge. The sparseness of the forest and redness of the soil is due to the many fires that have swept the island. The first recorded fire was in 1771, when the French suspected the English of arson. However, it seems more likely that fire is part of the natural cycle in the palm forest, helping new, vigorous plants to establish themselves and ridding out the old and dead vegetation.

A leper colony was established in 1833 at **Anse St José** on the south coast of the island. The old Creole-style **Doctor's House** (open daily 9am–5pm) is still intact though most of the leprosarium buildings lie in ruins. A footpath leads from here to **Baie Laraie**. The causeway across the bay encloses a turtle pond where turtles were once kept prior to slaughter and export. Today, you can still spot the occasional one swimming into and out of the pond on the tides. You can also watch the colourful reef fish from here without getting wet.

A board walk follows the margins of the bay through mangroves where large *Cardisoma* crabs and colourful fiddler crabs are dominant. The path emerges at Baie Laraie, where there is a Tortoise Conservation Project. The young tortoises are kept in pens, while the adults over five years are allowed to roam wild. These animals have been transferred from Aldabra, which has the world's largest giant tortoise population. A mangrove boardwalk has been laid out behind the project buildings.

Day trips to the island can be arranged through most Praslin hotels and tour operators, and are often combined with a visit to Cousin Island nature reserve *(see page 325).*

COUSIN, COUSINE AND ARIDE

*A Special Reserve and a haven for land birds and seabirds,
Cousin has been the centre for recovery programmes for
some of the rarest birds in the world*

Map
on page
326

These islands belong to the birds. Cousin and Cousine are the breeding ground for hundreds of thousands of seabirds; Aride is home to over a million. All three are a refuge for rare land birds, most notably the Seychelles warbler and Seychelles magpie-robin. Thanks to the efforts of conservationists, particularly the Royal Society for Nature Conservation (RSNC), Government of Seychelles and BirdLife International, both species have been saved from extinction.

COUSIN

In the mid-1960s, **Cousin Island ❶** came on the market. As a coconut plantation of insignificant proportions with no other source of income it was not deemed to be a particularly desirable investment. However, it emerged that Cousin was the final refuge of the Seychelles brush warbler, which was down to the last couple of dozen specimens. An international appeal was launched by conservationists and interest in the island grew as did the owner's price. It was finally purchased by the RSNC on behalf of BirdLife International for £15,500 ($25,000), a small price for saving one of the rarest birds in the world. Today it is managed locally by Nature Seychelles.

LEFT: the waters around Aride are often choppy and landing is not as easy as it looks.
BELOW: fairy tern.

Cousin is now a nature reserve for many other bird and animal species. It is easily visited from Praslin, being just 2 km (1¼ miles) from Amitié on the west coast, and is accessible all year round (Mon–Thur, mornings only), though landing is generally easier during the southeast monsoon (May to October) when Praslin provides shelter from the strong trade winds. This is also the best time to visit to see the greatest numbers of nesting seabirds.

Most Praslin hotels and many independent boat owners arrange trips which are often combined with afternoon visits to Curieuse and St Pierre islands to make a full-day excursion. There is a resident Nature Seychelles warden and several knowledgeable rangers who provide guided tours that last about 90 minutes. Tours are given in French, English and Kreol. Visitors are not permitted to explore the island unaccompanied and there is no overnight accommodation available.

Bird life

To minimise the risk of rats or other pests getting ashore no boats are allowed to land directly; instead, visitors transfer to the island boat to land directly onto the sandy shore. As the noise of the engine is cut, the noise of the seabirds takes over. Seven species thrive on the island: four species of tern (lesser noddy, brown noddy, bridled tern and fairy tern), two shearwaters (Audubon's and wedge-tailed) and the white-tailed tropicbird.

However, it is the land birds for which Cousin is most famous, the Seychelles warbler in particular. The cessation of plantation activity and the regeneration of the native vegetation led to a rapid recovery in its numbers. The future of this tiny wren-like bird has been deemed secure enough to remove it from the current world Red Data list of critically endangered species. It is a remarkable bird in that the sex of its offspring is determined by food availability. When food is plentiful, 80 percent of chicks are males, which leave soon after fledging to seek territories of their own. When food is scarce, nearly 90 percent will be female, which remain to help parents with future broods.

The Seychelles magpie-robin, a distinctive black and white bird, was once found on most of the granitic islands, but was wiped out by a combination of direct persecution and introduced predators, which had confined the bird to Frégate by the 1930s. Attempts to establish a breeding population on Cousin began in 1994, then on Cousine the following year, met with success. Today, this charming, tame endemic is often spotted hopping along the tourist paths. Nevertheless, it remains one of the rarest birds on earth. A third rare endemic, the Seychelles fody, breeds here and on just four other islands (Cousine, Frégate, Aride and D'Arros).

The dense population of seabirds on Cousin supports a large number of skinks.

Flora and other fauna

Of the 11 reptile varieties on Cousin, skinks are the most common. These bronze-coloured lizards feed on dead chicks and eggs. Hermit crabs are also common in the undergrowth and you'll probably spot one of the few giant tortoises that roam the island. Cousin is also one of the few places a visitor stands a reasonable chance of seeing a hawksbill turtle as Seychelles is the only place on earth where these animals come out by day *(see box opposite)*.

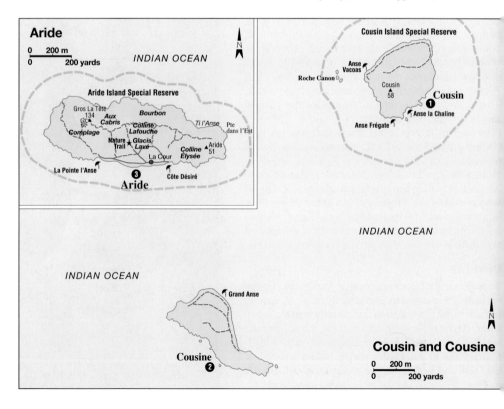

The vegetation is dominated by indigenous species. These include the *bwa torti* (tortoise tree), so called because its fruits look like the carapace of a tortoise. They are also eaten by Cousin's resident tortoises, not put off by their unpleasant smell. Also common here is the remarkable pisonia that flowers to coincide with the peaks of activity in the lesser noddy nesting colony; its sticky seeds attach themselves to the birds' feathers, the soft, malleable leaves make good nesting material and the horizontal branches, ideal nest sites.

Map on page 326

COUSINE

Cousin's sister island is a more exclusive destination. It is a privately owned nature reserve with four colonial-style chalets that can accommodate up to eight guests at a time *(see Travel Tips)*. It is a rare opportunity to experience living on an island teeming with wildlife. Attractions on **Cousine ❷** include hawksbill turtles that come ashore to lay their eggs, mainly between September and January, along the sandy beach which fringes the eastern coast. Endemic birds include the Seychelles magpie-robin and Seychelles warbler, while many thousands of seabirds also breed here including the largest population of wedge-tailed shearwaters in Seychelles. Daytrippers are not usually allowed to visit, but you can get a good view of the island from the hill-top on Cousin.

These islands belong to the birds.

ARIDE

Lying about 10 km (6 miles) north of Praslin, **Aride ❸** is the most northerly of the granitic isles and arguably the most unspoilt island of the Indian Ocean. The name Aride (so called because there are no streams or other sources of freshwater) first appeared on French charts drawn up after exploratory voyages

BELOW: newly hatched turtle – if it survives, it will be up to 40 years before it returns to nest.

HAWKSBILL TURTLES

Though famous for birds, Cousin is also one of the most important breeding sites for hawksbill turtles, with possibly the longest-running monitoring programme (30 years) anywhere in the world. Elsewhere, the hawksbill turtle has been greatly reduced following years of exploitation – not for the flesh, which is sometimes poisonous, but for the shell which, until the early 1990s, was made into trinkets sold to tourists. It will take decades for populations to recover as hawksbills do not breed until 25–40 years of age.

In Seychelles, the turtles nest in daylight hours from August to April. A single female may emerge up to six times per season to lay her eggs at intervals of 14 days. Each nest may contain up to 180 eggs. Older turtles lay even more eggs, more frequently. They hatch after about 60 days. The young turtles that emerge scurry straight to the sea, but not all of them make it. On the way, some fall victim to crabs, others to seabirds. Those that reach the sea are still not safe, as many will be eaten by large fish. As a result, very few survive to adulthood. Recent research includes attaching transmitters to adult turtles linked to satellites in order to discover the mystery of where they spend their time outside the breeding season.

in 1770 and 1771, but the island had no settlers until 1861. Thereafter, it was run as a plantation until 1973 when it was purchased by Christopher Cadbury of chocolate fame (1908–95), a keen conservationist and at the forefront of campaigns to set up nature reserves on Cousin, La Digue and Aride. But it was his purchase of Aride island, given to the Royal Society for Nature Conservation, and its establishment as a nature reserve in 1979 for which he is most remembered. An engraved granite plaque on La Pointe l'Anse, is dedicated to his memory.

TIP

The landing on Cousin is a wet one, so put on beachwear or cotton shorts and a T-shirt – they'll soon dry off in the sun – and pack camera equipment in plastic splash-proof bags. A pair of solid walking shoes for the nature trail is also a good idea.

The island is covered in a rich flora and fauna and all species can be seen from the set nature trail. This begins at the settlement of **La Cour**, crosses the flat coastal plateau and winds uphill to a **viewing point** at the peak of Gros La Tête, 134 metres (435 ft), where the cliffs drop dramatically to the sea. From here you can see hundreds of frigatebirds, noted for their huge wingspan which can stretch to 2 metres (6½ ft), soaring over the sea. On clear days, the coral island of Denis is just visible on the horizon, but where the waves crash against the foot of Aride's cliffs are the last granite rocks before India and Sri Lanka. Once on the hill, visitors are not allowed to deviate from the path as the ground either side is riddled with the burrows of nesting shearwaters, which are easily inadvertently destroyed. You return to the Visitors Shelter at the beach in time for lunch with the afternoon free to swim, snorkel or explore the plateau.

The reserve is open three days a week, usually Sunday, Wednesday and Thursday, 10am-3pm, but days and times vary according to weather conditions *(see Travel Tips)*. The island warden and local rangers, the only inhabitants, give guided tours lasting about two hours. Most of the larger hotels organise day trips (the crossing from Praslin takes about 45 minutes), and lunch and the entrance fee to the reserve are included in the price.

BELOW: helicopter and schooner off Cousin island.

A million seabirds

Like Cousin and Cousine, Aride is a rat-free zone and consequently has remained a haven for vast numbers of seabirds. Ten species breed on Aride; more than the rest of the granitic islands combined. Chief among these is the sooty tern, numbering 300,000 birds. Aride has the world's largest colony of the lesser noddy, sheltering almost 200,000 pairs, as well as the largest surviving colony of the rare roseate tern in the Indian Ocean. The breeding season of terns and noddies coincides with the southeast monsoon, which lasts from March to October. All in all, there are over a million breeding birds milling about the island, making Aride an extremely noisy place at this time of year.

The elegant fairy tern, symbol of Air Seychelles, nests throughout the year, as does the white-tailed tropicbird, one of the most beautiful of all seabirds. They can be seen all over the island but you need to walk to the top of the hill to find the few pairs of red-tailed tropicbirds breeding in the only site outside the Aldabra group. Completing the seabird scene are the wedge-tailed shearwater and Audubon's shearwater. Shearwaters leave their burrows before dawn, returning after nightfall and are more likely to be encountered at sea en route to Aride.

Under the canopy

Indigenous vegetation was reintroduced to replace the monoculture of coconut palms. With the reappearance of a forest canopy, two species of land bird, the Seychelles sunbird and Seychelles blue pigeon, which disappeared when the indigenous trees were removed, have now returned. The Seychelles warbler needed more of a helping hand. Since the transfer of 29 birds from Cousin in 1988 numbers have rocketed to around 2,000 so that Aride now holds more than 80 percent of the world population. In January 2002, two more rare endemic birds, the Seychelles magpie-robin and the Seychelles fody, were transferred to Aride and, within a short time, both began to breed. This means Aride can now boast more breeding native species than any other island.

Map on page 326

The prolific seabird life supports an enormous number of lizards. Two endemic forms dominate, Seychelles skink and the larger Wright's skink. Large millipedes may also be seen on the hillside; they should not be handled as they emit an obnoxious spray.

Among the most beautiful of Seychelles' endemic plants is Wright's gardenia, and Aride is the only place in the world where it occurs naturally. Its large white flowers, spotted with magenta, have a delicate fragrance and appear precisely 10 days after heavy rain.

There are mice on Aride and hares on Cousin, but Cousine is the only granite island with no alien mammals. The cats that once overran the island ravaging the bird life have been successfully eliminated.

Reef fish

The naturalist Peter Scott, visiting Aride in 1986, recorded 88 species of reef fish in little more than 1½ hours in the water. Since then, other visitors and successive wardens have added to the list which now records over 380 species – more than on any other granite island. Dolphins are also seen around the island. ❑

BELOW:
male frigatebird,
inflating his pouch
for display.

GIANTS OF THE SKY

After a long, hot walk to the viewing point near the summit at Grolatet, it is refreshing to emerge from the woodland onto the bare granite cliffs and feel the cooling breeze. Here, the enormous frigatebirds soar on outstretched wings, occasionally harrying other seabirds as they return to feed their young, forcing them to relinquish their catches. Though notorious as pirates, frigatebirds are quite capable of catching their own fish. Using their long tails as rudders they steer with amazing agility. Yet they are primitive birds unable to land on the surface of the sea as they lack webbed feet to swim. Their feathers also lack waterproofing and quickly become waterlogged. These seabirds spend much of their lives wandering several thousand kilometres from breeding colonies across open ocean. They cannot even walk on their tiny stunted legs and once they land on a branch are literally rooted to the spot. Once aloft, they cruise with barely a flicker of their enormous 2-metre (6½-ft) wingspan. Their bones are incredibly light, only around 5 percent of their total weight, and they weigh little more than a kilogram (just over 2lb), about the same as a small chicken. This gives them the lowest wing loading (weight per wing area) of any bird in the world.

LA DIGUE

*La Digue is no longer the sleepy backwater it once was,
but life still proceeds at an agreeably slow pace
in the middle of magnificent scenery*

Map
on page
332

n the early days of tourism in Seychelles, La Digue was billed as the island
that time forgot, where life went along at a pace little faster than that of its
ox carts, then the only form of public transport. Today, La Digue's ox carts
re more of a tourist diversion than a necessity – bicycles and pick-up trucks and
ne or two cars now share the tracks beneath the palms. Tourism rubs shoulders
vith the traditional way of life and has combined with it to raise living standards.
Nevertheless, having no airstrip and a tiny population, the island retains its "out
f the rat race" atmosphere and friendliness.

The fourth largest island of the granitic group, La Digue is generally con-
idered to be one of the most beautiful of the Seychelles islands and should not
e missed. The spectacular coast, with its huge boulders towering over perfect
eaches, has been used as a backdrop for many a film and fashion shoot. It is
ess than half the size of Praslin, just 4 km (2½ miles) to the west, but rises
almost as high to 333 metres (1,093 ft) at Nid d'Aigles. The island population
s also less than half that of Praslin with around 2,000 inhabitants concentrated
nainly on the west coast between La Passe and La Réunion. Most tourist
ccommodation is here too.

xploring La Digue

here is no airstrip on the island, but it's no more than
30-minute sail away from Praslin *(see Travel Tips)*.
A day trip is feasible, but to experience the island fully
nd soak up the atmosphere it is worth staying for at
east two nights. Ferries from Baie Ste Anne arrive at
he tranquil harbour of **La Passe ❶**, a haven for
achts and schooners that shelter beneath the palm-
ringed shore. There are a number of grand plantation-
tyle houses at La Passe, gracefully growing old and,
n the whole, well maintained. The quiet fish market
y the jetty turns into a hive of activity when the fish-
rmen bring in their catches. Nearby is a small **café**
ext to a **Tourist Information Centre.**

You'll see very few cars here – there are only a
ouple of taxis and no hire cars – but La Digue is
mall enough (10 sq km/6 sq miles) to do without
em. *Camions*, or open-sided lorries with fitted seats
four of them in all – pass for buses. There are no set
metables and they meander around the island
ccording to the requirements of drivers and passen-
ers. The flat coastal plateau and its beaches as far as
'Union Estate *(see page 333)* is easily explored on
oot. Cycling is quicker, of course, and will enable
ou to travel further afield; south to Grand Anse or
ound the northern rim and south again to Anse
ourmis. To pedal at top speed from La Passe to L'U-
on Estate takes less than 10 minutes, but the whole

LEFT: Anse
Source d'Argent.
BELOW: ox-cart taxi.

TIP

When cycling round La Digue, take care on the mountain tracks, particularly after the rains when they can become slippery with mud. Wind-blown sand on the east coast road can also be hazardous.

point of La Digue is that no one does anything at top speed. There are plenty of bikes for hire at the jetty, including children's models, but these are of varying quality and it's a good idea to examine a few, the brakes in particular before settling on one.

Inland loop

Whether you're walking or cycling, the southbound road from La Passe is a good place to begin your exploration of the island (turn right on leaving the jetty). Looking out to sea as you head towards Réunion, the other main settlement, there is a view of **La Digue Cross**, a monument erected on top of granite rocks in the bay in memory of people who drowned while attempting to land on La Digue.

The road swings inland to round the chalets of **La Digue Island Lodge**, an upmarket resort. It then runs parallel to the coast to a T-junction at Pont Bill. A left turning takes you to the **Veuve Reserve ❷**. Named after the beautiful Sey-

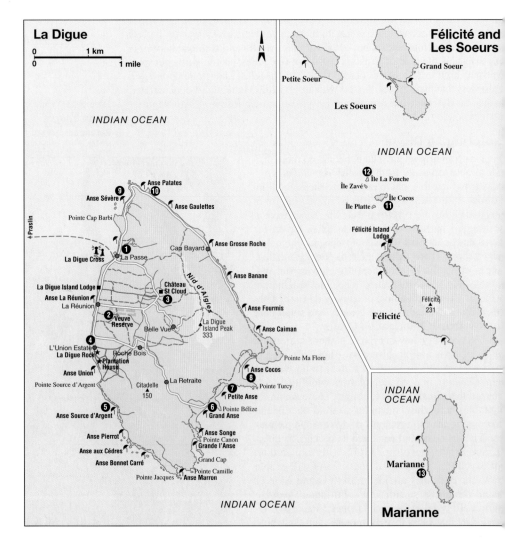

helles paradise flycatcher, the symbol of La Digue, the reserve was set up to reserve some of the last remaining takamaka and Indian almond *(badanmyen)* trees in which it feeds and nests. This habitat is under tremendous pressure from the island's growing population and boat-building industry. *Veuve (Vev* in Creol) means "widow", a reference to the magnificent, long black tail feathers of the male, reminiscent of a widow's black veil. The female by contrast lacks the elongated tail feathers and is chestnut and white with a black hood. Once widespread in the Praslin group, the paradise flycatcher has survived as a breeding bird only on La Digue, though a few sightings have been reported on neighbouring Félicité. They can be seen almost anywhere on the coastal plateau in the early morning, but chances of a sighting in the reserve are more or less guaranteed in the early morning and late afternoon. A Visitor's Centre at the reserve entrance provides information on the birds and the warden gives useful pointers on where they can be spotted. Entry is free and the path that begins at the roadside Visitor's Centre is navigable both on foot and by bike.

Map on page 332

Continuing inland from the reserve, the road bends northwards to run parallel with the coast road leading to **Château St Cloud ❸**, a grand and enchanting building that now houses a small hotel *(see Travel Tips)*. It was built at the height of the Napoleonic wars as the plantation house of a vanilla farm. Vanilla was introduced to La Digue in 1866 and quickly overtook coconuts as the most lucrative commodity. The development of synthetic vanillin in the early 19th century caused the industry to crash bringing hardship to the islanders. Ruins of the slaves' quarters and remnants of the vanilla factory can still be seen.

Sorting and cleaning vanilla pods.

A road near the chateau heads up the steep hillside to **Belle Vue**, just below the summit of Nid d'Aigles. It is too steep to ride a bicycle and a tough walk except in the cool of early morning or late afternoon. The easiest way to tackle this road is by taxi. It is worth the fare for the fabulous view over the coastal plateau and out towards Praslin.

BELOW: La Digue Island Lodge restaurant.

South of the Flycatcher Reserve the road leads back to the coast and turns southward once more past two art galleries, and the pretty Catholic church of **Notre Dame de l'Assumption.** Beyond these, the track leads to **L'Union Estate ❹** (open daily 8am–6.30pm; entrance fee), an old plantation. Here, there is a working *kalorifer* where copra (dried coconut) is heated and dried, and a coconut oil press pulled by an ox. Other features include **La Digue Rock**, a towering granite boulder appearing like a natural sculpture, giant tortoises, horse riding (strictly within the plantation grounds) and a picturesque **plantation house**. The old colonial **cemetery** nearby, where the early settlers are buried, is also worth a look.

The best beach

On the far side of the plantation reserve is one of Seychelles' most beautiful beaches, **Anse Source d'Argent ❺** (Bay of the Source of Silver). It is reached by following the palm-shaded trail that runs past La Digue Rock and the plantation house. There are no facilities here at all, but that is part of its beauty. The silver white sands are framed by giant granite boulders and perfectly positioned palms – the ultimate in exotic back-

drops and a popular spot for fashion shoots. A coastal path, easy to follow on foot, continues southward past a series of equally beautiful coves.

East to Grand and Petite Anse

Bicycles are an efficient form of transport on La Digue.

Near the entrance to L'Union Estate, the road turns inland and cuts through an area of marshland known as **La Mare Soupape** (*soupap* is the Kreol name for the terrapins, or mud turtles, that inhabit the area). Beyond the marsh, the road climbs steeply and it is quite an effort to cycle or walk to the crest of the hill. Perseverance is rewarded with stunning views as the road descends through thick vegetation to the velvety sands, granite outcrops and turquoise waters of **Grand Anse** , the island's largest beach. It's a perfect place to relax and picnic, but the sea can be wild and dangerous, particularly between June and September when the waves create a powerful undertow.

A footpath leads northeast of Grand Anse towards two more magical bays. Often deserted, the white sands of **Petite Anse** ❼ and **Anse Cocos** ❽ are also surrounded by spectacular rock formations. Like Grand Anse, however, currents are strong and swimming can be dangerous. Unless you are particularly adventurous it is not worth exploring further than Anse Cocos where the track turns inland crossing **Pointe Ma Flore** – which offers a lovely view over Anse Cocos and the northeast coast – to Anse Caiman then peters out before you reach the road at Anse Fourmis.

La Passe to Anse Fourmis

The easiest way to reach Anse Fourmis is by cycling the 4 km (2½ miles) around the northern coast from La Passe. Though walking is also easy, the route has no

nuch in the way of shelter from the hot sun. The wild, unspoilt scenery is the main attraction. The beaches en route are all beautiful, though not all of them are good for swimming. The first of these is **Anse Sévère ❾** which lies beyond the promontory of Pointe Cap Barbi, followed a little further on by the rockier bay of **Anse Patates ❿**. Both beaches are good for swimming and snorkelling (snorkelling can be difficult at low tide due to the swell over the shallow reef but is relatively easy a couple of hours either side of high tide). The corals are not fantastic but fish life is prolific, particularly around the rocks where the waters teem with butterflyfish, angelfish, parrotfish, squirrel fish, Moorish idols, batfish and hawkfish.

Continuing south, you'll pass a succession of small, rocky bays, washed by rougher seas – **Anse Gaulettes, Anse Grosse Roche** and **Anse Banane**. The road comes to a dead end at **Anse Fourmis**. Here, in calm weather, snorkelling is good around the rocks.

Islands north of La Digue

The waters around the neighbouring islands of Félicité, Marianne, Petite Soeur, Grand Soeur, Île Cocos, Île La Fouche and Île Zavé are rich in bird and marine life. All are within close proximity of La Digue and make ideal day-trip destinations, offering a choice of activities: swimming, diving, snorkelling, birdwatching, fishing, or just relaxing and eating. (All the islands, except Félicité, can also be reached by boat from Praslin.) Excursions to these largely uninhabited islands can be arranged through your hotel, the tourist information office at La Passe jetty or at one of the roadside stalls offering trips. Itineraries can be flexible if you discuss priorities in advance with the boat owner

Map on page 332

TIP

The restaurant at Grand Anse, Loutier Coco (daily 9am–5.30pm), serves creole cuisine, sandwiches and omelettes at reasonable prices.

BELOW: hard day at the bar, Grand Anse.

Map on page 332

and lunch and soft drinks are usually included. Most operators require a min imum of four people per trip.

For snorkelling, the best site is the tiny **Île Cocos ⓫**. Access to the water around this Marine National Park was forbidden to visitors during the 1980s because of the damage to its coral reefs caused by tourists. The corals are now slowly recovering and it is still a beautiful site. Seabirds are the main attraction on **Île La Fouche ⓬** a rocky islet off the north coast of Île Cocos and **Île Zavé**; the latter, lying south of Île La Fouche, is little more than a jumble of rocks but holds five breeding species of seabird: the wedge-tailed shearwater, the bridled tern, the lesser noddy, the brown noddy and the fairy tern. This is also an excellent snorkelling site, weather permitting. There are large numbers of parrotfish, sweetlips and groupers. Whale sharks are com monly seen around November.

Just north of Cocos, **Marianne ⓭** could have been Robinson Crusoe's very island. Uninhabited and blanketed with coconut palms, it has a single beach on the western coast where small boats can land. **Petite Soeur** and **Grand Soeur** are also uninhabited. Landing is difficult on Petite Soeur, but there is a beach either side of Grand Soeur and, according to the season, one or the other is usually sheltered.

There are no day trips to **Félicité Island**, 3 km (1½ miles) northeast of La Digue. It is owned and managed by La Digue Island Lodge and can only be vis ited by renting the whole island *(see Travel Tips)*. Guests to this exclusive hide away stay in one of the two plantation-style houses and bask in total seclusion on La Penice beach. Deep sea fishing, windsurfing, boat (sailing) trips and snorkelling are all laid on – the island even has its own tennis court.

BELOW: sorting a bumper haul.
RIGHT: L'Union Estate.

DEPORTED TO PARADISE

In 1798 there was a rebellion in the French colony of Réunion. The insurrection, led by a former sergeant Etienne Belleville, and a priest, Jean Lafosse, marched on the capital, St-Denis, protesting against taxation levels and rumours that the island was to be given to the English The revolt was easily quashed, and the decision taken to exile the dozen or so ringleaders to a suitable location somewhere on the coast of India. They were put aboard the *Laurette* under the command of Captain Loiseau, but were never to reach India. Loiseau later claimed that they had to seek shelter from bad weather at Mahé. Holding the crew at knifepoint, the deportees mutinied and forced them to sail the ship to La Digue, where they went ashore letting the *Laurette* sail on to Praslin.

This story is probably a cover-up. As the deportees told it, they thought La Digue made as good a place of exile as any, and Loiseau did little to dissuade them. In fact, more than half of the newcomers did settle peace fully on La Digue, their families joining them later. Among those who stayed was Célestin Payet, and to this day the Payets are one of the leading families of the island Belleville and Lafosse, the rebellion leaders, both returned to Réunion in the early 1800s.

BIRD AND DENIS ISLANDS

Each of these tiny coral islands on the rim of the Seychelles Bank has a cosy island lodge. Remote but noisy, Bird Island is for bird lovers, while exclusive Denis Island is a refuge for escapists

Map on page 340

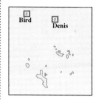

Although very similar on first appearance, Bird and Denis Islands have developed along different lines in recent times. Both have been in private ownership for many years, having once been plantations. Denis is now an island playground for tourists keen on watersports and game fishing. Bird, once a major source of seabirds' eggs for local cuisine, is now managed for eco-tourism. Whichever approach you prefer, these dream islands are just a 30-minute flight from Mahé.

Bird Island

Bird Island is also known as Île aux Vaches ("Island of Cows") after the dugongs or "sea cows" that once thrived in its waters. Because it was an excellent source of oil, this marine mammal was soon exterminated. It was named Bird Island by the British, after the millions of seabirds that flock here to breed. The secret of Bird Island is its simplicity. Lying 96 km (60 miles) north of Mahé, it is relatively remote. There is only one flight a day, so the minimum stay is two nights here, though many visitors opt to spend longer than they originally planned. For many, it becomes addictive: 35 percent of guests are return visitors, who come back periodically to wash away the strains of modern life.

The ethos of the island resort is firmly based on the ideal that a balance is possible between man and nature. Visitors are free to wander wherever they wish, providing they do not harm or disturb the wildlife. Organised sports and activities are deliberately kept to a minimum. You can walk, go bird-watching, swim, snorkel, go game fishing, play table tennis or billiards, or just laze in the sun and do nothing. The more energetic might wish to go in search of Esmeralda, the famous giant tortoise. He (the name's deceptive) once held the record as the heaviest land tortoise in the world.

Turtles and terns

Guests are also encouraged to help with the islands' turtle conservation projects. Hawksbill turtles come ashore to lay eggs between October and February (see page 327), and green turtles from April to October. There is a tagging programme, and "turtle-spotting" (hawksbill turtles lay their eggs in daylight) or nest watching gives an exciting dimension to an island walk. Since nests are closely monitored, some visitors are treated to the unforgettable sight of hatchlings struggling down to the sea.

Birds, appropriately, are the chief attraction and the best time to see them is in the breeding season between April and October. The island's most famous attrac-

LEFT:
sooty tern colony.
BELOW:
Bird Island trail.

tion is the enormous **sooty tern colony** ❶ which occupies one sixth of the islan during these months. The colony was once harvested for seabird eggs, considere a great delicacy by the Seychellois. In more recent years the birds have come t be appreciated more for the spectacle they provide than for their culinary value

Bird Island is also a good place for birdwatchers outside the breeding seasor Being on the edge of the Seychelles Bank, it is often a first landfall for migrant and many rare species have been seen here. Regulars include turnstones, whic are tame enough to peck about your feet, and there is a chance to glimpse roller bee-eaters, cuckoos and other species from far across the ocean.

Relaxing at the Lodge

At the height of the nesting period Bird Island is home to over a million birds.

The only place to stay here is **Bird Island Lodge** ❷ made up of 24 woode chalets strung along the idyllic beach on the west side of the island. Fron here you can watch columns of spiralling birds in their thousands, circling ove the colony. There is a delightful bar at the main building of the Lodge i which to relax, and the cuisine, with strong creole influences, is superb. Mos of the dishes on the menu are prepared with produce of the island. Imagine th delights of chicken soup with coconut milk, lemon grass and ginger, or fres sailfish steaks grilled on a barbecue under the stars. The chef can cater to any special requirements and vegetarians claim Bird offers the best special dishe in Seychelles *(see Travel Tips)*.

BELOW: rustic chalets, perfectly positioned for bird-watching.

Denis Island

Similar in size to its sister island, Denis lies 80 km (50 miles) north c Mahé. As with Bird Island, there is only one place to stay, and the minimur

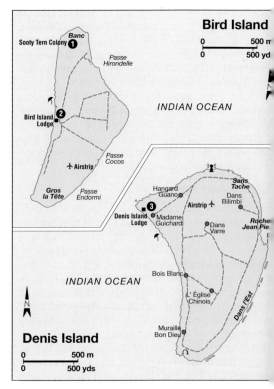

Bird Island

Banc
Sooty Tern Colony ❶

Passe Hirondelle

0   500 m
0   500 yd

Bird Island Lodge ❷

INDIAN OCEAN

Passe Cocos

✈ Airstrip

Gros la Tête   Passe Endormi

Hangard Guano●
Airstrip ✈
Sans Tache
Dans Bilimbi

Denis Island Lodge ●   Madame Guichard

●Dans Varre

Roche Jean Pie

❸

Bois Blanc●

INDIAN OCEAN

L' Église Chinois

N

Muraille Bon Dieu

Dans l'Est

Denis Island

0   500 m
0   500 yds

ooking is three days. **Denis Island Lodge ❸** is one of the best places
you can stay in the islands. The chalets are scattered amid the palms just
behind the beach, and the delicious cuisine is based around homegrown
produce and fresh fish. Close to the hotel is a large enclosure sheltering tor-
oises. After just a few hours in this quiet and stunningly beautiful refuge,
the world outside seems to lose all importance.

Map
on page
340

When early navigators wanted to stake a claim on an island for their country, they could lay a "possession stone" if they had one handy; if not, they
popped a deed of possession in a bottle and buried it. Somewhere on Denis
Island such a bottle may still lie hidden, dating from the visit of Denis de Tro-
briand in 1773, who claimed the island for France and blessed it with his name.
It is now the property of a local travel agency, Masons Travel.

The lighthouse, dating from 1910, is still operational. It is open to the public and the view from the top is magnificent.

Denis is more wooded than Bird, the latter having been cleared for the sake
of the breeding sooties, who prefer to nest on bare soil. The thick forest is
dominated by palm trees, interspersed with takamaka and casuarina trees.

*Both Bird and Denis
are popular game-
fishing destinations.*

Watersports

Situated on the edge of the Seychelles Bank, where the sea bottom plunges
away to 2,000 metres (6,600 ft), Denis Island has become a top game fishing destination where several records have been broken for dogtooth tuna
and bonito. Other catches-of-the-day might include barracuda or sailfish.
Diving has also become big here in recent years and there are two resident
divemasters.   ❑

BELOW: marlin are
plentiful in season.

THE OUTER ISLANDS

Still remote and visited by just a handful of people each year, these island groups have an unsurpassed beauty, and are scattered with the traces of a way of life that is rapidly being forgotten

Maps:
344, 348,
and 350

Even in our shrinking world, Seychelles' so-called "outer islands" are, for the most part, remote, uninhabited and possessed of an unspoilt beauty which those fortunate enough to have experienced find compelling. There are few who come away unmoved by these serene, isolated worlds; their encircling pristine beaches, vivid blue lagoons, kaleidoscopic reef life and the stillness beneath the palms which is only disturbed by the sigh of the waves.

The Outer Islands are divided into four main groups. From east to west they are the Amirantes Group, the Alphonse Group, the Farquhar Group and the Aldabra Group. In the early 20th century, these distant outposts were important elements in the economy of the Inner Islands. Schooners plied slowly from isle to isle collecting exotic produce for home consumption or export, returning with holds filled with coconuts, dried sea cucumber, green sea snail, guano and tortoiseshell. All that remains of the former trading posts and settlements are a few crumbling buildings and scattered ruins, which offer nothing more than a hint of what the way of life was like here. Today only a handful of the Outer Islands are inhabited, their tiny settlements peopled with hardy Seychellois "ilois" (island workers) on contract, fishing or collecting and processing copra.

Although tourism is playing an increasingly important role, the Outer Islands remain largely unexplored. Shops and nightlife are non-existent, and the beaches and sea are routinely breathtaking and pristine. There is excellent game fishing, particularly around Poivre, and fly-fishing, especially in the St François lagoon. The diving is spectacular off Desroches and Alphonse, and around Assumption Island. Aldabra Atoll is a major wildlife attraction, being home to thousands of giant tortoises, while the whole area is rich in birdlife.

Sail away

There are two ways to visit the Outer Islands: either on a charter boat or by basing yourself at one of the hotels. Desroches and Alphonse are currently the only two islands with hotels, though others are planned. It is also possible to stay at the Research Station on Aldabra and, if money is no object, you can book the entire islands of D'Arros and St Joseph Atoll for yourself. There are an increasing number of habitable boats visiting the area and these have the flexibility to go to all but D'Arros and Rémire, which are private. All the islands are within a short distance of each other and, depending on how long you want to spend at each, they can be visited in a few days. Chartering is fairly expensive due to logistics and the small scale of things, but not over the top (*see Travel Tips*). Whether you plan to base yourself on land or charter a boat, you should plan your trip to the Outer Islands

LEFT: at anchor in calm waters.
BELOW: preparing the catch for a barbecue supper.

in advance of going to Seychelles. It is difficult, though not entirely impossible to turn up and book an Outer Island excursion.

THE AMIRANTES GROUP

Of all the island groups, this is the closest to Mahé stretching from African Bank to the north, 235 km (146 miles) from Mahé, down to Desnoeufs Island 325 km (200 miles) southwest of Mahé. The islands were discovered during Vasco d' Gama's second great voyage in 1502, by which time he had been promoted to admiral, hence the name Ilhas do Amirante (Islands of the Admiral). Now largely uninhabited, the islands were once important components in the economy o' Seychelles, producing copra, tortoiseshell, turtle meat, seabird eggs and guano for local use and export. Life on these remote scraps of land was tough and lonely. As world markets changed, their relatively small harvests of goods became uneconomic to gather, and one by one they were abandoned to nature

Desroches

A Desroches Island punch.

The biggest island in the group is Desroches, a long thin strip of land with a fabulous sheltered lagoon and miles of sand, which make it the perfect get-away-from-it-all island. The flight from Mahé takes 40 minutes and lands at the grassy airstrip at the western end of the island by the **Desroches Island Resort ❶**, the only hotel in the Amirantes. There could hardly be a greater contrast between the arduous life of an *îlois* in the 19th century, and the luxury of a holiday at this exclusive island lodge nestling under the palms of an old coconut plantation. The chalets skirting the beach provide accommodation for no more than 40 guests

Most of the 50 or so inhabitants of Desroches are contract workers, mainly

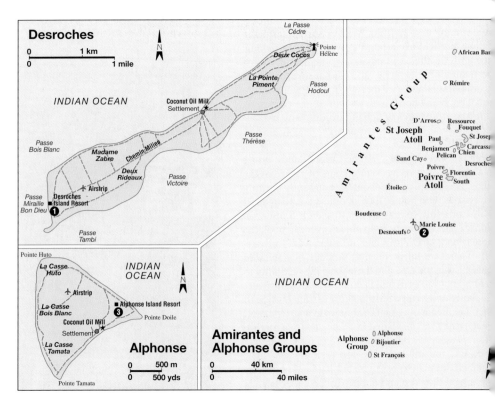

from Mahé, engaged in agriculture. They live at **Settlement**, 2 km (1 mile) northeast of the resort. Hotel guests and visitors on charter boats are free to visit this area which is a good place to get a feel for island life in colonial times. Look out for the old copra drier and the circle where an oil press once stood. The little lock up, with its barred doors, was the destination for any falling foul of island justice. Not surprisingly, the most common offence on these remote islands was drunkenness. The old hospital, if you can call it that, was little more than a room with a bed and a few basic medicines. In the early days, these would simply be medicinal plants that could be grown around the village, such as castor oil and datura.

Diving off Desroches is excellent, especially between November and April, and the island is famous among the diving fraternity for the amazing **Desroches Drop** – the edge of a coral plateau which forms the southern rim of the island, pitted with gulleys and deep caves (these can only be explored under the supervision of a PADI divemaster). The dive centre here runs courses for beginners and caters for other watersports (canoeing, windsurfing, sailing, snorkelling). A boat can also be chartered for game fishing trips or visits to nearby islands. The big game fishing is sensational, the waters rich in tuna, bonito, kingfish and sailfish. The hotel also has its own floodlit tennis court and hires bicycles. The flat island is perfect for exploring by bike. The lodge produces a map with basically two routes – coastal and inland.

Southern islands and atolls

Only a day's sail from Desroches, **Poivre Atoll** is the largest atoll in the Amirantes group. It is made up of three islands – Poivre, South Island (joined

Map on page 344

Louis Poiret, the mystery man who claimed he was Louis XVII, the lost king of France (see page 248) came to Poivre in 1804 where he was apprenticed at the cotton gin.

BELOW: a close encounter.

together at low tide by a man-made causeway) and Florentin – all with first class beaches. Although it was a coconut plantation before it was abandoned, in its early days its major production was cotton. Plans for the building of an island resort are in the pipeline, but at present, there is nothing here except a small settlement on Poivre. One of the most beautiful of the Amirantes islands, Poivre is named after the former governor of Mauritius (1763–72), Pierre Poivre, who was responsible for introducing spices to Seychelles *(see page 247)*. It is famous for its deep sea fishing and diving and, although it is privately owned, a limited number of visitors are allowed access, provided they have been given permission in advance (permission from Islands Development Company, New Port, Victoria; tel: 224640).

Crusing on a charter yacht is one of the best ways to explore the Outer Islands.

Étoile and **Boudeuse** are tiny uninhabited islands with nothing but breeding terns, notably the sooty tern and roseate tern, while Boudeuse has a huge colony of masked booby. They have the same uncanny beauty, enhanced by a sense of real isolation, as African Banks *(see below)*. You can only visit by charter boat, and landing is only possible in very calm conditions.

Marie Louise ❷ is in some ways the prettiest of the Amirantes, a coral island version of the granitic islands of Aride and Cousin, with large populations of seabirds. It has an airstrip to serve the small settlement, but there are no regular flights and no facilities for visitors. It is simply a beautiful place to include on your charter itinerary.

The southernmost island of the Amirantes group is **Desnoeufs**, famous in Seychelles for the vast numbers of sooty terns that breed here, the eggs of which are considered a delicacy in the granitics. Egg-collecting is limited to half the island. This restriction will hopefully ensure that a sufficient number of birds are

left to breed successfully. Outside the egg-collecting season, the island is abandoned. Again, visiting is only possible on a charter boat; even then it's difficult to get ashore. Landing should not be attempted by any but an experienced boatman or strong swimmer.

Northern islands and atolls

African Banks is a tiny island with nothing but a lighthouse. The landscape of sweeping white sand hovers like a mirage on the brightest turquoise and ultramarine waters you have ever seen. Seabirds breed here in considerable numbers. The sands are criss-crossed by turtle tracks as if a safari rally had been held during the night. The urge to go ashore and explore makes landing irresistible.

Rémire was originally named Eagle Island, after a ship sent here in 1771 by the British in Bombay to find out what the French were up to in Seychelles. Today it is the personal retreat of President Albert René, and visitors must have special permission to land here by boat or plane. If you do obtain permission to visit, it is an island of gentle beauty, with shaded paths through the woodland and attractive beaches all around.

D'Arros and neighbouring **St Joseph Atoll** (the property of the same private owner) were important coconut-producing islands during the early years of the 20th century, often yielding over 40,000 nuts a month. D'Arros is an oval-shaped platform reef. It has an

airstrip and a guest house offering an exclusive retreat which has been a haven for heads of state, wealthy Arabs and film stars. **St Joseph Atoll,** separated from D'Arros by a deep channel, is made up of 13 small islets, which together make up less than 1 sq km of land. They are all deserted, but some have old colonial ruins which are interesting to visit and speculate upon. Diving here is excellent.

THE ALPHONSE GROUP

The Alphonse Group consists of two neighbouring atolls, **Alphonse Atoll** and **St François Atoll**.

Alphonse Atoll

Alphonse was a productive plantation in its heyday, generating 100,000 coconuts a month on a regular basis during the 1930s. The plantation was abandoned in recent times, and the island is now leased to **Alphonse Island Resort ❸** whose 25 chalets skirt the tranquil lagoon. There is an **airstrip** for transfers from Mahé, an hour's flight away. (Visitors on charter boats need advance permission from the Island Development Company on Mahé.)

The resort's Dive Centre offers facilities for diving the wall of Alphonse where forests of gorgonian fan corals, sharks, rays and huge schools of predatory fish such as barracuda, as well as a host of colourful reef fish, may be seen. The best snorkelling is at the pass into the lagoon, but this is a long way out and can only be reached by boat. Special snorkelling trips can be arranged by the hotel.

Exploring the island on foot is simple; the paths are clear, there is no climbing involved and little danger of getting lost. The Alphonse Island Resort

Just south of St Joseph Atoll is a tiny deserted tuft of land called Sand Cay. It has no vegetation and is often submerged by high spring tides, but it is a popular destination for roosting terns. It is often seen covered with up to seven different species.

BELOW: the D'Arros guest house.

arranges day-trips to nearby Bijoutier and St François, the uninhabited islands of St Francois Atoll.

St François Atoll

Alphonse is shaped like an arrowhead. Two of its three points are named after ships: Pointe Doille is named after a guano vessel that used to call here and Pointe Tamatave is named after a British steamship that ran aground in 1903.

To reach the other islands from Alphonse you must cross the **Canal la Mort** – "Death Channel"! The water here is deep, cold and treacherous with powerful currents. The 5-km (3-mile) journey is worth it, however, to reach the near-perfection of **Bijoutier.** The name means "little jewel" and that is just what this island is. Perfectly round, capped with bright green vegetation, fringed with the whitest of coral beaches and encircled by purple reefs and turquoise sea, this is the closest any island comes to the paradise ideal.

St François is surrounded by a fearsome reef, girdled by shipwrecks. At least six are still visible on the horizon, a grim reminder that the waters in these parts should be treated with respect. It is possible to enter the huge lagoon of St François in safety through **La Passe Traversé.** Over the coral crest, the tranquil lagoon waters are fairly shallow and a world away from the ferocity of the waters beyond the reef. The enormous plain of sand, left dry at low tide, is a feeding ground for hundreds of wading birds. Apart from its beauty and birdlife, the biggest attraction of St François is fly-fishing in the lagoon.

THE FARQUHAR GROUP

BELOW: Bijoutier, a jewel in Seychelles' crown.

The Farquhar group, which comprises Providence Atoll, St Pierre island and Farquhar Atoll, is about 700 km (435 miles) from Mahé. The islands are only accessible by sea, but with the growth of habitable cruising they are no longer entirely out of reach. There are also plans to build a hotel on Farquhar and it is

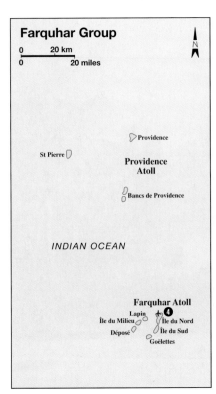

Farquhar Group

0   20 km
0   20 miles

N

▷ Providence

St Pierre ◗

Providence
Atoll

Bancs de Providence

INDIAN OCEAN

Farquhar Atoll
Lapin
Île du Milieu   Île du Nord
Déposé   Île du Sud
Goélettes

already possible to charter a plane from Islands Development Company (IDC) and use an 8-room facility in an existing building.

Providence Atoll

This is a long, thin atoll oriented roughly north-south. **Providence**, the main island, lies at its northern tip, while across 40 km (25 miles) of shallow water lies **Bancs de Providence** at its southern extreme. Most of the reef is out of sight of land and, consequently, many a ship has foundered here. The huge shallow lagoon attracts hundreds of grey herons and this is the only place in Seychelles where herons outnumber all other bird species. Providence has a small transient human population employed by IDC in copra production, but Bancs de Providence is strictly for the birds and turtles.

St Pierre

Due west of Providence is the extremely strange raised coral platform of **St Pierre**, rising to about 10 metres (33 ft) above sea level. There is no beach at high tide and landing is only safe when the tide recedes to reveal a tiny sandy corner in the northeast. This island, now abandoned, was once mined for guano and you can still see the walls of the rotting stores and the twisted metal of what was once a quay.

Farquhar Atoll

South of Providence are the 10 islands of **Farquhar Atoll ❹**. The lagoon is a popular anchorage for yachts and schooners. On the main island, Île du Nord, there is a small settlement where a little copra is still produced. The island also

Maps on pages 344 & 348

TIP

When tides are low, a good pair of plastic shoes or similar footwear is essential for wading ashore across reef flats with sharp coral fragments and possibly poisonous cone shells.

BELOW: burning coconut husks on Farquhar.

has an airstrip. Many of the trees on neighbouring Île du Sud have been turned white by the droppings of hundreds of red-footed boobies which nest here. The southern tip of the atoll, Goëlettes, is also the most southerly island of Seychelles. It is swept almost bare of vegetation by the strong southeasterly winds, but is a haven for seabirds with 260,000 pairs of sooty terns and a healthy number of black-naped terns, a species that breeds only on coral atolls.

The name Aldabra may originate from the Arabic al-khadra, "the green", due to the reflection cast by the shallow lagoon waters on clouds above the atoll, a sight probably familiar to Arab traders between Comoros and the Middle East.

THE ALDABRA GROUP

Aldabra is the most remote and most interesting of all the Outer Island groups. Geographically a part of Seychelles, these islands lie closer to Madagascar than they do to Mahé, more than 1,000 km (625 miles) away. The archipelago is made up of **Astove** and **Cosmoledo Atoll**, lying due west of Farquhar Atoll, and **Assumption** and the **Aldabra Atoll** beyond. There are no hotels on the Aldabra group which, apart from visiting scientists and the occasional small cruiseship or charter boat from Mahé, sees few visitors. For the most part the only footprints in the sand belong to the birds.

Aldabra Atoll

Aldabra ❺ is the world's largest raised coral atoll; the exposed coral cap of a volcanic seamount rising more than 4 km (2 miles) from the ocean floor. Geologically, it is part of a chain that includes the Comoros. It is made up of four main islands – Picard, Polymnie, Malabar and Grand Terre – and a number of other small islets, stretching 32 km (20 miles) from east to west. This ring of coral islands encloses a vast lagoon which is fed by several channels that carry in new life with each tide.

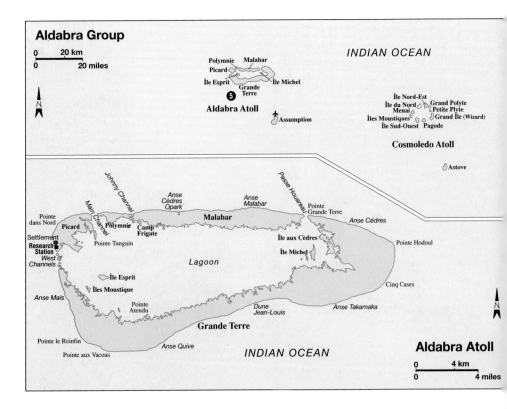

Virtually untouched by the modern world, Aldabra Atoll is now listed as a UNESCO World Heritage Site. It does not possess the tranquil beauty of the archetypal tropical idyll as seen elsewhere in Seychelles, but has the atmosphere of an untamed wilderness lost in time. Its survival owes less to design than to its inhospitable terrain. Much of the interior is covered with sharp, jagged rocks and impenetrable scrub.

The atoll is home to nearly 95 percent of the world's giant tortoise population with an estimated 100,000 animals. In addition, around 2,500 green turtles come ashore to breed each year as do smaller numbers of hawksbill turtle. Living alongside them is the Aldabra rail, the last surviving flightless bird of the Indian Ocean. Most of the other land birds are unique species. It has the world's second largest colony of frigatebirds, with 10,000 breeding pairs, and the world's only oceanic colony of Caspian tern.

About 40 of the plant species are endemic, including the beautiful Aldabra lily. However, the vegetation is dominated by salt-resistant pemphis scrub, capable of surviving in the harsh conditions, and throwing a dense prickly blanket over much of the land surface. Around the inner rim of the lagoon is a dense thicket of mangroves.

Marine life is concentrated around the channels. Snorkelling or diving can be exhilarating here on the incoming tides that run at 10 km (6 knots) per hour or more, taking swimmers on a roller coaster ride that sweeps them past sharks, rays, groupers and other exotic fish. This is not for the inexperienced and should never be attempted without a small boat to accompany your group.

There is a small **Research Station** on Picard with a warden and staff of around ten employed by the SIF (Seychelles Islands Foundation). There is also an accommodation block of six twin rooms for visiting scientists. When no scientists are in residence (which is most of the time) these rooms are available for visitors, but you need to apply in advance for permission from SIF on Mahé. Otherwise the atoll, one third of the land mass of Seychelles, is uninhabited. Except for Picard, Polymnie, Western Malabar and Camp Frigate, access to the atoll, even for resident visitors, is prohibited.

Maps on pages 348 & 350

The Assumption airstrip departure lounge.

Cosmoledo, Astove and Assumption

Cosmoledo Atoll has Seychelles' largest populations of red-footed booby, masked booby and sooty tern. It is also the last breeding site for the brown booby, exterminated elsewhere in the islands. The marine life around Cosmoledo and Astove is very rich, making for excellent diving territory.

West of Cosmoledo is the barren island of **Assumption**. Guano mining wiped out most of the bird life here, though a small human population remains, connected by air to Mahé. Flights are few and far between except when officials are flown out to clear a cruise-ship, or passengers to join a dive boat based in the area from November to April. Nevertheless, the reefs here are largely intact and, as elsewhere in the group, diving is excellent. Advance permission to visit is required from IDC (Islands Development Company) on Mahé. ❑

BELOW: Cosmoledo.

☀ INSIGHT GUIDES
TRAVEL TIPS

Insight FlexiMaps

Maps in Insight Guides are tailored to complement the text. But when you're on the road you sometimes need the big picture that only a large-scale map can provide. This new range of durable Insight Fleximaps has been designed to meet just that need.

Detailed, clear cartography
makes the comprehensive route and city maps easy to follow, highlights all the major tourist sites and provides valuable motoring information plus a full index.

Informative and easy to use
with additional text and photographs covering a destination's top 10 essential sites, plus useful addresses, facts about the destination and handy tips on getting around.

Laminated finish
allows you to mark your route on the map using a non-permanent marker pen, and wipe it off. It makes the maps more durable and easier to fold than traditional maps.

The world's most popular destinations
are covered by the 125 titles in the series – and new destinations are being added all the time. They include Alaska, Amsterdam, Bangkok, Barbados, Beijing, Brussels, Dallas/Fort Worth, Florence, Hong Kong, Ireland, Madrid, New York, Orlando, Peru, Prague, Rio, Rome, San Francisco, Sydney, Thailand, Turkey, Venice, and Vienna.

🕮 INSIGHT GUIDES
The world's largest collection of visual travel guides

CONTENTS

Mauritius and Rodrigues

The Place

Area: Pear-shaped Mauritius is 1,865 sq km (720 sq miles) and is the same size as the county of Surrey in England. Its fish-shaped neighbour, Rodrigues, lying 653 km (405 miles) to the east, is a mere 110 sq km (43 sq miles).

Situation: The Mascarene Islands of Mauritius and Rodrigues lie in the western Indian Ocean between latitude 19° and 22° south, just inside the Tropic of Capricorn, and longitude 55° and 64° east. Their nearest neighbour is Madagascar lying 805 km (500 miles) to the west. Mauritius includes the islands of Agalega and St Brandon in the Cargados Carajos group and claims sovereignty, with Réunion, over the turtle-rearing island of Tromelin, 560 km (347 miles) to the north. Diego Garcia in the Chagos Archipelago, 1,931 km (1,200 miles) to the northeast, used to belong to Mauritius but now forms part of the British Indian Ocean Territory (BIOT) and is the principal American military base in the Indian Ocean. It is closed to visitors.

Capitals: Mauritius – Port Louis; Rodrigues – Port Mathurin.

Population: Estimated at just over 1.1 million, Mauritius is one of the most densely populated islands in the world. Indo-Mauritians form the majority at 68 percent, followed by Creoles or people of mixed European and African origin (also referred to as the "general population") 27 percent, with Sino-Mauritians at 3 percent and Franco-Mauritians 2 percent. On Rodrigues there are only 37,000 people, mainly Creoles of African, Malagasy and French descent.

Metric Conversions

Mauritius is fully metric although you may still see road signs indicating miles rather than kilometres and some small shops may still weigh in pounds.

1 gram = 0.035 ounce
1 kilogram (1,000 grams) = 2.2 lb
1 millimetre = 0.039 inch
1 centimetre = 0.393 inch
1 litre = 1.76 pints
4.5 litres = 1 gallon
8 kilometres = 5 miles
1 metre = 3.28 feet
1 kilometre = 0.62 mile
1 ounce = 28.5 grams
1 pound (16 ounces) = 453 grams
1 pint = 0.568 litre
1 gallon = 4.5 litres
1 inch = 2.54 centimetres
1 foot (12 inches) = 0.3048 metres (30.48 centimetres)
1 yard (3 feet) = 0.9144 metres
1 mile (1,760 yards) = 1.609 kilometres

Language: Kreol is the *lingua franca* of the Mascarene Islands. However, in Mauritius the official language is English; French is also spoken and many Indian and Chinese languages such as Bhojpuri (a sort of creolised Hindi), Tamil, Urdu, Telegu, Marathi, Gujurati, Mandarin and Cantonese.

Religion: Hinduism (52 percent), Christianity (28 percent, most of whom are Roman Catholic) and Islam (16.5 percent). Since the majority of Sino-Mauritians are Roman Catholics, Buddhism is diminishing although Chinese festivals are still celebrated. Many religious festivals are public holidays and give an indication of the delicate balance needed to preserve each culture. Rodrigues is mostly Roman Catholic.

Time Zone: Four hours ahead of Greenwich Mean Time. Daylight hours: November to April 5.30am–7pm; May to October 6.45am–5.45pm.

Currency: Mauritius rupee (R) divided into 100 cents (c). There are 1, 5 and 10 rupee coins and 20 and 50 cent coins. Notes come in the following denominations: R25, 50, 100, 200, 500, 1,000 and 2,000.

Weights and Measures: The metric system is used in the Mascarenes, though in Mauritius and Rodrigues, you may come across road signs in miles and the occasional shop still weighing in pounds.

Electricity: 220 volts throughout the Mascarene Islands. In Mauritius and Rodrigues square three-pin plugs are used as in the UK.

International dialling codes: 230 for both Mauritius and Rodrigues. To call from Mauritius dial 00 095.

Climate

Mauritius and Rodrigues enjoy a tropical climate with two seasons: summer and winter. The hot and humid summer months from November to May produce prolonged sunshine with temperatures of up to 35°C (95°F) on the coasts broken by short heavy bursts of rainfall. Humidity is high even at night.

From May to October, temperatures can climb up to 25°C (77°F) with little rain, cooler nights and less humidity. The southeast trade winds blow all year keeping the south and east coasts fresher during the summer but it can get uncomfortably windy during the rest of the year.

For visitors who like to walk, tour and explore, the best time to go is October and November. These are the driest months which provide less humidity than high summer and are outside the cyclone season. The differences in Mauritius' altitude, topography and wind direction produce varied micro-climates; the towns on the central plateau can be cloud-capped, damp and cooler while the coast is clear and warm.

Cyclones can occur between November and April. They are born hundreds of miles to the northeast of Mauritius and take days to meander westwards. Various weather stations track their route and warnings that a cyclone may develop are broadcast days in advance. Most pass by harmlessly bringing only heavy rain and winds which clear the air after a spell of very hot humid weather. Others may have more devastating effects and you should listen to all cyclone warnings and comply with any directions or advice.

Cyclone Warnings

In the southwestern region of the Indian Ocean the following terms describe the intensity of different cyclonic disturbances:

• **Tropical depression:** speed of gusts are less than 90 km (56 miles) per hour.
• **Moderate tropical depression:** speed of gusts are 90–134 km (56–83 miles) per hour.
• **Strong tropical depression:** speed of gusts are 135–179 km (84–111 miles) per hour.
• **Tropical cyclone:** speed of gusts are 180–250 km (112–155 miles) per hour.
• **Tropical cyclone of strong intensity:** speed of gusts are 251–335 km (156–208 miles) per hour.
• **Tropical cyclone of very strong intensity:** speed of gusts are more than 335 km (208 miles) per hour.

When a cyclone approaches the islands, the Meteorological Office regularly broadcasts cyclone bulletins and red flags are raised on public buildings to denote their intensity:

• **One red flag:** Warning Class I – low risk of gust up to 120 km (75 miles) per hour.
• **Two red flags:** Warning Class II – increased risk of gusts to 120 km (75 miles) per hour.
• **Three red flags:** Warning Class III – great danger of gusts to 120 km (75 miles) per hour.
• **Four red flags:** Warning Class IV – gusts of 120 km (75 miles) per hour have been registered.

Weather information: tel: 302 6071
Cyclone information: tel: 96

Government

The government of the Republic of Mauritius is based on a British parliamentary-style democracy but still retains traditional links with Africa, India and Europe. The constitution allows for the appointment of a president (in whom executive power is invested) and a prime minister. Elections are held every five years. Rodrigues, a former Mauritian dependency, is politically integrated with Mauritius and was granted regional autonomy in 2002.

Economy

In 1971 the Mauritian government created the Export Processing Zone (EPZ) as a means of diversification from sugar into manufacturing and textiles. Today, the textile industry is the driving force of the economic miracle and there are over 600 export-orientated companies involved in manufacturing and export of jewellery, leather goods and electronics. More recent activities include information technology, printing and publishing. The EPZ now competes with tourism in the nation's economy, followed by the sugar industry. The country is also self sufficient in agriculture through land rotation farming techniques and interline cropping. Sugar remains the most important agricultural activity and enough sugar is produced to meet a quota of at least 500,000 tonnes per year under the Lomé Convention. Serious drought in 1999 produced only 410,000 tonnes compared with 1998 figures of 627,000 tonnes.

Business Hours

Non-government offices: open 8am–4.30pm Mon–Fri; 9am–noon on Saturday.
Government offices: open 9am–4pm Mon–Fri; 9am–noon on Saturday.
Shops in Port Louis: open 9.30am–5pm Mon–Fri; 9am–noon on Saturday.

Shops in plateau towns: open from 10am–6pm every day; 10am–noon Thur–Sun.
Municipal markets: open from 6am–6pm Mon–Sat.

Public Holidays and Festivals

All public services are closed on public holidays. Many of these are religious festivals celebrated by various ethnic groups in Mauritius and some, but not all, shops and businesses are closed. In Rodrigues, Chinese-run shops (which are most shops) shut for a week during the Chinese Spring Festival. *(See pages 80–81 for more about Hindu festivals).*
January 1 and 2 New Year's Day
mid-January/February Cavadee (varies)
February 1 Abolition of Slavery
February/March Chinese Spring Festival (varies)
February/March Maha Shivaratree (varies)
March 12 Republic Day
March/April Ougadi (varies)
May 1 Labour Day
May/June Id El Fitr (varies)
August 15 Assumption Day
September Ganesh Chaturthi (varies)
October/November Divali (varies)
November 1 All Saints' Day
November 2 Arrival of Indentured Labourers
December 25 Christmas Day

Planning the Trip

Passports & Visas

Nationals of the EU, USA and all Commonwealth countries do not require visas, and entry as a tourist is for a maximum of three months. You will be asked to produce your return or onward ticket at Immigration and to provide an address in Mauritius.

Applications for longer stays should be made at the Passport and Immigration Department at Sterling House, rue Gislet Geoffrey, Port Louis; tel: 210 9312; fax: 210 9322; e-mail: piomain@intnet.mu. Take two passport-size photographs, a valid return ticket, evidence of funds to meet the cost of your stay and a letter from your host explaining why you want to extend your stay. Applications can be made Mon–Fri, 9am to 12 noon and 1pm to 4pm, and Saturdays from 9am to noon. There is no charge for an extension visa.

Customs

Travellers are allowed to bring in the following duty free items:
● 250 grams of tobacco (including cigars and cigarettes)
● 1 litre of spirits
● 2 litres of wine, ale or beer
● 250 ml of eau de toilette
● a reasonable amount of perfume
There are stiff penalties for the importation of illegal drugs.

Health & Insurance

Malaria has been eradicated in the Mascarenes and no vaccinations are necessary unless you are coming from an infected area.

The cost of private treatment in Mauritius is substantially less than in Europe. Shop around for an insurance policy which suits your circumstances and in the event of a medical claim ensure that you keep all receipts and documentation.

HEALTH HAZARDS

In Mauritius avoid wading in muddy waters without wearing protective shoes. This is the habitat of the laff or stone fish which if trodden upon emits a poisonous venom from its spines. Local fishermen resort to a poultice remedy but immediate removal to hospital is necessary as the wound, if untreated, can be fatal. In Rodrigues the only nasties you may encounter are large centipedes. They frequent dark corners in old buildings and can emit a painful sting.

Money Matters

Major currencies, major credit cards and travellers cheques are accepted in banks, bureaux de change, most hotels and some shops. There is no restriction on the amount of foreign currency you can bring in to the country. Banks offer a better rate of exchange than hotels. If you have a surplus of rupees on departure you can change them back into your own currency but keep any bank receipts as you can only export a maximum of R350.

BANKS

Banks are open 9.15am–3.15pm Monday to Thursday and 9.15am–3.30pm on Friday. In tourist areas and Port Louis they are also open on Saturday 9.15–11.15am.

Bank of Mauritius has small branches everywhere and branches of **Barclays** and HSBC can be found in Grand Baie and other tourist areas. The only bank in Le Morne is a branch of MCB (Mauritius Commercial Bank). Banks at the

airport open to coincide with arrivals and departures of international flights.

Change facilities are widely available at bureau de change offices and opening times are 3.15–5pm Monday to Friday; 9am–5pm on Saturdays; 9am–noon on Sundays and public holidays. You can use your credit card to withdraw cash from ATMs (automatic teller machines). Before you leave home make sure that you know your PIN number.

TAX

Value Added Tax (TVA) of 12 percent is added to goods and services, including hotel and restaurant bills, but there is no VAT on foodstuffs and books. Duty-free goods are available everywhere but you can't take them with you at the time of purchase; they are sent to the airport for you to collect on departure.

What to Bring

The emphasis is on smart casual wear such as loose cotton shorts, shirts, t-shirts and dresses around town and in the evenings. For the feet light sandals are appropriate and comfortable. You should also bring a pair of plastic water shoes for protection against injury from sharp coral.

Women are expected to cover up when venturing from beach to hotel and swimsuits should not be worn around town or in hotel dining rooms. Male visitors need not bring a jacket and tie unless they plan to attend formal functions or dine in the smartest hotels and restaurants.

Most hotels used by tour operators have a dress code for dinner which specifies smart casual wear, but no shorts or t-shirts. You might need a light jumper or shawl for the evening breeze.

To protect yourself from the sun and rain, bring a hat, sunglasses and sun cream and a light mac or cape and a pocket torch in case of power cuts.

Indian Ocean Weddings

More and more couples are choosing to marry abroad and Mauritius and Seychelles are particularly popular destinations for tying the knot and honeymooning (*see* Romancing the Isles *page 35*).
• **Planning your wedding:** There are a number of specialised tour operators (*see right*) who can arrange everything for you, but they should be approached at least six months before your planned wedding date. Places get booked up well in advance and there's a certain amount of paperwork to deal with.

When shopping around for a tour operator, ask if there are any special deals. More often than not there will be some discounts or extras such as complimentary champagne on arrival or a room upgrade as it is assumed that as this is a celebration, you will be spending a little bit extra.
• **You will need:** Photocopies of the following documents must be sent to your destination around 10 weeks before the big day – and remember to take the originals with you.
• Birth certificates.
• Passports.
• If divorced, the relevant divorce papers.
• In the case of a widow/widower,

a death certificate and any previous marriage certificates.
• Proof of any change of name by deed poll, if relevant. This must be stamped and signed by a solicitor or relevant official according to your country.
• If either the bride or groom is adopted, an adoption certificate.
• For a religious wedding, christening certificates and a certificate of "Good Morality" from respective parish priests may be required. Church weddings may have to be backed up by a civil ceremony to be recognised by the law of the country in which you reside.
• **When to travel:** In Mauritius, couples must be on the island 24 hours before a civil wedding and 15 days before a religious wedding. In Seychelles the residency requirement is 11 days but on payment of SR100 (approx. £12) this will be waived and only three days will be necessary to sort out all the final details and let you acclimatise. This fee is often absorbed by the tour operator.
• **On arrival:** Once at your hotel, you will have a meeting with the wedding co-ordinator to decide on the final details such as the type of flowers you want and any extras. Then you will visit the local Civil Status Office to check

you have the correct documents and the Supreme Court where certificates are issued. It is also necessary in Mauritius to visit the Civil Office that oversees the district your hotel is in. Reputable hotels will arrange taxis for these trips.

Wedding Packages
Beachcomber Tours: tel: 01483 445610 (Mauritius only)
Elite Vacations: tel: 020 8864 4431
Indian Ocean Connections: tel: 01244 355320
Kuoni Travel: tel: 01306 747007
Silhouette Travel: tel: 020 8255 1738
Sunset Faraway Holidays: tel: 020 7498 9922
Thomas Cook Faraway: tel: 01733 418450
Tradewinds: tel: 0870 751 0009
• **Going it alone:** If you want to arrange your wedding abroad independently, contact:
Mauritius: Registrar of Civil Status, 7th Level, Emmanuel Anquetil Building, Sir S. Ramgoolam Street, Port Louis, Mauritius. Tel: 00 230 201 1727
Seychelles: The Registrar, Civil Status Office, PO Box 430, Victoria, Mahé. Tel: 00 248 224030

Tourist Offices

Mauritius Tourism Promotion Authority offices (MTPA):
UK: 32–33 Elvaston Place, London SW7 5NW, tel: 020 7584 3666; fax: 020 7225 1135; e-mail: mtpa@btinternet.com
USA: Mauritius Embassy, Suite 441, 4301 Connecticut Avenue NW, Washington DC 20008, tel: (202) 244 1491/92; fax: (202) 966 0983
Australia: Mauritius High Commission, 2 Beale Crescent, Deakin, Canberra, Act 2600, tel: 06 281 1203; fax: 06 282 3235.
Tourist information can also be

obtained from high commissions and embassies and on the MTPA's website: www.mauritius.net

Getting There

BY AIR

Air Mauritius (airline code MK), the national carrier, flies from destinations in Europe (London, Paris, Frankfurt, Munich, Vienna, Brussels, Geneva, Zurich, Rome), Africa (Johannesburg, Durban, Cape Town, Nairobi, Comores, Antananarivo, Seychelles), Asia (Hong Kong, Singapore, Kuala Lumpur, Mumbai, Delhi) and

Australia (Perth, Melbourne), with frequent daily flights from Réunion.
Flights to Rodrigues are only available from Mauritius and Réunion.
Other international carriers are: Air Austral (UU), British Airways (BA), Air France (AF), Condor, South African Airways (SA), Air Seychelles and Singapore Airlines (SQ). Emirates also fly to Mauritius from Dubai.
Air Austral (tel: 00 33 1 44 95 11 30; fax: 00 33 1 44 95 11 37; e-mail: paris@air-austral.com), based in France, offers routings to Mayotte, South Africa (Jo'burg), the Comores, Madagascar, Seychelles, Réunion and Mauritius.

No charter airlines serve Mauritius directly but you can fly from Paris to Réunion on a charter flight *(see page 380)* booked through a French travel agency such as Nouvelles Frontières (www.newfrontiers.com) and fly on to Mauritius from there. Several planes a day fly between Réunion and Mauritius with Air Mauritius and Air Austral. It is important you have a recognised address to go to on arrival in Mauritius, or you will be denied entry into the country.

Airport tax is included in the price of Air Mauritius tickets and many package deals, but it is advisable to check. Passengers whose tickets do not include the airport tax will have to pay R300 in local currency on departure.

Airline contacts
Air Mauritius: tel: 207 7070; fax: 211 0366 (reservations); tel: 207 7171; fax: 211 4014 (sales). Also general sales agents for Air India, Royal Swazi, Scandinavian, Swissair and Thai Airways
Air Mauritius (Rodrigues): tel: 831 1632; fax: 831 1959 (prefix with 00 095 if dialling from Mauritius)
British Airways: tel: 202 8000; fax: 202 8080
Rogers Travel Ltd: tel: 202 6655; fax: 211 7667. Also general sales agents for Air France, Air Inter, Air Malawi, Saudi Arabian Airlines, South African Airways, Ansett Airlines of Australia, Union de Transport Aeriens
Ireland Blyth Ltd: tel: 202 8000; fax: 212 4050. Also general sales agents for British Airways, Air Madagascar, Cathay Pacific

Package tour operators
Many tour operators based throughout Europe, South Africa, Australia, Canada and the US offer package and specialist holidays to Mauritius. For details contact your local travel agent.

The following UK-based operators specialise in Mauritius:
Beachcomber Tours: tel: 01483 445610
Carrier Indian Ocean: tel: 01625 547030

Elegant Resorts: tel: 01244 897 888
Elite Vacations: tel: 020 8864 4431
Explore Worldwide: tel: 01252 760000.
This company offers a 15-day hiking holiday in both Réunion and Mauritius
Expressions: tel: 020 7435 8484
ITC Classics: tel: 01244 355320
Mauritian Connections: tel: 0870 741 9967
Sunset Faraway Holidays: tel: 020 7498 9922

FROM THE AIRPORT

Sir Seewoosagur Ramgoolam International Airport, abbreviated to SSR, is officially named after the first prime minister of Mauritius after independence. It occupies the area of Plaisance in the south, 48 km (30 miles) from Port Louis, and is often referred to simply as Plaisance. The international code for the airport is MRU, tel: 603 3030; fax: 637 3266.
Bus service: An hourly express bus service, often crowded with locals, links with Mahébourg and Port Louis between 6.30am and 6.30pm but is only convenient if you have no luggage.
Taxis: If a taxi is not equipped with a meter, which they should be, agree a price before starting any journey. A metered taxi ride to Rose Hill, for example, with two items of luggage, should work out at around R550. An unmetered ride for the same journey, depending on your bargaining skills, may work out slightly less.
Plaine Corail Airport, Rodrigues: tel: 831 6321; fax: 831 6301. As Rodrigues' airport is just a small strip in the south of the island, tour operators usually collect their own visitors. Independent travellers can take the Supercopter bus to Port Mathurin for R75. To return to the airport, call Ibrahim Nalla on 831 1859 for pick ups from any guest house or hotel location in and around Port Mathurin.

Maps
You can pick up pocket-size maps from most bookshops in Port Louis and most good hotels should have a stock of tourist maps at reception. These will only highlight tourist spots, however. French IGN produce a more detailed and accurate map (1:100,000) which is available from Stanfords, 12/14 Long Acre, Covent Garden, London WC2E 9LP; tel: 020 7836 1321; www.stanfords.co.uk

---

BY SEA

There are no international passenger shipping services to Mauritius although cruise ships occasionally call at Port Louis, either as part of a round-the-world trip or on a cruise from South Africa. Nor can you travel by sea between the Mascarenes and Seychelles, unless, of course, you are chartering a yacht.

The only regular passenger/cargo vessel is the MS *Mauritius Pride* which operates to and from Réunion six times per month. The journey takes about 12 hours and children travel half price. The ship also operates a service to Rodrigues two or three times per month *(see page 363)*.

If you are considering planning a long-distance sea trip, make sure you choose the right season. Long-haul ocean trips are not generally made during the cyclone season.

Practical Tips

Media

TV AND RADIO

The Mauritius Broadcasting Corporation (MBC) transmits television news in English at 7am, 5.40pm and 9pm and radio news at 8am, 3pm and 9pm daily. French TV comes from Réunion. BBC World Service can be received on various frequencies mainly in the morning and late evening. Skyvision and Canal Plus are available in most hotels.

PUBLICATIONS

English-language newspapers are hard to come by and imported publications such as *Newsweek* are expensive and often late. The *Côte Nord* magazine is distributed free in hotels and shops in the Grand Baie area and Beachcomber's house magazine, *Evasion*, contains interesting articles in both French and English. All are ideal for news, reviews and tourist information.

There are plenty of local newspapers, the most popular being the morning *L'Express* and the evening *Le Mauricien*. Both are published in French with some news items and adverts in English. There are no English-language newspapers printed in Mauritius.

The Mauritian Wildlife Foundation (tel: 211 1749/2228 or e-mail: mwfexec@bow.intnet.mu) issues an annual newsletter. Set up in 1984 the foundation aims to protect and manage the rare flora and fauna of Mauritius and to inform, educate and involve locals in all aspects of its work.

Postal Services

Post offices operate in towns and villages and are open from 8.15am to 11.15am and 12 noon to 4pm Mon–Fri and from 8am to 11.45am on Saturday. **Post Office Headquarters:** Quay Street, Port Louis; tel: 208 2851; fax: 212 9640.

Telecommunications

Information technology has taken off in leaps and bounds in recent years enabling telexes, faxes and e-mails to be sent from just about anywhere on the island. Making overseas calls from public telephone boxes in tourist areas rather than the hotels will avoid hefty surcharges.

Phonecards can be bought in shops and supermarkets in units of R30, R50, R100, R200 and R400. Alternatively you can make calls at **Mauritius Telecom Offices** at Rogers House, John Kennedy Street, Port Louis (tel: 208 1036), or at **Mauritius Telecom Tower** at Edith Cavell Street (tel: 203 7000), Port Louis. Both are open from 8.30am to 5pm Mon–Fri and 8.30am to 2pm on Saturday. Mauritius Telecom also operates a 24-hour service at their office at Cassis (tel: 208 0221).

All hotels have **email** and **internet** access. If you have a laptop, you can make arrangements with your hotel to plug it in to the system.

Embassies and High Commissions

If you are arrested or need legal representation contact your embassy or consulate. However, it should be stressed that officials can't advise on legal matters but may help you find an interpreter or arrange to contact friends or relatives. The main addresses are:

Australia High Commission: 2nd floor, Rogers House, John Kennedy Street, Port Louis; tel: 208 1700; fax: 208 8878
British Honorary Consul: Craft-Aid Centre, Camp du Roi,

If your own mobile/cellular phone does not function, you can rent a phone through Cellplus in Port Louis, tel: 203 7500 (Call free on 800-5000), or Emtel in Rose Hill, tel: 454 5400.

CYBERCAFES

Grand E Baie
Super U Commercial Centre
La Salette Street, Grand Baie;
tel: 263 0822; e-mail:
Netshopgb@servihoo.com
Cyber Ryder
Telecom tower, Port Louis;
tel: 203 7277; fax: 210 1164;
e-mail: cyberyder@intnet.mu
Cybercafe
Impasse Pot de Terre, Curepipe;
tel: 676 1863; fax: 676 3143;
e-mail: cyberyder@intnet.mu
Cyber 2000
Continent Commercial Centre,
Phoenix; tel: 698 5473;
fax: 698 5509; e-mail:
Cyber2000@intnet.mu
Orchard Cybercafe
Orchard Centre, Quatre Bornes;
tel: 424 0575

Local Tourist Offices

MPTA Tourist Office: Air Mauritius Centre, 11th Floor, John Kennedy Street, Port Louis; tel: 208 6397; fax: 212 5142; e-mail: mtpa@intnet.mu

Port Mathurin; tel: 831 1766; fax: 831 2276; e-mail: pdraper@intnet.mu
Canada High Commission: c/o Blanche Birger Company Ltd, Jules Koenig Street, Port Louis; tel: 208 0821; fax: 208 3391
United Kingdom High Commission: 7th floor, Les Cascades Building, Edith Cavell Street, Port Louis; tel: 208 9850; fax: 211 1369
United States Embassy: 4th floor, Rogers House, John Kennedy Street, Port Louis; tel: 208 2347; fax: 208 9534

There is a tourist office booth on the Port Louis waterfront (tel: 208 6397) and at Sir Seewoosagur Ramgoolam Airport (tel: 637 3635) which opens during arrivals and departures. There is no tourist office in Rodrigues.

Business Travellers

Business dress in Port Louis is fairly formal; women will feel more at ease in cotton dresses and men should wear lightweight suits or at least a shirt and a tie. It's considered good form to present your business card at the first meeting and shake hands. All business is conducted in English. Local business people do not object to being phoned at home before the working day but they do expect you to be punctual for appointments.

A useful publication for the business traveller is the annual *International Mauritius Directory* published in Mauritius and available from bookshops. Travellers from the UK will find that their laptop computer plugs are compatible with the square three-pin plug sockets in Mauritius.

Women Travellers

To find a woman travelling alone in these islands is unusual since most visitors are couples or families. At most you'll be regarded as strange when you explain why you're not with a friend, relation or husband but you're unlikely to be harassed, except perhaps by youths in questionable nightspots in Mauritius' Grand Baie area; elsewhere, opportunistic groping, unwanted attention or blatant propositioning is rare.

If you find yourself in an awkward situation, deal with it immediately in

Marriage Seekers

Men and women visiting on their own should be aware that some Mauritians may be courting you with marriage and a passport to living in another country in mind.

Photography

White sand, turquoise seas and blue skies contrasting with the colourful dress of the islanders provide stunning pictures but these are the very ingredients which may play havoc with auto-exposure programmes on single lens reflex and compact cameras. The dense dark green foliage against sunlit sky can induce similar problems resulting in over or under exposure and care in metering is required to provide the perfect shots one expects from such a photogenic location.

Great effects can be produced by shooting straight into the sun and a graduated grey filter allows this without over exposure.

What to take: Try to take all the film and equipment you might need with you. With high temperatures and humidity all equipment should be adequately protected with silicon crystals and kept in an insulated bag. A camera left in the midday sun for only a few minutes can result in fogged film.

All types of film and some accessories are available but be prepared for high prices.

Film processing is generally good but the range and size of prints is limited.

a positive way. Don't get involved in inane chatter, avoid eye contact – being polite but firm usually works. It's not a good idea to fend off advances with a few choice Kreol expletives as this tends to encourage more attention.

In Mauritius and Rodrigues it's not the done thing to sunbathe topless on any beach although more liberal behaviour is acceptable in Réunion where dress is not so conservative.

Serious incidents, such as rape and knife attacks on tourists (both male and female), have been reported in recent years in Grand Baie so walking alone at night is not recommended. And however friendly

a situation appears, never accept a lift from a stranger.

Travelling with Kids

Kids are welcome at restaurants, festivals and all places of worship throughout the Mascarene Islands. Luxury hotels in Mauritius cater specially for youngsters and offer supervised activities, special meals, babysitting services and family rooms and child discounts on excursions.

If you're travelling with very young children avoid December and January which may be too hot for them. Supermarkets stock a wide range of baby food and nappies but you should bring your own from home if you have a favourite brand.

Gay Travellers

Homosexuality, while tolerated, is not blatantly obvious in public places but any open displays of full blown affection, whether you're straight or gay, are likely to offend or attract jeers.

Travellers with Disabilities

Top-class hotels provide good facilities for disabled travellers but check with your travel agent before leaving home. Beyond the hotels, facilities are generally dire but disabled people joining an organised tour will find that islanders are willing to lend a helping hand.

Religious Services

Mosques, temples and churches often within close proximity of the other reflect the religious tolerance of the Mascarenes' multi-cultural society and respect should be shown by removing your shoes before entering a mosque or temple.

Emergency Numbers

Police: tel: 999
Fire: tel: 995
Ambulance: tel: 114

English services are held as follows:
Roman Catholic Mass: St Joseph's Chapel, Celicourt Antelme Street, Rose Hill, every Saturday (tel: 464 2944 for times)
Church of England: St Paul's Church, La Caverne, Vacoas; tel: 686 4819. 8.30am every Sunday (except the second Sunday of each month)
Presbyterian: St Columba's Church, Phoenix; tel: 696 4404.

In Rodrigues, there is one Hindu temple and one mosque. Most of the churches are in Port Mathurin. St Barnabas Church in Jenner Street holds an English service once a month on Sundays at 8.30am.

Medical Treatment

Emergency hospital treatment is free at public hospitals. They tend to be very crowded and most visitors go to a private clinic *(see below)*. Your hotel can provide a doctor in cases of sudden illness and help locate out-of-hours pharmacists. Western medicines or their equivalent and antibiotics are also available over the counter.

If you fall ill in Rodrigues, where facilities are very basic, you should return to Mauritius as soon as possible for treatment.

Dental facilities are very good and most practitioners speak English. Contact lens and spectacles are good value, of a high standard and prescriptions can be made up in a few days.

PRIVATE CLINICS

Clinique Mauricienne, Le Réduit; tel: 454 3063; fax: 464 8813
Clinique du Nord, Coastal Road, Tombeau Bay; tel: 247 2532; fax: 247 1254
Clinique Darné, G Guibert Street, Floréal; tel: 686 1477; fax: 696 3612
Med Point Clinic, Sayed Hossen Avenue, Quatre Bornes; tel: 426 7777; fax: 426 5050
Private ambulance: tel 426 8888

Tipping

The Mascarene Islands are not tip-conscious societies, although any tip for good service is always appreciated. In Mauritius tipping is not necessary if the 12 percent TVA tax has already been added to bills, but ask if unsure.

Airport porters often demand a tip and it's not a bad idea to give

them around R20 just to steer you through the airport and into a taxi; hotel porters are happy with R10; taxi drivers do not expect tips.

Security & Crime

Generally, Mauritians are a law-abiding people. However, you should take basic precautions as you would at home. Don't flaunt jewellery and money in public; never leave property on view in your car; always lock doors and windows when you go out, particularly in self-catering accommodation; and after dark don't give a lift to a stranger or go out walking alone.

English is spoken at all police stations in Mauritius but recently some tourists have complained that officers have been reluctant to help. If you are a victim of crime, try to get names and addresses of witnesses and report the matter to the police. In cases of theft ensure you have documentation for insurance purposes.

A Word on Etiquette

Social etiquette in Mauritius stems from the French *savoir-faire*, the British aplomb and the Asian desire to please, and throughout the Mascarene Islands, words like *bonjour*, "thank you" and *salam* (good-bye) are frequently heard in everyday life.

Handshaking is expected when meeting someone for the first time but allowing yourself to be kissed on each cheek shows that your host has really taken a liking to you.

Local political scandals can be discussed quite freely and often get a good airing in the press. You're more likely to witness laughter, infectious smiles and giggling than outright aggression, but use your own common sense

when choosing with whom to bring up touchy subjects such as slavery, colonialism and racist issues. Note also that in Mauritius, but not Réunion, it is considered very rude to refer to the Indian community as *malabars*.

The people of the Mascarenes accept Western whims, however strange some might appear to be, and will gladly pose for photographs, show you the way if you get lost and rescue you from trouble. However, they do tend to exaggerate and their laid-back attitude to life means that they are not often very good time-keepers. But if you show tolerance, respect and good humour you'll take home fond memories of a warm and welcoming people.

Getting Around

Driving

The British legacy of Mauritius and the Seychelles is most evident on the roads where driving is on the left and the roundabouts operate as in Britain with priority on the right. Not every local driver seems to be aware of this rule, however, and in practice he who hesitates least goes first. Beware of poultry, goats and dogs on the roads, hawkers and foragers with heavily overloaded bicycles. Scooters carrying entire families need to be given a wide berth! Public buses often drive dangerously fast on small, winding roads – make plenty of room as they will often cross the central line on sharp bends. If driving through the sugar cane areas, watch out for deep gulleys on either side of the road, especially at night.

Mauritians tend to sound their horns when overtaking or approaching a junction. It is meant as a friendly warning, not as a reprimand.

Rules of the road: 80 kph (50 mph) on "motorways" and 50 kph (30 mph) elsewhere. The wearing of

seatbelts is compulsory and there is no age restriction for front seat passengers.

The police should attend any personal injury accidents and where damage only is involved, exchange names and addresses and notify the car hire agency. In cases of doubt or difficulty call the police.

There is a strong presence of traffic police, particularly on the Mahébourg–Grand Baie road, where speeding is common and driving habits verge on the dangerous.

MAIN ROUTES

Mauritians refer to the road linking Mahébourg and Grand Baie as the "motorway" but it is really only a well-surfaced trunk road which crosses the island from south to north linking the plateau towns. Most of the 1,600 km (995 miles) of roads are surfaced, but many of the highways and minor roads are badly potholed. The best roads are the "motorway" and the road through Black River Gorges National Park, the worst are along the less touristy south coast.

Names of towns and villages may appear in French and/or English and can be poorly positioned or concealed by sugar cane. Roads are adequately signed (with UK-style signposts) but navigating through towns can be a challenge. Make sure you have a good map (available from tourist offices). Distances and speed limits are shown in kilometres and, more rarely, miles.

PARKING

Parking can be a nightmare at all times in Port Louis so head for the car park behind Caudan Waterfront. Short-term parking up to two hours is also available at the Port Louis Waterfront.

Parking restrictions apply in towns and to avoid being fined, display a parking coupon on your windscreen. These can be bought in booklets at petrol stations.

CAR HIRE

To hire a car you must be aged over 23 and have a full valid driving licence. Car hire rates usually include fully comprehensive insurance and collision damage waiver but always check first. Tyre punctures can be easily repaired for a few rupees at any garage. If you hire a motor cycle you should be provided with a crash helmet. If you only want a car for a short while to see round the island, consider hiring one with a driver-guide, who will know the best places to go and will relieve you of the anxiety of driving in a foreign country.

Major credit cards and cheques are becoming increasingly acceptable by smaller companies.

Car Hire Companies
Avis: Al-Madina Street, Port Louis; tel: 212 3472 and 208 1624; fax: 211 1420; e-mail: avis@bow.intnet.mu
Budget Rent a Car: S. Venkates-ananda Street, BP 125, Rose Hill; tel: 454-1666; fax: 454 1682; e-mail: mauritours@mauritours.intnet.mu
Europcar: Pailles; tel: 208 2115; fax: 208 4705; e-mail: europcar@intnet.mu
Hertz Mautourco: Gustave Collin Street, Forest Side; tel: 674 3695; fax: 675 6425; e-mail: mautourc@bow.intnet.mu
Société J.H.A. Arnulfy and Co: Labourdonnais Street, Mahébourg; tel: 631 9806; fax: 631 9991

By Bus

Buses are plentiful, inexpensive and generally reliable although the service is less frequent in the evening. There are two bus stations in Port Louis, one linking it with the north and the other with the plateau towns in the south. Fares range between R10 and R20 or up to R30 if travelling by express service.

Some of the older buses do not inspire confidence; they chug along belching out heavy black exhaust but get to their destination eventually. If you're in a hurry take

Driving Times

Airport–Belle Mare	1¼ hours
Belle Mare–Pamplemousses	55 mins
Belle Mare–Trou d'Eau Douce	30 mins
Belle Mare–Grand Baie (via the coast)	1 hour
Port Louis–Curepipe (without holdups)	40 mins
Le Morne–east coast (via interior)	2 hours

one of the express buses but always check the destination with the conductor. Queues are orderly and tickets are bought on board. Stop bells are located at each seat. Avoid travelling between 8am and 9am and 4pm and 5pm during the week when buses are very crowded, and carry small change for the fare.

Buses operate in urban regions from 5.30am to 8pm and in rural regions from 6.30am to 6.30pm. In the country buses will normally stop on request. Nightowls should note that the last bus from Port Louis to Curepipe via Rose Hill, Quatre Bornes and Vacoas leaves at 11pm. The Tourist Office can provide a comprehensive list of bus services operating throughout the island although in practice you'll find that they are so frequent during the day a timetable is not really necessary.

Citirama run a three-hour tour of Port Louis from the tourist office at the Port Louis Waterfront, which operates daily except Sundays (tel: 212 2484).

In Rodrigues bus services grind to a halt at around 4pm.

By Taxi

Taxis are equipped with meters but they are rarely switched on so always agree a price before starting a journey. Try to use them only for short journeys as the fare depends on the whims of the driver and includes the taxi's return fare to base. The official tariff should be displayed inside the vehicle, with waiting time chargeable for the first 15 minutes and every additional 15 minutes. Drivers do not expect to be tipped.

In practice drivers do not adhere to these rates and any complaints should be made to the Mauritius Tourist Promotion Authority or the National Transport Authority, Victoria Square, quoting the number plate, driver's name and details of the journey.

For longer journeys it may be cheaper to hire a taxi for the day and fix a price which should be less than a day's car hire. If you find a knowledgeable taxi driver who can

act as a guide, try to keep his custom by using him regularly.

Licensed "taxi trains" or shared taxis operate near bus stops in some towns and villages. They cover a prescribed route and the fare is divided between the number of passengers. The taxis are dilapidated and overloaded but travelling this way can be cheap, fun and fast with rates working out at not much more than the official bus fare.

Taxis are recognisable by black registration numbers on white plates. Unlicensed taxis or *taxis marrons* are instantly recognisable because they are nothing more than private cars i.e. they have white numbers on black plates and lurk near taxi stands, bus stations and the airport. They often incur the wrath of their licensed competitors; their rates are low because they're uninsured to carry passengers.

Taxis can be hired from licensed taxi stands. Some hotels have a special arrangement with taxi drivers who are expected to charge reasonable fares. However if you feel you are about to be ripped off, warn the driver that you will report him to the hotel. It usually works.

In Rodrigues there are only four taxis servicing the island.

On Your Bike

Many visitors hire bicycles in Grand Baie. Several villages and resorts are only a few miles away and can easily be reached by bike. Most good hotels and tour operators such as White Sand Tours, tel: 212 3712 and Mauritours, tel: 467 9700 organise bike rental.

By Helicopter

Air Mauritius helicopters undertake transfers and regular sightseeing tours with prices depending on flying time and route. Current tariffs start at R13,500 per helicopter which can accommodate up to four people. Transfers from the airport to the north of the island are R8,400 per person and for the rest

of the island R6,900 per person.

Reservations can be made in your home country through Air Mauritius (tel: 603 3754; fax: 637 4104), travel agents or e-mail: helicopter@airmauritius.intnet.mu

Sightseeing Tours

There are numerous tour operators but the following provide a wide range of sightseeing tours and other services and have hospitality desks at major hotels:
Grand Bay Travel and Tours: Coast Road, Grand Baie; tel: 265 5261; fax: 265 5798
Mauritours: 5 Venkatasananda Street, Rose Hill; tel: 467 9700; fax: 454 1682; e-mail: mauritours@mauritours.intnet.mu
MTTB/Mautourco: 84 Gustav Colin Street, Forest Side; tel: 670 4301; fax: 674 3720; e-mail: mtco@mautourco.com
White Sand Tours: Ground Floor, IBL House, Caudan, Port Louis; tel: 212 6092/3/4/5; fax: 212 6096; e-mail: wstt@intent.mu

Island Hopping

Tour operators organise excursions to both Rodrigues and Réunion depending on sailings. To travel on the MS *Mauritius Pride*, it is advisable to book directly, as soon as you arrive in Mauritius, through Mauritours which has desks in major hotels. Better still, make arrangements through your own travel agent before you leave your home country, as you are unlikely to get a cabin in first class at short notice and the airline-style seats in economy class sell fast. Sailings between Mauritius and Rodrigues are between two and three times a month and it goes six times a month to Réunion.

Another alternative is the *Mauritius Trochetia*, which cruises regularly between Mauritius, Réunion, Rodrigues and Madagascar. It takes up to 112 passengers and there are 54 cabins, a bar, a shop, a swimming pool and a children's corner. In Mauritius, details of sailings can be obtained from **Mauritius Shipping Corporation**, Suite 417–418 St James Court, St Denis Street, Port Louis (tel: 210 5944; fax: 210 5176) or through your travel agent.

In Réunion contact **SCOAM**, 4 avenue du 14 juillet 1789, 97420, Le Port (tel: 42 19 45; fax: 43 25 47 or e-mail: pax@scoam.fr)

The *Spirit of Port Louis*, a catamaran with seating for more than 200 passengers, operates twice weekly (Tuesday and Saturday) between Mauritius and Réunion. The voyage takes around six hours depending on weather conditions. In Mauritius contact a reputable travel agent, such as Mauritours. Tickets can be purchased at most travel agents.

Boat trips from Rodrigues to the nature islands of Ile aux Cocos and Ile aux Chats can be organised through your hotel or tour companies such as **Rod Tours** in Port Mathurin (tel: 831 2249; fax: 831 2267; e-mail: rodtours@intnet.mu). Bookings must be made in advance as there are restrictions on the number of visitors at a time.

Where to Stay

Choosing a Hotel

Hotels owned by **Beachcomber** (www.beachcomber-hotels.com), **Sun International** (www.sunresort.com) and **Naiade Resort** (www.naiade.com) groups provide exceptionally high standards and facilities, including watersports which are free except for scuba diving and game fishing.

Many of the top hotels, such as the Prince Maurice and Royal Palm, offer a personalised service where they will make a point of knowing your name and will use it in the bar or reception. The beds are super king size and bathrobes, and slippers are usually provided.

Less grand hotels also provide high standards while guest houses may appeal to independent travellers. Many of the hotels have a "mini club" for children's activities.

Breakfast is not always included in the price and any extra meals may have to be ordered in advance. Not all hotels are available through all operators, so you may have to shop around if you prefer to stay in one particular establishment. For further information on accommodation contact the MTPA in your home country *(see page 357)*.

All hotels have their own security guards. Visitors have complained that access as a non-resident

Price Guide

Prices are all for two sharing a double room and include breakfast:

$$$$	more than R10,000
$$$	R5,000–R10,000
$$	R3,000–R5,000
$	less than R3,000

depends on the whims of the guards, but happily this policy is being abandoned and entry is far more relaxed.

Hotel Listings

PORT LOUIS AND THE NORTH

Port Louis
Labourdonnais Waterfront Hotel
Caudan
tel: 202 4000; fax: 202 4040
e-mail: lwh@intnet.mu
First class facilities in first class location within walking distance of shops, cinemas and restaurants. **$$**
Hotel St Georges
19 rue St Georges
tel: 211 2581; fax: 211 0885
Sixty air-conditioned rooms situated in quiet area. Increasingly popular with business travellers although you may find the xenophobic management rather off-putting. **$**

Balaclava
Colonial Beach Hotel
tel: 261 5187; fax: 261 5247;
e-mail: cbeach@intnet.mu
Reasonably priced small family hotel overlooking a lagoon and reef rich in corals and marine life. Ideal as a base for snorkelling enthusiasts. **$**
Maritim Hotel
tel: 204 1000; fax: 204 1020
e-mail: info.mau@maritim.com
Luxurious resort overlooking Turtle Bay, popular with businessmen and holidaymakers. Environmentally friendly policy of changing towels only when requested rather than twice a day as in other hotels. The Maritim Diving Centre attached is well equipped and offers a full programme of excursions. **$$$**
Oberoi
Turtle Bay, Pointe aux Piments
tel: 204 3600; fax: 204 3625
e-mail: reservations@oberoi.intnet. mu
Luxurious collection of 76 single-storey, thatch-roof villas and rooms enclosed by volcanic stone walls. Appealing to empty nesters and honeymooners. Beautiful grounds and pools adorned with Balinese

statues and exclusive restaurant for private dining. **$$$$**
Plaza Beach Resort
tel: 204 3333; fax: 204 3344
e-mail: radplaza@intnet.mu
Relaxing ambience for residents and non-residents who wish to use its facilities. 198 sea-facing rooms, including Executive Club accommodation for business travellers, three restaurants, casino, health club and mini club for 3–12 year olds. **$$$$**

Cap Malheureux
Coin de Mire Village Hotel
tel: 262 7304; fax: 262 7305
e-mail: veranda@intnet.mu
Picturesque cottage-style hotel set in spacious gardens. Pleasant sandy beach nearby. **$**
Marina Resort
tel: 204 8800; fax: 204 7650
e-mail: marinah@intnet.mu
Set in beautiful gardens along three secluded coves overlooking lagoon and offshore islands, this bungalow resort is under new management and promotes a child-friendly policy. Two restaurants, kids club and a good choice for families and couples looking for a quiet holiday. **$$**
Hotel des Mascareignes
tel: 262 7373; fax: 262 7372
Comfortable complex in landscaped gardens with swimming pool across the road from the beach. **$**
Paradise Cove
tel: 204 4000; fax: 204 4040
e-mail: pcove@intnet.mu
A member of the Small Luxury Hotels of the World, this hotel is intimate, relaxed and tranquil. Tropical gardens, private beaches and waterfalls overlooking Coin de Mire. Dive centre. **$$$**

Grand Baie
Colonial Coconut Hotel
Pointe aux Canonniers
tel: 263 8720; fax: 263 7116;
e-mail: ccoconut@intnet.mu
A charmingly run colonial villa with old-style ambience. Renovated bungalow-style accommodation with thatched roofs. Lovely views of Grand Baie, but beach not much to write home about. Creole buffet served every Wednesday. **$**

Hotel Le Canonnier
Pointe aux Canonniers
tel: 209 7000; fax: 263 7864;
e-mail: canonnier@bchot.com
Beachcomber hotel with 173 rooms on isolated headland surrounded by three beaches; lush gardens; swimming pool, restaurants and its own diving centre. Good choice for families and couples. **$$$**
Royal Palm Hotel
tel: 209 8300; fax: 263 8455;
e-mail: royalpalm@bchot.com
A member of the Leading Hotels of the World and Beachcomber owned. Pure five-star luxury, super-efficient staff, exceptional cuisine, discreet service and a favourite with royalty, celebrities and statesmen. Not the best place for children however. **$$$$**
Verandah Bungalow Village
tel: 263 8015; fax: 263 7369
e-mail: veranda@intnet.mu
Small and comfortable complex overlooking Grand Baie with pub, night club, restaurants and shop, including the Islandive Diving Centre. **$$**

Grand Gaube
Calodyne Sur Mer
Mirabelle Avenue, Coastal Road
tel: 282 1590; fax: 282 1363
email: calodynesurmer@intnet.mu
56 fully equipped colonial style bungalows complex set in beach-fronted gardens with views of Coin de Mire island. Ideal for upmarket clientele seeking combination of self-catering and hotel facilities. Kids club, a la carte restaurant and bar. **$$$**
Legends
tel: 204 9191; fax: 288 2828
e-mail: legends@naiade.intnet.mu
Naiade Resort's latest acquisition, this chic hotel, located in a spectacular sandy bay, is based on the principles of feng shui, with plenty of use of water, earth, wood, fire and metal. 199 rooms and suites, 3 restaurants, thalassotherapy spa and centrally located pool bar and lounge. **$$$**
Paul et Virginie Hotel
tel: 288 0215; fax: 288 9233
e-mail: pauletvirginie@intnet.mu
This 80-room hotel stands on the

beach and offers a wide range of watersports and tennis. There are two swimming pools, two restaurants and two bars. **$$$**

Trou aux Biches
Sandonna Villa
tel: 265 5523; fax: 283 7313
Just 500 metres (550 yd) from the beach, this small guest house offers comfortable accommodation and friendly service. **$**
Trou aux Biches Village Hotel
tel: 204 6565; fax: 265 6530
Dominating 2 km (1 mile) of beach. Great for families and couples. Consistent high standard of the Beachcomber group with 197 rooms and several restaurants. Own dive centre and boathouse providing all watersports facilities, casino and golf course. **$$$**

EAST COAST

Belle Mare/Palmar
Beau Rivage
tel: 402 2000; fax: 415 2020
e-mail: brivage@intnet.mu
Young at heart and lively best describes this hotel which has a magnificent swimming pool overlooking a lagoon. Cigar lounge, piano bar and jazz sessions on Thursday nights in the Club Savanne. Four restaurants and gourmet grocery on site. **$$$$**
Belle Mare Plage Golf Hotel and Resort
Poste de Flacq
tel: 415 1083/4/5; fax: 415 1082
e-mail:
resa@bellemareplagehotel.com
Very popular with golf enthusiasts and plays host to major tournaments. The oldest resort on the island recently benefitted from major refurbishment. Luxurious private villas with individual pools and sun deck appeal to those seeking absolute privacy. Good facilities for children and excellent swimming. The Neptune Diving Centre is next door. **$$$$**
Le Palmar
Coastal Road
tel: 415 1041; fax: 415 1043
e-mail: palmarbeach@intnet.mu

Small and friendly with 70 air-conditioned rooms. Swimming pool, watersports and dive centre. Relaxing atmosphere. **$$**

La Residence
tel: 401 8888; fax: 415 5888
e-mail: hotel@theresidence.com
Luxurious hotel on a vast scale with magnificent pool overlooking sparkling white beaches. Each guest is appointed a butler on arrival. Past guests include the Princess Royal and Sir Peter Ustinov. **$$$$**

Le Surcouf Village Hotel
tel: 415 1800; fax: 415 1860
Cottage-style complex in spacious tropical gardens. Peaceful atmosphere by a sparkling lagoon. **$**

Mahébourg
Le Preskil Beach Resort Hotel
Pointe Jerôme
tel: 604 1000; fax: 631 9603
www.lepreskil.intnet.mu
The former Croix du Sud Hotel is being rebuilt following a devastating fire, and re-opens with a new name in September 2003. The isolated beachside bungalow resort faces the idyllic Île aux Aigrettes and is just a 15-minute drive from the airport. Diving centre and watersports. **$$**

Poste de Flacq
Coco Beach Hotel
tel: 415 1010; fax: 415 1888
e-mail: infococo@sunresort.com
Close to St Géran, with sea-facing rooms set in 33 hectares (80 acres) of landscaped gardens containing giant tortoises. Ideal for young families, the hotel has Disneyesque décor and child-friendly atmosphere with plenty of kids entertainment. **$$$**

Prince Maurice
tel: 413 9100; fax: 413 9129
e-mail: info@princemaurice.com
This five-star de luxe hotel has a peaceful atmosphere, induced with the help of water pools and the judicious use of natural light. A smell of spices pervades and all suites are equipped with video, CD player, personal fax and some have private swimming pools. Own golf course. **$$$$**

St Géran
tel: 401 1688; fax: 401 1668
e-mail: infostg@sunresort.com
The resort complex, completely refurbished for the Millennium, includes casino, golf course, dive centre, three restaurants and every luxury imaginable – at a five-star de luxe price. All rooms look out over the sea. Member of Leading Hotels of the World. **$$$$**

Price Guide

Prices are all for two sharing a double room and include breakfast:

$$$$	more than R10,000
$$$	R5,000–R10,000
$$	R3,000–R5,000
$	less than R3,000

Trou d'Eau Douce
Silver Beach Hotel
tel: 419 2600; fax: 419 2604
e-mail: silverbeach@intnet.mu
Small unpretentious 60-roomed hotel overlooking beautiful beach. Staff sometimes appear to be too laid-back so don't expect fast service. **$**

Le Touessrok
tel: 419 2451; fax: 419 2025
e-mail: info@sunresort.com
www.touessrok.com
In a spectacular setting down a long drive, this hotel, opposite the Île aux Cerfs, benefitted from major refurbishment in 2002. It has several restaurants, a central pool, and the use of a private island with plenty of watersports on offer. **$$$$**

Le Tropical Hotel
tel: 419 2300; fax: 419 2302
e-mail: tropical@naiade.intnet.mu
All-inclusive rates, ideal for couples and families, in a peaceful location with views of bay and mountains. Good sega show on Thursdays. **$**

SOUTH COAST

Blue Bay
Blue Lagoon Beach Hotel
tel: 631 9529; fax: 631 9045
e-mail: blbhotel@intnet.mu
Just 15 minutes from the airport

and a stone's throw from the beach. Welcoming atmosphere and very reasonably priced. Nightly buffet is worth booking in advance. **$**

Shandrani
tel: 603 4343; fax: 637 4313
www.shandrani@bchot.com
e-mail: shandrani@bchot.com
A luxurious hotel on its own peninsula in 30 hectares (75 acres) of gardens. 180 bedrooms and four restaurants. Superb diving. **$$$$**

Chemin Grenier
Villas Pointe aux Roches
tel: 625 5112; fax: 625 6110
e-mail: paroches@intnet.mu
A remote location offering a relaxed atmosphere with individual bungalows on the beach. Bus service right outside serves villages along the south coast. **$$**

WEST COAST

Black River
Island Sports Club Hotel
La Balise
tel: 483 6768; fax: 483 6547
e-mail: islsprt@intnet.mu
Reasonably priced accommodation and very popular with repeat UK visitors. Conveniently located for big game fishing and within walking distance of local restaurants. **$$**

Tamarin Hotel
Tamarin
tel: 683 6581; fax: 683 6927
e-mail: tamhot@intnet.mu
Facing the beach at Tamarin in a quiet location, this rambling 32-room hotel has a swimming pool and restaurant but few other facilities. Appeals to budget travellers. **$**

Flic en Flac/Wolmar
Hilton Mauritius Resort
tel: 403 1000; fax: 403 1111
e-mail: info.mauritius@hilton.com
www.hilton.com
This five-star hotel on Flic en Flac beach features 193 rooms, each with an ocean view and balcony, a fitness club, helipad and wedding pavilion along with several restaurants and all the watersport facilities you would expect. **$$$$**

Le Pearle Beach Hotel
tel: 453 8428; fax: 453 8405
e-mail: pearle@intnet.mu
Newly refurbished hotel overlooking
the beach. Beautiful restaurant and
pool area but narrow beach. **$$**

La Pirogue
Wolmar
tel: 453 8441; fax: 453 8449
e-mail: infolap@sunresort.com
Lively Sun International luxury class
hotel with everything for the
hedonist. Casino, restaurants,
entertainment programme, land and
watersports including its own dive
centre. Non-residents can use
casino and facilities. **$$$$**

Sands Resort
Wolmar
tel: 403 1200; fax: 453 5300
e-mail: thesands@intnet.mu
Catering to a child-free clientele,
this luxuriously appointed hotel
overlooks a dazzlingly white sandy
beach with views of Tamarin Bay. It
has 92 rooms, a welcoming buffet
restaurant and fine dining in an
intimate à la carte restaurant. Spa
and health centre. **$$$**

Sofitel Imperial
Wolmar
tel: 453 8700; fax: 453 8320
e-mail: sofitel@intnet.mu
Benefiting from a strong Thai
influence and lots of decorative
woodwork, this elegant, spacious
hotel was completely refurbished in
2002. Designed around a central
swimming pool and next to a lovely
broad beach. Three restaurants,
pool and dive centre. **$$$$**

Sugar Beach Resort
tel: 453 9090; fax: 453 9100
e-mail: infosbr@sunresort.com
Grand colonial-style Sun
International hotel with spacious
accommodation and beautifully kept
lawns. The magnificent swimming
pool is a focal point for holiday
entertainment. Longest beach on
the island with a coral reef quite
close to the shore. Plenty of
watersports on offer. **$$$$**

Villas Caroline
tel: 453 8411; fax: 453 8144
e-mail: caroline@intnet.mu
Delightful complex of self-catering
bungalows and double rooms right
on the nicest stretch of beach in

the area. Welcoming atmosphere
and a good location for divers and
snorkellers as the reef is close to
the shore. Within five minutes' walk
of the bus station to Port Louis and
plateau towns. **$**

Le Morne

Berjaya Le Morne
tel: 450 5800; fax: 450 6070
e-mail: berjaya@intnet.mu
Luxury resort hotel built in
Malaysian style on the south side of
Le Morne peninsula. Full
entertainment programme and
superb facilities. Ideal for young
families, couples and popular with
Italian tour groups. Dive centre. **$$$**

Dinarobin Hotel
tel: 401 4900; fax: 401 4901
e-mail: dinarobin@bchot.com
www.dinarobin-hotel.com
Beachcomber's latest hotel to open
on Le Morne peninsula will appeal
to golfers, families and beach
lovers. Attractive complex of 172
sea-facing suites reflects Mauritian
style and architecture. Spa centre
and three restaurants, with further
eateries available at adjacent Le
Paradis Hotel *(see below)*. **$$$**

Le Paradis
tel: 401 5050; fax: 450 5140
e-mail: paradis@bchot.com
www.paradis-hotel.com
Lovely Beachcomber property
covering 150 hectares (370 acres)
The resort skirts one of the best
beaches on the island, fringed with
shady palm trees, and has a superb
18-hole golf course, which doubles
as a helicopter landing pad. It also
has three restaurants, casino,
gymnasium, and offers a range of
water and land sports. Good choice
for families and couples. Nothing to
stop non-residents turning up for
tea and a swim. **$$$$**

Les Pavillons Hotel
tel: 401 4000; fax: 450 5248
e-mail: pavillons@naiade.com
www.naiade.com
The public areas are beautifully
furnished in this friendly hotel.
Spacious accommodation in well-
equipped suites and rooms.
Excellent sega show on Tuesdays
and fine restaurants serving
European and local cuisine. **$$$**

PLATEAU TOWNS

Quatre Bornes

Gold Crest Hotel
St Jean Road
tel: 454 5945; fax: 454 9599
Long-established business-class
hotel with 59 well-appointed rooms
and centrally located. Excellent
value for money. **$**

El Monaco Hotel
St Jean Road
tel: 425 2608; fax: 425 1072
A good alternative to the Gold
Crest Hotel, this one has 93 rooms
with private facilities. Swimming
pool in the garden, bar and
restaurant and conference facilities.
$

Rose Hill

Auberge de Rose Hill
275 Royal Road; tel: 464 5832
Near the Plaza Theatre this small
26-room hotel offers basic
accommodation. Popular with
visitors from Réunion. **$**

RODRIGUES

Les Cocotiers
Anse aux Anglais
tel: 831 1058; fax: 831 1800
e-mail: lescocotiers@intnet.mu
This former guest house, now
a comfortable 3-star hotel managed
by Naiade Resorts, has 42
delightful air-conditioned rooms,
swimming pool and open-sided
restaurant overlooking the lagoon.
$$

Cotton Bay
Pointe Coton
tel: 831 8000/2/4;
fax: 831 8003/8030
e-mail: cottonb@intnet.mu
Superb location on the beach. Its
isolation may appeal to
honeymooners. **$**

Escale Vacances
Fond la Digue, Port Mathurin
tel: 831 2555/6; fax: 831 2075
e-mail: escale.vac@intnet.mu
Ideal location in town. Warm
and welcoming accommodation.
Try local food and Chinese
dishes cooked by the Chinese chef.
$$

Mourouk Ebony
Pate Reynieux
tel: 831 6351/4; fax: 831 6355
e-mail: ebony@intnet.mu
Perched atop a gentle cliff
overlooking the lagoon. Typical
Rodriguan ambiance and excellent
restaurant. **$$**

Self-catering

Self-catering holidays are becoming
increasingly popular, particularly with
repeat visitors to Mauritius. Many
comfortable beachside bungalows
are available for short- or long-term
rental and the deal may include maid
service. Details can be obtained from
the MTPA in your home country *(see
page 357)*. Rental agencies in Grand
Baie, such as **Ocean Villas** (tel: 263
8567; fax: 240 8797; e-mail:
koala@bow.intnet.mu) or **Grand Baie
Travel & Tours** (tel: 265 5261;
fax: 265 5798; e-mail:
gbtt@intnet.mu) can help you find
cheaper accommodation, otherwise
look for the sign *à louer* outside
properties or consult the local
newspaper.

There are many bungalows to
rent in Flic en Flac where you can
pay around R6,000 a week for two
people, or a whole bungalow for five
people for around R9,000 a week.
Self-catering apartments, studios
and beach-front properties are also
available. Contact the Flic en Flac
Tourist Agency, Royal Road, Flic en
Flac; tel: 230 453 9389;
fax: 230 453 8416;
e-mail: ffagency@intnet.mu

The following UK-based operators
also specialise in self-catering
accommodation:
Twin Towers: tel: 0113 279 5955;
fax: 0113 279 6442; e-mail: info@
mauritiustwintravel.com
Planet Mauritius: tel: 01582
841757; fax: 01582 841757
www.planet–mauritius.com
The **Residence Tamaris**
(tel: 831 2715; fax: 831 2720) at
Camp du Roi in Rodrigues will
appeal to self-caterers. The 25
modern bright apartments are
fully equipped with kitchenette
and TV and come with daily
maid service.

Where to Eat

Eating out is sheer pleasure in
Mauritius and gives an opportunity
to savour the colour and tradition of
Mauritian fare, as well as being a
great alternative to hotel dining. The
service, quality of cooking and
reasonable prices all add to the
enjoyment. Dress is casually
informal, the atmosphere is relaxed
and there are scores of restaurants
to choose from. Restaurants
generally close by 11pm and
booking is recommended in only a
few places.

By the beach and elsewhere **food
stalls** sell fresh fruit cut in pieces
and sold in bags for a few rupees –
a cocktail may include cucumber and
mango spiced up with some chilli, if
you choose. Stalls also fry up *mine
frit* and *boulettes* (fish and potato
croquettes), or *dholpuri* (Indian flat
bread stuffed with curried lentils).

Fish tends to dominate **hotel
menus**, but usually there's a wide

What to Drink

Rum is the national drink, the
most popular being Green Island
rum. Other brands are Old Mill
and Spiced Gold (more like a
liqueur). Imported alcohol is very
expensive as it carries 300
percent tax. Hotels don't have
very good wine lists and many
people tend to drink beer.
Phoenix beer is Mauritian and is
a very palatable lager. Most of
the wine is from South Africa
although some is made in
Mauritius with imported grapes
and is cheaper.

Citronelle – hot water spiced
with lemon grass and ginger – is
often offered after dinner to
cleanse the palate.

choice of meats as well from wild
boar to lamb. Many of the chefs
are European and so there is often
an international bent to meals.
Most hotels have special Mauritian
buffets or an Indian evening once
a week.

Fast food restaurants are on the
increase inevitably, with Kentucky
Fried Chicken being the most popular
and McDonald's opening new
branches in Port Louis, Grand Baie
and Phoenix. Pizzas are available at
Caudan Waterfront, Port Louis.

PORT LOUIS AND THE NORTH

Port Louis
La Bonne Marmite
18 Sir William Newton Street
tel: 212 2403
Housed in an attractive creole
building and sharing premises with
the Rocking Boat Pub, this is a busy
lunchtime venue serving local,
Indian, European and Chinese fare.
Closed at weekends. **$$**
Le Boulevard
Happy World House
Sir William Newton Street
tel: 208 8325
Inexpensive and cheerful salad bar.
Ideal for quick snacks and lots of
vegetarian appeal. **$**
Carri Poulé
Duke of Edinburgh Avenue
tel: 212 1295
The best Indian food in town.
Popular lunchtime venue for
businessmen and tourists. Also
open for dinner on Friday and
Saturday 7–11pm. Reservations
highly recommended. **$$**
Keg & Marlin
Les Docks Building
Caudan Waterfront; tel: 211 6821
English-style pub and restaurant in
fashionable location on the
waterfront. Open every day from
noon till late. **$$**
Lai Min
56–58 Royal Road; tel: 242 0042
Chinese dishes that are simply out
of this world served in exotic
surroundings. Open daily 11.30am
to 2.30pm and 6.30pm to
9.30pm. **$$$**

Domaine des Pailles

Cannelle Rouge (creole cuisine), **La Dolce Vita** (Italian), **Fu Xiao** (Chinese) and **Indra** (Indian) are among the island's finest restaurants located all together in one complex just outside Port Louis at Domaine des Pailles. Open for lunch and dinner, reservations can be made centrally on tel: 212 4225; fax: 212 4226. **Clos St Louis** serves French and creole food in the stylish surroundings of a grand colonial mansion. Book ahead on 212 4225. **$$$**

Cap Malheureux
Coin de Mire Restaurant
Coast Road; tel: 262 8070
Smugglers cove-style eaterie with authentic creole atmosphere and views of Coin de Mire island. The grilled pork makes a superb sizzling starter before a choice from the extensive menu. **$$**

Grand Baie
Café de la Plage
Sunset Boulevard; tel: 263 7041
Fashionable hangout for Grand Baie groupies and a good venue for relaxing over a snack and a drink. alternatively you can dine in the thatch-roofed restaurant right on the beach. **$$**
La Charette
Royal Road; tel: 263 8976
Chefs from Bombay produce some really varied curries in this reasonably priced restaurant. **$$**
Don Camillo
Coast Road; tel: 263 8540
Located near the fuel station in Grand Baie. Welcoming Swiss owner offers tasty pizzas and pastas and delicious garlic bread in a convivial atmosphere. Try the *gratin de fruits de mers* followed by scrumptious fish brochettes. **$$**
La Pagode
Coast Road; tel: 263 8733
People watch and gorge on various Chinese dishes on the verandah of this restaurant overlooking the main road. Popular with Mauritians. Excellent value for

money and child-friendly. Try the *saucisse chinoise* (spring rolls) and fantastic crab. **$$**
Sakura
Royal Road; tel: 263 8092
Elegant Japanese restaurant specialising in Teppan Yaki, Tempura, Sushi and Sukiyaki. Advance notice required for some dishes and reservations recommended. Closed Sunday. **$$$**

Pereybère
Caféteria Péreybère
Coast Road; tel: 263 8539
For snacks, drinks and lunch this popular beachside café/restaurant offers real value for money. The *poisson gingembre* is well worth trying. **$**
Nirvana
tel: 262 6711
People travel miles to feast here on great Indian food. The lobster massala is divine and there's an unusual selection of Indian sweets. Busy on Friday and Saturday so book ahead. Closed Sunday. **$$**

Price Guide

Prices are for two people including soft drinks or beer:
$$$$ R1,000 plus
$$$ R600–R1,000
$$ R400–R600
$ less than R400

Le Tanjore
Coast Road; tel: 263 6030
Adjacent to the Ventura Hotel, this restaurant turns out authentic Muglai cuisine, European and local specialities. Good for vegetarians. **$$**

Trou aux Biches
Le Pescatore
Coast Road, tel: 265 6337
Fine dining and wines in elegant surroundings with an Italian Mauritian touch. Unmissable for succulent seafood and worth trying the seafood lasagne. **$$$**
Souvenir Snack
tel: 265 7047
Just across the road from Trou aux Biches police station, gargantuan portions of *mine frit* (fried noodles)

and tasty rice-based dishes are served in an authentic creole atmosphere. **$**
Trou aux Biches Gourmet Club
Coast Road; tel: 265 6092
Creative creole cookery by one of Mauritius' top chefs. Booking recommended. **$$$**

EAST COAST

Anse Jonchée
Paranamour Restaurant
Domaine du Chasseur;
tel: 634 5097
Offers panoramic views of Grand Port Sud Est. Watch Mauritian curries being cooked by Indian women and then walk off the excesses along wooded paths bounded by indigenous species of flora. Only open for lunch. Reservations recommended unless you go as part of a tour group. **$$**

Belle Mare
Chez Manuel
Royal Road, St Julien Village;
tel: 418 3599; fax: 418 3888
Well worth the taxi ride to get to this inland village to sample the superb Chinese and local dishes. Open daily except Sunday. Reservations highly recommended. **$$$**
Symon's Restaurant
Pointe de Flacq; tel: 415 1135
Restaurant specialising in seafood, creole and Chinese cuisine. Popular lunch and dinner menu with guests staying at hotels along the east coast. **$$**

In the Treetops

Le Chamarel (tel: 483 6421) and **Varangue sur Morne** (tel: 483 6010) are two superb restaurants serving creole and European food in the Black River Gorges area. They make you feel as if you are dining in the treetops and have distant views of the lagoon. Ideal lunch stops if visiting the Chamarel and Plaine Champagne areas, but it is advisable to book in advance. **$$**

Trou d'Eau Douce
Restaurant Sept Chemins
Sept Croisées
tel: 419 2766
Lunch or dine in upstairs restaurant. Excellent creole specialities in very informal atmosphere. Open daily for lunch and dinner. **$**

SOUTH COAST

Souillac
Le Batelage
tel: 625 6083
Souillac's only restaurant in the refurbished warehouse in the "Tourist Village" overlooking the river. Good for European and creole specialities. **$**
The Hungry Crocodile
La Vanille Crocodile Park, Riviere des Anguilles; tel: 626 2503/2843
Try the crocodile croquettes! Or play safe with *croque monsieur* and some interesting creole goodies, such as samousas, washed down with wine from the extensive list. **$$**

WEST COAST

Black River
La Bonne Chute
On the forecourt of the Caltex Petrol Station, Tamarin; tel: 483 6552
Don't be put off by the strange address. This long established restaurant, often used for wedding receptions, serves excellent creole and European cuisine. **$$**
Pavillon de Chine
Black River Village; tel: 483 5787
Serves tasty creole food and excellent South African wines. There is a good family atmosphere and a supply of bamboo high chairs for toddlers. Watch the world go by from the verandah. **$$**

Price Guide

Prices are for two people including soft drinks or beer:
$$$$ R1,000 plus
$$$ R600–R1,000
$$ R400–R600
$ less than R400

Pavillon de Jade
Royal Road, Trois Bras, Black River; tel: 483 6151
Colourful Chinese restaurant serving excellent food to hungry walkers visiting Black River Gorges. Car parking facilities. **$$**

Le Morne
Le Domino Seafood Restaurant
tel: 483 6675
Set on the slopes of Le Morne mountain, this restaurant has lovely views of Benitiers Island. Serves wide selection of Chinese, European and local dishes. Closed evenings. **$$$**

Flic en Flac
Mer de Chine
tel: 453 8208
Great Chinese goodies in this friendly restaurant. Excellent value. **$$**

PLATEAU TOWNS

Curepipe
La Nouvelle Potinière
Hillcrest Building, Sir Winston Churchill Street; tel: 676 2648
Excellent French restaurant of long-standing reputation. Consistently high standard of food and service. **$$**

Floréal
La Clef des Champs
Queen Mary Ave, tel: 686 3458
Gourmet French cuisine with Creole touch in the sophisticated colonial-style setting. Reservations recommended. **$$$**

Quatre Bornes
Café Dragon Vert
La Louise, tel: 424 4564
The best Chinese platter in the plateau towns. Also serves a good range of European and local cuisine. Unhurried atmosphere but book ahead at weekends. **$$**
Tannur
St Jean Road; tel: 465 3140
Try the butter chicken and massala dishes and finish off with the sweet called *kulfi* at this authentic Indian restaurant. No alchol served. **$$**

Rose Hill
Hotel School of Mauritius
tel: 465 8298
Be a guinea pig and eat in the restaurant at the Hotel School of Mauritius. Here, student waiters practise the art of serving meals prepared by student cooks. There are two public lunch sittings at 1pm and 2pm, but reservations are essential.

RODRIGUES

Port Mathurin
Le Capitaine
Johnston Street; tel: 831 1581
Doubles up as a disco and restaurant. Try seafood, chicken croquettes or go for the popular *menu du jour*. **$$**
Le Gourmet
Duncan Street; tel: 831 1571
Opens for lunch only and does a good line in Chinese food. **$$**
Paille en Queue
Duncan Street; tel: 831 1616
Opposite Le Gourmet, serves excellent Rodriguan curries. **$$**

La Mangue
John's Resto
tel: 831 6306
The restaurant is noted for fresh seafood and Chinese specialities but if you're after something special, order in advance. **$$**

Nightlife

There is usually something going on somewhere in Mauritius, whether it be a hotel dinner show, a sega performance, a Hindu, Chinese, Muslim or Christian festival *(see page 355)* or some kind of play or theatrical show. For up-to-date information on cultural events and evening entertainment consult the local tourist office or your hotel receptionist. Most tourist hotels offer Las Vegas-style cabarets, sanitised sega shows, live music and themed cultural programmes and some have casinos. The Mauritius Tourism Promotion Authority also produce a *What's On In Mauritius* guide which is issued free. Information is basic, but the main bars, nightclubs and casinos are listed.

Nightclubs

Mauritius is not hot on nightlife, though the Caudan Waterfront has brought new life to the capital which, for the most part, goes quiet after dark. Party animals can find a clutch of cyclone-proof discos, with names like Speedy, sprouting in sugar cane fields behind **Grand Baie** – although some are the haunts of prostitutes and sailors. More upmarket nightclubs can be found at the Caudan Waterfront in **Port Louis**. Discos and nightclubs usually open only on Friday and Saturday nights.

In **Rodrigues** look out for hand-written bills advertising the **Grande Soirée Dansante**, dance nights organised in the town's three discotheques when everyone from babes in arms to robust Rodriguan grannies bop to seggae and reggae. For clean family fun make for the alfresco disco **Les Cocotiers** next to Residence Tamaris, but for rum, rhythm and red-blooded recreation, try **Le Capitaine** or **Ebony Nightclub**.

Cinema

Most films shown in Mauritius are in French and a few cinemas also show Hindi and Tamil films. The island's best cinema for English speakers is by the harbour at the **Caudan Waterfront** which shows the latest films in both English and French. Consult the local newspaper for times and programmes. **Rose Hill** also has a cinema. English films are sometimes shown in the cinema in Port Mathurin, Rodrigues.

Casinos

If you're feeling lucky, head for the **Caudan Waterfront** casino or the Casino de Maurice in **Curepipe** and try your luck at roulette and blackjack, or pump your money into one of the many slot machines. Many of the top hotels also have their own casinos including **La Pirogue** in Wolmar, **Trou-aux-Biches Village Hotel**, **St Géran** in Poste de Flacq, **Domaine les Pailles** near Port Louis and **Berjaya Resort Hotel** in Le Morne. None of the casinos require you to show your passport and entry is free, but you are expected to dress smartly. Casinos are open every day from 10am to 4am.

Theatres

Productions by the Réunion-based theatre company, **Centre Dramatique de l'Océan Indien**, are frequently staged at one of the island's two theatres: **Plaza Theatre**, Rose Hill; **Théâtre de Port Louis**, Intendance Street, Port Louis.

Sport

Throughout the year football and athletics attract huge crowds and for details of these and other sporting events consult the Tourist Office, local newspapers or the general secretary of the **Mauritius Amateur Athletics Association** at Le Réduit, tel: 464 2256.

The Mascarene Islands regularly take part in the **Indian Ocean Island Games** a sort of mini-olympics event involving Mauritius, Réunion, Madagascar, Seychelles and the Comores Islands, held every four years and hosted in turns by a member nation.

Outdoor Activities

Mauritius is ideal for watersports, some of which are more strenuous and daring than others. The coral reefs provide a fascinating and magnificent underwater landscape and many establishments offer snorkelling and diving expeditions. Undersea walks, submarine excursions and glass-bottom boat trips may be more appealing to the less adventurous.

Offshore breezes provide ideal conditions for windsurfing on the west coast and sailing, and the glassy lagoons and sheltered bays are perfect for water skiing, paragliding, pedalo trips and kayaking. Big game fishing is popular out in the Indian Ocean and you are unlikely to return from a trip empty handed.

On dry land, the many nature reserves offer not only a network of hiking trails but the possibility of spotting some of the indigenous wildlife rescued from extinction. Horse-riding and mountain biking are also available. **Mauritours** (tel: 467 9700; fax: 454 1682) has a desk at many hotels and can organise a wide range of sporting activities for you.

For a fun family day out, try the **Belle Mare Water Park** (Coastal Road, Belle Mare; tel: 415 2626; fax: 415 2929; e-mail: lewaterpark@intnet.mu; daily in summer 10am–5.30pm and winter 10am–5pm; entrance fee). The complex includes food kiosks, fast food outlets, children's and adult pools, giant water slides, Jacuzzi and wave pool.

Watersports

DIVING & SNORKELLING

Nearly 30 dive centres are attached to hotels and offer excursions to shipwrecks and dive sites. Many cater for all levels, from beginners to experienced divers, and some provide night dives. Check out the website www.mauritius-info.com/sports/index.htm or contact the **Mauritian Scuba Diving Association**, tel: 454 0011; e-mail: msda@intnet.mu. The following are a selection:
Beachcomber Fishing Club, Le Morne, Black River; tel: 450 5142 Also specialists in big game fishing.
Blue Water Diving Centre, Le

Corsaire, Trou aux Biches; tel: 265 7186
Paradise Diving Centre, Coastal Road, Grand Baie; tel: 265 6070
La Pirogue Diving Centre, Wolmar; tel: 453 8441
Good for learners.
Villas Caroline Diving Centre, Flic en Flac; tel: 453 8450
Old hands will find plenty of specialist diving, including night diving. Owned and managed by Pierre Szalay, President of the Mauritius Scuba Diving Association.

Trou aux Biches has several good dive centres. Hughes Vitry, based at the Blue Water Diving Centre next door to the popular fish restaurant Le Pescatore (*see page 368*), is a well-known undersea photographer and may take you on a "shark dive".

Rodrigues
Bouba Dive Centre
Mourouk Ebony Hotel, Pate Reynieux; tel: 831 9063; e-mail: ebony@intnet.mu
Cotton Dive Centre, Cotton Bay Hotel; tel: 831 6000/1/2; e-mail: diverod@intnet.mu
Rodrigues Underwater Group
Pointe Monier-Rodrigues; tel: 831 2032

Equipped for Snorkelling

Many hotels and dive centres provide snorkelling equipment, but if you plan on doing a lot of underwater exploration, it is always better to invest in your own. Snorkels and masks are widely available, but before parting with your money, make sure the snorkel mouthpiece is soft and comfortable and check the mask fits properly. You can do this by holding it in place without putting the strap over your head, then breathing in through your nose. If the mask stays on with the suction, it should be fine; if air escapes then try another one.
Identifying fish: a host of different species of tropical fish make their home in the coral reefs and there

are a number of excellent books to assist with the identification of the common species. For snorkellers it would be well worth getting hold of a "fish watchers slate" – a plastic card printed with colour drawings of the 40 most common species, as this can be taken into the sea.
Sun protection and safety: remember to cover yourself with plenty of waterproof, high-factor sun cream and it's also a good idea to wear a t-shirt while snorkelling to avoid sunburn on your back. If there are jet skis or other motorised craft in the area, it is sensible to mark your location by tying a brightly coloured float to your waist or foot.

BIG GAME FISHING

The best time for game fishing is from October to April when marlin, espadon, tuna and the big wahoo are plentiful. The Marlin World Cup competition is held at the Centre de Pêche in November. Fishing trips last for a minimum of six hours and take five rods at a time. Book through your hotel or tour operator or directly through the following companies:
Centre de Pêche de l'Île Maurice Hotel Club, Black River; tel: 483 6522/5060
Island Sports Club La Balise; tel: 683 5353; e-mail: islsprt@intnet.mu
Killer Fishing, Coastal Road, Trou aux Biches; tel: 265 6595
Organisation de Pêche du Nord, Corsaire Club, Royal Road, Trou aux Biches; tel: 265 5209
La Pirogue Big Game Fishing, Flic en Flac; tel: 453 8441
Surcouf, Trou d'Eau Douce; tel: 419 3198

Rodrigues
Sailfish Ltd, Port Mathurin; tel: 831 1623
BDPM Fishing Co Ltd, Port Mathurin; tel: 831 2790

SAILING & CRUISING

Hobie Cats (small catamarans) can be booked on the beach at most hotels. The following yacht charter companies offer half or full day excursions in large sail boats such as Le Pacha. Reservations can be made through hotels or direct with:
Centre Sport Nautique Ltd, Sunset Boulevard, Royal Road, Grand Baie; tel: 263 8017; tel/fax: 263 7479
Also organises Hobie Cat sailing, kayaking, pedalo trips and other excursions.
Croisières Australes, c/o Maurtourco, Gustave Collin Street, Forest Side, Curepipe; tel: 674 3695
Croisières Turquoises Ltd, Riche en Eau SE; tel: 633 5835
Day-long cruises on a catamaran.

In the Dry

If you don't like getting your face wet but don't want to miss out on the beauties of a coral reef, try a solar-powered undersea walk. Wearing a specially designed helmet which supplies you with fresh air from the surface, you can even wear your spectacles or contact lenses. And it is suitable for children as young as seven.

Captain Nemo's Undersea Walk Kiosk next to Caltex petrol station, Grand Baie; Black River; Belle Mare tel: 263 7819/3077 and (after hours) 423 8822. Or book through your hotel or tour operator. Open daily from 9am.

Aquaventure Blue Mare Plage Hotel, tel: 415 1515; fax: 415 1993 More undersea walking.

Blue Safari Submarine, Royal Road, Grand Baie; tel: 263 3333; fax: 263 3334; e-mail: bluesaf@intnet.mu; www.bluesaf.com An air-conditioned hour-long trip in a submarine under the sea. Open daily, 9am–9pm.

Le Nessee, Croisières Australes, 84 Gustave Collin Street, Forest Side; tel: 674 3695; fax: 674 3720 A one-hour trip in a semi-submersible. Departs four times a day from 9.30am and once at night at 7pm.

Cruising Experience Ltd, in Flic en Flac; tel: 453 8888; fax: 453 9688 Live music, food and drink on board a catamaran with a choice of three cruises.

Océane Croisières, Trou d'Eau Douce; tel/fax: 419 2767/419 7743 Cruise along the southeast coast, stopping off for a snorkel and a visit to the Île aux Cerfs.

Yacht Charters, Royal Road, Grand Baie; tel: 263 8395 A day-long cruise on the 150-year-old sailing ship *Isla Mauritia* with a stop for a barbecue lunch on the beach.

WINDSURFING & SURFING

Surfing is best on the west coast, around Tamarin and also Le Morne. Most beach hotels supply windsurfing boards or you can book directly through **Centre Sport Nautique Ltd** in Grand Baie (tel: 263 8017; tel/fax: 263 7479).

Hiking, Trekking and Adventure

For general information on hiking trails around the island, contact The Director of the National Parks and Conservation Service at the Ministry of Agriculture and Natural Resources, Le Réduit; tel: 464 4016; fax: 464 2993.

Le Petrin Information Centre near Grand Bassin (open daily, 9am–4pm) has trained staff who can provide up-to-date information on walks and conditions of trails in the Black River Gorges National Park, such as the 7-km (4-mile) round walk from Le Petrin through the Macchabe Forest (spectacular views). Another walk from Le Petrin is to the Tamarin Falls near Curepipe. Or go to the **Black River Visitor Centre** (open daily 9am–4pm) near the gorges.

Green View Rando at Sir Edgar Laurent Avenue, St Clement, Curepipe (tel: 675 2941; e-mail: gvrando@intnet.mu) organises guided walking tours to Le Pouce mountain and elsewhere.

Wolmar Nature Reserve in Flic en Flac (tel: 453 8463/9334) offers a natural wilderness where walkers can see plenty of wildlife and tropical flora. There are also some good mountain biking trails here. Guided tours can be arranged through La Pirogue Hotel close by (tel: 453 8441) and other local hotels. They also provide mountain bikes and will hire them out to non-residents.

Espace Adventure, tel: 696 3001; fax: 674 3720 Adventurous inland nature trails for off-road enthusiasts in specially adapted Land Rovers, with guide. Some tours include lunch in local homes.

Vertical World Ltd, tel: 254 6607; fax: 395 3207 Specialists in hiking, exploring canyons and rock climbing.

Yemaya Ltd, tel: 283 8187; fax: 283 0180 Hiking, mountain biking and sea kayaking.

Quad Biking, Domaine du Chasseur Grand Port; tel: 634 5097; fax: 634 5261 An unusual way to discover the interior with a guide by "quad biking" through sugar-cane fields and forests.

Kart Loisir, La Joulliette Lane, Petite Rivière; tel: 233 2223; fax: 233 2225; e-mail: kartloisir@intnet.mu Well designed 900-metre go-kart track for speed lovers. The complex includes an Italian and traditional style restaurant, a swimming pool with lovely views of Pointe aux Sables and Coin de Mire, a bar and a nightclub.

Abseiling and Canyoning

If you want to try your hand at abseiling head for the Tamarind Falls. Organised excursions include a picnic lunch for groups of 8 plus two guides. For more details contact MTTB, tel: 670 4301; fax: 674 3720.

Eco-tourism

The **Île aux Aigrettes Nature Reserve**, opposite Mahébourg on the east coast, is home to a large population of pink pigeons and an assortment of reptiles. It is in the process of gradually being restored to its natural original state. However, visitors are encouraged to see it for themselves either through **White Sand Tours** (tel: 212 3712), or the **Mauritius Wildlife Foundation** (MWF) directly (tel: 211 1749 or 211 2228).

Golf

Several of the hotels have their own golf courses and they have a golf club house and can store golf equipment:

Belle Mare Plage Golf Hotel and Resort, tel: 415 1083:

Championship 18-hole course – the best on the island.
Le Paradis, Le Morne; tel: 401 5050; fax: 450 5140; e-mail: parahot@intnet.mu
An 18-hole course on which the odd helicopter lands from time to time.
Nine-hole courses:
Coco Beach, Poste de Flacq; Maritim Hotel, Balaclava; St Géran Hotel, Pointe de Flacq; Shandrani Hotel, Blue Bay; Sofitel Imperial, Flic en Flac; Trou aux Biches Hotel.
Mini golf:
Put Put Rodrigues (tel/fax: 831 2356) in Rodrigues is a mini-golf course at Port Mathurin on the waterfront.

Horse-riding

Horse-riding – whether it be along the beach, in a nature reserve or up in the hills, for beginners or the experienced – can be arranged through your hotel or tour operator or through **Mauritours**, tel: 467 9700; fax: 454 1682/3.

Shopping

What to Buy

You could be spoilt for choice in your wanderings round the new shopping malls in Mauritius where local products and handicrafts stand alongside luxury imported goods. Haggling in markets is perfectly acceptable. Shops tend to have fixed prices but may offer you a small discount for bulk or major purchases.
Model ships *(see box below)* and **wooden handcarvings** make good buys. Replicas of wooden creole houses and hand-carved salad bowls, miniature tropical fruits and the inevitable dodo can be bought everywhere.
Textiles and **clothing** are of top quality – good buys to look for are woollens, t-shirts, saris, silk and cotton shirts and casual wear. In upmarket shops you'll find rich tapestries, murals, rugs and cushions, embroidered tablecloths and napkins, quilted wall hangings and pottery depicting scenes from Mauritian life.
Markets sell *tentes* or baskets made from the vacoas or pandanus leaf, coconut leaf, raffia, aloe, bamboo and banana fibre which serve as useful shopping bags as they are very strong and hardwearing.
Costume jewellery Unusual buys include pieces made from mother of pearl, coconut or local dried seeds; gold jewellery, mounted with precious stones. Raw materials such as straw, wood and fabrics turn up as appealing patchwork creole dolls representing people from the various ethnic groups.
Flowers Long-lasting cut andreanums and anthuriums, in small, medium or large blooms,

travel well and can be bought at the airport in convenient pre-packaged boxes, just prior to your flight. Alternatively, you can visit the plantations and order flowers from there.
Glass blowing demonstrations from recycled glass can be seen at the Glass Gallery, next to the Mauritius Breweries at Phoenix, between 9am and 11am and 1pm and 3pm. Slender vases and ornaments can be bought from the adjacent shop (open Mon–Fri 8am–4.30pm; Saturdays till 1pm; tel: 696 3360).
Chinese goods such as kimonos, silks and *objets* made from brass, jade and porcelain can be found in specialised shops, particularly in Curepipe.
Mauritian food specialities such as spices, sugar, tea and smoked marlin don't cost the earth and make nice gifts.
There are **art galleries** dotted all over the island where you can pick up paintings and handicrafts by local artists and artisans.

Shopping Centres

Caudan Waterfront, Port Louis Some of the best shops on the island. Several clothes shops and duty free *(see box)*.
Currimjee Arcades, Royal Road, Curepipe.

Model Ships

Making intricate model boats and ships – including replicas of famous galleys – is an art in Mauritius and can be bought from workshops dotted around the island ranging from the affordable to the very expensive. The **Historic Marine**'s factory is at Zone Industrielle de St Antoine, Goodlands, where marine furniture in teak and mahogany is also made.
    You can also watch model ships being made in the **Comajora** factory, La Brasserie Road, Forest Side, Curepipe, and at **Ceuneau** just outside Grand Baie.

Small centre with a few clothes and duty-free shops.

La Sablonnière, Bernardin de St Pierre Street, Curepipe.
Large shopping emporium where you can buy oriental carpets, objets d'arts and furnishings duty free.

Le Continent, Phoenix
Large American-style shopping centre with an enormous supermarket and street of other shops, but not many clothes outlets.

Orchard Centre, Quatre Bornes
More glitzy inside than out. Lots of clothes stores.

Port Louis Waterfront, Port Louis
Boutiques selling everything from bonsai to arts and crafts.

Sunset Boulevard, Grand Baie
A mixture of shops with some good clothes stores.

Duty Free

Remember to take your passport and airline ticket when shopping for duty-free goods outside the airport and that they must be paid for in foreign currency or by credit card. Duty-free shops will arrange for your purchases to be delivered to the airport before your departure, but you must allow at least one day for the formalities to be completed.

Mauritius Shopping Paradise has duty-free outlets in Port Louis, Grand Baie and the airport, but other names to look for are Sashena Trading, Etoile d'Argent, Linea Azzura Shop, Parure and Bijouterie Bienvenue for perfumes, photographic equipment, cosmetics, sportswear, shoes and jewellery.

Some duty-free shops

Adamas Diamond Duty Free Boutique, Mangalkhan, Floréal; tel: 686 5783; fax: 686 6243

ATVA Gems Factory Showroom, 32 Mon Desir, Bone Terre, Vacoas; tel: 425 7815/7585; fax: 425 7594

Caudan Waterfront, Port Louis; tel: 211 7294

Mauritius Shopping Paradise, Paille en Queue Shopping Centre, John Kennedy Street, Port Louis; tel: 211 6835; fax: 211 6696

Mizumoto (for cultured pearls), 12

Belmont House, Intendance Street; tel: 212 8339

Poncini Duty Free Boutique, 2 Jules Koenig Street, tel: 212 4723; fax: 208 8850

Shiv Duty Free Jewellery, Le Pavillon Cinema Complex Shop C14, tel: 211 7294

Tara Cashmere, Espace Ocean, Grand Baie; Caudan Waterfront, Port Louis.

Bookshops

Publications in both French and English are widely available in the island's bookshops.

Bookcourt Ltd, Caudan Waterfront, Port Louis; tel: 211 9262

Le Cygne, 307 Royal Road, Rose Hill; tel 464 2444
Browse all day in this well-stocked bookshop tucked in the arcades at Rose Hill. Choose your books over a cup of tea or coffee at the back of the shop.

IPBD, Cité Malherbes, Curepipe; tel: 674 4098/4099; fax: 674 4100

Libraire Allot, Currimjee Arcade, Royal Road, Curepipe; tel: 676 1253; Sir William Newton Street, Port Louis; tel: 212 7132

Papyrus, Royal Road, Grand Baie; tel 263 7070

Trèfles, Currimjee Arcade, Royal Road, Curepipe; tel: 676 3025

Textiles & Clothes

A shopping complex beneath the Floreal Textile Museum (see page 155) sells quality garments made from raw imported materials such as cashmere, cotton and silk:

Floreal Textile Museum
Floreal Square, Floreal
Open Mon–Fri 9am–5pm, Sat 9.30am–1pm; tel: 698 8016.
Men fare rather better than women in **made-to-measure outfits** and you can select from a wide range of imported or local cloth to make top quality trousers and shirts. A wool worsted three-piece suit can be made for less than £200. **House of Caustat** (rue Chasteauneuf, Curepipe; tel: 676 1195; fax: 686 5441) is considered to be the best mens' tailor in Mauritius, with a

client list which includes guests of the Royal Palm Hotel. Suits can be made up in 24–48 hours at **Karl Kaiser** (Europe's Hugo Boss) but your tailor will expect you to have one or two fittings before the final stitches are put in place. They will keep measurements on file, if asked, so that new or repeat orders can be made in advance.

Bargain designer clothing

Mauritians make up the clothes for many European designers and often have stock left over that is sold at a third of the normal price, such as Bonair, Floreal Knitwear, Shibani and Tara.

Rodrigues

In **Rodrigues**, a **Saturday market** selling everything under the sun from souvenirs to homemade chutneys and fresh produce operates on Fishermen Lane, Port Mathurin from 6–10am. You can buy baskets made from vacoas leaves at the **Women's Handicraft Centre** in Mont Lubin and other handicrafts at **Craft-Aid** in Port Mathurin.

Language

Over a dozen languages are spoken by the various ethnic groups living in Mauritius, Réunion and Seychelles but Kreol is spoken by most of the islanders *(see feature* Lingua Franca *on page 23)*. This colourful language, which has evolved from French to have its own grammar and a vocabulary enriched from several languages, is so popular that it is threatening to render obsolete other widely spoken tongues such as Bhojpuri and Hakka, the ancestral languages of north Indians, and most of the Chinese.

Other minority languages you may hear on the streets of Mauritius include Marathi, Tamil (Madras), Telegu and Hindi. A small number of Muslims speak Gujerati.

In Mauritius, which was a British colony until 1968, French dominates at the expense of English. Newspapers, shop signs and street names are mostly in French. English-speaking films are also dubbed in French. Government forms and road signs, however, are in English. People in tourism and commerce speak English out of necessity but the standard is variable.

Unlike Seychelles, which has elevated Kreol to the status of an official language used in schools and the media, in Mauritius it is merely a means of verbal communication and is consequently undervalued. Because the grammar of Mauritian Kreol has never been taught in schools, and there is no universally accepted way of writing it, many Mauritians assume that Kreol has no rules. In fact, it is a sophisticated language, with its own tenses and grammatical forms and a simplified pronunciation of French terms that gives Kreol a unique means of making double-entendres. This is exploited to the full in sega lyrics and in island humour.

In Seychelles, English is widely spoken, especially in hotels, shops and offices. Many Seychellois speaking to each other drift effortlessly between English and Kreol often within the same sentence. A few words of Kreol are useful away from tourist sites and Victoria, particularly when talking to older Seychellois.

Pronunciation Tips

Do not try to imitate a French accent. Indeed, the best approach is not to try speaking with an accent. Do not worry too much about the frills of the French language, such as tenses, declining verbs and the gender of objects that have no place in Kreol. If you run into difficulty do not worry about using English for most nouns, as these are likely to be well understood.

Common features of Indian Ocean Kreol include the use of the word *ban* as a marker of plurality: thus *ban zenfants* means children and *ban zil* is islands. The word *zot* means you in the plural form.

Kreol Institute

The Seychellois take their Kreol seriously and have set up an institute devoted to the preservation of the language and the promotion of Creole culture. The Kreol Institute (Lenstiti Kreol) near the Craft Village at Anse aux Pins on Mahé, has just over 20 staff members who run several departments, namely literature, research, promotion, graphics, documentation, and education and training.

The premises are used for creole functions throughout the year, from plays and poetry workshops to masked balls and karaoke nights. The institute is also the central venue for the Creole Festival, held every year in October *(for details, see page 412)*.

Common Words and Phrases

Airport *Erport*
Bank *Labank*
Bed *Lili*
Breakfast *Ti dezennen*
Bus stop *Bestop*
Excuse me *Eskiz*
Good morning *Bonzour*
Good afternoon/evening *Bonswar*
Goodbye *Orevwar*
Key *Lakle*
Later *Plitar*
Meal *Manze*
No *Non*
Now *Konmela*
Please *Silvouple*
Room *Lasanm*
Swimming pool *Pisin*
Thank you *Mersi*
Today *Ozordi*
Tomorrow *Demen*
Towel *Servyet*
Yes *Wi*
Yesterday *Yer*

Do you speak English? *Ou kapab koz angle?*
How are you? *Konman sava?*
I'm fine, thank you *Mon byen mersi*
I'm staying at a hotel *Mon reste lotel.*
I don't know *Mon pa konnen.*
I don't understand *Mon pa konpran.*
Please speak more slowly *Koze pli lantman silvouple.*
Where can I get a taxi? *Kote mon kapab ganny en taksi?*

Emergencies

Call an ambulance *Apel lanbilans*
Call the police *Apel lapolis!*
Fire! *Dife!*
Help! *Sekour!*
I am not well *Mon pa byen*
They've had an accident *Zot in ganny en aksidan*
We need a doctor *Nou bezwen en dokter*
Where can I find a telephone? *Kote mon pou ganny en telefonn?*
Where is the nearest clinic? *Kote klinik pli pre silvouple?*

Shopping

chemist *farmasi*
Do you accept credit cards? *Eski ou pran kart kredi?*
Have you got...? *Eski ou annan...?*
How much is it? *Konbyen sa?*
I'm just looking *Mon pe rode selman.*
I'll take this one *Mon pran sa enn.*
It is too expensive *I tro ser.*
market *bazar*
money *larzan*
newspaper *gazet*
post office *lapos*
shop *laboutik*
Where can I find a bank? *Kote labank?*

Sightseeing

church *legliz*
closed *fermen*
garden *zarden*
lake *lak*

mountain *montanny*
open *ouver*
river *larivyer*
town *lavil*
village *vilaz*
waterfall *kaskad*

At the Restaurant

bill *kont*
dinner *dinen*
fork *forset*
glass *ver*
knife *kouto*
lunch *dezenen*
menu *meni*
plate *lasyet*
spoon *kwiyer*

WHAT TO ORDER

bef **beef**
labyer **beer**
dipen **bread**
diber **butter**
gato **cake**

fromaz **cheese**
poul **chicken**
lasos piman **chilli sauce**
kafe **coffee**
kari/cari/carri **curry**
deser **dessert**
kannar **duck**
dizef **eggs**
pwason **fish**
zifri **fruit juice**
ayskrim **ice cream**
dile **milk**
palmis **millionaire's salad**
delo mineral **mineral water**
fri delapasyon **passion fruit juice**
dipwav **pepper**
lavyann koson **pork**
diri **rice**
ronm **rum**
disel **salt**
delo gaze **sparkling water**
stek **steak**
disik **sugar**
dite **tea**
diven **wine**

Numbers, Days and Months

Numbers

0	*zero*
1	*enn*
2	*de*
3	*trwa*
4	*kat*
5	*senk*
6	*sis*
7	*set*
8	*wit*
9	*nef*
10	*dis*
11	*onz*
12	*douz*
13	*trez*
14	*katorz*
15	*kenz*
16	*sez*
17	*diset*
18	*diswit*
19	*disnef*
20	*ven*
30	*trant*
35	*transenk*
40	*karant*
50	*senkant*
60	*swasant*
70	*swasandis*
80	*katreven*
90	*katrevendis*
100	*san*
1000	*mil*

Days

Monday *Lendi*
Tuesday *Mardi*
Wednesday *Merkredi*
Thursday *Zedi*
Friday *Vandredi*
Saturday *Sanmdi*
Sunday *Dimans*

Months

January *Zanvye*
February *Fevriye*
March *Mars*
April *Avril*
May *Me*
June *Zen*
July *Zilyet*
August *Out*
September *Septanm*
October *Oktob*
November *Novanm*
December *Desanm*

FRUIT AND VEGETABLES

brenzel **aubergine/eggplant**
zavoka **avocado**
bannann **banana**
friyapen **breadfruit**
kokonm **cucumber**
fri **fruit**
lay **garlic**
mang **mango**
zanannan **pineapple**
ponmdeter **potatoes**
tomat **tomatoes**
legim **vegetables**

FISH AND SEAFOOD

palourd **clams**
krab **crab**
vieille rouge **grouper**
oumar **lobster**
zourit **octopus**
cateaux **parrot fish**
kanmaron **prawn/shrimp**
bourgeois/bourzwa **red snapper**
ton **tuna**
karang/carangue **trevally**
cordonnier **surgeon fish**

LOCAL SPECIALITIES

Mauritius

bol renversée **spicy meat and rice**
bouyon bred **clear soup made of edible leaves**
bredes **spinach-like vegetable**
carri de poulet aux grains **chicken curry with red beans and wheat**
cochon marron **wild boar**
dite lavani **vanilla tea**
espadron fime **smoked sailfish**
fooyang **Chinese omelette**
gateaux piments **fried lentils and chillis**
gros pois **fat butter beans**
kari koko **curry with coconut milk**
meefoon **fine noodles**
mine frit **fried noodles**
pain frit **fried bread with sugar**
rougaille **Mediterranean-style meat or fish stew**

Réunion

achards **vegetable pickles**
bonbon piment **chilli cake**
cari de bichiques **young alevin fish curry**
cabri au massalé **kid goat massala**
gratin chouchou **christophene bake**
manioc frit **fried manioc**
tarte bredes chouchou **vegetable pie**
rougailles **spicy chutney**

Seychelles

kari koko zourit **mild octopus curry**
ladob **creamy banana and sweet potato dessert**
palourd **small clam-like shellfish in garlic butter**
tectec **tiny white shellfish**

Further Reading

MASCARENE ISLANDS

GENERAL

Bourbon Journal by Walter Besant. London (1933).
Short and amusing diary of a British schoolteacher who holidayed in Réunion and climbed Piton de Neiges.
Culture Shock! Mauritius by Roseline NgCheong-Lum. Kuperard (1997).
Cultural insights into Mauritius – good reading for anyone intending to work or stay long term.
Golden Bats & Pink Pigeons by Gerald Durrell. William Collins (1977).
A hilarious account of Durrell's travels to Mauritius and Rodrigues in search of specimens for his Jersey Zoo.
History of the Indian Ocean by August Toussaint. Routledge (1996)
A general background history of countries in and around the Indian Ocean with a good reference to pirates, the Anglo-French conflict and British supremacy of the Mascarenes and Seychelles.
Islands in a Forgotten Sea by T.V. Bulpin. Books of Africa, Cape Town (1969).
One of the finest books you'll come across for an overview of pirates and corsairs in the western Indian Ocean, including history and development of the Mascarenes and Seychelles to the 1960s.
Six months in Réunion by P. Beaton. London (1860).
Life in Réunion as seen by a British reverend.
Studies of Mascarene Island Birds edited by A.W. Diamond. Cambridge University Press (1987).
Academic study of the dodo, solitaire and other extinct birds of Mauritius and Rodrigues.
Sub Tropical Rambles in the Land of the Aphanapteryx by Nicholas

Pike. London (1873).
Highly readable and often amusing account of experiences in Mauritius by the US Consul to Mauritius.
The Age of Kali: Indian Travels and Encounters by William Dalrymple. HarperCollins (1998).
Contains an interesting chapter on Réunion and Creole beliefs in black magic.
The Dive Sites of Mauritius by Alan Mountain. New Holland (1995).
A well-illustrated comprehensive guide to diving and snorkelling in Mauritius.
The Island of Rodrigues by Alfred North-Coombes. Mauritius (1971).
A most readable history and background to Rodrigues by the Mauritian-born author whose interest goes back to 1937 when he was posted there as a civil servant.
Underwater Mauritius by A.J. Venter. Ashanti Publishing (1989).
The author describes some amazing dive sites in Mauritius, Rodrigues and the Seychelles.
Voyages and Adventures by Francois Leguat. London (1707).
Written by Rodrigues' first settler and acknowledged as Rodrigues' first guide book this book is a must for anyone going there. Ask your public library to order it for you.
The full story of Jewish detainees in Mauritius is described in ***The Mauritius Shekel*** by Genevieve Pitot.

FICTION

Paul et Virginie by Bernadin de St Pierre (translated by Raymond Hein). Editions l'Ocean Indien.
This romantic novel tells the story of the ill-fated St Géran which sank off the coast of Mauritius in August 1744.
The Book of Colour by Julia Blackburn. Jonathan Cape (1995).
Set largely in Mauritius this is the story of the author's meditation on the lives of her father and grandfather which unfolds with surreal precision.
The Mauritius Command by Patrick O'Brian. Collins (1977).
Naval adventures around Mauritius during the Napoleonic Wars.

Réunion

Area: Réunion, the largest of the Mascarene trio and almost round in shape, covers an area of 2,512 sq km (970 sq miles).
Situation: Just 164 km (103 miles) to the southwest of Mauritius.
Capital: St-Denis.
Population: Estimated at 700,000, Réunion's population has a similar mix of people to Mauritius and Rodrigues, but in different proportions. The majority are Creoles and French Europeans, followed by Indians or *malbars*, and Chinese.
Language: The official language is French *(a list of useful words and phrases appears on page 394).* Kreol is widely spoken, but rarely written. Few people speak English.
Religion: Mostly Roman Catholicism and many Indians are also Tamil. Fewer people are Muslims and Buddhists.
Currency: The euro.
Weights and Measures: The metric system is used in Réunion. For a conversion chart see page 354.
Electricity: 220V, but standard European round two-pin plugs are used, so visitors from the UK and outside Europe should take an adaptor.
Time zone: Standard time for all the Mascarene Islands is four hours ahead of Greenwich Mean Time.
International Dialling Code: Dial the international code followed by the Réunion country code, 262.

Climate

Like Mauritius and Rodrigues, Réunion also enjoys two seasons; the hot rainy season from

Cyclone Warnings

In Réunion, there are three levels of cyclone warning:
● *Vigilance cyclonique* (cyclone watch): an early warning system advising people to stock up on basic goods (ie food, candles, water) and to listen to broadcasts on TV and radio.
● *Alerte orange* (orange alert): cyclone approaching within the next 24 hours. Schools close but some businesses remain open and everyone is advised to bring moveable objects and animals indoors and to batten down windows and doors.
● *Alerte rouge* (red alert): imminent danger. Driving is banned and everyone must stay indoors and listen to the radio.
Cyclone information: tel: 08 97 65 01 01. Weather information for the next 24 hours and hourly updates is available in French on 08 36 68 08 08 or on the website: www.meteo.fr

December to April and the cool dry season between May and November. On the coast the temperatures are similar to Mauritius, averaging at around 21°C (70°F) in winter and 28°C (81°F) in summer, but on the high plains and mountains variations between 4°C (39°F) and 25°C (77°F) depending on altitude and season are normal. At heights approaching 2,000 metres (6,500 ft) temperatures can drop to below freezing at night.

Cyclones in the Indian Ocean are the worst in the northern hemisphere and usually occur between December and April. On average between 10 and 12 cyclones hit the southwestern Indian Ocean a year causing devastation as they pass over land. Réunion tends to suffer more than Mauritius as the many rivers flood, washing away anything in their path.

Government

Réunion is an overseas French territory or *Département d'Outre Mer*

(DOM). The island's affairs are the responsibility of the French Minister for DOM-TOM and are administered by a prefect and an elected council. Réunion is represented in the National Assembly in Paris by five deputies, and in the French Senate by three councillors.

Economy

Like Mauritius, Réunion has a guaranteed market and fixed prices for sugar. However, much of Réunion's goods are imported from France resulting in inflation and high prices. In 2002 the unemployment figure was a startling 40 percent. Industrial zones have been created at Le Port, St-Denis and St-Pierre. Tourism is a growth industry, with nearly 200,000 tourists a year, mostly from France.

Business Hours

Shops and offices are open every day, except Sunday, from 8am to 6pm, and many close for lunch from noon to 2.30pm. Museums also close for an hour at lunchtime.

Public Holidays

Most shops and businesses are closed on *jours feriés* (public holidays) which are the same as France except for the extra day celebrating the abolition of slavery.
January 1 New Year's Day *(Jour de l'An)*
March/April Easter Monday *(Pâques)*
May 1 Labour Day *(Fête du Travail)*
May 8 Victory Day *(Victoire 1945)*
Ascension Day *(Ascension)*
May Whit Monday *(Pentecôte)*
July 14 Bastille Day *(Fête National)*
August 15 Assumption *(Assomption)*
November 1 All Saints Day *(Toussaint)*
November 11 Armistice Day
December 20 Abolition of Slavery Day *(Abolition de l'Esclavage)*
December 25 Christmas Day *(Noël)*

Planning the Trip

Passports & Visas

French and European Union (EU) nationals must be in possession of a valid identity card or passport. Others need a valid passport and a return or onward ticket and may be asked for an address in Réunion. Entry is normally granted without visa for three months for nationals of the EU, USA, Canada and New Zealand. Australians and South Africans and other nationals must have a visa. Check your situation with the French Embassy.

Applications for visa extensions can be made at the Service de l'Etats Civile et des Etrangers at La Préfecture, St-Denis; tel: 40 75 80.

For **customs allowances** see *Planning the Trip – Mauritius, page 356*.

Health & Insurance

Medical services in Réunion are excellent and with nearly 1,600 doctors, 300 pharmacies and an efficient emergency service you will find yourself in good hands should you happen to fall ill. The cost of treatment is on a par with metropolitan France. There is no need for vaccinations (unless you are coming from an infected area) as malaria has been eradicated from the island since 1948.

Make sure you are adequately insured before you leave home and in the event of a medical claim keep all receipts and documentation. Drinking water in hotels is fine but you can also order bottled water.

There are no dangerous animals in Réunion apart from sharks which frequent the waters around the north and east coasts. Mosquitos can be a pest especially at night during the summer; these can be kept at bay with a plug-in diffuser *(un diffuseur electrique)* which can be bought locally.

Money Matters

Major credit cards are accepted in most hotels, shops and restaurants but it's wise to keep a surplus of euros, particularly if you're heading for the Cirques where there are no banks. You can use your credit card to withdraw cash from ATMs (automatic teller machines) but memorise your PIN number before leaving home.

All banks have exchange facilities but there are hefty charges for changing foreign currency and travellers' cheques, and you may have some difficulty settling bills with Eurocheques. To save costs it may be better to buy euro travellers' cheques before leaving home.

You will need a 1 euro coin for a trolley at the airport before you reach the bureau de change.

BANKS

Major banks are open Mon–Fri from 8am–4pm. A foreign exchange counter operates at Roland Garros Airport Mon–Fri from 10am–1.30pm and 3–6.30pm and on Sat from 8.30–11.30am.

TAX

Value Added Tax (TVA) of 9.5 percent is added to goods and services but not on foodstuffs and books. Duty-free goods are not available in Réunion except at the airport. There is no hotel or restaurant tax, although service may be included in the bill.

What to Bring

In the mountainous interior the climate is much cooler so take something warm, and the evenings can be fresh along the coast, so a light wrap, jacket or cardigan may be necessary. Réunion is quite laid-back about dress: casual wear such as loose cotton shorts, shirts, t-shirts and dresses around town and in the evenings are acceptable but not swimsuits. Men may need a tie for a smart occasion. In St-Gilles-les-Bains women are allowed to sunbathe topless on the beach.

For the feet light sandals are advisable and a pair of plastic water shoes will protect against injury from sharp coral. A pair of good walking boots is essential to bring if you are planning on doing any hiking in the mountains *(see Hiking Along the Grandes Randonnées on page 186)* or a pair of comfortable but sturdy shoes for short walks.

Tourist Offices

Tourist information for Réunion is centralised by the Comité du Tourisme de la Réunion (CTR) in France and by the French Tourist Offices in other countries (e-mail: ctr@la-reunion-tourisme.com; www.la-reunion-tourisme.com – in French and English).

France: Comité du Tourisme de la Réunion, 90 rue de la Boétie, 75008 Paris; tel: 01 40 75 02 79; fax: 01 40 75 02 73; e-mail: ctrparis@aol.com
UK: Maison de la France, 178 Piccadilly, London W1V 0AL; tel: 020 7399 3520; fax: 020 7493 6594; e-mail: info@mdlf.co.uk
Australia: Maison de la France, 25 Bligh Street, Sydney, NSW 2000; tel: 02 9231 5243; fax: 02 9221 8682; e-mail: france@bigpond.net.au
Canada: Maison de la France, Suite 490, 1981 Avenue McGill College, Montreal, Quebec H3A 2W9; tel: 514 288 4264; fax: 514 845 4868; e-mail: mfrance@attcanada.net
USA: French Tourist Office:
New York: 444, Madison Avenue, 16th Floor, New York NY 10022; tel: 212 838 7800; fax: 212 838 7855
Los Angeles: 9454 Wilshire Blvd. Ste 715, Beverly Hills, Los Angeles, CA 90212-2967; tel: 310 271 2693; fax: 310 276 2835.

Getting There

BY AIR

There are two airports in Réunion; **Roland Garros Airport** (tel: 48 80 68), 10 km (6 miles) from St-Denis and **Pierrefonds** (tel: 96 80 00) on the west coast, 5 km (3 miles) from St-Pierre. The national carrier is Air France (AF). Swissair, Sabena, Austrian Airlines and British Airways also offer special pre-routing fares for passengers to and from Réunion, if flying via Paris.

Regular daily flights operate between Mauritius and Réunion with Air Mauritius (MK) and Air Austral (UU), which also operates flights to Réunion from Africa and the African islands (Johannesburg, Moroni, Mayotte, Seychelles and several destinations in Madagascar). Based in France *(see details below)*, Air Austral offers routings to the Comores, South Africa, Madagascar, Seychelles, Réunion and Mauritius.

Air Austral: 122 rue de la Boétie 75008 Paris, tel: 01 44 95 11 30; fax: 01 44 95 11 37; e-mail: paris@air-austral.com

Airline charter companies
Airlib Bat 363, BP854 94551, Orly Aerogare Cedex.
Group reservations tel: 0820 835 835 or contact Opera Agency, 45 avenue de l'Opera, 75002, Paris; tel: 01 53 45 48 00; www.airlib.fr
Corsair: 2 avenue Charles Lindbergh, 94528 Rungis; tel: 01 49 79 75 08 (information, sales and discounts)
Website: www.newfrontiers.com; or www.nouvelles-frontieres.fr
Minitel: 36 15 NF or 36 16 NF

Airline offices in Réunion
Air Austral: 4 rue de Nice BP 611, 97473 St-Denis; tel: 0262 90 90 90; fax: 0262 90 90 91; Roland Garros Airport: 0262 48 80 20
Air France: 7 avenue de la Victoire BP 845, 97477 St-Denis; tel: 0262 40 38 38; fax: 0262 40 38 40; Roland Garros Airport: 0262 40 38 38

Package Deals

Many tour operators based throughout Europe, South Africa, Australia, Canada and the US offer package and specialist holidays, such as trekking or golfing, to Réunion. For details contact Maison de la France or your local travel agent.

The following UK-based operators specialise in Réunion:
Partnership Travel: tel: 020 8343 3446; fax: 020 8343 3439
Elite Vacations: tel: 020 8864 4431
Explore Worldwide: tel: 01252 760000. This company offers a 15-day hiking holiday in both Réunion and Mauritius.
Mauritian Connections: tel: 0161 865 7275
Sunset Faraway Holidays: tel: 020 7498 9922

Air Madagascar: 2 rue Victor Mac-Auliffe, 97461 St-Denis; tel: 0262 21 05 21; fax: 0262 21 10 08
Air Mauritius: 13 rue Charles Gounod, 97400 St-Denis; tel: 0262 94 83 83; fax: 0262 94 13 23; Roland Garros Airport: 0262 48 80 18
Air Lib: 7 rue Jean Chatel, 97400 St-Denis; tel: 0262 94 77 77; fax: 0262 20 07 16; Roland Garros Airport: 0262 48 80 99
Corsair (Aerolyon and Nouvelles Frontières): 37 rue Juliette Dodu 97400 St-Denis; tel: 0262 94 82 82; fax: 0262 40 96 72; Roland Garros Airport: 0262 48 17 51.

FROM THE AIRPORT

You can hire a car *(see page 383)* or take a taxi from the airport but expect to pay between €15 to €22.50 and €4.20 or more if travelling after 8pm or on public holidays. A cheaper alternative at €4 is the *car jaune* (yellow bus) to St-Denis which departs at regular intervals between 7.30am and 8.30pm.

Practical Tips

Media

All television programmes are in French and there are many private TV and local radio stations – 102FM plays mostly British and American music. The biggest range of imported English publications is sold at Le Tabac du Rallye, avenue de la Victoire, off the Barachois in St-Denis. Locally produced daily papers are *Le Quotidien*, which publish a page of news in English on Wednesday, *Journal de l'Île* and *Témoignages*.

Postal Services

Look for La Poste or PTT signs indicating the post office. As in France, the post office offers a wide range of services, including the sale of *telecartes* (telephone cards) for €7 or €14. Most *tabacs* (tobacconists) sell stamps and *telecartes*.

All towns have a post office and poste restante service (open Mon–Fri 8am–6pm; Sat 8am–noon. Most close for lunch between noon and 2pm. There is a post office at Roland Garros Airport (open Mon–Fri 9.30am–12.30pm and 1.30–4.30pm; Sat 8–11am).

The **main post office** in St-Denis is at rue Maréchal Leclerc and rue Juliette Dodu.

Telecommunications

It is cheaper to use a public telephone outside peak times (Mon–Fri 8am–6pm; Sat 8am–noon) than to phone from the hotel.

Agreements between mobile phone companies overseas enable subscribers to use a mobile phone in Réunion. Check with your service provider before leaving home. Most hotels offer internet access and e-mailing facilities. If you have a laptop computer, you can make arrangements with your hotel to plug it in to their system. Remember to bring an adaptor if your plug is not compatible.

CYBERCAFES

L'Entrepôt
82 rue Juliette Dodu, St-Denis
tel: 0262 20 94 80
e-mail: entrepot@stor.fr
Le Web Kafe
Place Antoine Roussin, St-Benoit
tel: 0262 92 96 72
Espace Multimedia
81 rue Archambaud, St-Pierre
tel: 0262 25 44 44
Souris Net
Galerie Ah-Kouen, 70 avenue du Général de Gaulle, St-Gilles-les-Bains; tel: 0262 33 26 60

Local Tourist Offices

Most main towns have a tourist office which can book gîte accommodation and supply maps. Ask for the free *cartapoche* (pocket map) which folds to less than credit card size. The free tourist information publications *RUN* and *Practical Guide* are published in English as well as French and are widely available.

The North
St-Denis Tourist Office:
53 rue Pasteur; tel: 0262 41 83 00; fax: 0262 21 37 76.
Open Mon–Sat 8.30am–1pm and 2–6pm.
Gîtes de France and **Maison de la Montagne** are housed at 10 Place Sarda Garriga; tel: 0262 90 78 78.
CTR: 4 Place 20 Decembre 1948, BP 615, 97472 St-Denis Cedex; tel: 0262 21 00 41; fax: 0262 21 00 21
La Possession Tourist Office:
24 rue Evariste de Parny, BP 94, 97419 La Possession; tel: 0262 22 26 66; fax: 0262 22 25 17
Open Mon 1.30–5.30pm, Tues–Fri 8.30am–5pm, Sat 8.30am–noon.

West Coast
St-Leu Tourist Office:
Bâtiment Espace Laleu, 1 rue Barrelier, 97436, St-Leu; tel: 0262 34 63 90; fax; 0262 34 96 45
Open Mon 1.30–5.30pm, Tues–Fri 9am–noon and 1.30–5.30pm, Sat 9am–noon and 2–5pm.
Etang-Salé Tourist Office:
74 avenue Octave-Bénard, 97427 Etang-Salé; tel: 0262 26 67 32; fax: 0262 26 67 92
Open Mon–Sat 8.30am–noon and 2.30–6pm.

East Coast
Sainte-Suzanne Tourist Office:
65 avenue Pierre Mendes-France 97441, Ste-Suzanne; tel: 0262 52 13 54; fax: 0262 52 13 63
Open Mon–Fri 8am–noon and 1–5pm, Sat 8am–5pm.
St-André District Tourist Office:
68 Centre-Commercial, 97440 St-André; tel: 0262 46 91 63; fax: 0262 46 52 16
Open Tues–Sat 8.30am–noon and 1.30–5.30pm.
St-Benoit Tourist Office:
Place de L'Eglise, 97437 Ste-Anne; tel/fax: 0262 51 02 57
Open Mon–Fri 9am–noon and 2–5pm, Sat 9am–noon.

South Coast
Entre-Deux Tourist Office: 9 rue Fortuné-Horau, 97414 Entre-Deux; tel: 0262 39 69 80; fax: 0262 39 69 83. Open Mon–Sat 8am–5pm, Sun and public hols 9am–1pm.
St-Pierre Tourist Office: 17 Bd Hubert-Delisle, 97410 St- Pierre; tel: 0262 25 02 36; fax: 0262 25 82 76.
Nov–Apr Mon–Fri 9am–5.45pm, Sat 9am–3.45pm; May–Oct Mon–Fri 9am–5.15pm, Sat 9am–3.45pm.
St-Philippe Tourist Office:
64 rue Leconte-de-Lisle, 97422 St-Philippe; tel: 0262 37 10 43; fax: 0262 37 10 97.
Open Mon–Fri 9am–5pm; Sat, Sun and public hols 9am–4pm.

High Plains
Pays d'Acceuil des Hautes-Plaines:
Domaine des Tourelles, 97431 Plaine-des-Palmistes; tel: 0262 51 39 92; fax: 0262 51 45 33

Open Mon–Fri 9am–6pm; Sat, Sun and public hols 10am–5pm. Closed Tues.
St-Pierre/Le Tarnpon Tourist Office: 11 Angle des rues de Volcan et de Genêts, 97418 Plaine des Cafres (next door to the Maison du Volcan); tel: 0262 59 09 82; fax: 0262 59 22 18.
Open Mon 1.30–5.30pm Tues–Sat 8am–12.30pm, 1.30–5.30pm, Sun 8.30am–12.30pm.

The Cirques
Cilaos Tourist Office and **Maison de la Montagne:** 2 bis, rue Victor MacAuliffe, 97413 Cilaos; tel: 0262 31 71 71; fax: 0262 31 78 18
Open Mon–Sat 8.30am– 12.30pm and 1.30–5.30pm, Sun and public hols 9am–1pm.
Tourist Office Salazie:
Centre d'Artisanal d'Hell-Bourg; tel: 0262 47 89 89; fax: 0262 47 89 70. Open Mon–Thur 8am–4pm, Fri 8am–3pm.

Consulates

As Réunion isn't an independent country, only a few countries have diplomatic representation. These include Germany, Belgium, India, Italy, Madagascar, Norway and Switzerland. The nearest consulates for other countries are in Mauritius. For the addresses of the UK, US and Australian consulates, *see page 359.*

Business Travellers

Men need not wear a jacket and tie in the tropics but for formal meetings they may feel more comfortable in a short-sleeved shirt and tie. Women should wear cotton dresses or skirts. Business will usually be conducted in French; however, there is usually at least one member of a meeting who will speak English.

Most business people on short stays favour the hotels in St-Denis although business facilities such as fax, internet, minitel and conference rooms are available throughout the island. Meetings are best scheduled for the morning, and remember that everybody stops for the two-hour lunch break between noon and 2pm as in France.

Réunion has a cell phone network with fairly good coverage. Users should contact their own service provider before leaving home to arrange access. **Chamber of Commerce and Industry:** 5 bis, rue de Paris, PO Box 120, 97463 St-Denis Cedex; tel: 0262 21 53 66; fax: 0262 41 80 34

Travelling with Kids

Children are welcome everywhere. Many hotels cater specially for youngsters and offer supervised activities, special meals, babysitting services, family rooms and child discounts on excursions.

If you are travelling with very young children avoid December and January which may be too hot for them. Supermarkets stock European baby food and nappies.

Gay Travellers

Homosexuality, while tolerated, is not made obvious in public places. Any open displays of affection, straight or gay, are likely to offend or attract jeers. Here is a list of the main gay bars and clubs:

L'Annexe Gay Club (bar): 378 bis rue Saint-Louis, 97460 St-Paul; tel: 0262 02 62 45 50 31
Bar Karaoke – le "Cherwaines": rue Auguste Babet, 97410 St-Pierre
Le Queen (club): rue Maréchal Leclerc, 97400 St-Denis
Le Must (club): rue Méziaire Guignard, 97410 St-Pierre

Emergency Numbers

Ambulance: tel: 15
Police: tel: 17
Fire: tel: 18
In less urgent cases of difficulty, English-speaking visitors should go to the **Air Mauritius office** in St-Denis at 13, Rue Gounod; tel: 0262 94 83 83; fax: 0262 94 13 23.

Le 21ème Parallèle (restaurant): rue Général de Gaulle, 97434 St-Gilles-Les-Bains

Religious Services

Réunion is 95 percent Roman Catholic. Catholic church services are always in French. At mosques and temples the proceedings are likely to be in French too.

Medical Treatment

In theory the E111 form is accepted, but in practice difficulties may be encountered, particularly with urgent treatment. Tourists are strongly advised to take out a comprehensive travel insurance. Most large towns have a hospital and/or private clinic and plenty of doctors.

GENERAL HOSPITALS

Centre Hospitalier Départemental (CHD) Félix Guyon, Bellepierre, 97400 St-Denis; tel: 0262 90 77 00; fax: 0262 90 77 01
Hôpital des Enfants Association Saint François d'Assise 60 rue Bertin, 97400 St-Denis; tel: 0262 90 87 00; fax: 0262 90 87 10
Centre Hospitalier Sud de la Réunion, avenue Président Mitterrand, St-Pierre; tel: 0262 96 09 69; fax: 0262 25 92 44

PRIVATE CLINICS

Clinique de Saint Clothilde, 127 Route Bois de Nèfles, 97400 St-Denis; tel: 0262 48 20 20; fax: 0262 48 20 80
Clinique Océane, 8 rue de Paris, 97400 St-Denis; tel: 0262 40 60 80; fax: 0262 40 60 68

Tipping

A service charge is normally added to restaurant bills. When service is not included *(service non compris)*, a 10 percent tip is perfectly acceptable. Taxi drivers do not expect to be tipped.

Security & Crime

In general, the Réunionnais are willing to help anyone in distress. However, as with everywhere you should take the same basic precautions that you would at home. Don't flaunt expensive jewellery and money in public places; never leave property on view in your car; always be aware of your personal safety; lock doors and windows when you go out, particularly in self-catering accommodation; and after dark don't give a lift to a stranger or go out walking alone.

If you become a victim of crime, try to remain calm, take stock of the situation and get names and addresses of witnesses. Report the matter to the police and in cases of theft ensure you have all the documentation for insurance purposes. However, English is not spoken by the police, so if you have a problem ask at your hotel or your holiday representative to find an interpreter for you.

Getting Around

Driving

Whether travelling by hire car or public bus getting around Réunion is easy thanks to an excellent well-signposted road system. Driving is on the right, as in France. The speed limit is 110 kph (68 mph) dropping to 50 kph (30 mph) in towns and built-up areas. Avoid driving during the rush hours, particularly the main coastal route, which can become a four-lane traffic jam, and the winding roads in the Cirques can be very busy during the peak holiday season.

Hazards: Pedestrians also use the roads, even the four-lane *route nationales,* and it is not practical to drive fast on the winding mountain roads, so it is advisable to drive slowly everywhere. However, the locals tend to treat all roads as race tracks. They also tend to jump the traffic lights, so beware! Look out for cyclists at night riding without lights.

Road conditions: The main coastal route is well-maintained, but the surfaces of the high roads are not so good and are often narrow and winding – the road to Cilaos has 450 bends in it.

In heavy rain the coast road between St-Denis and La Possession can disappear under water in 10 minutes.

CAR HIRE

Most companies ask for a full driving licence from your home country, a credit card or cash deposit, and in some cases insist on full payment in advance. Hirers should be at least 21 years old. For reliability, it's best to choose a company belonging to the French National Car Syndicate (CNPA). The companies below are all members and have desks at the airport, but there are many others which offer seasonal special deals.

Car Hire companies
Au Bas Prix: 35 rue Suffren, St-Paul; tel: 0262 22 69 89; fax: 0262 22 54 27
Budget: 2 rue Pierre Auber-ZI du Chaudron, Ste-Clothilde; tel: 0262 28 92 00; fax: 0262 28 93 00
ERL: 128 rue Général-de-Gaulle, St-Gilles-les-Bains; tel: 0262 24 02 25; fax: 0262 24 06 02
Europcar: Gillot, La Ferme, Ste-Marie; tel: 0262 93 14 15; fax: 0262 93 14 14
Hertz Locamac: 82 rue de la Republique, St-Denis; tel: 0262 53 22 55; fax: 0262 53 26 34
Pop's Cars: Hotel Apolonia, St-Leu; tel: 0262 34 72 10; fax: 0262 34 62 98

By Bus

Réunion's buses are a comfortable and cost effective means of travel. As there are no stop bells, be prepared to clap your hands to alert the driver when you want to get off or just shout *devant* (ahead). There are 12 lines or routes which interconnect with towns. Buses start running at around 5am with last departures being between 7pm and 8pm. For bus schedules and information call the following stations:

St-Denis: tel: 0262 41 51 10
St-André: tel: 0262 46 80 00
St-Benoit: tel: 0262 50 10 69
St-Paul: tel: 0262 22 54 38
St-Pierre: tel: 0262 35 67 28
St-Joseph: tel: 0262 56 03 90

By Taxi

Taxis in Réunion are an expensive alternative to buses and cars. The fare between St-Denis and Boucan-Canot (40 km/25 miles) for example, can cost around €38. However, if you're a woman travelling alone after dark they are probably the safest way of getting around. Cheaper deals can be had if you negotiate a fare for a whole day's hire and split the cost between several passengers. Tipping is not obligatory. Taxis can be hired at taxi ranks in main towns or by telephone, or through your hotel.

Driving Times

Depending on the time you are travelling and the weather conditions, here is an estimate of how long it will take you to drive between different parts of the island:

St-Denis–west coast	40–80 km/25–50 miles	40–65 mins
St-Denis–Hell-Bourg	55 km/34 miles	1 hour 10 mins
St-Denis–volcano	150 km/93 miles	2¾ hours
St-Denis–Cilaos (centre)	113 km/70 miles	2 hours
St-Gilles–Hell-Bourg	100 km/62 miles	1½–2 hours
St-Gilles–volcano	100 km/62 miles	2 hours
St-Gilles–Cilaos (centre)	75 km/47 miles	1½ hours
Hell-Bourg–west coast	90–107 km/58–68 miles	1 hour 30 mins
Hell-Bourg–volcano	135 km/84 miles	2–2½ hours
St-Pierre–Hell-Bourg	96 km/62 miles	2 hours
St-Pierre–west coast	40–54 km/25–34 miles	30–45 mins

To Roland Garros Airport:

St-Denis	14 km/9 miles	20 minutes
St-Gilles	51 km/32 miles	45 minutes
Hell-Bourg	41 km/26 miles	1 hour
St-Pierre	91 km/57 miles	2 hours

Helicopter Tours

A wonderful way to see the grandeur of the island's volcanic landscape is to go on a helicopter trip *(see page 220)*.
Helilagon: Altiport de l'Eperon, St-Paul; tel: 0262 55 55 55; fax: 0262 22 86 78.
Heli-Réunion: Roland Garros Airport, St-Denis; tel: 0262 93 11 11; fax: 0262 29 51 70 and at Route de l'Hermitage, St-Gilles-les-Bains; tel: 0262 24 00 00.

Sightseeing Tours

A range of sightseeing tours is available through the following travel agents based on the island:
Atlas Voyages: 104 avenue du Général de Gaulle, St-Gilles-les-Bains; tel: 0262 33 02 20; fax: 0262 33 08 48; e-mail: atlas@wanadoo.fr
Bourbon Tourisme: 1 Lot Aquarium/Local 14; rue du Général de Gaulle, Port de St Gilles-les-Bains; tel: 0262 33 08 70; fax: 0262 41 03 09; e-mail: bourbon.tourisme@travel-run.com
Euro-Voyages Réunion: 20 rue de l'Est, St-Denis; tel: 0262 21 89 00; fax: 41 30 00; e-mail: eurovoyager@wanadoo.fr
Nouvelles Frontieres: Residence Claire 1, 31 Place Paul Julius Benard, St-Gilles-les-Bains; tel: 0262 33 11 99; fax: 0262 33 11 98 e-mail: nf.stgilles@wanadoo.fr
Objectif: 28 rue Summer, St-Gilles-les-Bains; tel: 0262 33 08 37; fax: 0262 33 08 38; e-mail: objectif.reunion@wanadoo.fr
Papangue Tours: 5 rue de Nice St-Denis; tel: 0262 41 61 92; fax: 0262 41 61 96; e-mail: papangueprod@wanadoo.fr

Where to Stay

Choosing a Hotel

Most of Réunion's 60 classified hotels are on the west coast and in St-Denis. They all meet French standards, are clean, comfortable and well-run and many cater for French package tourists. Book well in advance as hotels fill quickly during the high season. However if you are coming from Mauritius, don't expect the same kind of quality or service. The staff are generally not so warm and friendly.

Price Guide

Prices are all for a room for two for one night including breakfast:
€€€ = more than €100
€€ = €50–€100
€ = less than €50

Hotel Listings

THE NORTH

St-Denis
Central Hôtel
37 rue de la Compagnie; tel: 0262 94 18 08; fax: 0262 21 64 33
Small and friendly family hotel close to shops in city centre. €€
Domaine des Jamroses
6 Chemin du Colorado, La Montagne; tel: 0262 23 59 00; fax: 0262 23 93 37
In a 2-hectare (5-acre) tropical park with sea views 8 km (5 miles) from the capital, this grand creole house has 12 rooms, a gourmet restaurant, swimming pool and sporting facilities. €€€
Mercure Créolia
14 rue Stade Montgaillard; tel: 0262 94 26 26; fax: 0262 94 27 27
With impressive views over St-Denis, this modern hotel has a gastronomic restaurant, swimming pool, tennis court, sauna. Entertainment on some evenings. €€€
Le Saint-Denis
2 rue Doret; tel: 0262 21 80 20; fax: 0262 21 97 41
Fully refurbished this four-star hotel is right in the centre facing the sea next to Le Barachois gardens. Casino. Popular with business travellers. Tacky bar with crooning singers. €€€

THE EAST

St-Benoit
Armony
Route Nationale 2, La Marine, tel: 0262 50 86 50; fax: 0262 50 86 60
Ideal starting point for Réunion's inland attractions. Special weekend and weekly rates. Swimming pool and fine restaurant. €€
Hostellerie de la Confiance
60 Chemin de la Confiance; tel: 0262 50 90 50; fax: 0262 50 97 27
This seven-roomed hotel stands in a 100-year-old garden. Gourmet restaurant, swimming pool and honeymoon suite. €€

THE SOUTH

St-Pierre
Demotel
8 Allée des Lataniers, Grand-Bois; tel: 0262 31 11 60; fax: 0262 31 17 51
Bungalow-style hotel with 30 rooms between St-Pierre and Grand-Bois beaches. Facilities include helicopter flights, nearby golf course and evening entertainment. French and creole cuisine in seaside restaurant. €€/€€€
Le Sterne-Protea
Boulevard Hubert Delisle; tel: 0262 25 70 00; fax: 0262 25 70 66
In the heart of St-Pierre and facing the beach but only a 10-minute drive to the 18-hole Golf Club de Bourbon. Evening entertainment three times a week. €€€

St-Philippe
Le Baril
Route Nationale 2; tel: 0262 37 01
04; fax: 0262 37 07 62
Overlooking the wild south coast
and volcanic lava flows. Swimming
pool and cosy restaurant serving
French and creole food. €€

THE WEST

St-Gilles-les-Bains
Les Aigrettes
Chemin Bottard; tel: 0262 33 05
05; fax: 0262 24 30 50
Mid-range hotel overlooking the
harbour. Free shuttle bus to
St-Gilles-les-Bains and beaches. €€
Grand Hotel des Mascareignes
Boucan-Canot; tel: 0262 24 36 24;
fax: 0262 24 37 24
Popular with package tourists.
Across the road from Boucan-Canot
beach. Swimming pool, tennis
courts and nightly entertainment.
Good views from rooms. €€€
Maharani
28 Route du Boucan; tel: 0262 33
06 06; fax: 0262 24 32 97
Atmospheric hotel with 55 spacious
rooms right on the beach. Two
restaurants with evening
entertainment. €€€
Marina
6 Allée des Pailles en Queue, Lot
Champagne; tel: 0262 33 07 07;
fax: 0262 33 07 00
Close to Boucan Canot beach.
Ten rooms. Private car park and
car rental available. Discounts
available on stays of more than one
week. €€
Le Saint-Alexis
44 Route de Boucan Canot; tel:
0262 24 42 04; fax: 0262 24 00 13
One of Réunion's most expensive
hotels right on the beach. Swimming
pool, giant jacuzzi and restaurant.
Evening entertainment Thursday to
Saturday. €€€
Villas du Lagon
28 rue du Lagon L'Hermitage
tel: 0262 70 00 00; fax: 0262
70 00 07
Pleasant holiday resort complex,
comprising 23 villas and 174 rooms
in lush gardens by the lagoon.
Facilities include large pool, 3

Bedding Down in the Mountains

On a hike that lasts for more than
a day you can plan your overnight
stays in an assortment of lodgings
en route, from the very basic to
the more comfortable. For
information and reservations,
contact local tourist offices or
Maison de la Montagne, 10 Place
Sarda-Garriga, St-Denis; tel: 0262
90 78 78; fax: 0262 41 84 29, or
in Cilaos at 2 Rue MacAuliffe; tel:
0262 31 71 71; fax: 0262 31 80
54. Two sheets, a pillow and two
blankets are provided in all gîtes.

● **Gîte d'étape:** basic overnight
gîte offering dormitory-style
lodging and breakfast and makeshift kitchens where guests can
cook up their own pot noodles.
● **Gîte de montagne:** dormitory
bunk-bed accommodation in an
isolated location, sometimes

without a shower or hot water and
in dry periods no water at all.
Basic self-catering facilities
although meals can be provided if
booked.
● **Refuge:** private basic lodging
with an evening meal provided by
the owner and sometimes
breakfast.
● **Chambre d'hôte:** bed and
breakfast in someone's home.
Evening meals can also be
provided as a *table d'hôte* (*see*
Country Cooking *box, page 387*).
● **Gîte rural:** self-catering cottage
located in the countryside. They
are normally well equipped and
probably the best option for
families or groups.
● **Abris:** shelters on trekking
routes consisting of only a roof
under which you can pitch your
own tent.

restaurants and mini-club for 3–12
year olds. €€€

Maïdo
Parc-Hotel du Maïdo
Route du Maïdo, La Petite France;
tel: 0262 32 52 52; fax: 0262
32 52 00
Bungalow-style accommodation,
set in parkland with views of the
sea. Ideal location for exploring
walking trails around Le Maïdo.
Horse-riding and mountain biking
facilities. €€

St-Leu
Apolonia
Boulevard Bonnier; tel: 0262 34 62
62; fax: 0262 34 61 61
Large hotel near the sea. Rooms
comfortable if impersonal. Free
activities include surfing, body
boarding, mountain biking and
water aerobics. Excursions can be
booked at reception. Gourmet
restaurant. €€€
Iloha
Pointe des Châteaux; tel: 0262 34
89 89; fax: 0262 34 89 90
Comfortable bungalows with
kitchenette and some double
rooms overlooking the bay.

Pleasant open-air bar and
restaurant next to the swimming
pool. €€

VOLCANO AND HIGH PLAINS

La Plaine-des-Palmistes
Les Azalées
80 rue République; tel: 0262 51 34
24; fax: 0262 28 17 97
Good value, unpretentious 36-room
hotel, 1,100 metres (3,600 ft) above
sea level. Children's play area.
Special deals on three-night stays. €
Hotel des Plaines
156 rue République; tel: 0262 51
35 67; fax: 0262 51 44 24
Charming small hotel in the heart of
Plaine-des-Palmistes. €€

VOLCANO AND THE CIRQUES

La Plaine-des-Cafres
Adret
137 Route Forestière du Volcan; tel:
0262 59 00 85; fax: 0262 59 09 34
Ideal choice for volcano watchers
and explorers in simple

accommodation. Visits to volcano with experienced guides and pleasant restaurant serving fresh farm products. €

Auberge du Volcan
PK 27, Route Nationale 3, Bourg-Murat; tel: 0262 27 50 91; fax: 0262 59 17 21
Next door to La Maison du Volcan, this good value hotel is a popular choice with package and independent holidaymakers and serves typical creole fare in the restaurant. €

L'Ecrin
PK 27, Route Nationale 3, Bourg-Murat; tel: 0262 59 02 02; fax: 0262 59 36 10
Centrally located for outdoor leisure pursuits this complex consists of 13 bungalow-style accommodations. Special rates are offered for hiking groups. €–€€

Les Géraniums
Route Nationale 3, 24ème km; tel: 0262 59 11 06; fax: 0262 59 21 83
Close to Maison du Volcan with superb views of Piton des Neiges. Ideal for walking excursions. The gourmet restaurant is a welcome sight after an activity-packed day. €€

Cilaos
Hôtel du Cirque
27 rue du Pere Boiteau; tel: 0262 31 70 68; fax: 0262 31 80 46
This 35-room hotel has pleasant balconies overlooking the main street and a terraced restaurant. Special weekend deals include half-board. €€

Hotel des Neiges
1 rue de la Mare à Joncs; tel: 0262 31 72 33; fax: 0262 31 72 98
Spacious and simple rooms, under the shadow of the Piton des Neiges. Two restaurants to choose from –

Price Guide

Prices are all for a room for two for one night including breakfast:
€€€ = more than €100
€€ = €50–€100
€ = less than €50

Le Marla and La Grange *(see page 388).* €€
Le Vieux Cep
2 rue des Trois Mares; tel: 0262 31 71 89; fax: 0262 31 77 68
This centrally located mid-range hotel is comfortable and the restaurant serves fine French and creole cuisine. €€

Salazie
Le Relais des Cimes
rue Général de Gaulle, Hell-Bourg; tel: 0262 47 81 58; fax: 0262 47 82 11
Simple and pleasant rooms in typical creole house. The restaurant serves the best French and creole meals in the area. The Chinese-run general store directly opposite sells everything you need for treks, including camera batteries. €€

Camping

Standards vary in community-run campsites and you should be prepared for poor security and facilities. Alternatively, you can camp in the wild provided you have permission from the landowner. Two community-managed campsites open year round are at **Colorado** (tel: 0262 23 74 12) and at **Rivière des Roches** (tel: 0262 51 58 59). If you're heading to Salazie, it's worth booking a place at the privately run **Camping à la Ferme**, Chemin Bras-Sec, Ilet à Vidot (tel/fax: 0262 47 83 06; mobile: 0692 088586) The site provides fully equipped tents, toilet/shower and kitchen facilities, and is run by a local guide.

Self-catering

Good value furnished flats can be rented on a weekly basis by contacting owners listed in the locally published guide *RUN*. Alternatively you can contact **Relais Départmental des Gîtes de France** 10 Place du Barachois, St-Denis (tel: 0262 90 78 90; fax: 0262 41 84 29) and ask for their illustrated booklet called *Vacances en Gîtes de France* which lists full details and photographs of

self-catering accommodation in *gîtes ruraux* (rural gîtes), bed and breakfast in *chambres d'hôtes* and farm guest houses *(ferme auberges)*.

Youth Hostels

To stay in one of Réunion's three youth hostels *(auberges de jeunesse)* you need to buy French Youth Hostelling membership from the hostel or contact the **Fédération of Youth Hostels** at 42 rue du Général de Gaulle, St-Denis (tel: 0262 41 15 34; fax: 0262 41 72 17). Daily rates on either full or half board are reduced depending on the length of stay and number of hostellers. As a price guide one to four people on half board can expect to pay around €25 per person. There are youth hostels at: **Hell-Bourg:** tel: 0262 47 82 65
Bernica: tel: 0262 22 89 75
Entre-Deux: tel: 0262 39 59 20
Readers in the UK can also apply to the YHA for international membership. Contact YHA (England and Wales) Ltd., Trevalyan House, 8 Sts Stephen's Hill, St. Alban's, Herts. AL1 2DY; tel: 0870 870 8808; fax: 01727 844 126

Family Holiday Villages (VVF)

There are two VVFs *(Villages Vacances Famille)* in Réunion geared to families or groups who can choose from an inexpensive range of studio, bungalow or dormitory-style accommodation. A group joining fee of around €16 is payable before bookings can be made at the following:

St-Gilles-les-Bains
VVF St-Gilles "Le Village de Corail"
90 avenue de Bourbon
tel: 0262 24 29 39; fax: 0262 24 41 02

Cilaos
VVF "Le Village des Sources"
rue Fleurs Jaunes; tel: 0262 31 71 39; fax: 0262 31 80 85

Where to Eat

Some of Réunion's best restaurants form part of the **Saveurs et Senteurs de la Réunion** (Flavours and Fragrances) group which is affiliated to the Guild of French Provinces Restaurateurs. These restaurants are often attached to hotels and mainly specialise in both French cuisine and local creole specialities, such as *cari* (curry), *chou chou* (christophene), *brèdes* (a spinach-like vegetable), and pork, chicken and seafood dishes. But don't overlook the many crêperies, bars and cafés and markets for mouthwatering morsels of freshly cooked snacks such as samosas and *boulettes* (fried spiced meat or fish ball). Most restaurants keep to standard lunch times from noon to 2.30pm and offer a fixed-price *menu du jour*. Buying a meal in restaurants outside these times is virtually impossible and you will have to wait till the evening. Many restaurants are closed on Monday *(see pages 174–5 for more about Réunion's cuisine).*

THE NORTH

St-Denis

L'Hélios
88 rue Pasteur; tel: 0262 20 21 50
Fish restaurant with a 1950s' film-star theme. Eat inside or on the outdoor terrace. Specialities include French and creole cuisine. €€

La Nouvelle-Orléans
12 rue de la Compagnie;
tel: 0262 20 27 74
Gourmet restaurant specialising in French and creole cuisine in a sophisticated atmosphere and popular with lunchtime business travellers and tourists. Reservations recommended. €€€

Roland Garros
2 Place du 20 décembre, Barachois; tel: 0262 41 44 37
For fine wining and dining in sophisticated air-conditioned restaurant. Try the *menu du jour* or sip drinks on the outdoor terrace. €€€

La Terrasse
39 rue Félix-Guyon; tel: 0262 20 07 85; fax: 0262 21 93 45
Serves superb French and creole food, including salads, pizzas, grills and Corsican specialities. You can enjoy theme nights and karaoke evenings too in this typical creole building. €€

Le Vésuvio
7 rue Maréchal-Leclerc;
tel: 0262 21 44 54
Opposite St-Denis' *grand marché*, this Italian-style restaurant is a popular lunchtime and evening

Price Guide
Prices are for two without wine:
€€€ = more than €30
€€ = €15–€30
€ = less than €15

haunt, renowned for its pizzas. Open until midnight. €

THE WEST

St-Gilles-les-Bains

Chez Loulou
86 rue Général de Gaulle;
tel: 0262 24 46 36
Typical creole ambiance in this long-established restaurant and pâtisserie. Specialities include *cabri massale*, *rougail de saucisses*, lobster curry and local punch. €€

Loïk-Olivier Pâtisserie
5 rue de la Plage;
tel: 0262 24 33 73
Prizewinning Réunion pastry cook, Loïk-Olivier, turns out first class patisserie and breakfasts at his shop overlooking the sea. Open from 6.30am to 7pm. €€

Le Massilia
Plage de l'Hermitage;
tel: 0262 33 81 38
Beachside fish restaurant noted for French and creole cuisine. Try the delicious bouillabaisse, grilled fish and shellfish. Fixed price menus. €€–€€€

My Fun Beach
Mail de Rodrigues, Hermitage;
tel: 0262 33 00 99
Just 100 metres (330 ft) from the sea this friendly restaurant turns out delicious crêpes, French cuisine and some Belgian goodies. €€

Paul et Virginie
15 rue de la Plage;
tel: 0262 33 04 53
Wonderful panoramic views from the terrace of this beachside restaurant. Grilled meats and fish and a range of French and creole dishes from Mauritius and Réunion prepared by a Mauritian chef. Closed Monday. €–€€

San Remo
1 Place des Coquillages
Boucan-Canot; tel: 0262 24 42 85

Country Cooking

Many of the island's farmers and country dwellers offer lunches at good value for hungry trekkers at their homes. Usually the food is traditional creole and in some establishments eaten with the hosts. Contact **Maison de la Montagne** *(see page 385)* or the local tourist office for details. It's advisable to book in advance especially for Sunday lunch.

● **Fermes auberges:** inn-farms where a traditional creole meal is cooked with local produce. Contact

Relais Agriculture et Tourisme, 24 Rue de la Source, 97464 St-Denis (tel: 0262 94 25 94; fax: 0262 21 31 56) for a list of the island's 16 *fermes auberges.*

● **Table d'hôte:** traditional creole meals are served at the large family table of the host seating up to 20 people. Popular on Sundays.

● **Auberge de campagne:** a country inn at which the farmer can cater for up to 80 people with traditionally cooked home-grown produce.

Relaxed open-air dining in this Italian-run pizzeria within walking distance of the Grand Hotel des Mascareignes. Try the range of homemade pastas and pizzas or go for grilled meat or fish. €€

Le Tandjore
28 Route du Boucan-Canot;
tel: 0262 33 06 06
Upmarket Indian restaurant attached to the Hotel Maharani offering tandoori dishes and French and creole food. Try the grilled lobster for a special treat or book a table for the Friday Indian dinner and dance show. Closed Monday. €€€

St-Leu
Le Lagon
2 bis rue du Lagon;
tel: 0262 34 79 13
Right on the beach and serving a good range of local, Indian and Malagasy food. €€–€€€

Le Palais d'Asie
5 rue de l'Etang;
tel: 0262 34 80 41
Welcoming Chinese restaurant which also serves snacks and ice creams. Take-away service or sit down meals. €€

THE SOUTH

St Pierre
Café de la Gare
17 boulevard Hubert-Delisle;
tel: 0262 35 24 44
On the seafront, this trendy

Pint of "dodo"

The name of the local beer is Bourbon which has an emblem of the dodo, hence a bottle of beer is referred to as un dodo. For draught beer, ask for un pression. Wine is popular and as well as being produced in Cilaos, it is also imported from France. But rum in an assortment of concoctions is a speciality of Réunion – as rhum arrangée, rum flavoured with spices and fruit, or punch creole, rum blended wth fruit, cane syrup and juice.

watering-hole used to be the old railway station. Ideal for people-watching from the open-air terrace and next door to the tourist office. €€

Le Retro
34 boulevard Hubert-Delisle;
tel: 0262 25 33 06
Expensive but worth trying for first-class service and creole and French cuisine. €€€

Basse Vallée
Le Cap Méchant
Basse Vallée; tel: 0262 37 00 61
Typical Creole menu and seafood including grilled lobster, against an ocean backdrop. Closed Sunday night and Monday. €€€

St-Philippe
Chez Laurent
26 Route Nationale 2, Le Baril, near St-Philippe; tel: 0262 37 07 03
Small and welcoming restaurant ideal for creole or Indian lunch or take-away baguettes. €

THE EAST

St-André
Beau Rivage
Vieille Eglise, Champ-Borne;
tel: 0262 46 08 66
Reasonably priced restaurant specialising in Indian, Chinese, French and creole cuisine. Closed Sunday evening and Monday. €€

La Coupole
Centre Commercial "Les Cocoteraies"; tel: 0262 46 94 77
Popular and centrally located restaurant specialising in creole, French and Chinese cuisine. SS

St-Benoit
L'Hostellerie de la Confiance
60 Chemin de la Confiance;
tel: 0262 50 90 50
Romantic inland hotel restaurant popular with honeymooners. Noted for its creole cuisine gastronomique. €€

Piton-Ste-Rose
Anse des Cascades
tel: 0262 47 20 42
Informal easy-going atmosphere in

this restaurant specialising in French and creole cuisine. Closed evenings. €€

VOLCANO AND THE CIRQUES

Salazie
P'tit Bambou
Opposite the church at Salazie;
tel: 0262 47 51 51
Tasty home products turned into delicious creole cuisine with mounds of white rice. Closed Wednesday. €€

Le Relais des Cimes
rue Général de Gaulle, Hell-Bourg;
tel: 0262 47 81 58
The finest restaurant in the area and has rooms attached. €€

Cilaos
La Grange
2 Chemin Saul; tel: 0262 31 70 38
Lakeside views of Mare à Joncs and wonderful countryside at this restaurant. Creole specialities include gratin de papayes vertes and sweet potatoes drizzled with chocolate. €€€

Le Marla
1 rue de la Mare à Joncs;
tel: 0262 31 72 33
Typical creole fare in a pleasant dining room of the Hotel des Neiges (see page 386). This is the place to try Cilaos' famous lentils, wine and the delicious dessert, gâteau banane. €€€

Plaine-des-Cafres
Auberge du Volcan
27ème km, Bourg-Murat;
tel: 0262 27 50 91
Centrally located restaurant and bar at Bourg-Murat and ideal lunch stop when returning from the volcano. Traditional cuisine, creole specialities and French food served in lively atmosphere. Menu du jour or à la carte. Open daily from 6.30am. €€

Culture

Music & Dance

Scarcely a week goes by without some form of entertainment being staged in Réunion's theatres and cultural centres. A most unusual venue is St-Denis' **Palaxa Theatre** (tel: 0262 21 87 58), a converted warehouse seating 300 people and noted for late-night folk music and unusual sounds from Réunion and the Indian Ocean islands.

The **Centre Dramatique de l'Océan Indien** is an innovative theatre company based at the **Theatre du Grand Marché** in St-Denis (tel: 0262 20 33 99) and is host to many small theatrical companies from around the world. Contact the Tourist Office for further information or consult the free *RUN* guide for listings of other gigs, concerts, dance-shows, plays and musical events. You can also get a free monthly newsletter called *Trajectoires* containing details of theatre, jazz and classical music performances from the **Office Departmental de la Culture** (tel: 0262 41 11 41; fax: 0262 41 55 71) in St-Denis.

Nightlife

There are three late-night casinos and dozens of pubs, clubs and discotheques to choose from with the highest concentration in St-Denis, St-Gilles-les-Bains and St-Pierre. Many nightclubs open on Fridays, Saturdays and the day before a public holiday at around 10pm but really get going after midnight closing only when the last revellers stagger home in the morning. Most clubs have a cover charge of about €15, and alcoholic drinks can cost half as much again.

Festivals & Sporting Events

Réunion has a year round cultural programme: fire walking, Cavadee and Dipavali are practised by the Tamil community in various parts of the island and dates may vary. Wine, fruit and handicraft festivals take place in villages and towns while sporting events can be watched virtually year round.

The international surfing community come to the west coast during June, and October/November is the time for the Grand Raid, a gruelling 125-km (77-mile) mountain running race, the Maido Run, an international paragliding competition, and the International Cross Country race at St-Denis. For details of these and other events contact the Tourist Office.

Museums

Among Réunion's newest attractions are the following museums:

The **Musée de la Vraie Fraternité** (True Fraternity Museum; 28 bd de la Providence, St Denis; tel: 0262 21 06 71, fax: 0262 41 54 80; Wed and Sat 9am–5pm; entrance fee) is a social history museum displaying local costume and remains of the island's first printing press.

At **Turmeric House** (14 Chemin du Rond, Plaine des Grègues, St Joseph; tel: 0262 37 54 66; fax: 0262 65 04 68; daily 9am–noon and 1–5pm. Free) you can discover how turmeric – a spice much used in local cuisine – is processed, sampling such local products as candied orange and sweet and sour ginger on the way.

The **Ecomusée Salazie** (60 rue du Général de Gaulle, Hell-Bourg; tel: 0262 47 89 28; fax: 0262 47 86 17; Mon–Sun 9am–4pm; entrance fee) houses a collection of archive photographs, news cuttings and videos relating to Salazie. The entrance ticket includes a guided tour of 18 typical Creole houses in Hell-Bourg each displaying information boards on its architectural origins. In French only.

Outdoor Activities

The dramatic volcanic mountainous landscape of Réunion provides a magnificent arena for a vast variety of sports and outdoor activities, as does the surrounding sea whipped up by the trade winds, becalmed in the lagoons and concealing an underwater world of coral reefs and marine creatures. This really is an island which has something for everyone from the seekers of high adventure to those with more of a sense of self preservation *(see* Island of Adventures *on pages 183–187)*. Activities on offer include hang-gliding and paragliding *(parapente)* over breathtaking scenery, canyoning down the gorges, hiking, climbing and mountain biking, or horse-trekking and rambling on the more gentler slopes. For full details of all mountain activities, practical information, accommodation and maps contact: **La Maison de la Montagne**, 10 Place du Barachoise, St-Denis; tel: 0262 90 78 78; fax: 0262 41 84 29, or their branch in Cilaos at 2 rue Mac-Auliffe 97413; tel: 0262 31 71 71; fax: 0262 31 80 54.

Safety Measures

To avoid accidents and disappointments, follow the rules of the mountain as drawn up by the Maison de la Montagne *(see page 184)*.
● Check the weather forecast before going; tel: 08 36 68 08 08 or 08 36 68 02 02 (in French).
● Keep the Mountain Rescue Police (Peleton de Gendarmerie de Haute Montagne) number to hand: tel: 0262 930 930.

On offer on the water are sailing, surfing, windsurfing and a whole range of watersports in the lagoons, or game fishing out to sea and scuba diving under it. Alternatively, life in the open can be enjoyed just as much on a catamaran cruise as a golf course.

Adventure Sports on Land & Sea

The following organisations offer a whole range of adventure sports and provide equipment, qualified guides and instructors. It's best to make reservations in advance:

Austral Aventure: 4 Chemin Enilorac, Le Guillaume, tel: 0262 32 40 29; fax: 0262 32 34 04
For hiking, hang-gliding, paragliding, canyoning, river sports and mountain climbing.

Jacaranda: 34 Allée des Mangiers, La Montagne; tel: 0262 23 82 58
Hiking, canyoning, climbing, mountain biking, kayaking.

Kalanoro: BP 23, Bras-Panon; tel: 0262 50 74 75

La Maison de la Montagne: *see page 390*

Maham: Place Artisanale, Hell-Bourg; tel: 0262 47 82 82
Hiking, canyoning, mountain biking, horse-trekking and scuba diving. Qualified English-speaking instructors.

Run Evasion: 23 rue du Père Boiteau, Cilaos; tel: 0262 31 83 57; fax: 0262 31 80 72
Mountain biking, guided rides, rambling, hiking, canyoning.

Réunion Sensations: La Saline-les-Bains; tel: 0262 33 17 58; and Cilaos; tel: 0262 31 84 84
Sports on offer include canyoning, heli-canyoning, climbing and mountain biking.

Paragliding & Microlighting

Azurtech, La pointe des Châteaux: St-Leu Cedex; tel: 0262 34 91 89; fax: 0262 38 01 86

Bourbon Parapente: 1 rue Tabaillet, St-Leu; tel: 0262 87 58 74; fax: 0262 34 32 57

Felix ULM Run: Base ULM de Cambaie. St Paul; tel: 0262 45 58 38; fax: 0262 45 63 08
Microlight flights.

Lit d'Air Ecole de Parapente: 40 rue Bertin, St Denis; tel: 0262 692 60 01 23

Les Passagers du Vent: rue A. Artaud, Le Port; tel: 0262 42 95 95
Microlighting, hang-gliding and paragliding.

Cimes Loisirs: BP 930, St Denis; tel/fax: 0262 97 14 22
Paragliding and other activities.

Parapente Réunion: Pente-école 4; Montée des Colimaçons, St-Leu; tel: 0262 24 87 84; fax: 0262 24 87 15
Paragliding school for beginners and advanced courses. Qualified, English-speaking instructors. Take-off is usually on the slopes of Les Colimaçons. On the D12.

Mountain Biking

Known as *vélo tout terrain* (VTT), the sport has become so popular that seven specially marked trails have been created for enthusiasts. The

following operators hire equipment and organise guided rides:

Telenavette: 146 bis, rue route de Crève-Coeur St Paul; tel: 0262 692 21 11 11

Rando Bike: 100 Route du Volcan, Plaine-des-Cafres; tel: 0262 59 15 88

Run Evasion: 23 rue du Pere Boiteau, Cilaos; tel: 0262 31 83 57

VTT Réunion: 34 route du Tevelave, Les Avirons; tel: 0262 38 01 97

Horse-riding & Trekking

You need not be an experienced rider to go on a pony trek as the Réunion Mérens horse is a gentle, easy-going breed. For half-day to three-day treks with a guide contact:

Centre Equestre Alti-Mérens: Notre Dame de la Paix; tel: 0262 59 18 84

Centre Equestre du Maïdo: 350 Route du Maïdo, Le Guillaume-St-Paul; tel: 0262 32 49 15

Ferme Equestre de Grand Etang: Route Nationale 3, Pont Payet, St-Benoit; tel: 0262 50 90 03

Planning a Trekking Holiday

Accommodation: There are various types of accommodation (*see* Where to Stay *page 384*) but not nearly enough to satisfy demand during July and August, when it seems the whole of France comes to Réunion, so it makes sense to book as early as possible. May to June and September are less frenetic times and accommodation is not so scarce.

Catering: In Mafate, where the only way of getting around is on foot, the grocer store or *épicerie* is rather like a beacon in the wilderness luring a hungry trekker to happiness with a basic range of goodies. Hard cheese if you find yourself at Ilet à Bourse but there are three *épiceries* at La Nouvelle and one each at Marla, Roche Plate, Grand Place les Hauts, Ilet a Malheur and Aurère.

In and around Cilaos cirque, particularly at Dimitile, Le Pavillon and Ilet Haute, you should make

sure you have your own food. Other areas you should know about for their absence of sustenance are Belouve on the GR1 and Roche Ecrit, Piton des Neiges, Basse Vallée and Grand Bassin on the GR2 and anywhere along the banks of the Rivière des Remparts.

What to take on a trek:
● enough water and food
● warm sweater
● waterproof cape or jacket
● hat, sunglasses and suncream
● good walking shoes or boots and pack a pair of soft shoes to change into
● torch, pocket knife, whistle and basic medical kit

For staying out overnight if camping:
● sleeping bag and tent
● crockery, cutlery
● minimal cooking utensils
● toiletries eg loo paper

Horse-riding centres:
Centre d'Equitation du Colorado: La Montagne; tel: 0262 23 62 51
Centre Equestre Eldorado: Allée Montignac, Etang-Salé; tel: 0262 26 56 53

Hiking & Trekking

Hiking excursions of varying lengths from half a day to a week with qualified English-speaking guides can be arranged through **Maison de la Montagne** *(see page 389)* who can help plan your route and organise accommodation. It's worth asking for the services of a *guide pei* (native guide) from the tourist office in rue Victor Mac Aciliffe, Cilaos (tel: 0262 31 78 03) or by phoning a central number: 0262 90 78 78. These guides are born and bred in the Cirques, know every nook and cranny, and keep you entertained with folklore and legend. As well as the companies listed under "Adventure Sports on Land & Sea" *(left)*, the following also organise treks and hikes:
Altitudes Australes: Residence Ixora, 196 Route Nationale 1, L'Hermitage-les-Bains; tel: 0262 33 84 93
Anne le Garrec: 73 Allée des Roberts, St-André; tel: 0262 58 37 44
Maham: Place Artisanale, Hell-Bourg; tel: 0262 47 82 82

Heli-canyoning

For those who find canyoning too tame and want to experience the higher, steeper and inaccessible canyons, heli-canyoning is the answer. After flying to the top of a canyon you are suspended from the helicopter as you shoot to the bottom, contact **Réunion Sensations** *(see left)* for more details.

Golf

There are three golf courses and a mini-golf:

Golf Club de Bourbon: 140 Les Sables, L'Etang-Salé; tel: 0262 26 33 39
Website: www.golf-bourbon.com
Golf du Colorado: Zone de Loisirs du Colorado, La Montagne; tel: 0262 23 79 50
Golf du Bassin Bleu: Villèle, St-Gilles-les-Hauts; tel: 0262 55 53 58.
Mini-Golf du Lagon: Plage de l'Hermitage, 3 Allée des Îles Eparses, St-Gilles-les-Bains; tel: 0262 22 92 98
Open daily during the school holidays; closed Tuesday and Friday during term time.

Big Game Fishing

The best time for catching the big ones, such as blue marlin, sailfish, bluefin tuna and sea bream, is from October to May, although you can go all year round. Fully equipped boats for up to six people leave from the harbours at St-Gilles, Pointe des Galets and St-Pierre. A picnic and drinks are often included in the price:
Réunion Fishing Club: 5 rue du Grand Large, St-Gilles-les-Bains; tel: 0262 24 36 10
Réunion Pêche au Gros: 5 Chemin Souris Blanche, Trois Bassins; tel: 0262 33 33 99; fax: 0262 33 82 21
Deep sea fishing in two boats, *Alopia* and *Octopus II.*

Scuba Diving

Many of Réunion's dive companies operate from St-Gilles-les-Bains offering PADI, NAUI and CMAS courses and a chance to see the magnificent coral landscape and marine life under the Indian Ocean:
Abyss Plongée: 7 boulevard Bonnier, St-Leu; tel: 0262 34 79 79
Aress: Centre de Plongée Beuchat, St-Gilles-les-Bains; tel: 0262 24 23 30
Atlantis: Route de Colimaçons, Pointe-des-Châteaux, St-Leu; tel: 0262 34 77 47
Bleu Marine Réunion: Port de St-Gilles; tel: 0262 24 22 00
Corail Plongée: Zone Portuaire, St-Gilles-les-Bains; tel: 0262 24 37 25

Cruising

Either take to the water the easy way and watch the sun go down over cocktails from the deck of the 22-metre (72-ft) ketch *Hnoss* or learn to sail a catamaran yourself, through **La Compagnie des Alizés**; tel: 65 60 00.

Sub Excelsus: 1 ZA Pointe des Châteaux; tel/fax: 0262 34 73 65

Surfing

International surfers descend on Réunion between March and September to ride out the big waves found on the west coast. One of the best spots, described as a world-class break, is for experienced surfers only and is in front of the town of St-Leu. At Etang-Salé some amazing left-hand waves rising to almost 90 degrees provide ace surfing conditions and are best tried out in the earling morning. A two-hour intoductory surfing course in French at **Ecole de Body Board et Surf des Roches Noires** at St-Gilles-les-Bains (tel: 0262 24 63 28) or at **Ecole de Surf Trois-Bassins** at Ravine Trois-Bassins (tel: 0262 66 02 45) costs around €31.

Other Watersports

Windsurf boards, hobie cats and **glass bottom boats** can be hired at St-Gilles-les-Bains through **Blue Sail** (tel: 0262 33 17 39). **Waterskiers** of all levels can hire equipment from the **Ski Nautique Club de St-Paul** (tel: 0262 45 42 87).

Shopping

You're unlikely to find the bargains in clothing that you can get in Mauritius but Réunion excels in producing original handicrafts. These items are the work of cottage industries throughout the island and end up for sale in many retail outlets. Things to look for are miniature replicas of **creole houses** made from fragranced wood, toiletries and perfumes made from **essential oils** such as citronelle and geranium, and **tentes** or baskets woven from pandanus leaves.

Gourmets may like to shop for a range of local **speciality foods** such as local jams, compôtes, confectionery, spices and **traditional drinks** such as rum, punch and liqueurs, and sweet wine from Cilaos. For something typically Réunionnais call at **Loïk-Olivier's Pâtisserie** at 5 rue de la Plage in St-Gilles-les-Bains and ask to try his renowned *canne en sucre*, a sort of sweetmeat *(see page 176)*, before buying some to take home.

Tourist offices (Syndicats d'Initiative) sell products from the region; look for **Gol chairs** *(see page 212)* at Etang-Salé-les-Bains, **vanilla** products at St-André and **fruity wines** and lentils at Cilaos.

For a full range of **island crafts** in St-Denis, visit **Galerie Artisanale LaCaze** at 10 Place Sarda-Garriga (Barachois) in St-Denis, or **Galerie Artisanale** in Espace Continent supermarket in St-Clotilde near Roland Garros airport.

No visit to Réunion would be complete without a souvenir of the volcano. There's a good range of postcards, decorative pieces of basalt, photographs and illustrated books on volcanology at **Boutique du Volcan** (next door to La Maison du Volcan at Bourg-Murat).

Nuns in Cilaos have been embroidering for over a century. There is now an embroidery school here and many skilled craftswomen who embroider everything from lovely christening robes, to tablecloths and napkins, all in natural white or beige. No two pieces are the same and each piece can take up to several months to produce – hence the price. The best selection can be found at **Maison de la Broderie**, in rue des Ecoles, Cilaos.

Further Reading

Most books written about Réunion are in French but there are several books in English which cover the Mascarenes and include Réunion. These are listed on page 377.

Language

It is worth trying to master a few simple phrases in French before holidaying in Réunion. The fact that you have made an effort is likely to get you a better response. Pronunciation is the key; they really will not understand if you get it very wrong. Remember to **emphasise each syllable**, but not to pronounce the last consonant of a word as a rule (this includes the plural "s") and always to drop your "h"s. Whether to use "**vous**" or "**tu**" is a vexed question; increasingly the familiar form of "tu" is used by many people. However it is better to be too formal, and use "vous" if in doubt. It is very important to be polite; always address people as **Madame** or **Monsieur**, and address them by their surnames until you are confident first names are acceptable. When entering a shop always say, "Bonjour Monsieur/Madame," and "Merci, au revoir," when leaving.

Words & Phrases

How much is it? *C'est combien?*
What is your name? *Comment vous appelez-vous?*
My name is... *Je m'appelle...*
Do you speak English? *Parlez-vous anglais?*
I am English/American *Je suis anglais/américain*
I don't understand *Je ne comprends pas*
Please speak more slowly *Parlez plus lentement, s'il vous plaît*
Can you help me? *Pouvez-vous m'aider?*
I'm looking for... *Je cherche*
Where is...? *Où est...?*
I'm sorry *Excusez-moi/Pardon*
I don't know *Je ne sais pas*
No problem *Pas de problème*

Have a good day! *Bonne journée!*
That's it *C'est ça*
Here it is *Voici*
There it is *Voilà*
Let's go *On y va. Allons-y*
See you tomorrow *A demain*
See you soon *A bientôt*
yes *oui*
no *non*
please *s'il vous plaît*
thank you *merci*
(very much) *(beaucoup)*
you're welcome *de rien*
excuse me *excusez-moi*
hello *bonjour*
OK *d'accord*
goodbye *au revoir*
good evening *bonsoir*
here *ici*
there *là*
today *aujourd'hui*
yesterday *hier*
tomorrow *demain*
now *maintenant*
later *plus tard*
this morning *ce matin*
this afternoon *cet après-midi*
this evening *ce soir*

On Arrival

I want to get off at... *Je voudrais descendre à...*
Is there a bus to...? *Est-ce qui'il ya un bus...?*
How far is...? *A quelle distance se trouve...?*
airport *l'aéroport*
bus station *la gare routière*
bus *l'autobus, le car*
bus stop *l'arrêt*
ticket *le billet*
hitchhiking *l'autostop*
toilets *les toilettes*

The Alphabet

Learning the pronunciation of the French alphabet is a good idea. In particular, learn how to spell out your name.
a=ah, b=bay, c=say, d=day e=er, f=ef, g=zhay, h=ash. i=ee, j=zhee, k=ka, l=el, m=em, n =en, o=oh, p=pay, q=kew, r=ehr, s=ess, t=tay, u=ew, v=vay, w=dooblah vay, x-=eex, y ee grek, z=zed

This is the hotel address *C'est l'adresse de l'hôtel*
I'd like a (single/double) room... *Je voudrais une chambre (pour une/deux personnes) ...*
....with shower *avec douche*
....with a bath *avec salle de bain*
....with a view *avec vue*
Does that include breakfast? *Le prix comprend-il le petit déjeuner?*
May I see the room? *Je peux voir la chambre?*
washbasin *le lavabo*
bed *le lit*
key *la cléf*
lift/elevator *l'ascenseur*
air conditioned *climatisé*

On the Road

Where is the nearest garage? *Où est le garage le plus proche?*
Our car has broken down *Notre voiture est en panne*
the road to... *la route pour...*
left *gauche*
right *droite*
straight on *tout droit*
far *loin*
near *près d'ici*
opposite *en face*
beside *à côté de*
car park *parking*
at the end *au bout*
on foot *à pied*
by car *en voiture*
town map *le plan*
road map *la carte*
street *la rue*
square *la place*
give way *céder le passage*
dead end *impasse*
no parking *stationnement interdit*
petrol *l'essence*
unleaded *sans plomb*
diesel *le gasoil*
water/oil *l'eau/l'huile*
puncture *un pneu crevé*
bulb *l'ampoule*
wipers *les essuies-glace*

Shopping

Where is the nearest bank (post office)? *Où est la banque/Poste la plus proche?*
I'd like to buy *Je voudrais acheter*
How much is it? *C'est combien?*

Emergencies

Help! *Au secours!*
Stop! *Arrêtez!*
Call a doctor *Appelez un médecin*
Call an ambulance *Appelez une ambulance*
Call the police *Appelez la police*
Call the fire brigade *Appelez les pompiers*
Where is the nearest telephone? *Où est le téléphone le plus proche?*
Where is the nearest hospital? *Où est l'hôpital le plus proche?*
I am sick *Je suis malade*
I have lost my passport/purse *J'ai perdu mon passeport/porte-monnaie*

Do you take credit cards? *Est-ce que vous acceptez les cartes de crédit?*
I'm just looking *Je regarde seulement*
Have you got...? *Avez-vous...?*
I'll take it *Je le prends*
I'll take this one/that one *Je prends celui-ci/celui-là*
What size is it? *C'est de quelle taille?*
Anything else? *Avec ça?*
size (clothes) *la taille*
size (shoes) *la pointure*
cheap *bon marché*
expensive *cher*
enough *assez*
too much *trop*
each *la pièce (eg €5 la pièce)*
bill *la note*
chemist *la pharmacie*
bakery *la boulangerie*
bookshop *la librairie*
grocery *l'alimentation/l'épicerie*
tobacconist *tabac*
market *le marché*

Sightseeing

town *la ville*
church *l'église*
town hall *l'hôtel de ville/la mairie*
colonial mansion *grand domaine*
sugar factory *l'usine sucrière*
museum *la musée*
exhibition *l'exposition*
tourist information office *l'office de tourisme/le syndicat d'initiative*
free *gratuit*

open *ouvert*
closed *fermé*
every day *tous les jours*
all year *toute l'année*
all day *toute la journée*

At the Restaurant

Table d'hôte (the "host's table") is one set menu served at a set price. Prix fixe is a fixed-price menu. A la carte means dishes from the menu are chosen and charged separately.
breakfast *le petit déjeuner*
lunch *le déjeuner*
dinner *le dîner*
meal *le repas*
first course *l'entrée/les hors d'oeuvre*
main course *le plat principal*
made to order *sur commande*
drink included *boisson compris*
wine list *la carte des vins*
the bill *l'addition*
fork *la fourchette*
knife *le couteau*
spoon *la cuillère*
plate *l'assiette*
glass *le verre*
napkin *la serviette*
ashtray *le cendrier*

BREAKFAST AND SNACKS

baguette long thin loaf
pain bread
petits pains rolls
beurre butter
poivre pepper
sel salt
sucre sugar
confiture jam
oeufs eggs
...à la coque boiled eggs
...au bacon bacon and eggs
...au jambon ham and eggs
...sur le plat fried eggs
...brouillés scrambled eggs
tartine bread with butter

Non, non, garçon

Garçon is the word for waiter but is never used directly; say *Monsieur* or *Madame* to attract his or her attention.

False Friends

False friends are words that look like English words but mean something different.
le car motorcoach, also railway carriage
le conducteur bus driver
la monnaie change (coins)
l'argent money/silver
ça marche can sometimes mean walk, but is usually used to mean working (the TV, the car etc.) or going well
actuel "present time" *(la situation actuelle* the present situation)
rester to stay
location hiring/renting
personne person or nobody, according to context
le médecin doctor

yaourt yoghurt
crêpe pancake
croque-monsieur ham and cheese toasted sandwich
croque-madame ...with a fried egg on top

MEAT AND FISH

La Viande Meat
bleu rare
à point medium
bien cuit well done
grillé grilled
agneau lamb
bifteck steak
canard duck
entrecôte beef rib steak
farci stuffed
faux-filet sirloin
feuilleté puff pastry
grillade grilled meat
jambon ham
lapin rabbit
lardon small pieces of bacon, often added to salads
magret de canard breast of duck
médaillon round meat
porc pork
poulet chicken
poussin young chicken
rognons kidneys
rôti roast
saucisse fresh sausage
saucisson salami

Poissons Fish
anchois anchovies
calmars squid
coquillage shellfish
crevette prawn, shrimp
fruits de mer seafood
homard lobster
langouste crayfish
langoustine large prawn
thon tuna

FRUIT & VEGETABLES

ananas pineapple
banane banana
citron lemon
citron vert lime
fruit fruit
fruit de la passion passion fruit
goyane guava
grenaclelle passionfruit
mangue mango
noix de coco coconut
pamplemousse grapefruit
pêche peach
poire pear
pomme apple
raisin grape
ail garlic
avocat avocado
carotte carrot
cassava manioc
chips potato crisps
chou cabbage
chou chou christophine
concombre cucumber
cru raw

Table Talk

I am a vegetarian *Je suis végétarien*
I am on a diet *Je suis au régime*
What do you recommend? *Que'est-ce que vous recommandez?*
Do you have local specialities? *Avez-vous des spécialités locales?*
I'd like to order *Je voudrais commander*
That is not what I ordered *Ce n'est pas ce que j'ai commandé*
Is service included? *Est-ce que le service est compris?*
May I have more wine? *Encore du vin, s'il vous plaît?*
Enjoy your meal *Bon appétit!*

crudités **raw vegetables**
frites **chips, French fries**
haricots **beans (red or white)**
légumes **vegetables**
lentilles **lentils**
oignon **onion**
patate douce **sweet potato**
petit pois **peas**
piments **chillies**
pomme de terre **potato**
riz **rice**
salade verte **green salad**
tomate **tomato**

In the Café

If you sit at the bar, drinks will be cheaper than at a table. Settle the bill when you leave; the waiter may leave a slip of paper on the table to keep track of the bill.
drinks les boissons
coffee café

...with milk or cream au lait or crème
...decaffeinated déca/décaféiné
...black/espresso express/noir
...American filtered coffee filtre
tea thé
...herb infusion tisane
hot chocolate chocolat chaud
milk lait
mineral water eau minérale
fizzy gazeux
non-fizzy non-gazeux
fizzy lemonade limonade
fresh lemon juice served with sugar citron pressée
full (eg full cream milk) entier
fresh or cold frais, fraîche
beer bière
...bottled en bouteille
...on tap à la pression
orange juice jus d'orange
white wine with cassis, blackcurrant liqueur kir

Numbers, Days and Months

Numbers

0	zéro	101	cent et un
1	un, une	110	cent dix
2	deux	1000	mille
3	trois	1000,000	un million
4	quatre		
5	cinq		Note that the number 1 is
6	six		often written as an upside down
7	sept		V and the number 7 is usually
8	huit		crossed
9	neuf		
10	dix		

Days

Monday lundi
Tuesday mardi
Wednesday mercredi
Thursday jeudi
Friday vendredi
Saturday samedi
Sunday dimanche

Months

January janvier
February février
March mars
April avril
May mai
June juin
July juillet
August août
September septembre
October octobre
November novembre
December décembre

11	onze
12	douze
13	treize
14	quatorze
15	quinze
16	seize
17	dix-sept
18	dix-huit
19	dix-neuf
20	vingt
21	vingt et un
22	vingt-deux
30	trente
40	quarante
50	cinquante
60	soixante
70	soixante-dix
80	quatre-vingts
90	quatre-vingt-dix
100	cent

Time

At what time? A quelle heure?
When? Quand?
What time is it? Quelle heure est-il?
● Note that the French generally use the 24-hour clock.

kir with champagne kir royale
with ice avec des glaçons
red rouge
white blanc
rose rosé
dry brut
sweet doux
sparkling wine crémant
house wine vin de maison
local wine vin de pays
pitcher carafe/pichet
...of water/wine d'eau/de vin
half litre demi-carafe
quarter litre quart
mixed panaché
after dinner drink digestif
cheers! santé!
hangover gueule de bois

On the Telephone

How do I make an outside call? Comment est-ce que je peux téléphoner à l'exterieur?
I want to make an international (local) call Je voudrais une communication pour l'étranger (une communication locale)
What is the dialling code? Quel est l'indicatif?
I'd like an alarm call for 8 tomorrow morning. Je voudrais être réveillé à huit heures demain martin
Who's calling? C'est qui à l'appareil?
Hold on, please Ne quittez pas s'il vous plaît
The line is busy La ligne est occupée
I must have dialled the wrong number J'ai dû faire un faux numéro

Seasons

spring le printemps
summer l'été
autumn l'automne
winter l'hiver

Seychelles

The Place

Area: The islands of Seychelles cover a land area of 455 sq km (176 sq miles), spread over an Exclusive Economic Zone of 1,340,000 sq km (517,000 sq miles).
Situation: The main populated islands of Mahé, Praslin and La Digue lie approximately 1,600 km (1,000 miles) east of Africa and 1,600 km (1,000 miles) northeast of Madagascar. The archipelago lies between latitude 4° south and 10° south and between longitude 46° east and 54° east.
Capital: Victoria on Mahé.
Population: Around 81,000, of whom 72,000 live on Mahé, 6,000 on Praslin, 2,000 on La Digue, 135 on Silhouette and very small numbers on other islands, most of which are uninhabited.
Language: Kreol, English and French are all official languages. All Seychellois speak Kreol – a Kreol Institute has been established to support the language *(see page 375)* – and English is understood by most, especially the young and especially on Mahé. The English-speaking visitor will have no difficulty in communicating in English in hotels, shops and offices. A few words of Kreol can be useful away from tourist sites, particularly when talking to older Seychellois *(see pages 375–77 for some useful words and phrases).*
Religion: Most Seychellois profess to be Roman Catholics, albeit with a relaxed attitude to some of the rules. The vast majority of regular churchgoers are women dressed in their Sunday best. The second largest Christian denomination is the Anglican Church. There are also communities of Seventh Day Adventists, Pentecostal Assembly Church, Hindus, Muslims and Bahais.
Currency: Seychelles rupee (SR), divided into 100 cents.
Weights and measures: The metric system is used in Seychelles. *(See page 354 for conversions).*
Electricity: 240 volts using three square-pin sockets, same as UK.
Time zone: Seychelles is four hours ahead of Greenwich Mean Time and three hours ahead of British Summer Time. The sun shines for approximately 12 hours a day – sunrise is between 6 and 6.30am and sunset between 6 and 6.30pm.
International dialling code: To call Seychelles from abroad dial the international access code followed by 248 then the number you want (there are no area codes in Seychelles). To call overseas from Seychelles the international access code is 00.

Climate

There are no seasons equivalent to winter, spring or autumn. The climate is tropical: hot and humid year round with temperatures in the region of 24°–30°C (75°–86°F), fluctuating very little from one month to the next or during the day. Rainfall is high, with heavy showers possible at any time of year, particularly during the northwest monsoon from November to April, reaching a peak from mid-December to the end of January. Humidity is highest from March to April.

Rainfall and humidity are lowest during the southeast monsoon from May to October. This season brings stronger, more consistent winds producing heavy swells at sea particularly at its peak from July to September. Unpleasant for those without a strong stomach at sea, but the cooling breeze and lower rainfall makes this the best time for walking.

Rainfall on coral islands is much lower than on the granitic islands due to the influence of relief. In the southern islands, there is a marked seasonal drought (September to October rainfall on Aldabra averages just 17 mm/¾ in compared to 300 mm/12 in on Mahé).

The islands lie outside the cyclone belt that brings turbulent conditions to the south from January to March. However, strong winds and heavy rain around this time often indicate a cyclone further south and, very occasionally, one may reach the southernmost islands of Seychelles.

Geography

A figure of 115 islands is often quoted as the number of islands in Seychelles. However, the Constitution of Seychelles lists 155. These can be divided into five main groups, the granitic islands, the Amirantes, the Alphonse Group, the Farquhar Group and the Aldabra Group.

The 40 **granitic islands** are the world's only oceanic islands of continental rock. They occupy the shallow waters of the submerged Seychelles Bank. The granite rocks have been dated from about 750 million years ago. Included in this group are **Silhouette** and **North Island,** both of similar physical appearance though they are built from much younger syenite, dated from around 63 million years ago. Two coral cays, **Bird** and **Denis,** lie on the northern rim of the Seychelles Bank. All these islands are sometimes grouped together and called **Central Seychelles.** They are not central geographically but are certainly central in terms of human importance, being home to all but a few Seychellois.

The coral islands of the Amirantes, Alphonse Group, Farquhar Group and Aldabra Group are known collectively as the **Outer Islands,** due to their isolation from the main population centres of the granitics. The **Amirantes** chain of 26 islands and the **Alphonse Group** of three islands lie to the southwest of the granitic islands. The Amirantes islands lie on a shallow bank that varies in depth from about 11 metres (36 ft) near the rim to 70 metres (230 ft) in the centre. A deep channel separates this bank from the Alphonse Group but the islands are otherwise similar in origin and appearance and more conveniently grouped together as a linear chain.

South of the Alphonse Group, the next point of land, Providence, in the **Farquhar Group** lies 300 km (188 miles) southwest of St François. The group of 13 islands comprises **Providence Atoll** (with two islands), **Farquhar Atoll** (10 islands) and the raised coral platform island of **St Pierre**.

The **Aldabra Group** of raised coral islands lie due west of Farquhar Atoll. The group is made up of one platform island, **Assumption** and three atolls, **Astove** (with just one island), **Cosmoledo** (19 islands) and **Aldabra** (46 islands) giving a total of 67 islands in the group.

Two isolated coral islands south of the granitics, **Coetivy** and **Platte**, do not fit into any of the major groupings.

Government

Seychelles is a republic with a democratically elected president and National Assembly. The president appoints an unelected cabinet of ministers. Legislation is framed by the cabinet and presented to the National Assembly for approval.

Three main political parties are represented in the National Assembly, the **Seychelles People's Progressive Front (SPPF)**, **Democratic Party (DP)** and **Seychelles National Party (SNP)**, members being elected mainly in a first past the post system with a top-up system based on proportional representation. Elections for both president and the National Assembly take place roughly every five years.

Economy

Tourism is the mainstay of the Seychelles economy, although commercial fishing has been rapidly catching up in recent years. During

Business Hours

● **Office hours:** Mon–Fri 8am–4pm.
● **Shops:** Victoria: 8.30 or 9am–5 or 5.30pm and on Sat 8.30am–12.30pm. Some shops will close for lunch 12.30am–1.30pm. Elsewhere, small shops are likely to remain open much longer hours.
● **Banks:** Victoria: Mon–Fri 8.30am–2.30pm, Sat 8.30–11am, closed Sun. Praslin: 8.30am–1.30pm, Sat 8.30–11am, closed Sun. La Digue: Barclays Bank opens only on Mondays, Wednesdays and Fridays 10.30am–2pm.

the latter half of the 1990s, after a decade of growth, the number of visitors to Seychelles levelled off at around 130,000 per year. During the same period, foreign exchange earnings from fishing more than quadrupled, most of the increase being attributable to the expansion of tuna canning on Mahé. The waters of Seychelles are rich fishing grounds and Port Victoria is the principal transhipment port of the Indian Ocean.

All this is in marked contrast to the era prior to the opening of Seychelles International Airport, which ushered in the era of tourism in 1972 and provided the commercial links on which the fishing industry also depends. A small amount of cinnamon bark is still exported – it was once a main export along with copra – but otherwise, Seychelles is no longer an agricultural producer of any significance.

On Praslin and La Digue, other than those self-employed as fishermen or farmers, the main employment is connected to the tourism industry. Tourism has been kind to Seychelles and raised income to levels equivalent to a middle income country. Health and education are free. Levels of literacy and infant mortality rates are equivalent to Western standards.

However, the Seychelles economy

has been plagued by a shortage of foreign exchange. The government has introduced increasingly tight controls in an attempt to balance the books. Up until the 1990s this was never a problem, in part due to a Cold War dividend in the form of direct aid from both East and West. The super powers attempted to court Seychelles because of the strategic position of the islands beneath political hotspots in the Middle East and Asia and because, despite the tiny size of the country, they still had an all-important vote at institutions such as the United Nations. When the Soviet Union dissolved, Russia could no longer afford the handouts. The West had other priorities and Seychellois were simply too well off to merit much attention. The US Embassy closed its doors as did a US satellite tracking station, which has now been dismantled. Millions of dollars of income were lost overnight. Seychelles was on its own.

In truth many of the problems of the economy are home grown. Private companies complain of the restrictions placed upon them and point to the size of the public sector in such a small country. The speed with which fiscal measures are introduced, tinkered with, withdrawn and then introduced in another form have been blamed for an uncertainty that has made potential investors nervous. Above all, foreign investors have hesitated to put money in when there is doubt surrounding the prospects of obtaining a return in foreign exchange. The government has run substantial budget deficits and shown a propensity to invest in ambitious capital projects that produce little or no real revenue. After the years of plenty, belt tightening has proved a difficult concept to swallow.

Yet some innovative measures have produced hope that the country will find its way out of the mire one day. An offshore sector has attracted considerable interest. An Investment Promotion Act has been introduced extending guaranteed incentives to new companies generating foreign exchange. There is a willingness to forge partnerships with the private sector. Tourism is likely to remain in the top spot with an increased emphasis on high quality and high returns with other sectors playing substantial supporting roles. Seychelles as a place to do business has a lot going for it.

Public Holidays

January 1/2 New Year's Day
March/April Good Friday, Easter Monday
May 1 Labour Day
June Corpus Christi (Thursday after Trinity Sunday), Liberation Day (5), National Day (18), Independence Day (29)
August 15 Assumption/La Digue Festival
November 1 All Saints Day
December Immaculate Conception (8), Christmas Day (25)

Planning the Trip

Passport & Visas

No visas are necessary for visitors from any country, only a valid passport and a return air ticket. A Visitors' Permit is issued on arrival. This is the tear-off portion of the arrivals card distributed on international flights prior to landing. It should be retained and presented along with your passport upon departure. Valid for 30 days, the Visitors' Permit may be extended for up to three months at no charge by completing an application form available from **Immigration Division**, First Floor, Independence House, Victoria. Processing takes about one week. A fee is payable for extensions beyond three months.

Health & Insurance

Seychelles has a healthy climate. No vaccinations are essential though some doctors, erring on the side of caution, will recommend typhoid and polio injections. There is no yellow fever or malaria in Seychelles. The cabins of all flights to Seychelles are sprayed prior to landing to keep such diseases out. If arriving from a country where yellow fever occurs, such as Kenya, you will be required to produce a certificate of vaccination on arrival.

Money Matters

The **Seychelles rupee** comes in notes of SR100, SR50, SR25 and SR10. Be careful with SR50 and SR10 notes which are similar in colour and sometimes muddled. Coins come in denominations of SR5, SR1, 25 cents, 10 cents and 5 cents. Prices in shops may be in

amounts that do not end in units of 5 cents and unless paying by credit card will be rounded up or down in your change (usually up!).

In 2003, the exchange rate was roughly SR5.40 to US$1.

Credit cards are accepted at hotels, many guest houses and the larger restaurants. Visa and Mastercard are most commonly accepted. Diners Club and American Express are also accepted at many locations.

Changing **foreign currency** on the black market is illegal. To change rupees back into foreign exchange, it is essential to retain bank receipts. You will get a higher rate of exchange for travellers' cheques than for currency and better at banks than at hotels. The **Saymore Bureau de Change** situated by the customs exit offers the most competitive rate of exchange.

TAX

There is no hotel and restaurant tax but a trades tax is applied to almost all goods which is non-refundable. Only at the **duty free shop** in Victoria and at **Seychelles International Airport** are goods exempt of trades tax.

Customs

Visitors are allowed to import free of tax two litres of alcohol, 200 cigarettes or 250 g of tobacco, 125 cc of perfume and 250 cc of eau de toilette. The importation of fruit, seeds, vegetables and meat products is strictly prohibited. Spear fishing equipment and firearms are also prohibited. Penalties for possession of drugs are severe.

What to Bring

Lightweight cotton clothes are standard; waterproof kagoul or umbrella; plastic sandals to protect against spiny sea urchins and broken coral washed up on the water's edge; walking shoes for forests and nature trails; sunglasses, sun hat, high factor sun protection lotion.

Some hotels require men to wear long trousers in their restaurants in the evening. Otherwise, dress is casual. With very few exceptions, no one wears a tie in Seychelles from the president downwards. It is too hot even at night for a jacket. A good pair of binoculars for birdwatching will be useful, as will a torch as power cuts are possible.

Etiquette

Seychellois do not like to see scantily clad visitors walking around their towns and villages. Dress respectfully in churches and other holy places. Be sensitive about photographing the local people. It's always polite to ask first. Sunbathing topless is acceptable on the beaches.

Tourist Offices

For information before you go on every aspect of Seychelles, contact the **Seychelles Tourist Office** in your home country:
UK: 36 Southwark Bridge Road, London SE1 9EU, tel: 020 7202 6363; fax: 020 7928 0722; e-mail: seychelles@hillsbalfour.com
France: Economic and Commercial Section, Seychelles Embassy, 51 avenue Mozar, 75016, Paris; tel: 00331 42 30 02 67; fax: 00331 42 30 02 68; e-mail: stoparis@worldnet.fr
Ireland: Luxury Destinations, Plunkett Chambers, 21–23 Oliver Plunkett Street, Cork, tel: 21 4 32 23 44; fax: 21 4 27 20 99; e-mail: luxdest@indigo.ie
South Africa: 480 Cork Avenue, Ferndale 2194; tel: 00 27 11 791 0300; fax: 00 27 11 791 0052. e-mail: sto.seychelles@intekom.eo.zq
There are also offices in Dubai, Germany, India, Italy, Kenya, Spain, Sweden and Switzerland.

Useful Websites

www.aspureasitgets.com
www.kokonet.sc
www.nation.sc
www.sey.net
www.seychelles.net
www.airseychelles.com
www.virtualseychelles.sc

Best Times to Go

● **For diving:** March to May; September to November – best sea conditions, clear and calm, although diving is good all year.
● **For birdwatching:** April – start of the breeding season; May to September – sooty terns nest on Bird island; October – migration begins.
● **For hiking:** May to September – drier and less humid.
● **For surfing/windsurfing:** June to September – when the strong southeast trade winds blow.
● **For fishing:** October to April when the gentle northwest trades blow. But for those with good sea legs, fish are plentiful all year round.
● **For sailing:** all year round.

MAPS

Excellent maps are available for every island from the Survey Division, Ground Floor, Independence House, Independence Avenue, Victoria, Mahé.

Photography

Films, film processing and camera equipment are available in Victoria from Photo Eden (Kodak) and Kim Koon (Fuji) both in Independence Avenue. Many hotel shops also stock films. *(See page 360 for some photography tips.)* However, film is often expensive, and developing and printing is sometimes of poor quality in Seychelles.

Getting There

Aeroflot, Air France, Air Seychelles, British Airways, Condor and Kenya Airways all fly to the Seychelles. **Air Austral** (tel: 00 33 1 41 92 01 30; fax: 00 33 1 41 92 01 37), based in France, offers an **Indian Ocean Air Pass**, allowing flexible travel between Nairobi, the Comores, Madagascar, Seychelles, Réunion and Mauritius. All international flights arrive at **Seychelles International Airport**, Mahé. The

Domestic Terminal north of the international departure terminal, serves Air Seychelles' and IDC flights *(see box below)*.
It is essential to reconfirm your return flight at least 72 hours prior to departure. **Airport tax:** US$50 tax is payable (SR250 for residents of Seychelles) on departure. This may be paid in advance through your tour operator or from a bank at the airport at check-in time. The banks are situated to the right as you face the check-in desks. These counters may not open as early as the check-in counters but it is fine to check in first, the tax receipt being presentable upon proceeding to the departure lounge.

Airline contacts
Aeroflot: tel: 225005; fax: 224170
Air Austral: tel: 323262; fax: 323223
Air France: tel: 322414; fax: 224960
Air India: tel: 322414; fax: 321366
Air Mauritius: tel: 322414; fax: 323951
Air Seychelles: tel: 381000; fax: 224305
Alitalia: tel: 288888; fax: 225273
British Airways: tel: 224910; fax: 225596
Kenya Airways: tel: 322536; fax: 322989
Lufthansa: tel: 224907

Inter-island Flights

The small Air Seychelles planes make regular trips throughout the day from the Domestic Terminal on Mahé to Praslin, and operate a single flight daily to Bird and Denis (chartered by the hotels on these islands through which bookings must be made). IDC operate scheduled flights most days to Alphonse and Desroches plus charter flights to other outer islands:

● Mahé – Praslin	15 mins
● Mahé – Bird	25 mins
● Mahé – Denis	25 mins
● Mahé – Frégate	15 mins
● Mahé – Alphonse	1 hour
● Mahé – Desroches	50 mins

Practical Tips

Package tour operators

Many tour operators in Europe, South Africa, Australia, Canada and the US offer package and specialist holidays to Seychelles, such as diving, birdwatching or weddings *(see* Indian Ocean Weddings *box on page 357).*

The following UK-based operators specialise in Seychelles:

Aardvark Safaris Ltd: (island hopping combined with an African Safari); tel: 01980 849160

Abercrombie & Kent Ltd: (tailor-made luxury travel); tel: 0845 0700610

Aquatours Ltd (diving holidays): tel: 020 8398 0505

Cox & Kings Ltd: (upmarket travel); tel: 020 7873 5000

Cresta Yachts Ltd (sailing holidays): tel: 020 7730 9962

Elite Vacations Ltd: tel: 020 8864 4431

Frontiers International Ltd: (fly-fishing) tel: 020 7493 0798

Hayes & Jarvis Ltd: tel: 0870 898 9890

Indian Ocean Connections: tel: 01244 355502 (brochure line); 01244 3555320 (reservations)

Island Holidays (birdwatching): tel: 0800 253 534/01764 670107

Jarvis Seychelles: (tailor-made travel); tel: 01492 53 2222

Just Seychelles Ltd: tel: 020 7240 8595

Kuoni Travel: tel: 01306 740888

Naturetrek: (wildlife); tel: 01962 733051

Planit World Travel: tel: 08705 133606/01293 596603

Seychelles European Reservations: tel: 0208 7512156

Seychelles Experience: tel: 01202 419219

Seychelles Travel: tel: 01202 877330

Sunset Faraway Holidays: tel: 020 7498 9922

Tropical Locations: tel: 020 7724 6644

Tropical Places: tel: 0870 1664915

Worldwide Journeys and Expeditions: (tailor-made and special interest); tel: 020 7386 4646

Media

TV AND RADIO

Radio Seychelles, owned by the government, and the private station Paradise FM are the only exclusively local radio stations. There is a BBC relay station on Mahé and BBC World Service broadcasts are transmitted on 102.6 FM, receivable over much of Mahé and nearby islands.

The only terrestrial TV station is Seychelles Broadcasting Corporation (SBC), which shows CNN and BBC news programmes in the mornings. The more upmarket hotels offer satellite television and a variety of channels as well as in-house video films.

In the Outer Islands, no local radio or TV broadcasts can be received, but some satellite TV channels are received at hotels.

PUBLICATIONS

The government-owned *Seychelles Nation* is published daily except Sundays with articles in English, French and Kreol. It has the latest cinema, TV and radio listings. The independent newspaper *Regar*, published weekly on Thursday, offers an alternative view of life in Seychelles and is mainly in English.

British Sunday newspapers and many international magazines may be purchased at **Antigone Trading** in Passage des Palmes, Victoria. The papers are usually on the shelves by Monday afternoon.

Silhouette, the in-flight magazine of Air Seychelles, carries excellent features on the islands. Other local magazines are *New Wave* (which also covers Mauritius and Réunion) and *Seychelles Today*.

Postal Services

The main post office in Victoria is on Independence Avenue next to the clock tower (open Mon–Fri 8.30am–4pm and Sat 8.30am–noon). There are sub-post offices at Grand Anse on Praslin and La Passe on La Digue. Public postboxes are situated outside most police stations. Hotels will sell stamps and post your mail. Airmail collections are made at 3pm Mon–Fri and at noon on Sat.

Telecommunications

International calls can be made from **Cable & Wireless** offices at Mercury House, Francis Rachel Street, Victoria (Mon–Sat 7am–9pm). Telex and fax services are also provided. Calls can be made from hotels, though surcharges are high. Most payphones take only phonecards obtainable from Cable & Wireless. Some of the remoter islands without phone lines are setting up satellite phone links.

Local Tourist Offices

The Seychelles Tourism Marketing Authority has its head office at Bel Ombre Road, Bel Ombre, Mahé (Mon–Fri 9am–5pm; tel: 620000; fax: 620620; e-mail: seychelles@ aspureasitgets.com). There are also information offices on Mahé, Praslin and La Digue, from which many brochures and leaflets are available.

Mahé: Independence House, Victoria (Mon–Fri 8am–5pm, Sat 9am–noon;

tel: 620801; e-mail: info@aspureasitgets.com)

Praslin: Praslin Airport, Amitié (Mon–Fri 8am–5pm, Sat 8am–3pm, Sunday and Public Holidays 8am–1pm;

tel: 233571, e-mail: praslin@seychelles.sc)

La Digue: La Passe (Mon–Fri

8am–5pm, Sat 9am–noon and 3pm–5pm, Sunday and public holidays 9am–noon; tel: 234393; e-mail:info@aspureasitgets.com

Local tour operators

7°South: Kingsgate House, Victoria; tel: 322682; fax: 321322; e-mail: 7south@seychelles.net; www.7south.net
Creole Holidays: Kingsgate House, Victoria; tel: 224900; fax: 225817; e-mail: info@creoleholidays.sc
Masons Travel: Michel Building, Victoria; tel: 322642; fax: 324173; e-mail: masons@seychelles.net; www.masonstravel.com
Premier Holidays: Premier Building, Victoria; tel: 225777; fax: 225888; e-mail: premier@seychelles.net
Travel Services Seychelles (TSS): Mahé Trading Building, Victoria; tel: 322414; fax: 322401 e-mail: tss@tss.sc; www.tss.sc

Embassies & Consulates

● **British High Commission**, Oliaji Trade Centre, Victoria; tel: 225225
● **French Embassy**, Victoria House, Victoria; tel: 382500
● **United States Consulate**, Victoria House, Victoria; tel: 225256.

Business Travellers

Short-sleeved shirt and trousers are standard wear for businessmen. There is no need for a jacket or tie, both impractical in the tropical climate. Appointment times may be taken with a pinch of salt. In particular, being kept waiting for a meeting with any government official may be taken as the norm.

Travelling with Kids

Seychellois love children and Seychelles is a very safe place for a family holiday. There is no problem taking well-behaved children into any restaurant in Seychelles. However, parents should note there are few amusements for children

away from the beach. The larger hotels offer a baby-sitting service, though it is usually necessary to give a little notice.

Travellers with Disabilities

Most of the larger hotels are geared to accommodate wheelchairs but away from these there are few special facilities. It is very difficult to get around Victoria by wheelchair due to the narrowness of the busy pavements.

Medical Treatment

Essential healthcare services are free of charge to Seychelles residents while for visitors a small charge is made. There are a large number of local clinics, particularly on Mahé, that visitors may attend though the waiting time can be frustratingly lengthy. This is particularly true on a Monday morning when the start of the working week coincides with a remarkable peak in illnesses. Treatment at clinics is usually basic.

For those who prefer to spend much of the day somewhere other than sitting on a wooden bench in a waiting room, private doctors are very good and not expensive. On Mahé there is a **tourist doctor** on call 24 hours, who will visit you at your hotel (tel: 515657) if necessary, otherwise normal consultation hours are 8am–4pm. A small fee will be charged. It is possible to call in to see a private doctor without an appointment, but a phone call may save waiting time.

HOSPITALS

Victoria Hospital: Mont Fleuri, Mahé; tel: 388000
Anse Royale Hospital: Anse Royale, Mahé; tel: 371222
Praslin Hospital: tel: 232333
Logan Hospital: La Digue; tel: 224255
Silhouette Hospital: Silhouette; tel: 224110

PRIVATE TREATMENT

Dr Chetty: Quincy Street, Victoria; tel: 321911 or Le Niol, Mahé; tel: 266670. Open Mon–Fri 8am–1pm and 2.30pm–5pm, Sat 8am–noon, closed Sun. Grand Anse Clinic: tel: 233633
Le Chantier Medical Services: Le Chantier, Victoria; tel: 324008. Open Mon–Fri 8am–1pm and 2pm–5pm, Sat 8am–noon, closed Sun.
Le Chantier Dental Clinic: as above; tel: 224354. Open Mon–Fri 8am–4pm; closed Sat and Sun.
Dr Albert Maurice: Le Chantier, Mahé; tel: 323866. Open Mon–Fri 7.30am–4pm, closed Sat and Sun.
Oceangate Dental Clinic: Dr Derick Samsoodin, Oceangate House, Victoria, tel: 224852

PHARMACIES

Behram's Pharmacy: Victoria Arcade, Victoria; tel: 225559
Le Chantier: as above; tel: 224093 There are no pharmacies on Praslin, so go to the hospital dispensary.

Emergencies

Police, fire, ambulance: tel: 999

Tipping

Tipping is not essential, but is always appreciated at 5–10 percent of the bill. Often, a service charge is included in restaurant bills.

Security & Crime

Seychelles is very safe, though crime is not unknown. Some visitors are lulled into a false sense of security by the friendliness of the locals. They make the mistake of leaving their valuables unguarded on the beach while taking a swim, with inevitable consequences. Take the same precautions that you would at home to prevent your holiday being spoiled.

Getting Around

Most of the granitic islands may be visited from bases on either Mahé or Praslin. Mahé is the base for trips to islands of Ste Anne Marine National Park, Silhouette, North and Thérèse. Praslin is the base for trips to Aride, Cousin, St Pierre and Curieuse. Either Praslin or La Digue may be used as a base for visits to Petit Soeur, Grand Soeur, Marianne and Cocos. La Digue may be visited on a day trip from Praslin but a longer stay is preferable to enjoy the atmosphere of the island. To visit Bird, Denis and any of the Outer Islands requires overnight accommodation.

By Air

Air Seychelles (tel: 381000) offers internal flights to Praslin throughout the day. The same planes are chartered to the resorts of Frégate Island, Bird Island and Denis Island for guests and staff (no day trips by air are possible). **Islands Development Company (IDC)** (tel: 224640; fax: 224467) also operates planes to Desroches and Alphonse for the resorts of these islands. IDC planes may be chartered to other islands where airstrips exist. There are no facilities on planes and no in-flight services.

BY HELICOPTER

Helicopter Seychelles (tel: 373900; fax: 373055) offers flights between helistops on Mahé (Domestic Terminal, Victoria Inter-Island Quay and Plantation Club), Praslin (Amitie airfield, Lemuria Resort), La Digue (L'Union Estate), Denis Island, Félicité Island,

Frégate Island, Silhouette Island and North Island. Helicopters accommodate a pilot and four passengers. Children over the age of two require their own seat by law. Passengers should avoid taking more than 10 kilos (22 lb) of baggage without prior consultation.

By Sea

Ferries operate between Mahé, from **Inter-Island Quay**, Victoria, Praslin (Baie Ste Anne) and La Digue (La Passe jetty). Between Mahé and Praslin there is a choice between a fast catamaran, *Cat Cocos*, operating daily and taking one hour, or a more leisurely local **schooner** taking three hours. *Cat Cocos*, an Australian-built 25-metre (82-ft) high-tech vessel, has an upper deck Club Lounge for 34 passengers and a main cabin for 125, both air-conditioned. There is also an exterior sun deck and a bar and snack service available. It is advisable to book, particularly at weekends when there is considerable local traffic: **Mahé** – tel: 324843; **Praslin** – tel: 233438; **La Digue** – tel: 234411.

Schooners between Mahé and Praslin or La Digue only operate from Mon–Fri. They are geared more towards the carriage of cargo than passenger comfort, but they are the cheapest form of travel. Schooner departure times and prices are posted at the notice board of **Le Marinier Restaurant** on Mahé's Inter-Island Quay.

Ferries are the main form of transport between Praslin and La Digue and they operate daily. Departures from Praslin at 7am, 9am, 10am, 11am, 2.30pm, 4pm and 5.15pm and from La Digue at 7.30am, 9.30am, 10.30am, noon, 3pm, 4.30pm and 5.45pm. It is essential to book seats in advance (tel: 233229).

BY YACHT OR MOTORBOAT

Day trips or trips of several days on a yacht or motorboat can be arranged to most islands. Contact

Marine Charter Association (tel: 322126) or a local tour operator *(see page 400)* for a tailor-made excursion.

By Bus

Buses are cheap and reasonably good but times and routes are geared to local requirements, not tourists. On Mahé, if travelling at peak periods you may have to stand and at other times, particularly weekends and public holidays, you may have a long wait at bus stops. Buses are less frequent on Praslin. On La Digue buses take the form of open-sided covered lorries *(camions)* that roam the island with no fixed timetable. Elsewhere there are no buses. Buses on Mahé operate mainly between 5.30am and 8pm and on Praslin between 6am and 6.30pm.

By Taxi

There are plenty of metered taxis available on Mahé but not so many in Praslin. It is often necessary to ask the driver to turn on the meter to avoid any argument over the fare at your destination. If the meter is broken (often the case) a fare should be agreed in advance. On Mahé taxis can be found at the airport, Victoria taxi rank in Albert Street (next to Camion Hall) and by the clock tower in Independence Avenue. Your hotel will also organise one for you.

Taxi drivers can often make very good, amusing and informative guides to the islands and can be hired by the hour or day for negotiable rates, which you must agree on before setting off. On La Digue most people get around on bicycles (ask at your hotel); there are only two unmetered motorised taxis, and many more ox-carts, which pass for taxis. They may be encountered driving up and down at La Passe or at the jetty when a ferry arrives from Praslin. None of the other islands has taxis.

Driving

In common with other former British colonies, cars drive on the left in Seychelles. Standards of driving are not high. Drivers tend to roam onto the wrong side of the road with alarming frequency, veering to the left only when absolutely essential. Tourists unfamiliar with driving on the left sometimes forget which country they are in and create added confusion.

The absence of pavements and the narrowness of roads mean that pedestrians are often added obstacles, particularly at weekends and public holidays when the drink has flowed a little too freely. The rush hour around Victoria should be avoided if possible (either side of 8am and 4pm). None of this should deter you from taking to the road, however – certainly the best way to explore both Mahé and Praslin.

Roads on Mahé are very good. Praslin roads are good between Grand Anse, Baie Ste Anne and Anse Volbert, but deteriorate en route to Anse La Blague and Anse Lazio.

Speed limits are 40 kph (25 mph) in towns and villages and 65 kph (40 mph) elsewhere, except for Mahé's east coast road where the limit is 80 kph (50 mph).

CAR HIRE

Cars may be hired only on Mahé and Praslin and several car hire companies are represented at Seychelles International Airport and at the larger hotels. You can arrange to hire a car before you leave home through your tour operator. A national licence is required, though an international licence is also acceptable if you have one. Vehicle standards are variable and, whenever possible, it is useful to inspect prior to making a commitment. Vehicles can be delivered or re-delivered to any point, mutually agreed with the hire company. Mini mokes are commonly used. These are

open-sided, which can be a disadvantage in wet weather and also means that not all valuables may be locked away safely. Jeeps and saloon cars are widely available from most car hire firms.

Service stations
Victoria Service Station, Mahé: open daily 5.30am–11pm
Airport Service Station, Mahé: open daily 6am–9pm
Anse Royale Filling Station, Mahé: open daily 7am–6.30pm
Baie Lazare Petrol Station, Mahé: open Mon–Sat 7am–7pm, Sun and public holidays 7am–noon
Beau Vallon Service Station, Mahé: open daily 6am–9pm
Baie Ste Anne Filling Station, Praslin: open daily 7am–6pm
Grand Anse Service Station, Praslin: open Mon–Sat 7.30am–6pm, Sun and public holidays 7.30am–noon

---

PARKING

Parking is free in Seychelles except in the centre of Victoria. Even here, there is a free car park on Francis Rachel Street next to the sports stadium, convenient for most requirements. To park on other Victoria streets and car parks requires advance purchase of parking coupons, available through most retail outlets. Traffic police have little to do in Victoria and failure to observe the rules where payment is required will almost invariably lead to a fine.

Where to Stay

Choosing a Hotel

Hotels are generally small and exclusive in Seychelles, so prices are usually high and you get a better deal with a package. But they are in beautiful spots and often provide bungalow accommodation. Some establishments offer self-catering accommodation with a restaurant as an option and there are a growing number of guest houses. Contact the **Seychelles Tourism Marketing Authority** (tel: 620000; fax: 620620; e-mail: seychelle@ aspureasitgets.com) for a list. Supplements may be applied during the peak seasons at Easter, Christmas and New Year and August. There is no service charge or tax but to ensure the flow of foreign exchange, visitors are required to pay their hotel accounts in some form of foreign currency, usually by credit card, but cash and travellers' cheques are also acceptable. No camping is permitted in Seychelles.

Hotel Listings

MAHÉ

Beau Vallon
Beau Vallon Bay Beach Resort
tel: 247141; fax: 247943; e-mail: bhrsem@seychelles.net; www.seychelles.net/berjaya
One of the larger Berjaya hotels with good facilities including dive centre, watersports, tennis court and casino. Separate restaurants offer pizzas and snacks, plus Chinese, Japanese and international cuisine. **$$**
Coral Strand
tel: 621000; fax: 247517; email: coralres@seychelles.net
A dependable, friendly hotel on

Beau Vallon beach. Well located for various activities including watersports, glass bottom boat, game fishing and diving. **$$**

Fisherman's Cove
tel: 247247; fax: 247742;
e-mail: fishres@seychelles.net;
www.lemeridien-fishcov.com
A beautiful Le Meridien hotel right on Beau Vallon beach. 62 rooms, facilities include tennis courts and watersports. **$$$$**

Glacis

Le Northolme Hotel
tel: 261222; fax: 261223;
e-mail: northolm@seychelles.net
A charming small hotel situated above a small, secluded cove, complete with beauty salon and dive centre. This is one of the oldest hotels in Seychelles and though compact and a little ragged around the edges, it retains a character all of its own. **$$$**

Sunset Beach Hotel
tel: 261111; fax: 261221;
e-mail: sunset@seychelles.net;
www.sunset-beach.com
A small, quiet, exclusive hotel featuring Spanish-style rooms and one luxury villa on a beautiful secluded bay. Shady terrace. **$$$**

Anse Forbans

Allamanda Hotel
tel: 366266; fax: 366175
e-mail: amanda@seychelles.net;
www.wsf.fr/seychelles
A small, attractive 10-room hotel on the beach with beach bar and restaurant. The excellent Sunday buffet is very popular with locals. **$$**

Bel Air

Bel Air Hotel
tel: 224416; fax: 224923;
e-mail: belair@seychelles.net;
www. seychelles.net/belair
More of a guest house than a hotel, this is situated on the edge of Victoria and is ideal for those visiting Seychelles on business. **$**

Port Glaud

Mahé Beach Resort
tel: 378451; fax: 378117;
e-mail: bmbsm@seychelles.net;
www. seychelles.net/berjaya

Price Guide

Prices are for two sharing a double room for one night and include breakfast:
$$$$ more than SR4,000
$$$ SR2,000–SR4,000
$$ SR1,000–SR2,000
$ less than SR1,000

A large Berjaya hotel in beautiful landscaped grounds with good facilities and a casino. **$$**

Barbarons

Barbarons Hotel
tel: 378253; fax: 378484;
e-mail: merbbh@seychelles.net
A large 122-room hotel on the west coast with good amenities, including a big swimming pool with a children's pool and a free shuttle service to a nearby casino. **$$**

Château d'Eau
tel: 378177; fax: 378388
A quiet but beautiful small hotel on an excellent beach in a peaceful location. **$$$**

Baie Lazare

Plantation Club
tel: 361361; fax: 361333;
e-mail: resa2@plantation club.sc;
www.plantationclub.com
A large, sprawling hotel with a choice of 200 rooms from standard to "presidential suite" and a choice of restaurants including the excellent but expensive Lazares. Own casino, pool, tennis courts, gym, hairdresser, fitness centre and dive centre. Nice beach, but not safe for swimming at times. **$$$**

Anse Intendance

Banyan Tree Resort
tel: 366557; fax: 383600;
e-mail: banyanseychelles@slh.com
www.banyantree.com
The most modern hotel on Mahé (opened 2001) and the highest of standards. There are 37 villas and one Presidential villa, all set in lush tropical surroundings on a hillside overlooking a beautiful beach in a quiet corner of the main island. **$$$$**

Anse Soleil

Anse Soleil Beachcomber
tel: 361461; fax: 361460;
e-mail: asbeachr@seychelles.net.
Good value for money in a superb setting. Off the beaten track, so what you save on accommodation might have to go towards car hire. **$$**

PRASLIN

Anse Bois de Rose

Black Parrot
tel: 233900; fax: 233919
Just 12 luxury suites, with four-poster and king-size beds, and many amenities. Each suite has a balcony with a stunning sea view. **$$$$**

Coco de Mer
tel: 233900; fax: 233919
e-mail: cocodemer@seychelles.net;
www.cocodemer.com. Facilities include watersports, tennis court and fitness centre. Bars include Fisherman's Wharf on a jetty with delightful views. **$$$**

Pointe Cabris

Château de Feuilles
tel: 233916; fax: 233916
e-mail: info@chateau.com.sc
www.chateau.com.sc
A small, luxurious hotel with a variety of accommodation from rooms to individual chalets. The restaurant has a fixed menu featuring fish dishes. **$$$$**

Anse La Farine

Emerald Cove Hotel
tel: 232323; fax: 232300;
e-mail: emerald@seychelles.net;
www.emerald.sc
Overlooking Round Island, Praslin and Baie Ste Anne on a beautiful beach accessible by sea only. The 42 rooms vary in facilities and price from moderate and good to expensive and very good. Amenities include dive centre and volleyball. **$$**

Anse Kerlan

Lemuria Resort
tel: 281281; fax: 281001
e-mail: lemuria@seychelles.net
www.constancehotels.com
A five-star facility in a spectacular

location spread over 36 hectares (90 acres), with three beaches. In 2002, eight luxury villas and an opulent Presidential villa were added to the 88 existing suites. A choice of restaurants and bars plus excellent amenities including an 18-hole golf course, tennis, dive centre, watersports and fitness centre. $$$$

Anse Gouvernement
L'Archipel
tel: 232242; fax: 232072
e-mail: archipel@seychelles.net
An excellent small hotel with magnificent architecture, set on a secluded sheltered beach. A variety of watersports facilities are offered and the restaurant is good too. $$$

Anse Petite Cour
La Reserve
tel: 232211; fax: 232166;
e-mail: lrmk@seychelles.net;
www.lareserve-seychelles.com
A pleasant hotel with good facilities and thatched bungalows on the beach. A minimum five-day stay is required. $$$$

Anse St Saveur
Villa Flamboyant
tel: 233036; fax: 233036;
e-mail: vila@seychelles.net
Colonial-style guest house set in 2 hectares (5 acres) of beautiful gardens and trees by the beach. Home cooking with home-grown organic produce. the sea can be seaweedy between June and October. No children under 12. $

Anse Volbert
Acajou Hotel
tel: 232400; fax: 232401;
e-mail: acajou@seychelles.net;
www.seychelles.net/acajou

A small hotel with 28 spacious rooms in two blocks constructed from mahogany (from South African plantations). Rooms have a balcony facing the sea, air-conditioning and the usual amenities. $$$
Paradise Sun Hotel
tel: 232255; fax: 232019;
e-mail: paradise@seychelles.net;
www.paradise-sun.com
A medium-sized hotel with good watersports facilities and an excellent dive centre. $$$
Praslin Beach Resort
tel: 232222; fax: 232244;
e-mail: bpb@seychelles.net;
www.seychelles.net/berjaya
A large Berjaya hotel with good facilities next to an excellent beach. One of the few hotels on Praslin offering live entertainment. $$

Grand Anse
Hotel Marechiaro
tel: 233322; fax: 233337;
e-mail: merkler@seychelles.net;
www.co.za/marechiaro
Pleasant granite and timber chalets in a tranquil setting. Facilities include a dive centre, tennis court and watersports. $$$
Indian Ocean Lodge
tel: 233324; fax: 233911
e-mail: iol@seychelles.net
Creole-style, well-ventilated chalets in pleasant surroundings next to the beach. Relaxed atmosphere. $$$
Maison des Palmes
tel: 233411; fax: 233880; e-mail:
maisonp@seychelles; www.the-seychelles.com/maisondespalmes
A small friendly hotel with 24 rooms next to the beach on the outskirts of Grand Anse. Good facilities for watersports and excursions to neighbouring islands. $$

LA DIGUE

Anse La Réunion
Château St Cloud
tel: 234346; fax: 234545
e-mail: stcloud@seychelles.net
An old château plantation house, near the foot of the hills, which once produced vanilla. A tourist attraction in its own right (see page 325). $$

Choppy's Bungalows
tel: 234224; fax: 234088;
e-mail: choppys@seychelles.net;
www.the-seychelles.com/choppys
A small 10-room beach-side hotel with good facilities, close to the jetty. Weekly entertainment. $$$
La Digue Island Lodge
tel: 234232; fax: 234100
www.ladigue.sc
A charming, charismatic hotel by the beach, with A-frame chalets, rondavels and a restored colonial house painted bright yellow. $$$$

Anse Patates
Hotel l'Océan
tel: 234180; fax: 234308;
e-mail: ocean@seychelles.net;
www.seychelles.net/ocean
A small eight-room hotel with a commanding view on a headland, a short way from a sandy cove. Good facilities including air-conditioning. $$
Patatran Village
tel: 234333; fax: 234344;
e-mail: patatran@seychelles.sc
Eighteen chalets on a rocky headland overlooking the wild northeast coast of the island. Simple but comfortable rooms. Creole restaurant. $$$

L'Union
Paradise Flycatcher's Lodge
tel: 234422; fax: 234423;
e-mail: mcdurup@seychelles.net
Chalets, each of two units, with common dining area, living area and verandah. Quiet location, a few minutes from the beach. Can choose between self-catering or restaurant facilities. $$$

OTHER ISLANDS

There is only one hotel on each of the islands listed here:

Aldabra Research Station
for information contact Seychelles Islands Foundation, Premier Building, Victoria;
tel: 321735; fax: 324884;
e-mail: sif@seychelles.net
With no vessels visiting on a regular basis and no trips organised by tour operators as yet, visits require careful planning. Accommodation is

in simple rooms each with en-suite shower and toilet (though water may be rationed). **$$$**
Alphonse Island Resort
tel: 323220 (Victoria Head Office)
tel: 229030; fax: 229034
e-mail: alphonse@seychelles.net
A luxury hotel in a remote island setting. There are 25 spacious thatched chalets, 5 deluxe villas and a "presidential villa". All have air-conditioning, verandah and en-suites with jacuzzi. The presidential villa has two bedrooms with en-suite bathrooms, living room, dining area, kitchen and an external jacuzzi pool. **$$$$**
Anonyme Resort
tel: 380100 or 710111;
fax: 380101;
e-mail: anonyme@seychelles.net
A small resort of just seven luxury villas off the east coast of Mahé. Anonyme is an "outer Island" experience within sight of the international airport. When leaving you can even go direct to the airport check-in by boat. **$$$$**
Bird Island Lodge
tel: 224925; fax: 225074 (Mahé)
tel: 323322 (Bird)
e-mail: birdland@seychelles.net
www.BirdIslandSeychelles.com
Pleasant individual chalets with ceiling fans and basic facilities. The restaurant is excellent. **$$$**
Cousine Island Chalets
tel: 321107; fax: 321107
e-mail: cousine@seychelles.net
www.indianoceanislands.net
Peace and quiet come first, together with the promotion of conservation on this island of seabirds and rare land birds. The four chalets, all with sea views, are old French colonial style, equipped with everything from a refrigerator to a jacuzzi. **$$$$**
Denis Island Lodge
tel: 321143; fax: 321010
e-mail: denis@seychelles.net
Comfortable individual chalets with all the usual facilities. Good watersports facilities and diving available. **$$$$**
Desroches Island Lodge
tel: 229009 (Mahé Head Office)
tel: 229003; fax: 229002
e-mail: tssez02@seychelles.net

20 spacious, air-conditioned chalets. Good dive centre and non-motorised watersports. **$$$$**
Félicité Island
tel: 234233; fax: 234100
Exclusive accommodation in two houses (four rooms). No other visitors are allowed to the island other than guests and staff. Guests may use the Denis Island Lodge's facilities. **$$$$**
Frégate Island Private
tel: 324545 (Mahé Head Office)
tel: 323370
e-mail: fregate@seychelles.net
www.fregate.com
The only place to stay on this private island is exclusive in every respect *(see pages 301–303)*. Accommodation is limited to 16 luxury villas, each with sun terrace, and designed with integrated glass walls for views of the ocean. Furnished with rare antiques and Asian artworks. Access to seven beaches and all watersports facilities. Maximum 40 guests. **$$$$**
Sainte Anne Resort
tel: 292000; fax: 292002;
e-mail: sainteanne@bchot.com;
www.sainteanne-resort.com.
This five-star resort opened in 2002 and is the only hotel on the island with a regular ferry to Victoria. There are 82 one-bedroom villas, four two-bedroom and one three-bedroom. Facilities include tennis, mountain bikes, diving, deep-sea fishing and various watersports. **$$$$**
Silhouette Island Lodge
tel: 344154; fax: 344178 (Mahé)
tel: 224003; fax: 224897 (Lodge)
e-mail: sillodge@seychelles.net
www.silhouette-seychelles.com
A small hotel with just 12 wooden, thatched bungalows with ceiling fans and good amenities. The hotel offers diving, fishing, walking and boat trips. **$$$**

Self-catering

MAHÉ

Blue Lagoon Chalets
tel: 371197; fax: 371565;
e-mail:blagoon@seychelles.net;
www.seychelles.net/bluelagoon.
A very small attractive development

with four well-equipped self-catering villas overlooking the tranquil waters of Anse à la Mouche. Two rooms have air-conditioning; all have ceiling fans. **$$**
Eden's Holiday Resort
Port Glaud;
tel: 378333; fax: 378160;
e-mail: eden@seychelles.net;
www.seychelles.nor/eden.
Excellent, well-equipped chalets in a quiet and beautiful location on the west coast. **$$**
Le Petit Village
Bel Ombre;
tel: 284969; fax: 247711;
e-mail: lepetit@seychelles.net;
www.seychelles.net/lepetit.
Spacious, well-equipped, air-conditioned, log-cabin self-catering units overlooking the sea. **$$**
Sun Resort and Properties
Beau Vallon;
tel: 285555; fax: 247224;
e-mail: xanadu@seychelles.net;
www.xanaduresort.com
Though geared up for self-catering, a restaurant offers breakfast and dinner should you change your mind. The complex is built around a good swimming pool and is just a two-minute stroll from Beau Vallon beach. **$$**
Xanadu Resort
Anse Cachée;
tel: 366522; fax: 366344;
e-mail: xanadu@seychelles.net;
www.xanaduresort.com
Beautiful, large, well-equipped chalets. Very quiet, private location in south Mahé. No shops within reasonable walking, but assistance with shopping available. **$$$**

PRASLIN

Villas de Mer
Grand Anse;
tel: 233972; fax: 233015
e-mail: britania@seychelles.net
Six villas in a well-kept garden by the beach, a short distance from Praslin airport and the shops of Grand Anse. **$$**

Where to Eat

One of the most attractive attributes of Seychelles is its cuisine. However, you need to know where to look to find it. There are no beach stalls as in so many other countries, fewer restaurants and if fast food is what you are looking for then you have come to the wrong place. There is no McDonald's – indeed nothing whatsoever very fast in Seychelles, though there are a few takeways (notably in Victoria).

Hotels offer a wide choice of meals to keep their clients from straying, often including a barbecue or a Seychellois buffet on certain evenings. However, to sample the finest local cuisine, a new twist on international flavours and to enjoy informal local surroundings, a trip to a restaurant outside your hotel is an excellent alternative.

Dress is very casual and the atmosphere generally very relaxed. Booking is unnecessary for lunch but advisable for evenings, indeed essential at some restaurants. Most will open around 6.30pm and by 10.30pm the shutters are beginning to go up. Fish dishes dominate though meat dishes, mainly chicken and beef, are almost always available. Authentic Seychelles curries are hot, but restaurants will offer chilli sauce on a separate dish to allow the customer to control the temperature.

MAHÉ

Victoria

Kaz Zanana
Revolution Avenue; tel: 324150
A charming, restored wood-built house in Victoria. Ideal for a toasted sandwich snack while in town. Excellent cakes. **$$**

Le Marinier
Inter-Island Quay; tel: 224 937
Not the place to linger when the air is filled with smells wafting across from the tuna cannery. However, it is quite the best place to sit and relax to enjoy a light meal, snack or just a drink while waiting for a ferry or yacht at the Victoria quayside. **$**

Pirates Arms
Independence Avenue; tel: 225001
Close to the clock tower, this is a popular meeting place to gossip and watch the world go by. Meals are fairly simple but good and there are usually one or two special dishes of the day on offer. **$$**

Sam's Pizzeria
Maison Suleman, Francis Rachel Street; 322499
A very good medium-priced restaurant with relaxed atmosphere and a varied menu. On the first floor overlooking the busy main street **$$**

Anse aux Pins

Vye Marmit Restaurant
Craft Village; tel: 376155
In a lovely setting, serving excellent creole cuisine on the verandah overlooking craft shops and a old plantation house. Mainly fish and seafood but some meat dishes. **$$$**

Anse Royale

Le Jardin du Roi
tel: 371313
Set among spice plants, fruit and ornamental trees, this restaurant is well worth a visit in its own right. The food is excellent, and reasonably priced – save room for the amazing ice creams; flavours include cinnamon and lemon grass. Curry buffet on Sunday. Advance booking advisable. Lunchtimes only. **$$**

Kaz Kreol
tel: 371680
A wide variety of inexpensive dishes, such as pasta, curries, salads and fish and chips, in a casual setting by the beach. **$$**

Anse aux Poules Bleus

La Sirène
tel: 361339
Not far from Michael Adams' studio, a simple and informal

beach restaurant at the southern end of the bay, serving good creole food. Open at lunchtimes only. **$$$**

Anse Boileau

Chez Plume
tel: 355050
Excellent seafood restaurant. Good desserts, unlike many restaurants, including superb Passion Fruit Soufflé. **$$$**

Bel Ombre

Le Corsaire
tel: 247171; mobile: 515171
Housed in a romantic steep-roofed stone and thatch building, overlooking the ocean, this restaurant offers international and creole cuisine. Open evenings only from 7.30pm, closed Monday. **$$$**

Price Guide

Prices are for two people including soft drinks or beer:

$$$$	SR400 plus
$$$	SR300–SR400
$$	SR200–SR300
$	less than SR200

La Scala
tel: 247535
This family-run restaurant is a popular choice among the local business community, so it is essential to book. Specialises in seafood and Italian, international and creole dishes at moderate prices. Evenings only, closed Sunday. **$$$**

St Louis

Marie Antoinette Restaurant
tel: 266222
This restaurant at the foot of Signal Hill is the best place to go for a creole feast in the perfect setting of an old planter's house. The food is consistently good, though the two-course set menu never varies. The first course alone involves five dishes: tuna steak, parrotfish in batter, grilled bourgeois, fish stew, and chicken curry with salad and rice. Dessert consists of fruit salad and ice cream followed by coffee. **$$**

Anse à la Mouche
Anchor Café
tel: 371289
The nearest thing in South Mahé to a fast food outlet, this is an informal restaurant, opposite the beach, offering simple snacks such as sausages, burgers, fish and chips and ice cream. **$**

Beau Vallon
Baobob Pizzeria
tel: 247167
At the northern end of the bay, this beach-side pizzeria with its stone benches and sandy floor, is a Seychelles institution. As well as dishing up good pizzas, it serves pasta dishes or fish and chips. It's difficult to get a table after 7pm and weekends can get crowded too. Lunchtime and evenings. **$**
The Boat House
tel: 247898
Excellent evening fish barbecue in informal surroundings. Commences 7.30pm (closed Monday). Very popular and booking essential. **$$**
La Fontaine
tel: 247841
Much quieter than the pizzeria, this romantic restaurant overloooking the beach serves excellent international and local cuisine. **$$$**
La Perle Noire
tel: 247046
A stone's throw from Coral Strand Hotel, an excellent restaurant serving Italian, international and creole dishes. Evenings only. **$$$**

Glacis
Copra House
tel: 241380
A takeaway and restaurant with excellent inexpensive local cuisine. Try the chicken kebabs or curries. Open daily for breakfast, lunch and dinner. **$**

Sans Soucis
Rose Garden Restaurant
tel: 225308
Set in the cooler mountains on the edge of Morne Seychellois National Park with spectacular views. Save room for the excellent desserts. Part of the secluded Rose Garden Hotel. **$$$**

PRASLIN

Anse à La Blague
La Vanille Beach Bar
tel: 232178
Good basic food served at tables on a terrace overlooking the sea. The menu is predominantly fish based, but meat dishes are also featured. **$$**

Anse Lazio
Bonbon Plume
tel: 232136
Cuisine with a strong French flavour mixed with local influences. Mainly fish and seafood served at wooden tables shaded by palm-thatched umbrellas next to this exceptionally beautiful beach. **$$$$**

Grand Anse
Britannia Restaurant
tel: 233215
If a walk to see black parrots sounds too much like hard work, relax at a table in the garden of this restaurant, order a drink and a meal and with luck the birds will come to you. Good value creole cuisine. **$$**
Capri Restaurant
tel: 233337
The best restaurant in the Grand Anse area of Praslin. Excellent Italian and creole cuisine in a garden setting. **$$$**

Grosse Roche, La Pointe
Les Rochers
tel: 233034
On its own beach, an excellent but expensive restaurant specialising in seafood. **$$$$**

Anse Bois de Rose
Black Parrot
tel: 233900
Excellent fish and seafood dishes served in a scenic setting overlooking a beautiful bay. A good venue for lunch and evening meals. **$$$**

Côte d'Or
La Goulue Café
tel: 232 223
A rustic, relaxed outdoor setting near the beach serving good quality mainly local dishes and snacks. Open noon–9pm. Closed Sunday. **$$**

Satellite Restaurants
Restaurants on Mahé's satellite islands – **Kapok Tree**, Île au Cerf; **Jolly Roger Bar & Restaurant**, Moyenne Island; **Chez Gaby**, Round Island; **Thérèse Island Restaurant** and **Piment Vert**, Anonyme Island – are usually only open for visitors on a full-day excursion organised by a local tour operator. They all serve a simple set buffet/barbecue-style menu in a delightful setting.

Tante Mimi
Casino des Isles; tel: 232500
A fabulous restaurant in a beautiful colonial-style building with interesting interior decor. Mainly international cuisine, possibly the best in Seychelles. In the evenings, will arrange collection and return to any Praslin hotel. Creole menu Wednesday evenings. Sunday lunch on the terrace. **$$$$**

LA DIGUE

Anse la Réunion
Zerof Restaurant and Takeaway
tel: 234439
Situated opposite the Vev Nature Reserve, serves a wide range of excellent creole dishes. Closes at 9.30pm. **$$**

Grand Anse
Loutier Coco
no phone
If you plan to eat out on this side of the island, this is the place to come for good value creole cuisine, sandwiches and omelettes. Closed evenings. **$$**

Outdoor Activities

Bird-watching

Birdwatchers are drawn to Seychelles for three reasons: the rarity value of the endemic land birds, the spectacular seabird colonies such as Bird Island and Cousin, and the chance of seeing unusual migrants. The land birds are, of course, present year-round, as indeed are many species of seabird. However, the huge tern colonies are at their best from May to September. October to December is the best time for migrants from Europe and Asia, when many unusual vagrants have been recorded including some not known anywhere else in the western Indian Ocean or Madagascar regions.

Top sites on the itinerary of any visiting birdwatcher should include the nature reserve islands of **Cousin** and **Aride**. On **Mahé**, the mudflats adjacent to the Seychelles Breweries is the best site for migrant waders such as **crab plover**, a northwest Indian Ocean speciality. The Plantation Club marsh on Mahé, and the pools of Lemuria Golf Course on Praslin and the wetlands of La Passe on La Digue are the best places to see **yellow bittern**, found nowhere else in the region.

On **Praslin**, **black parrots** may be seen early morning or late afternoon around the entrance to **Vallée de Mai** and in lowland fruit trees such as those around Villa Flamboyant. Birdwatching tours can be booked through local tour companies (see page 399–400). Several travel companies worldwide organise package birdwatching

holidays in Seychelles, such as **Island Holidays** and **Discover the World**.

Big Game Fishing

Fishing is a way of life in Seychelles (see Fishing on pages 276–77). Day charters for big game fishing may be organised from Mahé, Praslin, La Digue and on all the islands with single resorts. Customised safaris for up to six persons lasting three or more days may be booked with some.

For day trips, on Mahé, **The Boat House**, Beau Vallon (tel: 247464; mobile: 510269 or 514382; fax: 247955; e-mail: aircool@seychelles.sc; www.silhouette-island.com) operates three small vessels, and the magnificent vessel **Island Girl** (tel: 280000 or 515278; e-mail: island@seychelles.net; www.seychelles.net/islandcharters) also offers excellent facilities, as does Hermes Charters (tel: 225505 or 344088, e-mail: maurice@seychelles.net; www.charternet.com/fishers/hermes. On Praslin and La Digue, trips are organised by many small operators and by the operators of **Inter-Island Ferry Service** (tel: 232374).

The **Marine Charter Association** – PO Box 204, Victoria, Mahé; tel: 322126; fax: 224679 – is a member of the **International Game Fishing Association (IGFA)** and offers a wide selection of boats for hire, with a skipper, drinks and a light lunch. They will also team you up with others to make a party of four if wished, which is more economical than hiring the boat to yourself.

The boats should carry all the necessary safety equipment, first-aid kits and a radio link. Other big game fishing operators are:
Island Charters: Victoria; tel: 280000; mobile: 515278; fax: 324056; e-mail: speedy@vcsinet.com; www.seychelles.net/islandcharters
Marlin Charters: Providence, Mahé;

Scuba Safety

The Association of Professional Divers, Seychelles (APDS) has set guidelines for the safe and professional operation of diving centres. Many of its members are rated by the Professional Association of Diving Instructors (PADI) as five-star dive centres or resorts. All boats used for diving activities are properly licensed by the local authorities and, in addition to normal safety equipment, carry oxygen and additional emergency equipment. There is a two-man, twin-lock re-compression chamber at Victoria Hospital with a team of hyperbaric doctors and technicians available in the unlikely event of a diving accident.

tel: 373439; mobile: 511190; fax: 373632.
Striker: Beau Vallon, Mahé; tel: 247898; mobile: 511958; fax: 247797
Another event in which visitors may participate is the **National Fishing Competition** hosted by the Rotary Club of Victoria and held every April.

Diving & Snorkelling

The marine world is easily accessible in Seychelles with many APDS diving centres offering snorkelling (see Equipped for Snorkelling on page 371) and scuba diving facilities. If you are healthy and can swim, learning to snorkel or dive is easy and most dive centres offer introductory and certification courses.

Seychelles is one of the best places in the world to learn to dive and has several excellent dive centres. If you are not sure diving is for you, a one-day course is the best way to test the waters. These are offered by several excellent PADI (Professional Association of Diving Instructors) dive centres. You begin at 9am with a session in the hotel swimming pool to familiarise yourself with the equipment and learn basic techniques.

After lunch, you take a sea dive on a shallow reef accompanied at all times by an instructor. No certificate is issued, but if you decide to progress, this one-day experience counts as the first step towards obtaining further knowledge and skill on a second day. Successful completion of this stage leads to the PADI Scuba Diver Certificate, which allows you to dive to a limited depth under basic supervision. Two additional days completes your basic diving skills to give you a PADI Open Water Diver Licence. *(See* Underwater World *on pages 271–75).*

Association of Professional Divers Seychelles (APDS) and **Underwater Centre Seychelles:** PO Box 384, Victoria; tel: 345445; fax: 344223; e-mail: divesey@seychelles.net; website: www.diveseychelles.com.sc With centres at the **Coral Strand Hotel, Mahé** (tel: 247357)
Big Blue Divers: Vacoa Village, Mahé; tel: 261106
Bleu Marine Diving Centre: La Vanille Bungalows, Anse à La Blague, Praslin; tel: 560409
Island Ventures: tel: 247141; fax: 247943; e-mail: info@islandventures.net With centres at **Berjaya Beau Vallon Bay Hotel** (tel: 247165) and **Berjaya Mahé Beach Hotel** (tel: 378026).
Le Diable des Mers Diving Centre: Beau Vallon, Mahé; tel: 247104
Seychelles Travel *(see page 400)* can arrange diving package holidays from one week to three months and offer a 14-day Fantasia Diving Cruise to Aldabra.

Windows on the Reef

To see the wonders of the coral reef without getting wet there are two options. The first is a **glass bottom boat** which permits a vertical view of the reef from an open-sided flat-bottomed boat fitted with perspex panels along the central floor. Wooden benches run along each side of the vessel facing these viewing panels. The second

option is a **subsea viewer,** a semi-submersible vessel from which a horizontal view of the reef may be obtained. Glass bottom boats can enter extremely shallow water, though the passage of the vessel overhead scares away many fish, particularly the larger ones. Subsea viewers create less disturbance but cannot cross very shallow patches where reef life may proliferate. Some visitors find the subsea viewer claustrophobic.

Trips from Mahé to **Ste Anne Marine National Park** can be arranged through a local tour operator *(see page 400),* either for half a day or for a full day with lunch at one of the islands: Moyenne, Round or Cerf. The National Park is the headquarters of the Marine Parks Authority. However, the park has suffered greatly from the combined effects of El Niño in 1998, which killed more than 90 percent of corals and the extensive land reclamation along Mahé's east coast that produced some siltation resulting in reef damage.

Teddy's Glass Bottom Boat: Coral Strand Hotel, Beau Vallon, Mahé; tel: 261125; mobile: 511125. Can also be booked through most tour operators.

Live-aboard Cruising

It can be reasonably claimed that the best way to explore an island nation is by sea. A cruise on a live-aboard vessel is an ideal way to see a number of islands without having to move from hotel to hotel. It is also an excellent way to reach the more secluded bays and islands.

There are various options available depending on whether you wish to enjoy sailing, fishing, diving, watersports or simply get from A to B in the fastest possible time.

Most cruises begin from the Inter-Island Quay at Victoria. Many of the charter boats are moored next to the quay. Nearby, the **Seychelles Marine Charter Association** (tel: 322126) is also a useful source of information on the

availability of the smaller boats. Most vessels are licensed to operate solely within the Inner Islands, except for cruise ships and some specialist charter boats (especially dive boats). Moorings are available at Marine National Parks where a small fee is charged for entry. Some island nature reserves also charge a small fee for landing. Apart from the smaller, difficult to reach islands, secluded bays around the main islands are well worth exploring.

WHEN TO CRUISE

The southeast monsoon blows from May to October bringing steady winds. Wind strength is particularly high in July and August with rough seas. Unless you have a strong stomach this is not the best time to sail far afield, though a cruise around the mainly sheltered waters of Praslin and its satellite islands can be very pleasant. The northwest monsoon from November to April brings less consistent winds, which can be squally around mid-December to the end of January. Fortunately, however, Seychelles lies outside the cyclone belt.

ACTIVITIES ON BOARD

Diving facilities are offered by larger vessels (those of over 10 berths). This may be either the main activity, with perhaps three or four dives per day on offer, or an optional choice when opportunities arise within a set itinerary. Skippers of these vessels are usually qualified divemasters. Most vessels will at least offer snorkelling equipment, comprising mask, snorkel and fins.

Some of the larger vessels will also carry a range of watersports equipment including windsurfers and waterskis. Almost all will carry fishing tackle. Trailing a line in the water on sea passages is an excellent way to catch pelagic fish such as bonito

Mahé's Marine Parks

To explore the sea at **Port Launay National Marine Park**, Jamilah Big Game and Bottom Fishing have an outlet near Port Glaud offering snorkelling at **Baie Ternay** (also a National Marine Park) and excursions to the Inner Islands, while West Rand Holdings, a diving and water-sports centre a little further on, hires out jet skis and charter boats for trips. Jet skis are only allowed up to the marine park's boundary.

or dorado. At anchor, bottom fishing may also be offered with opportunities to catch fresh fish for supper.

Cruising is of course an activity in itself and one of the most important pieces of equipment on board is the ship's tender. This will be the only way to land on most beaches as only the largest populated islands have quays.

CHARTERING

At the smaller end of the scale, there are a range of monohulls and catamarans available for **bareboat charter**. Professional skippers who know the islands well may also be employed. Alternatively, a **set cruise** may be taken aboard a romantic twin-masted schooner or dedicated dive boat. Small, fast **motor-cruisers** are available for those who want to get to their destinations fast. All these options are offered by locally based operators but during the northern winter, cruise ships will also call at the islands.

You can organise yachting holidays around the islands with one week on board and another week in a hotel at home with companies such as:
Seychelles Travel: 01258 450983; www.seychelles-travel.co.uk

Sunsail Ltd: telesales: 02392 222222; www.sunsail.com
Yacht Connections: tel: 671667; fax: 671668; e-mail: ac@yacht-connections.co.uk; www. yacht-connections.co.uk

Charter companies in Seychelles
High Aspect Yacht Charter:
tel: 513911; fax: 322555; e-mail: kjones@highaspect.sc
High Aspect is a well-appointed 22-metre (72-ft) luxury yacht capable of exploring the furthest corners of Seychelles. Charters are flexible, the entire yacht being available for hire on a full board basis with an expert skipper who knows the islands well.
Indian Ocean Explorer:
tel: 345445; fax: 344223; e-mail; divesey@seychelles.net; www.divesychelles.com.sc
Indian Ocean Explorer is the only dedicated live aboard dive vessel in Seychelles. It is also the only vessel with regular cruises to islands of the Aldabra group, with departures from October to April. The remainder of the year includes whale shark special cruises and trips to the Amirantes.
Silhouette Cruises Ltd: tel: 324026 (office) or 514051 (ship mobile); fax: 380538; e-mail: cruises@seychelles.net; www.seychelles.net/cruises
Operates two Dutch-built twin-masted schooners, *Sea Shell* and *Sea Pearl*, carrying up to 18 passengers. These are the most beautiful ships in Seychelles. Cruises are for five or six days around the granitic islands. Guests may participate in sailing, though

vessels carry a full crew. Other activities include diving, fishing and watersports.
Sunsail (Seychelles) Ltd:
tel/fax: 225700; e-mail: ssseychl@seychelles.net; www.sunsail.com
A company with over 1,000 vessels world-wide in many holiday centres that you can book from home *(see above)*. The Seychelles fleet comprises monohulls, with up to nine berths, eight catamarans and one "super-luxury" Platinum-class catamaran with full crew. Other boats are available for bareboat charter, clients providing their own food and drink or with qualified skippers. Period or day charters may be arranged. The company offers a provisioning service if required. Advice on anchorages and other essential information is available.
VPM Yacht Charter:
tel/fax: 225676; e-mail: vpmsey@seychelles.net; www.vpm-boats.com
Another multi-national company with a Seychelles base, VPM operates a fleet of vessels, mainly catamarans. Some are available for bareboat charter and some for crewed charter. Crewed charters are skippered by professional sailors who know Seychelles waters well. A provisioning service is offered for bareboat charters.
Water World (Pty) Ltd:
tel: 373766; fax: 247607; e-mail: wworld@seychelles.net; www.seychelles.net/wworld
The ultra-modern high speed option. The motor-cruiser *Shamal*

Underwater Photography Festival

There are few events in Seychelles that you would want to plan your holiday dates around. One exception, if you are a diver, might be **SUBIOS**, a three-week festival of underwater images held each November, which is also one of the best months for diving due to the calm seas prevailing between the two monsoon winds. Entertainment,

centred around the main hotels of Mahé and Praslin, includes slide shows hosted by professional underwater photog-raphers and photography contests. Further details can be obtained from the **Ministry of Tourism**, Independence House, Victoria (tel: 611100) or **Underwater Centre Seychelles** (tel: 345445).

cruises at 24 knots with a top speed of 31 knots. It has just two standard cabins and one VIP cabin, all with en-suite facilities. Smaller vessels are also available for day charters.

Horse Riding

To enjoy the Seychelles scenery at a leisurely pace, you may ride a pure bred Arab horse along the western coast of Mahé, or up into the mountains. The coastal trip takes two hours, while hikes into the hills may take a full day with lunch provided. All rides are escorted and run daily, weather permitting, by **Magic Carpet Arab Horse Riding Club** (tel: 512380) situated at the southern end of **Anse aux Poules Bleues**, next to La Sirène restaurant. Make your reservation at least one day in advance. No experience is necessary. Take sun cream, as you will be out in direct sunlight for a fairly lengthy period. Riding boots are not necessary, but trousers are recommended to prevent rubbing. Trips may be tide-dependent, but early morning or late afternoon is best to avoid the midday heat.

A two-hour ride takes you along the shoreline of **Anse à la Mouche**. This is a shallow bay, though at high tide there is one point where the horses have to swim, so bring along some dry clothes to change into afterwards. The trip into the mountains follows the **Val d'Endor pass**, offering magnificent views of the island. The path is little used by vehicles and therefore affords safe, quiet riding. If taking a day trip you can reach Anse Bougainville on the east coast.

Away from Mahé, horses may be hired at L'Union Estate on **La Digue** for riding within the grounds of the estate only.

Scenic Flights

The majesty of the mountains, the variety of colours of the sea, secret beaches, coves and dramatic cliffs can only be fully appreciated from the air.

Helicopter Seychelles (tel: 373900) offers scenic flights from **Victoria Helistop** (next to Inter-Island Quay) and from **La Digue**.

Departure times from Victoria are flexible as are duration and routes. La Digue departures are every Friday and Sunday for 30 minutes. Praslin departures can also be arranged on Friday and Sunday when a helicopter is based at La Digue. There are four passenger seats, one next to the pilot and three at the rear. The best positions for photography are the rear window seats, which have small sliding windows permitting unimpeded shots.

Walking

The Ministry of Tourism has produced a series of booklets for nature walks on **Mahé**, **Praslin** and **La Digue**. These are not widely available, but may be purchased from the Tourist Office at Independence House, Victoria *(see page 400)*. All are well signposted, but a booklet will add to your appreciation of what you are seeing along the way.

Many are mountain walks, for which the best times for walking are the cooler months of June to September. The worst time is the height of the rains, mid-December to January, when paths are muddy and slippery. March and April can also be very tiring being hot and sticky with little or no cooling breeze. The cooler times of early morning or late afternoon are best for walking, but remember it gets dark quickly around 6.30pm. You should always take water and never drink from mountain streams on any of the islands, which may look crystal clear, but can harbour very unpleasant, harmful microscopic parasites. A hat is recommended for walks other than those through shaded forest.

It is not recommended to stray from mountain paths without a guide and to do a proper visit of the **mist forest** a guide is essential. The best

guided walks are offered by **Basil Beaudouin** (tel: 241790), who leads walks of varying difficulty, from one to two hours, to a full day. He is available to meet interested persons at the Coral Strand Hotel, every Monday at 6pm. His prices include a packed lunch, transport to the start, and from the finish of the walk, insurance and all the wealth of his knowledge of the islands, their flora and fauna.

Golf

The **Reef Golf Club** (club house tel: 376252), just south of the airport, has a nine-hole golf course, the only one on Mahé. Any golfer with a handicap wishing to enjoy a round is welcome. Competitions are held on Thursday and Saturday. It is generally not necessary to book except for Saturday, when you should put your name down by Thursday 6pm.

It is a lovely course in an old coconut plantation, kinder to golfers who slice than those that hook, the latter often ending up in the swamp. The best time to play is early from around 8.30am or after 3.30pm.

Praslin is the only other island with a golf course which is a championship 18-hole course (tel: 281281) at the new five-star **Lemuria**, a luxury resort *(see page 404)* and is open to non-residents.

Nightlife

Seychelles is not the place to come to for the nightlife. The little there is revolves around the hotels. On Mahé there are two tourist-friendly discos and two casinos. On Praslin there are two discos and one casino.

Flamboyant Discotheque: Bois de Rose Avenue on the outskirts of Victoria; tel: 321113
Top local musicians and bands play here on Friday nights.

Katiolo Club: Anse Faure, to the south of the airport; tel: 375453 Creole-style nightclub. Ladies Night on Friday until 11pm. Buffet on Saturday sometimes followed by an open-air disco, weather permitting until 3am.

The Dome Night Club: Baie Ste Anne, Praslin; tel: 232252. A non-smoking disco, with state-of-the-art lighting, featuring both local and international music. There are two bars, a games room and a snack shop. Open Friday, Saturday and the eve of public holidays, 10pm–4am

Jungle Disco: Grand Anse, Praslin; tel: 512683, features a variety of music, both local and international. There are three bars and a pool room. Snacks are available. Open Fri and Sat, 10pm–4am.

Casino des Seychelles: Beau Vallon Bay Hotel, Mahé; tel: 247272

Planter's Casino: Plantation Club, Baie Lazare, Mahé; tel: 361361

Casino des Isles: Côte d'Or, Praslin; tel: 232500

Shopping

The craft industry of Seychelles has shallow roots, having grown up to meet the demands of the tourist industry. This is not to say there are no items unique to Seychelles, for innovation has flourished. However, there are few traditional products on sale.

What to Buy

Art There are many art studios well worth visiting, most of which are mentioned in the Mahé, Praslin and La Digue chapters, including Michael Adams, Tom Bowers, George Camille, Gerard Devoud and Barbara Jenson *(see* An Arts Tour *on page 255)*. The Craft Village *(Le Village Artisanale)* at Anse aux Pins on the east coast of Mahé, is also a good place to see the work of local artists.

Batik Ron Gerlach uses an old Indonesian technique to produce beach robes, shirts and pareos in a range of attractive colours to his own, unique designs. His work reflects his love of nature (he is also Chairman of the Nature Protection Trust of Seychelles). His Mahé studio is at Beau Vallon Beach, almost opposite The Boat House.

Coco de Mer The world's largest seed, which could weigh as much as your baggage allowance when taken fresh from the tree, makes a novel souvenir when hollowed out. You can buy them at the Forestry Station, Fond B'Offay, Praslin (open Mon–Fri 8am–4pm). They are also available from souvenir shops but be sure the vendor gives you an export certificate, or you risk confiscation by customs at the airport.

Coconut crafts The coconut palm is the artisan's most versatile resource: its leaves are woven into

bags and baskets; the nut itself is made into napkin rings, candle holders and trinket pots; coconut oil is used to perfume soaps and bath oils; and the unusual spotted timber is used to make boxes, buttons and beads for necklaces. In the Craft Village, by the entrance to the old St Roch plantation house, is Maison Coco, a shop dedicated to the products of the coconut palm, housed in a building made out of palm tree products itself.

Jewellery Beautiful jewellery, combining gold with mother of pearl, sea shells and other local items is made by Kreolor (tel: 344551) who has shops at Camion Hall, Victoria and at La Passe, La Digue, and also sells at Café des Artes on Praslin. The sea shells used in the jewellery were acquired following the bankruptcy of a local button factory so there is no impact on the reefs, and there are enough to last another hundred years. The company also manufactures some highly original items combining granite, raffia seeds, coconut wood and espadon – the bill of sailfish discarded by fishermen, which can be made to look like ivory. These include placemats, trays, boxes, bracelets, mirrors and picture frames.

Pearls Praslin Ocean Farm Ltd (tel: 233150) culture pearls from the local black-tipped pearl oyster. They produce silvery blue, green, gold and black coloured pearls which are set in jewellery and also baby clams

Kreol Festival

The biggest cultural event of the year is the **Kreol Festival**, held in the last week of October. Creole artists from other countries of a similar culture, such as Mauritius and the Caribbean, gather in Victoria, which is decorated for the occasion. Dances, plays, concerts and processions are organised during the week, and everyone is encouraged to join in. For more details contact: the **Kreol Festival Committee**, Ministry of Education, Mont Fleuri, Mahé; tel: 225477.

plated with silver and gold. Their shop, Black Pearls of Seychelles, is opposite Praslin airstrip and is worth visiting not only to see the jewellery, but also their aquarium.
Model Boats From inexpensive to more than your airfare and hotel bills combined, La Marine produces a range of boats that can be seen at their Mahé workshop and at Souverains des Mers in Camion Hall, Victoria.
Perfume More than 100 local plants are used to produce three perfumes for Kreol Fleurage Parfums of North East Point, Mahé (tel: 241329). On sale at many hotel and souvenir shops – and Harrods in London.
Souvenirs and gifts One of the best places for souvenir shopping is the Codevar Craft Centre *(see page 285)* at Camion Hall in Albert Street, Victoria. Also in Victoria, Sunstroke Gallery on Market Street sells a range of beach wear, jewellery, printed table cloths and cushions while upstairs there is an art gallery featuring several excellent local artists. Outside the capital, the Craft Village is the other main centre on Mahé for gifts and souvenirs (see box). If you happen to be visiting Michael Adams' Studio at Anse aux Poules Bleus, Pineapple Studio next door sell their own original souvenirs, including beautifully hand-dyed pareos in individually woven hessian bags, painted sculptures and wall plaques of fish, beachwear, keyrings, letter racks and painted coconuts. (The shop is open weekdays until 4.30pm, but the owners live next door and will open up any time within reason.)

Wild Ginger, at the northern end of Mahé's Beau Vallon Bay next to The Boat House, is an excellent craft shop selling pottery, paintings, mobiles, glass plaques and lampshades, woven goods and sculptures.
Stained glass Les and Sharon Masterson produce beautiful jewel-like hangings, lamps, panels and windows at their studio Thoughts on the Sans Souci road near Victoria (tel: 224060). Some of their work is also on display at Fisherman's Cove Hotel, Mahé. Sharon's stained-glass windows decorate St Paul's Cathedral, Victoria, the Apostolic Church, Victoria and a wall at the Benedetti Gallery, Soho, New York.
Tea and spices Packets of spices may be purchased at many places including Victoria's market and Jardin du Roi, Mahé. The aptly named *Hellfire* – pickled hot chillies – and dried vanilla pods, also available at the market, make novel, genuinely local souvenirs to take home. Seychelles Tea Company sells packs of tea with cinnamon, lemon, orange and vanilla flavours, on sale in most supermarkets.

Further Reading

Aldabra, World Heritage Site by Mohamed Amin, Duncan Willets and Adrian Skerrett (Camerapix, 1995). The best guide to this little-known corner of Seychelles where giant tortoises still rule supreme.
Beautiful Plants of Seychelles by Adrian and Judith Skerrett (Camerapix, 1991). A photographically illustrated guide to some of the commoner plants to be found in Seychelles and, indeed, in many tropical countries.
Beyond the Reefs by William Travis (Arrow Books, reprinted 1990). Tales by an adventurer who abandoned his flying career to explore the Outer Islands of Seychelles.
Birds of Seychelles by Adrian Skerrett, Ian Bullock and Tony Disley (A&C Black, 2001). The only guide to all the birds recorded in Seychelles.
Insight Pocket Guide: Seychelles focuses on the top places to visit and the best things to do, and includes a large fold-out map. (Insight also produce a Fleximap to Seychelles, with a long-lasting laminated finish).
Journey through Seychelles photographs by Mohamed Amin and Duncan Willets, text by Adrian and Judith Skerrett (Camerapix, 1994). A colourful coffee table book, with text rich in tales of history and natural history.
Rivals in Eden by William McAteer (The Book Guild Ltd, 1991). Traces the early settlement of Seychelles and the intense struggle that took place between Britain and France to control the sea route to India, the results of which were to mould the future of the islands.
Trouble in Paradise by William McAteer (Pristine Books, 2000). The sequel to *Rivals in Eden*, following the story of Seychelles from the British takeover, through the 19th century and up to 1919.

ART & PHOTO CREDITS

Picture Spreads

INSIGHT GUIDE
MAURITIUS, Reunion & Seychelles

Cartographic Editor **Zoë Goodwin**
Production **Linton Donaldson**
Design Consultants
Carlotta Junger, Graham Mitchener
Picture Research
Hilary Genin, Monica Allende

Map Production Colin Earl
© 2003 Apa Publications GmbH & Co.
Verlag KG (Singapore branch)

Index

Numbers in italics refer to photographs

Insight Guides Website
www.insightguides.com

*Don't travel the
planet alone.
Keep in step with
Insight Guides'
walking eye,
just a click away*

INSIGHT GUIDES

The classic series that puts you in the picture

Alaska	Dominican Rep. & Haiti	London	Rio de Janeiro
Amazon Wildlife	Dublin	Los Angeles	Rome
American Southwest	East African Wildlife	Madeira	Russia
Amsterdam	Eastern Europe	Madrid	St Petersburg
Argentina	Ecuador	Malaysia	San Francisco
Arizona & Grand Canyon	Edinburgh	Mallorca & Ibiza	Sardinia
Asia, East	Egypt	Malta	Scandinavia
Asia, Southeast	England	Mauritius Réunion	Scotland
Australia	Finland	& Seychelles	Seattle
Austria	Florence	Melbourne	Sicily
Bahamas	Florida	Mexico	Singapore
Bali	France	Miami	South Africa
Baltic States	France, Southwest	Montreal	South America
Bangkok	French Riviera	Morocco	Spain
Barbados	Gambia & Senegal	Moscow	Spain, Northern
Barcelona	Germany	Namibia	Spain, Southern
Beijing	Glasgow	Nepal	Sri Lanka
Belgium	Gran Canaria	Netherlands	Sweden
Belize	Great Britain	New England	Switzerland
Berlin	Great Railway Journeys	New Orleans	Sydney
Bermuda	of Europe	New York City	Syria & Lebanon
Boston	Greece	New York State	Taiwan
Brazil	Greek Islands	New Zealand	Tenerife
Brittany	Guatemala, Belize	Nile	Texas
Brussels	& Yucatán	Normandy	Thailand
Buenos Aires	Hawaii	Norway	Tokyo
Burgundy	Hong Kong	Oman & The UAE	Trinidad & Tobago
Burma (Myanmar)	Hungary	Oxford	Tunisia
Cairo	Iceland	Pacific Northwest	Turkey
California	India	Pakistan	Tuscany
California, Southern	India, South	Paris	Umbria
Canada	Indonesia	Peru	USA: On The Road
Caribbean	Ireland	Philadelphia	USA: Western States
Caribbean Cruises	Israel	Philippines	US National Parks: West
Channel Islands	Istanbul	Poland	Venezuela
Chicago	Italy	Portugal	Venice
Chile	Italy, Northern	Prague	Vienna
China	Italy, Southern	Provence	Vietnam
Continental Europe	Jamaica	Puerto Rico	Wales
Corsica	Japan	Rajasthan	Walt Disney World/Orlando
Costa Rica	Jerusalem		
Crete	Jordan		
Cuba	Kenya		
Cyprus	Korea		
Czech & Slovak Republic	Laos & Cambodia		
Delhi, Jaipur & Agra	Las Vegas		
Denmark	Lisbon		

INSIGHT GUIDES

The world's largest collection of visual travel guides & maps